INSIDERS' GUIDE® SERIES

INSIDERS' GUIDE® TO

NEW ORLEANS

FOURTH EDITION

BECKY RETZ AND JAMES GAFFNEY

INSIDERS' GUIDE

GUILFORD, CONNECTICUT

AN IMPRINT OF GLOBE PEQUOT PRESS

All the information in this guidebook is subject to change. We recommend that you call ahead to obtain current information before traveling.

To buy books in quantity for corporate use or incentives, call **(800) 962–0973** or e-mail **premiums@GlobePequot.com**.

INSIDERS' GUIDE ®

Project editor: Lynn Zelem
Layout artist: Maggie Peterson
Text design: Sheryl Kober
Maps: XNR Productions, Inc. © Morris Book Publishing, LLC

ISSN 1543-8686
ISBN 978-0-7627-4187-8

Printed in the United States of America
10 9 8 7 6 5 4 3 2 1

CONTENTS

Directory of Maps

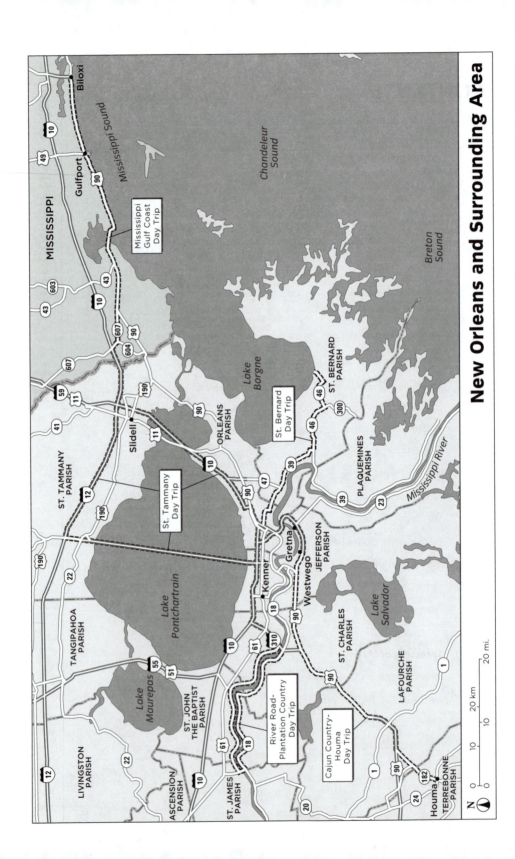

New Orleans and Surrounding Area

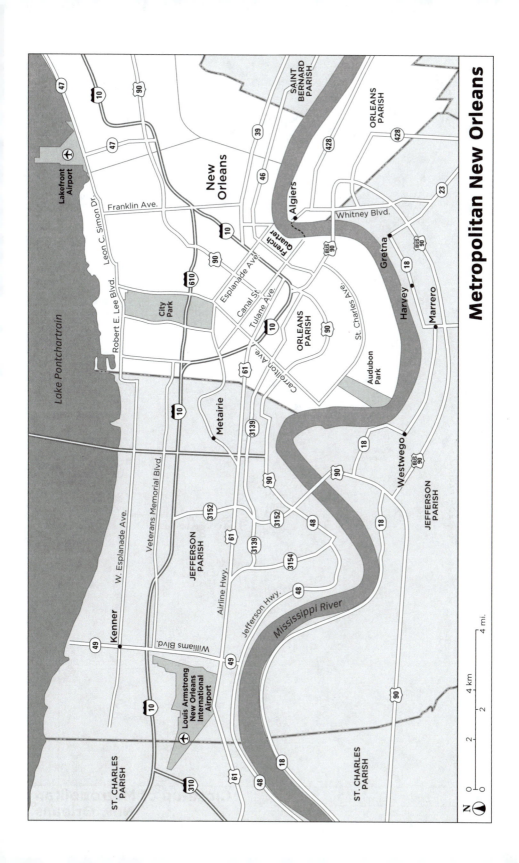

Metropolitan New Orleans

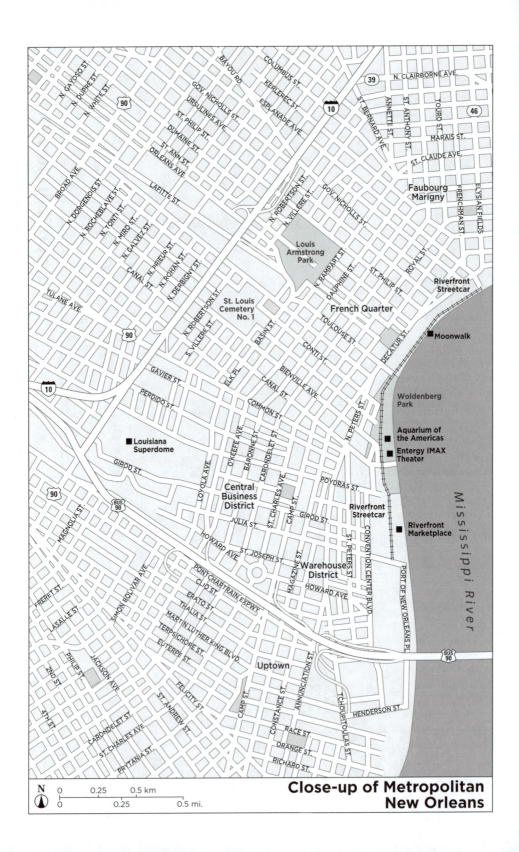

Close-up of Metropolitan New Orleans

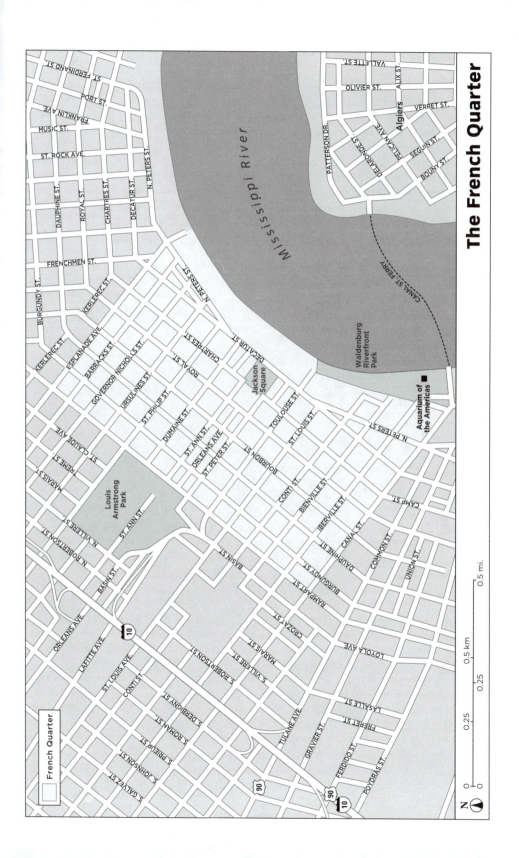

The French Quarter

PREFACE

New Orleans is a fiercely independent riverport and cultural island of good-natured people, rumbling streetcars, midnight mystery, courtyard romance, and simple pleasures. In fact, a city with this much color, historic architecture, oak-framed greenspaces, and renowned dining might be expected to be five times its size. But it's exactly this small-town compactness mixed with big-city possibilities that makes exploring this one-of-a-kind destination a pleasure—and a wise choice—for visitors.

Welcome to New Orleans.

Natives and transplants alike say New Orleans is hard to shake once it gets into your blood—which helps explain why most locals never leave and why so many who do wind up coming back. Compared with most other cities, coming to the Big Easy is like arriving at Oz—everything changes from humdrum sepia tones to vivid living color. Novice and seasoned globetrotters alike agree that New Orleans is among the most exciting and unique places in the world. It's hard to disagree after seeing this remarkably diverse city through the eyes of a visitor while pulling duty as informal tour guide for out-of-town friends and family. They marvel at the genuine warmth of the people, the aromas of its restaurant kitchens, and the richness of its multicultural heritage. This is not a city to be taken for granted.

Perhaps movies, TV, and other media have shaped your impressions of New Orleans. If so, you might have been led to think of this crown jewel of the Mississippi River as barely more than a nonstop party town in which Mardi Gras thrives 365 days a year and everyone speaks with Cajun accents. This couldn't be further from the truth. More so than ever, New Orleans is a sophisticated, cosmopolitan city rolling through the 21st century firmly rooted in its multiethnic tradition of devotion to family, religion, education, community, and hard work. And this 300-year-old child of the swamps has governed itself this way far longer than many places in the United States have even been in existence. If anything, the city's renowned *joie de vivre* is the result of our appreciation for the fragility of life, having weathered over the centuries numerous cataclysmic disasters, not the least of which are yellow fever epidemics, the Saints losing a Super Bowl play-off slot, and, most recently, Hurricane Katrina.

No matter how you slice the French bread, America should consider itself fortunate to count New Orleans as one of the top honeymoon hot spots and international tourism destinations in the world. As a convention town the Big Easy is second to none. If the city seems to bring a bounty of blessings to the national table, it's due largely to the effortless charm and indefatigable spirit of centuries-old Creole pride still evident in the people who call it home.

As for the nuts and bolts: The introduction in each chapter is designed to give readers a lay of the land, while Insider's tips will help visitors better navigate behind the scenes. Close-ups highlight aspects of the city that merit special attention. If you're a newcomer, the back chapters of the book deal with specific relocation concerns, such as real estate, child care, education, health care, media, and worship. Happy reading!

ACKNOWLEDGMENTS

There are a number of people without whose help this book would never have been written. I want to thank my mentors, Will Peneguy and Ed Tunstall, without whose encouragement writing may have simply become something I always wished I had done; my co-author, Jim Gaffney, for his talent in both writing and editing, and for the times he made my work read better than I wrote it; and Globe Pequot editor Lynn Zelem for being so easy to work with.

Personally, I'd like to thank my son Chris, for being the kind of person any mother would be proud to call her own, and the love of my life Steve, for providing constant inspiration and always being there when I need him.

—Becky Retz

A flame of eternal gratitude flickers in this author's window for his wife, Cathy Jacob Gaffney, a tireless proofreader, critic, and, ultimately, one-person cheering section throughout the research and writing phases of this update. Thank you for being a blessing in my life and for your unflinching faith in my ability to reach a goal.

Another individual instrumental in this endeavor is my coauthor, colleague, and friend Becky Retz, to whom I owe a world of thanks for recommending me for this project all those years ago. Others include historian William de Marigny Hyland, for teaching me the stories of the Isleños of lower St. Bernard Parish; the late Leonard J. Hansen, my mentor, colleague, and friend, for his support, encouragement, and guidance through the years; and the editors at Globe Pequot Press, for an excellent job editing the chapters.

A special debt of gratitude—one that can never adequately be repaid—goes to family members Claire and Larry Dejean and Francis and Sandie Jacob, who opened their homes and hearts to us for six weeks during our evacuation from New Orleans after Hurricane Katrina; and my sister and brother-in-law, Lynn and Michael Tomerlin, who literally helped us rebuild our lives and home upon returning to New Orleans following the worst natural disaster in U.S. history. Without them, well, god only knows.

Finally, to my fellow New Orleanians, thank you for teaching this Southern California transplant the true meaning of home—during the best and worst of times—over the past quarter century. I carry this lesson in my heart always.

—James Gaffney

HOW TO USE THIS BOOK

First, here's how *not* to use this book. A few years ago during Carnival, a woman was observed walking down Bourbon Street, which, at the time, was crowded with thousands of masked revelers—many dancing, others unabashedly trading flashes of flesh for trinkets thrown from balconies. There she strode, this woman, oblivious to the human sea of color and laughter surrounding her, because she never once glanced up from her guidebook. Don't do that.

Insiders' Guide to New Orleans follows a simple format. There's a Preface just to say "Where y'at?" (New Orleans-ese for "How do you do?") and a series of chapters designed to help you get acquainted with the city in order to make that upcoming visit the exceptional experience it should be. The Getting Here, Getting Around chapter offers the nuts and bolts of transportation—except, of course, what time your plane leaves. (Although we do tell you whom to call to find out.)

Like all unflinchingly peerless destinations, New Orleans has a long history peppered with fascinating people and their memorable stories. Read all about it as the History and Overview chapters unfold the tales of where we've been and where we are, respectively.

Need a place to stay? New Orleans has everything from swank chrome-and-glass high-rise hotels to charming antebellum inns decorated with antiques, the best of which can be found arranged alphabetically in Hotels and Bed-and-Breakfast Inns.

Now that we've got you settled in, the first thing you'll want to do is eat. Trust us. It's hard to find a bad meal in the Big Easy, but for the best locales check out Restaurants, listed alphabetically by area, to find out where New Orleanians go for the city's best jambalaya, gumbo, oyster po-boys, barbecue shrimp, and bread pudding, to name but a few indigenous delicacies.

For visitors with the right attitude, New Orleans is synonymous with fun. And if this city stands to teach you anything about what makes good cheer flow, we recommend memorizing the Nightlife text and working your way slowly to the head of the class. The next morning when you come to—er, wake up—check out the Attractions and Activities chapter, listed by categories, to discover exactly where we've got a whole lotta shakin' going on during daylight hours. If traveling to New Orleans with youngsters, God love 'ya, you'll be in need of Kidstuff. The Arts chapter outlines the city's cultural offerings, while Day Trips provides the low-down on great attractions on the city's outskirts.

Those planning to call New Orleans home, meantime, can get their compass bearings by checking out the Relocation chapter, featuring information on education, health care, worship and media.

Other practical ways to use this book include: as gift wrapping for two plane tickets tucked between the pages (this idea has more meaning if the tickets are to New Orleans); giving a separate copy to each friend that you missed while you were away with circles around the places that reminded you of them; or sticking it underneath a table leg to stop an annoying wobble. Just remember, the important first step in all of these plans is: Buy the book and buy often.

AREA OVERVIEW

Grace, it might be said, is one of those elusive conventions of human existence which explains that odd composure of the soul when it encounters a moment of near perfection. New Orleans, it might also be said, is a city of such grace. Eccentric. Serene. Self-possessed. Quixotic. Irrepressible. All the while it is easy on the eyes, has a good heart and a sense of humor, roots for the underdog, never forgets to ask how your mama's doing, and loves you just the way you are. Sounds like the perfect date.

This riverport checkerboard of working-class neighborhoods, middle-class enclaves, and Uptown society tumbles through life with the motto "Let the good times roll" and enjoys itself with more exuberance than just about any other place on Earth. While this is a predominately Catholic city steeped in religious tradition, it's also liberally mixed with a history of equal devotion to carefree pleasures best exemplified by the world's greatest free show on earth—Mardi Gras. For proof just hang out with festivalgoers on oak-lined St. Charles Avenue during a nighttime Carnival parade, as colorfully costumed float riders toss doubloons, panties, and plastic beads to a jubilant crowd shouting, "Throw me something, mister!" You'll get the picture.

For this and other reasons, the unsavory parallels of the outside real world, such as abstinence (except during Lent) and dispatch (unless we're hosting a World's Fair or major national convention), hold little interest. Instead, the newspaper obits are scanned daily so as not to miss paying last respects at a wake for even a distant relative or acquaintance. We trundle the kiddies off to City Park for a ride on the historic carousel's flying horses or to Bayou St. John to feed the ducks—just because we did the same thing when we were youngsters. And because this loosen-the-tie town has never cottoned to stuffy formalities, kids are taught early on to respect grown-ups by addressing them as, say, Miss Judy or Mister George. Last names are reserved for strangers.

This is a city of neighborhoods—and what neighborhoods. Uptown, for example, has its old money, stately oaks, Greek Revival and Italianate homes, streetcars, Tulane and Loyola Universities, Audubon Park and Zoo—not to mention the quasi-bohemian ambience of Magazine Street and its vintage clothing stores, antiques shops, art galleries, and restaurants. For proof just take an Uptown streetcar downtown past St. Charles Avenue's Garden District of drop-dead gorgeous mansions built by no-nonsense Americans arriving in the 19th century who wanted little to do with their freewheeling Creole counterparts in the French Quarter. You'll get the picture.

Meantime, the French Quarter bordering the Mississippi River is anchored by Jackson Square's sidewalk artists and palm readers, St. Louis Cathedral, paddle wheelers, Lucky Dog vendors, Royal Street antiques shops, the buzz of Bourbon Street, the French Market, and, of course, Cafe du Monde. Step inside one of the Quarter's historic, candlelit courtyards crumbling with history and lush with banana palms and fiery-red bougainvillea to discover why 19th-century aristocratic Creoles couldn't care less about the stand-offish American newcomers Uptown.

Over the centuries the world's great rivers have given birth to great cities, and this Mississippi River offspring—a wondrous amalgam born of French, Spanish, African, Caribbean, and early American cultures—is certainly no exception. Simply put, it's nearly impossible to pigeonhole this spirited, offbeat city. Just look at the nicknames given to New Orleans over the years: the Crescent City, the City that Care Forgot, the Big Easy, the Cradle of Jazz, America's most European city, Banana Republic, and the northernmost island in the Caribbean. New Orleans is also the birthplace of Creole cuisine and home to one of professional football's most losing teams. For the record, this colorful city also has green streetcars and red beans and rice.

Ties that bind in this overgrown small town include where you went to high school, potholed streets, Christmastime's Mr. Bingle, cafe au lait, and the sweat-defining summertime humidity. New Orleans cherishes its homegrown chefs much the same way Boston embraces its MIT math geniuses and L.A. its celluloid heroes. Writers ranging from William Faulkner and Tennessee Williams to John Kennedy Toole and Anne Rice have trawled the city's secret soul to hold up a mirror of words as poignant as anything Pablo Neruda ever wrote about his Chilean homeland. As Williams's character Blanche DuBois observes in *A Streetcar Named Desire:* "Don't you just love these long rainy afternoons in New Orleans when an hour isn't just an hour—but a little piece of eternity dropped into your hands . . . and who knows what to do with it?"

TUNE TOWN

In New Orleans music is everywhere there's a crowd, from Mardi Gras parades and seasonal festivals to nightclubs, jazz funerals, and Bourbon Street sidewalks.

Take your pick—zydeco, gospel, rhythm and blues, rock, salsa. Traditional jazz also is alive and well, thanks largely to the ranks of both older and younger musicians following the improvisational spirit of local pioneers Buddy Bolden, Sidney Bechet, Louis Armstrong, Joseph "King" Oliver, and Jelly Roll Morton, to name but a few.

A host of avant-garde and modern jazz masters continue to push the musical envelope. One of New Orleans' premier musical families is headed by pianist Ellis Marsalis and includes sons Wynton (who won two Grammys for best jazz and classical recordings in 1984), former *Tonight Show* bandleader Branford, and younger brothers Delfeayo and Jason. Listen to the Neville Brothers perform live and experience firsthand how four of the city's best-known ambassadors of the distinctive New Orleans sound fuse funk, soul, and rhythm and blues into an irresistible match made in heaven. The Big Easy can also brag that it was the home of Mahalia Jackson, Al Hirt, Pete Fountain, Louis Prima, the Dixie Cups, and Harry Connick Jr.

Rhythm and blues, too, found a spiritual home in New Orleans when native-born Antoine "Fats" Domino topped the charts in the 1950s. And if artists such as Irma Thomas, Clarence "Frogman" Henry, Allen Toussaint, Dr. John, and Marcia Ball ring a bell, it's because these award-winning native Louisianians can still be found gracing popular local venues like Tipitina's, Snug Harbor, House of Blues, and Howlin' Wolf. Gospel tips the heavenly scales with such nationally celebrated groups as the Zion Harmonizers and the 60-member Gospel Soul Children. Zydeco and Cajun bands offer up two-stepping music at Mulate's, Michaul's, and the Maple Leaf Bar. Rafter-shaking homegrown rock bands such as the Radiators and Cowboy Mouth also make the local rounds when not on national tours. Add to this mix the city's pulsating Latin music scene headed by the likes of Fredy Omar, Los Babies del Merengue, Julio and Cesar, and the Iguanas. As New Orleans rhythm and blues artist Ernie K-Doe once mused, "I'm not sure, but I'm almost positive that all music came from New Orleans." Either way, the city's legendary musicians past and present have lavished the Big Easy with a hip soul and a rhythmic heart that beats in time with the angels. Amen.

FOOD NATION

It's a safe bet you will roux the day you first tasted a perfectly seasoned crawfish étouffée in New Orleans. Dining in this self-styled Food Nation has always been, at its best, a social occasion and at its worst, an obsession. Jealous outsiders, including researchers at the Centers for Disease Control, have suggested that our love affair with food has resulted in waistlines with more spare tires than a junkyard and the life expectancy of a chicken at an Ozzy concert. To which we respond: "Shaddup and pass da' Tabasco."

Sure, many locals lean on the fat and sassy side. But, if the truth be told, New Orleanians are hardly the craven clutch of artery-clogged, gumbo-lapping nightcrawlers many nutritionists make us out to be. Still, where else in the world do people gather for a meal and rhapsodize about what they last ate (and where) and what they plan to eat next (and where)? Pull up a chair with locals at a Friday-night seafood blowout during Lent and marvel as hands blur while the pile of empty crawfish tails assumes Mt. McKinley heights. Initiate yourself with the tradition of dunking freshly baked French bread in the spicy melted buttah that bathes a dozen jumbo barbecued shrimp. See what we mean?

We compare notes and swap tales of dining lore with a thirst for detail that makes many locals walking food encyclopedias. New Orleans can't help it if the city has been flavored by more than its share of nationally acclaimed culinary wizards—for example, Paul Prudhomme, Leah Chase, Emeril Lagasse, and Susan Spicer. Plus, it's impossible not to be seduced by the city's multicultural menu of French, African, Cajun, Caribbean, and Spanish cooking traditions (with flourishes added by German, Irish, and Italian immigrants). At the drop of a hat, we pull up our socks to head to one of the city's old-line Creole institutions like Galatoire's or go as we are for a megaburger chowfest at a neighborhood eatery like Port of Call. We're blessed with lots of both.

Signature recipes range from andouille gumbo, sausage and chicken jambalaya, and crawfish bisque to sauce piquante, oysters Rockefeller, red beans and rice, courtbouillon, and Muffuletta sandwiches. And we've barely warmed up the cast-iron skillet. To turn salivary glands into water slides just add deep-fried shrimp po-boys, oysters on the half shell, soft-shell crab, and fresh fish from local waters served more ways than you can shake a net at. And no adult worth his or her culinary chops would be caught dead without at least a passing familiarity with menus at some of the city's heralded fine-dining establishments like Commander's Palace, Antoine's, Galatoire's, Emeril's, Restaurant August, and the Grill Room.

BEWITCHED AND BETWEEN

The "Isle d'Orleans" (as Napoleon called it) is strangely different than other U.S. and Southern cities. "You don't sound like a Southerner" is one of the most overheard comments made by newcomers to locals. That is because the only people here who have Southern accents are usually visitors from other Southern states. New Orleans speech inflections, especially in working-class neighborhoods, are more Brooklynese. Still, the city possesses its own vocabulary: "Lagniappe" (LAN-yap), for example, is "a little something extra", while a praline (PRAW-leen) is a bonbon of pecans browned in sugar. Order your po-boy (a huge French-loaf sandwich split down the middle and filled with meat or seafood) "dressed" if you want lettuce, tomato, and mayonnaise. Sidewalks are often called "banquettes," and "neutral grounds" are called medians everywhere else in the country. Grocery shopping is referred to as "making groceries" by old-timers, balconies are called galleries, gris-gris (GREE-GREE) is a voodoo charm, a cold drink is a soda, the Vieux Carre is the French Quarter, and Mardi Gras organizations are called krewes (pronounced just like "crews"). Red beans and rice is a popular Monday dish dating back to when homemakers slow-cooked this simple food on wash day. Snow cones are called snowballs and come in a gadzillion flavors (in New Orleans you can order yours topped with ice cream or, better yet, condensed milk).

The first thing you'll notice when you fly into New Orleans is how the town is built on a crescent—hence the moniker Crescent City—of the 2,350-mile Mississippi River, referred to as "the lawless stream" by Mark Twain in his book *Life on the Mississippi*. Second, swamps surround the city. In fact, an estimated 20 percent of the city's 365 square miles is unreclaimed swamp. If you find it odd that this "port city" is 102 miles from the Gulf of Mexico, so be it. New Orleans sits about 6 feet below sea level and, as a result of the high water table, is the only U.S. city to bury its dead in aboveground tombs. One of our "cities of the dead" is a former horse race track, and the tombs are arranged in the elliptical pattern of the original track. The late historian Mel Levitt, dean of New Orleans' TV news commentators, once estimated that New Orleans had roughly 3,000 bars, 41 cemeteries, and 700 churches of various denominations. Because New Orleans didn't have a zoning law until 1930, some visitors are shocked to see all three—saloon, church, and restaurant—on the same block. Locals find a certain efficiency to the arrangement, though. Another by-product of the city's low elevation and high water table are the numerous (and inescapable) potholes. City workers seem to have a devil of a time keeping up with repairs.

What else makes New Orleans unique? Insomniacs, nightcrawlers, conventioneers, all-purpose partygoers, and would-be vampires alike love this city partly because it's the only one in the country besides Las Vegas without a closing law. Many bars and some restaurants are open round the clock. How much of this is due to the fact that Louisiana was once a French colony and governed as a foreign province for almost 100 years under French and Spanish rule—or the fact that this is the only state that still bases its civil law on Roman (rather than Anglo-Saxon) law, practicing the Napoleonic Code? Not much.

WEATHER OR NOT YOU COME

Bring an umbrella, especially if you plan to visit this post-Katrina city of 310,000 residents (with a metropolitan-wide population of 1.1 million in 2008) during the hottest, most humid, and stickiest time of the year, which usually runs from May to September. Summer months in particular can torment even the most stalwart visitor accustomed to Central American jungles. And consider yourself forewarned: Hell hath no fury like New Orleans in August, so if you plan to visit during this unbearable month—good luck. Just walk outdoors and wait for the nanosecond it takes for your eyeglasses to steam over. Fortunately, the occasionally heavy afternoon thunderstorms during peak summer months sometimes help cool things down; at other times they make New Orleans feel like a mega sauna. Visitors soon come to understand why New Orleanians move a little slower (it's a life-saving strategy) and usually toward the nearest air conditioner. Winter months are mild, if not a little damp, compared with the rest of the country, but it's not uncommon for Santa to show up in Bermuda shorts and a tank top. Mid- to late-October and early spring—when temperatures are extremely pleasant—consistently draw rave reviews from locals and visitors alike.

In many ways the city is like a big family—tight-knit, full of warmth, occasionally given to infighting, and often leery of outsiders. New Orleanians are among the most genuine and friendly people encountered anywhere in the world. We are generous to a fault. After all, the word "lagniappe," meaning a little something extra, is part of the city's vocabulary. And like any family we bristle when misguided souls "from not here" mouth off about one of our foibles or idiosyncrasies. We're well aware of our shortcomings, thank you very much.

Once a lag-behind city, the Big Easy today has big dreams for the future. Evidence can be found in bustling Harrah's casino, the 1.1 million square feet of exhibit space at the Ernest N. Morial Convention Center, plus the 18,500-seat New Orleans Arena (adjacent to the Louisiana Superdome) for basketball and hockey games, Zephyr Field for AAA baseball (see Spectator Sports section in the Attractions and Activities chapter), and the Ogden Museum of Southern Art. Other additions and expansions include those at the D–Day Museum, the Maya-themed Jaguar Jungle exhibit at Audubon Zoo, the interactive Pacific Coast Adventures exhibit at the Aquarium of the Americas ("feel the spray from an orca's blowhole"), the Audubon Institute's 30,000-square-foot insectarium, and new hotel construction.

Year-round Old Testament-like plagues of cockroaches, termites, and mosquitoes still drive us crazy. But this is a city with a streak of kindness a mile wide. Simply put, New Orleans takes care of its own and gossips about them later. It understands the sliding-trombone poetry of a jazz funeral on a drizzly afternoon, as well as the long-gone echo of raucous ragtime and lusty laughter from a palm-flanked Storyville courtyard. Say what you will about New Orleans. This will always be a city where wild dreams slow-dance in the moon shadows till the sun comes up and the red azaleas look red once more.

GETTING HERE, GETTING AROUND

Getting around a city like New Orleans—where the West Bank just across the Mississippi River is actually south of the city, and South Carrollton and South Claiborne Avenues meet—can be a challenge for anyone with a logical mind.

First, never expect a local to give directions in terms of north, south, east, and west. The city just doesn't work that way. New Orleans follows a bend in the Mississippi River (thus its Crescent City moniker), and so, too, do its streets. Directions are generally given in terms of Uptown, Downtown, the river, and the lake. It's confusing, but you'll get the hang of it—in about five years.

This chapter should help. Plus, New Orleanians are generally very friendly and happy to help visitors find their way. Just ask.

GETTING TO NEW ORLEANS

The Airport

Louis Armstrong New Orleans International Airport (www.flymsy.com) is located about 12 miles outside the city in Kenner.

Airlines

Passenger airlines serving New Orleans include:

AIRTRAN
(800) 247-8726
www.airtran.com

AMERICAN AIRLINES
(800) 433-7300
www.aa.com

CONTINENTAL AIRLINES
(800) 523-3273
www.continental.com

DELTA AIRLINES
(800) 221-1212
www.delta.com

JETBLUE AIRWAYS
(800) 538-2583
www.jetblue.com

SOUTHWEST AIRLINES
(800) 435-9792
www.southwest.com

UNITED AIRLINES
(800) 241-6522
www.united.com

US AIRWAYS
(800) 428-4322
www.usairways.com

The Louis Armstrong New Orleans International Airport was originally named after aviator John Moisant, who died there. While competing in a 1910 contest, Moisant hit turbulence and crashed. The area eventually became a stockyard and was named for the pilot. When the stockyard was transformed into an airport, it was called Moisant Field. Today, the only reminder of Moisant is the airport code "MSY" on baggage tickets. "MSY" for Moisant Stockyard.

From the Airport

Taxis

The set rate for a ride from Louis Armstrong New Orleans International Airport to downtown New Orleans is $28 for up to two people or $12 per person for three to five. Pickup is on the lower level outside baggage claim.

Airport Shuttle Service

A one-way ticket downtown costs $13 (as does the return trip), with a three-bag-per-person limit. Pickup and ticket purchases are made on the lower level outside baggage claim. Call (504) 522-3500 or toll-free (866) 596-2699.

Jefferson Transit

AIRPORT-DOWNTOWN EXPRESS
(public bus)
www.jeffersontransit.org

This is by far the best deal. Only $1.60 gets you from the airport to Elk Place in the middle of the downtown Central Business District. Look for the bus outside Entrance #7 at the airport's upper level. It leaves approximately every 25 minutes on weekdays. The trip may take up to an hour.

This option becomes a lot more complicated on the weekends, however, when the bus stops several miles from downtown, forcing passengers and their luggage to transfer to another city bus to get to the CBD. Unless you are really hard-up for cash, find another mode of transportation if arriving on Saturday or Sunday.

Car Rental

A number of car rental agencies are located on the airport terminal's lower level. They are:

ALAMO
(877) 222-9075, (504) 469-0532
www.alamo.com

AVIS
(800) 331-1212, (504) 464-9511
www.avis.com

BUDGET
(800) 527-0700, (504) 467–1296
www.budget.com

DOLLAR
(800) 800-3665, (504) 467-2286
www.dollar.com

ENTERPRISE
(800) 261-7331, (504) 468-3018
www.enterprise.com

HERTZ
(800) 654-3131, (504) 468-3675
www.hertz.com

NATIONAL
(877) 222-9058, (504) 469-0532
www.nationalcar.com

THRIFTY
(800) 463-0800, (504) 463-0800
www.thrifty.com

Parking

The airport has 3,000 short-term and 2,500 long-term parking spaces. Rates are $2 for the first hour, $2 each additional half hour, and $13 to $16 per day. Call (504) 464-0204 for information.

Trains and Interstate Buses

It's easy to catch a train or bus in New Orleans because there's only one place to do it—the downtown Union Passenger Terminal (at the end of Loyola Avenue near the Superdome), home to Amtrak and Greyhound.

AMTRAK
Union Passenger Terminal
1001 Loyola Ave.
(800) 872-7245
www.amtrak.com

Amtrak offers three major lines through New Orleans: The daily City of New Orleans runs between the Big Easy and Chicago; the daily Crescent heads east, chugging all the way to New

York via Washington, D.C.; and the Sunset Limited travels from New Orleans to Los Angeles, thrice weekly, each way.

GREYHOUND
Union Passenger Terminal
1001 Loyola Ave.
(504) 525-6075, (800) 231-2222
www.greyhound.com
If you want to leave the driving to Greyhound, also make your way to Union Passenger Terminal. The ticket office is open daily. Call for schedules.

GETTING AROUND

OK, so now you're in the city. Have no fear, New Orleans is a pretty easy city to get around in once you learn the lay of the land. For traveling purposes, you will mostly be concerned with a few main areas of the city: Downtown, Uptown, and, to a lesser extent, the Lakefront. (There are a few outlying areas you may want to visit, and directions are provided with those individual listings.)

Parts of Town

Downtown covers the Central Business District, the Warehouse District, the French Quarter, and Faubourg Marigny. Uptown encompasses the Garden District, with all those beautiful St. Charles Avenue mansions, the University area, and the Riverbend. The Lakefront is the northernmost part of the city, located on Lake Pontchartrain. It is also where you'll find City Park.

The best part is that you can get to and from these areas without getting on the Interstate (I-10), which has a tendency to back up at any given hour.

French Quarter

What is now known as the French Quarter was the original City of New Orleans. It is a relatively small area on the Mississippi River. The French Quarter is 7 blocks "wide" from the Mississippi River to Rampart Street (so named for the wall, or "rampart," built to protect the fledgling city from Indian attacks) and 15 blocks "front to back" from

Canal Street to Esplanade Avenue. This is one of the few parts of the city where the streets are laid out in a proper grid, with loads of interesting shops, restaurants, art galleries, and wonderful street performers. When walking around, stay on the beaten path, especially at night. Crime is an issue, but just stick with the (sober) crowds and you should be fine.

> **i** When setting off on a French Quarter stroll, take along a pocket full of dollar bills with which to tip street performers. They are a major part of the French Quarter's charm, and you'll definitely get your money's worth.

Faubourg Marigny

Right "behind" the French Quarter (just downriver) is Faubourg Marigny. The city's first suburb, Faubourg (translates to "neighborhood") Marigny was created in 1805 when young Bernard Xavier Philippe de Marigny de Mandeville began subdividing the large plantation he had inherited from his father. Many of this funky little bohemian neighborhood's early architecture still remains and has been lovingly restored (often by locals who found themselves priced out of the French Quarter). The area boasts charming bed-and-breakfasts, terrific eateries, and some of the city's best music clubs.

Central Business District (CBD)

At the "front" (just upriver) of the French Quarter is Canal Street, which marks the edge of the Central Business District. Though Canal is still considered the city's main street, most of the bigger businesses moved to Poydras Street long ago. The three biggest streets to know for getting around downtown are Canal and Poydras Streets and Tulane Avenue. All three run parallel to one another and perpendicular to the Mississippi River. Also note that street names change at Canal Street. For example, after Carondelet Street crosses Canal Street, it becomes Bourbon Street in the French Quarter.

The Warehouse District

The Warehouse District is adjacent to the Central Business District and is basically indistinguishable from it, save for all those art galleries, New York designer stores, and chichi digs in converted textile mills, replete with doorpersons and valet parking, overlooking the Mississippi River. This is the newest hip place to live for the young professional with a penchant for dressing in black and smoking gold-tipped Russian cigarettes.

Uptown

Uptown is upriver from Downtown. Got that? Its main and by far most beautiful street is St. Charles Avenue, which runs from noisy Canal Street through the congested Central Business District and Warehouse District, all the way down the lap of luxury known as the Garden District, to the Riverbend. All roads Uptown lead to St. Charles Avenue. Confused as to which one is St. Charles? Just follow the streetcar. Or, better yet, ride it.

It's hard to miss St. Charles Avenue's Garden District mansions and university area, the latter so named because it is home to both Loyola and Tulane Universities, around the 6000 block. Directly across The Avenue (as St. Charles is often referred to because it really is all that) from the universities is Audubon Park. Walk through the park to find the must-see Audubon Zoo.

Don't walk through the park after dark.

A few blocks past the universities, St. Charles Avenue ends at the Riverbend. As the street, like the river, bends (hence the Riverbend name) it becomes Carrollton Avenue. If you like, you can drive down Carrollton all the way to City Park; the St. Charles streetcar line, however, ends before that.

The Lakefront

You may want to visit the Lakefront. Its West End boasts good, mostly down-home seafood restaurants, while the nearby shore of Lake Pontchartrain is a quiet, uncrowded area in which to relax. To get to the Lakefront from Downtown, take Canal Street away (northwest) from the Mississippi River. The street dead-ends, as it were, at Greenwood Cemetery. (The cemetery was built in an early attempt at urban planning to keep the city from growing any larger. Don't ask.) Take the dogleg—a right and immediate left—around the cemetery. You are now on Canal Boulevard, which can be taken all the way to the lake. To get to West End, take Canal Boulevard to Robert E. Lee Boulevard. Turn left and then right at the next stop light—Pontchartrain Boulevard.

That should basically get you around the city. There are a couple of outlying areas you may want to visit. You may have noticed that rather than counties, Louisiana is divided into parishes. Orleans Parish is made up of the City of New Orleans and a small area on the west bank of the Mississippi River called Algiers. On either side of Orleans Parish—on both the east and west banks—is Jefferson Parish.

i Although lovable in many respects, New Orleanians are notoriously bad drivers. Watch out for people running red lights, turning or changing lanes without signaling, and exhibiting particularly slow reaction time.

East Jefferson

East Jefferson, which includes Metairie (where the Zephyrs play) and Kenner (where the airport is), is best accessed by taking I–10 west. Yes, you take I–10 west to get to East Jefferson. Go figure. If traveling during peak traffic hours, it may be easier to take Airline Drive, which may well qualify as the least scenic route in America. Before I–10 was built, Airline Highway was the main road to Baton Rouge.

After the interstate was built, Airline Highway fell to pot. Local government recently tried to polish up the highway's tarnished image by changing a stretch of its name to Airline Drive, though they might have done better by first ridding this thoroughfare of its tumbledown motels, hubcap shops, and tattoo parlors. C'est la vie. What's important to know is that Airline—highway, drive, whatever—takes you on a straight shot from Downtown to New Orleans International Airport in Kenner. This is where Jimmy Swaggart got in trouble. Just remember: Friends don't let friends solicit prostitutes.

West Jefferson

There are two ways to get to West Jefferson, better known as the West Bank. There is a ferry landing where Canal Street meets the Mississippi River. The ferry goes to Algiers Point. The Canal Street Ferry costs $1 per car and is free for pedestrians. This is a really nice ride at night and offers a great view of the city. It's also a good way to get to any Algiers destination, such as Blaine Kern's Mardi Gras World, where Carnival floats are built and stored. Do not take the ferry if you're headed to any other parts of the West Bank.

To get to other parts of the West Bank, take the Mississippi River Bridge. (Its official name is the Crescent City Connection, but nobody calls it that.) This will connect you to the West Bank Expressway, which will get you anywhere else you want to go on the West Bank.

On the Move

REGIONAL TRANSIT AUTHORITY

www.norta.com

Use Regional Transit Authority (RTA) buses, which have citywide routes, for tooling around the city. Regular fare costs $1.25, $1.50 for express. Schedules are available from the RTA office, 2817 Canal St., by calling (504) 248-3900 or at the above Web site. The RTA also offers VisiTour Passes good for unlimited rides. Cost: $5 per day or $12 for three days; available at hotels and shopping areas. Call (504) 248-3900 for the vendor nearest you.

i International visitors who want to take advantage of the state's tax-free shopping program can turn in their refund paperwork (obtained from participating merchants at the checkout counter) before they leave town at the Tax Free Shopping office in Louis Armstrong New Orleans International Airport.

i Take the Canal Streetcar line all the way down Carrollton Avenue to City Park and the New Orleans Museum of Art, located at the end of the line. And before you ride back, also explore the surrounding historic Esplanade Ridge neighborhood—full of beautiful homes, charming restaurants, and the winding Bayou St. John.

Streetcars

The St. Charles Streetcar is a terrific way to see Uptown and one of the city's most enjoyable forms of transportation. Cost: $1.25. The Riverfront Streetcar doesn't offer much of a view, but if you're in the French Quarter and don't feel like walking all the way to the Aquarium of the Americas, climb aboard for $1.50.

There are two streetcars on the new Canal Streetcar line: cemeteries and City Park/Museum. Check the top front of the car to find out which one you're boarding. The Cemeteries car isn't as scary as it sounds. It simply runs the entire length of Canal Street, which ends at City Park Avenue, where a number of the city's cemeteries are located. As a visitor, you will be much more likely to want to ride the City Park/Museum car, which also follows Canal Street but turns right at Carrollton Avenue. This line ends at beautiful City Park, home to the New Orleans Museum of Art. Cost: $1.25.

Taxis

New Orleans is really not a cab-hailing town. If you need a taxi, most of the major downtown hotels have cab stands, or call for pickup. United Cab is the biggest taxi company. Call (504) 522-9771.

Driving

The two most important things to remember when driving around New Orleans are watch out for the potholes and don't break the law. The city is built below sea level atop a swamp, so everything sinks. Potholes are everywhere and there's no way to avoid them. Consequently, negotiating New Orleans streets is not unlike driving in a Third

Close-up

Streetcar

"They told me to take a streetcar named Desire, and then transfer to one called Cemeteries and ride six blocks and get off at—Elysian Fields!"

—Blanche DuBois, in Tennessee Williams's *A Streetcar Named Desire*

Say what you will, but as far as we're concerned you can never say enough about the poetry in motion that is a New Orleans streetcar. Even Tennessee Williams can be forgiven for futzing with the facts when he has Blanche DuBois get off the streetcar on Elysian Fields at the beginning of his famous play *A Streetcar Named Desire*. Truth is the streetcar never ran down Elysian Fields. Never. Anyone else who tried such a literary maneuver would have been hog-tied to the tracks of the City Park kiddie railroad. But Tennessee? Well, he's always been a different story.

The city's national historic landmark, which can trace its roots back to 1831, is the oldest continuously operated street railway system in the United States. But don't let that fact impress you any more than it did the city back in 1963 when it stopped running the streetcar down Canal Street in a regrettable move to save money by relying on public buses fueled by—then—cheap gas.

Today visitors can ride the clanging streetcars the 13.1 miles from Canal and Carondelet (pronounced *ca-ron-de-LET*) Streets, across from Bourbon Street in the French Quarter, all the way down St. Charles Avenue to the Riverbend, and then along Carrollton Avenue to Claiborne Avenue and Palmer Park and Playground—or vice versa. Cost is $1.25 per person for each leg of the 90-minute round-trip (exact change required).

Riding the streetcar is one of the best ways to leisurely soak up the oozing charm of St. Charles Avenue, not the least of which are the famous thoroughfare's canopies of moss-draped oak trees, Garden District mansions, Audubon Park, and Tulane and Loyola Universities.

The city's 35 streetcars were built between 1923 and 1924, and each carries 52 passengers. Sometimes it seems like more, though, during the after-school and after-work crush, as well

World country. Just relax and, most important, slow down.

Do not speed in New Orleans. Generally, the speed limit is 25 mph on undivided streets and 35 mph on divided streets. If you get pulled over for speeding, not only will it cost you an astronomical amount of money, but also an out-of-towner is much more likely than a local to be taken directly to jail to pay the fine.

Here are some other laws and safety tips to keep in mind:

- No open containers are allowed in vehicles.
- The police are really cracking down on drunk driving. Don't drink and drive or you'll find yourself in jail faster than you can say, "We'll have one for the road."
- Front-seat passengers and children under age 13 are required to wear safety belts.
- Emergency vehicles use red and blue lights. Do not pull over for a car with only flashing white lights. The Louisiana Office of Tourism recommends that anyone stopped by an unmarked "police" car should pull to a well-lighted, populated area. Ask to see official identification, or ask that a marked car be dispatched.

as during peak tourist times, including Mardi Gras and JazzFest. The best times to ride include late morning and early afternoon.

Whether picking up the streetcar at Canal Street or anywhere along St. Charles Avenue, passengers can get off at the Riverbend area (where the streetcar turns northeast from St. Charles Avenue and continues down Carrollton Avenue) and walk across the street and up onto the levee for a view of the Mississippi River. The original streetcar line, founded in 1935, was built to connect New Orleans with the city of Carrollton (where the Riverbend is located). There are several places to eat at the Riverbend, but the coolest is the Camellia Grill, an old-fashioned diner where everybody sits at the counter. They serve terrific burgers and omelettes that diners get to watch the cooks prepare on the grill right in front of them. The big white building across Carrollton Avenue from the diner is Lusher Elementary. It is the oldest building in America being used as a school. Originally, it was the courthouse for the Town of Carrollton.

Not to be outdone by the avenue line, are the seven red-with-gold-trim vintage streetcars unveiled in 1988, which run the 2.5-mile line along the city's riverfront from the lower French Quarter (Esplanade Avenue) to the Morial Convention Center (Julia Street). Truth is there is not a whole lot to see except the back of Jax Brewery and some less than photogenic wharfs. However, the riverfront streetcar is the only transportation from one end of the French Quarter to the other for sightseers with tired feet.

In 2004 the long-awaited return of streetcars to Canal Street came after an absence of 40 years. Just as it did originally, the 4.1-mile line runs the length of Canal Street, which separates the French Quarter and downtown, from the Mississippi River to the cemeteries. An additional milelong branch runs along Carrollton Avenue to City Park, home of the New Orleans Museum of Art.

And sometime in the near future, Tennessee Williams may be seen as a prophet, if the proposed three-mile extension of the Canal Street streetcar to the Industrial Canal is completed. The route, to follow North Rampart Street and St. Claude Avenue, would at long-last create a streetcar stop at Elysian Fields.

Parking

Parking is another hassle. Do not park illegally in the city. Always read the signs, especially during Mardi Gras and other special events. *Note:* If you are parking at the end of a block, a no parking sign at the other end may include the entire block. So check before you park. The most worry-free solution is put the car in a parking lot. They're everywhere.

If you do park on the street and your car is not there when you return, it may have been towed to the auto pound at 400 Claiborne Ave.

To find out, call (504) 565-7450. Be prepared to identify your car by license plate number, make, color, and location it was parked.

i **If you plan to use public transportation while in town, consider buying a pay-one-price VisiTour pass good for unlimited rides on city streetcars and buses. (See Regional Transit Authority listing for details.)**

HISTORY

Since the beginning, New Orleans has been a city that has survived, sometimes, it seems, despite the best efforts of man and God. It all started in 1682 when Robert Cavelier de LaSalle, while exploring the mostly unknown North American continent, entered the Mississippi River from the Illinois River, eventually making his way to the Gulf of Mexico. Along the route, he claimed this brave new world for the glory of France and named the region for King Louis XIV.

He then raced back to France, where the king's fledgling territory ran into its first obstacle. It seems Louis was not too crazy about LaSalle's idea of building a colonial empire for France by establishing a city on the river. All could have been lost then and there. But the king noticed that the land was adjacent to the Spanish claim of what would eventually become Texas—which just so happened to be owned by his brother-in-law and which Louie planned to get his hands on once his ailing kin kicked the bucket. It looked like smooth sailing for LaSalle—that is, until he got back to the New World and was unable to locate the mouth of the river again. Eventually he landed his crew in the pre-Texas region with the bright idea of hiking all the way back to Canada and retracing his steps. His crew, understandably, killed him. All of which goes to show how much people hate it when you give them bad directions.

It was another decade before anybody else in France had the guts to go near Louisiana, and it may have been even longer had the King of Spain not announced that all land bordering the Gulf of Mexico was his. So in 1698 Louis sent the Le Moyne brothers—Pierre Le Moyne, Sieur d'Iberville, and Jean-Baptiste Le Moyne, Sieur de Bienville (commonly referred to as Iberville and Bienville) to defend France's land claim. Of course, they had problems of their own, mostly in the form of a hurricane (which wiped out the first settlement in its second year) and fires. (In fact, the city's history is full of devastating fires, which is ironic considering that it is surrounded by water.) The first order of business was setting up a base of operations along the modern-day Mississippi Gulf Coast and naming Biloxi the capitol of the Louisiana Territory. It was now time to find the Mississippi River. But rather than risk mutiny and death as LaSalle had, the brothers enlisted the help of local Indians in their search.

Now these Native Americans, the Choctaws, were an interesting bunch. They were not the stereotypical proud warriors of old Western movies or even the spiritual peace-loving tribes of new Western movies. As the late historian John Chase put it, "Their outstanding characteristic was laziness; in truth it is doubtful that the world ever knew a class of people of whom it can more correctly be said that they didn't give a damn." Chase goes on to point out that although the region basically required an amphibious way of life, the Choctaws never learned to swim or even bathe. And whereas most Native Americans wore feathers at their head, the Choctaws attached them at the waist so that they stuck out in back like a tail.

This was a motley crew.

That bit of trivia concerning the Choctaw character is worth mentioning because it has some relevance to modern New Orleans. The city's population has long been known for its laissez-faire attitude toward just about every aspect of life, which most observers have attributed to the city's European roots (we even use French words to describe it). However, in light of what we now know about the Choctaws, it could be surmised that the City That Care Forgot started forgetting to care long before the Europeans arrived.

FIRE ON THE BAYOU

Back to the Le Moyne boys' search for the Mississippi River. The Choctaws were understandably a shy bunch and therefore difficult to make contact with. (Besides, what did they care?) The Frenchmen solved this problem by capturing an old brave who was too slow to get away and then planted him on the beach (where they knew his tribesmen could see him), presented him with gifts, and built a shelter and fire for his comfort. Unfortunately, as Chase writes in his book *Frenchmen, Desire, Good Children:* "[T]he roaring fire ignited the grass and burned the old man to a crisp."

This did not help their cause.

Almost unbelievably though, Bienville was eventually able to make friends with a group of Choctaws (maybe they hadn't heard about the other incident) who agreed to show him the way to the river when they finished hunting. Though he probably should have known better, Bienville marked the rendezvous point by lighting a fire—which, of course, raged out of control and burned down miles of forest. At this point, the French were forced to find the river on their own, which they eventually did.

During their journey up the river, about 100 miles inland the explorers came upon a tract of land at a bend in the river. To the north was what we know as Lake Pontchartrain. There was also a small stream (later called Bayou St. John) that led to the lake. Eighteen-year-old Bienville saw this as a perfect spot to establish a riverfront city. His older brother disagreed and went back to France. However, Bienville, with his youthful dream of a great river city, stayed behind and became commanding officer of the territory. But he had to wait nearly two decades to make his dream come true.

In 1717, a Scotsman named John Law persuaded the King of France that there was money to be made in Louisiana. The following year Bienville was promoted to territorial governor and instructed to establish a city on the river from which to protect France's New World empire. Of course, he knew just the spot. The City of New Orleans was promptly established and declared the new capital because of its strategic location and because, according to historian Chase, a French sergeant had fallen asleep with a pipe in his mouth and burned down Biloxi.

Back in France, Philip II (the former Duke of Chartres and the country's Regent during the infancy of Louis XV) was the inside man whose influence had assured royal approval of John Law's economic plan—a plan so sound that many called Law the inventor of inflation. Philip was also a despicable human being. When royal heirs began suspiciously dying near the end of Louis XIV's reign, it was Philip and his daughter (with whom he was accused of having an extremely close relationship) who were accused. However, the charges were never proven, and in his will the dying king named Philip France's Regent. By this time, Philip, a man of such objectionable character that his own mother's writings basically branded him a loser, had inherited the title of Duke of Orleans. He is the man for whom John Law named the new city.

And to think, all Bienville got named after him was a street.

A CITY OF CRIMINALS AND IRON LACE

Engineer Adrian de Pauger laid out the original city, which consisted of a central square with streets forming a grid around it. Today this area is known as the French Quarter with Jackson Square still at its center. As fate would have it, though, the building of the city was not easy going. Much of the land was swamp—perfect breeding ground for mosquitoes, snakes, and alligators. The Mississippi River often overflowed its banks, hurricanes visited from the Gulf and, of course, there were fires.

Then there were the people. In order to populate the new colony, John Law succeeded in getting two laws passed. One stated that anyone in a French prison, no matter what the crime, would be freed provided that he or she moved to Louisiana. Likewise, anyone who was out of work for three days was sent to a New World home. Therefore, much of the city's early European population was made up of criminals and ne'er-do-wells. Amazingly, the city not only survived, it thrived—perhaps because the land and these early settlers were made for each other.

New Orleans remained under French rule until 1762, when Louis XV ceded the territory to Spain. New Orleanians were enraged when the first Spanish governor, Don Antonio de Ulloa, arrived. In response, a mob of angry locals ran him out of town. The New Orleans Rebellion of 1768 marks the first American revolution against a European crown. King Carlos squelched the rebellion by sending in Don Alexander "Bloody" O'Reilly, who promptly executed the rebel leaders. Frenchmen Street in Faubourg Marigny (the neighborhood just downriver of the French Quarter) was named for these original American revolutionaries.

Although the city was never to adopt the Spanish language or culture, it did inherit the Spaniards' architecture. Two fires (wouldn't you know it), in 1788 and 1794, destroyed most of the original French buildings. These wooden structures were replaced, while the Spanish were running the city, with sturdier brick buildings constructed in the Spanish style—flush against the street with arched walkways, interior court-yards, and iron lace balconies. Many of these introductions remain, giving the French Quarter its decidedly Spanish look.

UH-OH, AMERICANS

Meanwhile, elsewhere on the continent, the big happening was the settling of the Ohio River Valley following the American Revolution. This was important to the development of the Crescent City because those frontiersmen from Tennessee and Kentucky soon found that the most practical way to get their goods to world markets was down the Mississippi River to the port town of New Orleans. The first river traffic consisted of rafts and flatboats. These crude crafts could not make the trip back up river, so after the boats were unloaded, they were broken apart and sold as lumber. Many of the wooden houses built in New Orleans at that time were made from these flatboats. The frontiersmen would then spend the next few weeks walking home.

It wasn't until the arrival of the second wave of river traffic—the keelboats—that the trouble really started. The Creoles, as early New Orleanians called themselves, had become quite a sophisticated bunch, and, generally speaking, life in New Orleans was rather genteel—especially when contrasted with the rowdy behavior of the keelboatmen. Unlike their predecessors, the keelboatmen (whose vessels could make the return trip upriver) were professional boatmen and, by all accounts, never in the mood to pass up trouble. They were known for brawling—and winning. Understandably, this did not go over well with locals, and there were constant run-ins with the authorities. Hostilities grew, and in 1798 the Spanish government ruled the New Orleans port off-limits to the keelboatmen.

The boatmen were mostly from Tennessee and Kentucky, both of which had recently been granted statehood. They went to the American government and threatened that if something were not done they would either take the port by force or secede from the Union. Meanwhile, Napoleon was now running France and had taken back Louisiana from Spain. (He did things like that.)

Back in Washington, President Thomas Jefferson decided that the best solution to the port problem was to buy New Orleans, which he had wanted to do since he took office two years earlier. Off went statesmen Robert Livingston and James Monroe to broker the deal with Napoleon, who was busy trying to conquer Europe and had little interest in his American territory—except as a source of income. (Taking over a continent is expensive.) So, in walk Livingston and Monroe authorized to pay up to $10 million for New Orleans, but only if the French emperor will throw in Florida. Napoleon promptly turns around and offers the entire Louisiana Territory (nearly 900,000 square miles) for $15 million—a price that works out to about four cents an acre. Livingston and Monroe had no authority to make such an agreement, no time to consult the president, and were pretty sure it was unconstitutional (which it turns out it was). However, they inked the deal, thus doubling the size of the United States and establishing the American tradition of never passing up a great sale.

The Louisiana Purchase was signed in 1803, and the next several years were pretty good ones for New Orleans. Americans and their money flooded into the city; New Orleans received both statehood and the steamboat in 1812; and along with the lifting of long-standing French-Spanish trade restrictions, the city became a boomtown.

AN "ECLECTIC" VICTORY

But another major battle lay ahead for New Orleans. By the second decade of the 19th century, the city's population had become quite eclectic. There were the Creoles of both French and Spanish extraction, the newly arrived Americans, a sizable black population made up of both slaves and free people of color (New Orleans had by far the largest population of pre-Civil War free people of color.), a handful of Choctaws and brutish keelboatmen, and a small band of pirates led by Jean Lafitte. Actually, Lafitte was more of a smuggler than a pirate, and many affluent New Orleanians were regular customers for his duty-free booty. Lafitte and his Baratarians were headquartered downriver of the city at Barataria Bay and were quite familiar with this swampy region—a fact the English would later bemoan.

America had been at war with England (once again) since, well, 1812. In 1814, British forces had employed the visually impressive Congreve rocket at the Battle of Bladensburg, which successfully scared away 5,000 raw American recruits. As a result, the British were able to take and burn Washington, inspiring Francis Scott Key to write about "the rockets' red glare, the bombs burst-

ing in air." The British were figuring on a similar victory in New Orleans, where the local troops, made up of the aforementioned eclectic group, were no more seasoned.

It was now early 1815, two weeks after the Americans and British had signed a peace treaty ending the War of 1812. Unfortunately, neither army was aware of this bit of trivia when they met in the swamps a few miles south of New Orleans in present-day Chalmette. General Sir Edward Michael Pakenham led 14,000 veteran British soldiers. Meanwhile, General Andrew Jackson commanded an estimated 2,800 irregulars, many of whom would not even have spoken to one another before this. Luckily Jackson's troops found they had one thing in common: They all hated the British.

When the smoke cleared, the score was unmistakable: 3,000 British soldiers killed, wounded, or captured; seven Americans killed, six wounded. No one is exactly sure why the completely unexpected defeat was so decisive. It has been suggested that in this particular battle, not knowing the rules of the game helped the Americans. The experienced British wore bright-red uniforms, marched in lines, and had bagpipers announcing their presence.

These traditional practices were meant to intimidate opponents. However, the uninitiated Americans didn't know that. They simply found that the bright colors, straight lines, and noise made the British easier to pick off. It also often has been mistakenly observed that the battle was nothing more than a waste of time and lives, as it took place after the treaty was signed. However, the British parliament had not yet ratified the treaty, and many historians believe that had that country's soldiers won the Battle of New Orleans, England may have rethought its peace agreement.

i LaSalle originally named the newly discovered territory "Louisiane" after the French King Louis XIV. The Spanish name was "Luisiana." The surviving "Louisiana" is a mingling of the two.

Close-up

Cemeteries

Laissez les bon temps rouler, let the good times roll, is an oft-heard phrase in New Orleans. And why wouldn't it be in a city that has, virtually since its emergence from the swamp, experienced almost nonstop reminders of how short life really is? The Big Easy has a long history of floods, fires, and epidemics (in 1853 alone 12,000 people died of yellow fever) that have inspired in locals the wisdom never to take life too seriously as well as the burning question: What do you do with all those bodies?

Actually, burying the dearly departed was a problem from the beginning. Because New Orleans lies below sea level, the only high ground was the natural silt levee created by the Mississippi River's annual overflow. Locals began burying the dead there until it occurred to them that the digging was weakening the city's only flood protection. In 1721 city engineer Adrien de Pauger designed St. Peter's Cemetery to be built on the outskirts of town.

This worked for a while, until the city began to grow toward and around the cemetery and folks decided that they did not like looking at graves while sitting on their front stoops. Officials responded by building a 5-foot brick wall around the cemetery. The wall was dedicated with much fanfare on All Saints' Day 1743. Participants arrived for the ceremony, also bearing flowers to commemorate the dead (as was the custom throughout Europe). All Saints' Day has been an important holiday in New Orleans ever since.

Residents made do with St. Peter's until 1788, a big year for natural disasters. First, the banks of the Mississippi overflowed, flooding the entire city; then, on Good Friday, 865 homes burned to the ground in a fire that destroyed most of New Orleans; and somewhere in the mix a variety of epidemics did what they do best, killing a large portion of the population. (Some people even consider this a worse year than 1979, when Mardi Gras was canceled because of a police strike.) As a result, the filled-to-overflowing cemetery had to be closed and covered with lime to avoid more pestilence.

New Orleans' oldest surviving "city of the dead," St. Louis No. 1, was built by royal decree the following year. However, mourners still faced the problem of burying their dead in, literally, watery graves. The decision was made to erect aboveground tombs, and because swamp-based New Orleans has no natural stone, they were constructed of brick. Unfortunately, in the city's subtropical climate, the bricks seemed to be competing with the bodies to see which would deteriorate first. To keep the tombs from falling apart, plaster was added to the outside and eventually painted white—a symbol of purity. (Although the idea that many of those good-time-loving Creoles made it to their graves pure seems naively optimistic.)

With the influx of Americans to the city following the 1803 signing of the Louisiana Purchase, accommodations had to be made for their dead, as well. The class system, which still exists in New Orleans culture to some degree, was reflected in the solution. The new Protestants would be buried at the back of the cemetery, behind the Catholic Creoles, with black people at the very end. (Sometimes, a person can't catch a break even when they're dead.)

These houses of the dead have changed little over the centuries. Generally the aboveground tomb is about 10 feet long with a 7-foot-long interior slab on which the coffin rests; the last 3 feet at the back of the structure are open from top to bottom. The tomb was not allowed to be opened for a year and a day after a body was placed inside to make certain that the "inhabitant" was past the point of spreading disease. Here, the burning sun of New Orleans' long, hot summers combines with the enclosed tomb to virtually cremate the body, leaving little behind by the next year. The remains that, well, remain are then pushed to the back, falling into that 3-foot hollow area, or *caveau,* before the next coffin is placed inside.

OK, so what if Uncle Herd kicks off just six months after MawMaw? Well, that's where the waiting wall comes in. That's right, the body would be placed in a sort of limbo lobby located within the outer walls of the cemetery until proper internment could safely take place. It may sound morbid, but it's a system that's worked for 200 years, and most of the city's families still own tombs. In fact, some interesting notables have made their permanent homes in St. Louis No. 1, including Etienne de Bore, the city's first appointed mayor and the first man to granulate sugar; Paul Morphy, North America's premiere chess champion, whose home is now a quaint little restaurant called Brennan's; and famed voodoo queen Marie Laveau. (The tomb bearing her name in St. Louis No. 2 is believed to be her daughter's).

And sometimes a resting place is considered interesting on the basis of who doesn't show up. The plot of William C. C. Claiborne, Louisiana's first governor, is also located in St. Louis No. 1. It contains the bodies of both his wives, with his brother-in-law in the middle. Nobody's quite sure how or why the governor's body ended up somewhere else.

On the edge of the city, Metairie Cemetery, full of grand and unusual monuments, represents a virtual who's who of dead New Orleanians. The long list of blue bloods includes nine Louisiana governors, eight mayors, and more than 50 kings of Carnival. There's also Mel Ott, New Orleans greatest contribution to the game of baseball. In his 22-year career with the New York Giants, Ott scored 1,859 runs (including 511 homers), tallied 1,860 RBIs, and maintained a lifetime average of .304. His lustrous career is in direct contrast to his tomb, which is one of the cemetery's more modest.

In his book *Proud, Peculiar New Orleans: The Inside Story,* Buddy Stall tells the tale of one of Metairie Cemetery's most interesting monuments and the man who built it. Daniel Moriarty, an Irish immigrant and successful businessman, was known as an inattentive and some say harsh husband to his wife, a woman several years his senior. Upon Mrs. Moriarty's death in 1887, his conscience apparently kicked in and he decided to build her the largest monument Metairie Cemetery had ever known. This was also a way for the Hibernian to thumb his nose at those members of New Orleans society who had snubbed him because his blood never managed to be the correct shade of blue.

The 85-foot monument featured a huge granite shaft topped with a cross and life-size statues of "the four graces." (When Moriarty put in his request for the statues and was told that there were, in fact, only three graces—Faith, Hope, and Charity—Moriarty said he didn't care and wanted four anyway.) The circular walk around the base was made of stones from various places around the country, each weighing 11 tons. The final cost for this 19th-century tomb was $185,000. However, Moriarty never finished paying for it.

Supposedly, Mrs. Moriarty was sensitive about her age and stipulated in her will that only the date of her death should appear on her tomb. Moriarty gave the information to the stonecutter who, after completing the work, realized that the information was off by a day. The cutter approached Moriarty and explained that an understandable mistake had been made by the widower in his time of grief but that it could be corrected for a paltry $2.50. Moriarty replied, "The hell with it, I've spent enough already."

Josie Arlington, the famed Storyville madam, is another interesting resident of Metairie Cemetery. Around the turn of the 20th century, a canal that ran past the cemetery featured red lights as markers, one of which ironically shone down on Arlington's tomb. Locals joked that Josie was working late.

It's hard to tell how big a role these very visible cities of the dead have played in the development of the New Orleans psyche. At the very least, their presence (there are more than 40 cemeteries within the city limits) seems to have instilled a certain cultural acceptance of the inevitability of death not found in communities where graveyards are kept as far away from the living as possible. And, perhaps they are partly responsible for the *joie de vivre* New Orleanians seem to possess from birth.

NEW ORLEANS' DEATH-DEFYING DEVELOPER

As for General Jackson, the battle made him a national hero who went on to become the seventh president of the United States (and a prominent statue in Jackson Square), which brings us to Micaela Leonard Almonester Baroness de Pontalba, one of the city's most interesting redheads. She was born in 1795, the daughter of 70-year-old Don Andres Almonester, a wealthy landowner. When she was 16, Micaela entered into an arranged marriage with her 20-year-old cousin Joseph Xavier Celestin Delfau de Pontalba of Paris, whom everyone apparently called Tin-Tin and whom Micaela had never met until the day of the wedding. Besides three children and intertwining lineages, the couple had nothing in common. And talk about in-law troubles—her father-in-law so disliked her that one day he shot her four times in the chest. (It would have been six times, but he missed twice.) Thinking her dead, he then fatally shot himself in the heart twice, although nobody's really sure how he got off that second shot. Miraculously, the baroness survived. Eventually, she left Paris, where the scandalous incident had taken place, and returned to New Orleans.

In 1848 she began building her legacy— two luxurious row houses flanking either side of Jackson Square. The identical three-story buildings would each accommodate 16 shops on the ground floor, with the second and third floors housing residences. She insisted that the initials AP (for Almonester-Pontalba) be designed into the balcony ironwork. The latter of the buildings was completed in 1851. Today, they are considered the oldest apartment houses in America. An interesting footnote: Local legend has it that although she and her husband did not get along, the baroness had a real thing for Andy Jackson.

Unfortunately, her affections were unrequited. However, she apparently had the last laugh. It seems that the building of her apartment houses sparked the city to make improvements to Jackson Square. This included finally completing the statue of General Andrew Jackson for which the cornerstone had been laid more than a decade earlier. To this day, the spurned baroness, wherever she may be, at least has the satisfaction of General Jackson forever tipping his hat in the direction of her house.

FORTUNES AND FEVERS

As a result of the Battle of New Orleans, the general got his statue and the baroness got her gesture. As for the city, the battle had finally done what peaceful coexistence never could: It united the various ethnic factions long enough for people to start making some real money. The port was jammed with business, cotton was king, and by 1850 New Orleans was the fourth largest city in the United States. Everything was coming up magnolias and crepe myrtles for the Crescent City. So, of course, it was time for another disaster.

Along came the yellow fever epidemic of 1853. Actually, mostly because it was built on a swamp, New Orleans was visited by yellow fever pretty much every year. But 1853 was the worst. More than 10,000 people died that summer— an average of more than 100 people a day. The worst was August 20, when 269 people perished. Homes were turned into hospitals and wagons were driven down the street with the drivers calling, "Bring out your dead." Piles of corpses lay rotting in cemeteries. Yellow fever outbreaks continued, but after the horrible summer of '53, God seemed to show mercy and the epidemics decreased in occasion and severity until they ended altogether in 1905.

Almost unbelievably, the local economy was doing so well that the dead were quickly replaced by newcomers eager to cash in on the city's prosperity. Of course, the only reason cotton (not to mention sugarcane) was king was because there were non-wage-earning slaves picking it. During this time New Orleans was one of the country's biggest slave markets. And the backs on which the city's prosperity had been built would eventually lead to its downfall. New

Orleans' glory days abruptly came to an end in 1861 with Louisiana's secession from the Union and the beginning of the Civil War, known on this side of the Mason-Dixon line as the War Between the States.

ℹ **Besides being the birthplace of jazz, New Orleans was home to another noteworthy American first. In 1859, on the corner of Bourbon and Toulouse Streets, the French Opera House was built. It was the residence of the continent's first permanent opera company.**

THE BUTLER DID IT

In 1862 Union troops occupied New Orleans and liked the place so much they stayed 15 years. The most prominent figure during this period was General Benjamin "Spoons" Butler, commander of the federal forces in New Orleans. He was much hated among the locals because of his liberal interpretation of the Confiscation Act of 1862. Butler seized at will a goodly amount of private property from homes, including many a family's silver service (thus his nickname).

The city's women, openly hostile toward occupying soldiers, would immediately get off a streetcar if soldiers boarded and sometimes literally spit in their faces. (Remember, the Creoles were an independent and spirited bunch.) In response, Butler passed an ordinance that any woman insulting or showing contempt for a soldier "shall be regarded and held liable to be treated as a woman of the town plying her avocation." Even Butler's closest advisors thought it a bit harsh to basically make it legal to punish a snubbing with rape. Needless to say, there was no more spitting and there is no record of the order ever being carried out.

However inhumane Butler was seen to be, New Orleans fared rather well compared with other occupied Southern cities. For the most part, citizens were allowed to go about their daily lives, and it was Butler who ordered the city scrubbed

from top to bottom, which is credited with eliminating yellow fever outbreaks during the war. Also, as authors Joan B. Garvey and Mary Lou Widmer write in *Beautiful Crescent: A History of New Orleans,* unlike Atlanta, New Orleans was never bombarded. "It was governed efficiently," write the authors, "and the physical comfort of the citizens was better during the federal administration than it had been under the Confederacy."

HOUSE OF THE RISING FUN

After the war, New Orleans went through the difficult period of Reconstruction and faced the challenge of rebuilding its economy without the help of free slave labor. Never having learned to type, the Big Easy fell back on what it was best at: fun. Vice was the name of the game in late 19th century New Orleans. Saloons and gambling establishments abounded and, by some counts, there was a house of ill repute on every city block. In 1898, in response to pleas from the police and the church community, city leaders decided that something had to be done to rein in this neverending party.

New Orleans businessman and alderman Sidney Story came up with a plan to create a regulated prostitution district. He left the wording of the ordinance to attorney Thomas McCaleb Hyman, whose challenge was to write a law legalizing prostitution that would stand up in court. The ingenious result was simple: The law said it was illegal for prostitutes to work *outside* the area bounded by North Robertson and North Basin Streets, from the Customs House to St. Louis Street. The ordinance made no mention of the legality of prostitution inside this area. The ordinance passed, and a church group soon filed suit. The case went all the way to the U.S. Supreme Court, which upheld the law's constitutionality. Of course, the respectable Mr. Story was appalled when he read in local newspaper accounts that this new sin sub-city had been dubbed Storyville.

Storyville's pleasure palaces thrived and were credited with not only satisfying the city's carnal cravings but also providing the incubator for an emerging new music—jazz. Although America's only original art form was actually born a few blocks away, it was in the ground-floor gambling and entertainment areas of Storyville's brothels (working girls were allowed to ply their trade upstairs only) that jazz received its first mainstream audience. In the early part of the 20th century, jazz pioneers such as Jelly Roll Morton and Louis Armstrong played in Storyville.

The prostitutes' biggest business had always come during Mardi Gras, and before the creation of Storyville, an annual prostitutes' costume party was established, known as "The Ball of the Two Well Known Gentlemen." The event was a huge success and grew larger each year until the curiosity of even the city's "proper ladies" got the best of them and they began wrangling invitations. The idea was that behind a mask, one could anonymously see firsthand the torrid behavior one could so self-righteously disapprove of later. In 1906, Josie Arlington, one of Storyville's most prominent madams, came up with a plan to deal with these unwanted highbrow guests. After everyone had arrived at the ball, Arlington had the place raided by some of her police buddies, who carted off to jail any woman who could not prove she was a prostitute. This highly embarrassing moment for those society women may be the only case in history in which a brothel was raided and women were arrested for not working there. Needless to say, there were no further intrusions at the prostitutes' ball.

Of course, all good things must come to an end. In 1917, Storyville was finally closed under pressure from the U.S. Secretary of War, who quoted a ban on open prostitution within five miles of a military installation. Within a year, writes local historian Buddy Stall in *Buddy Stall's New Orleans*, "venereal diseases were back because prostitutes were no longer required to obtain regular medical checkups, crimes against nature jumped up, unwed mothers were on the rise, and houses of ill repute sprang up all over town—including in the French Quarter and the elaborate Garden District."

HOOKED ON THE KINGFISH

During the first half of the 20th century, New Orleans saw its port become one of the world's busiest. River-flooding problems were finally for the most part stabilized with levees, and the Vieux Carré Commission was established to undertake preservation of the French Quarter. The most interesting and controversial figure in the state during this time was Huey P. Long. The Kingfish (a nickname he gave himself) was a political powerhouse. Elected governor in 1928, he came to represent the kind of savior people were looking for to rescue them from the ravages of the Depression. His book *Every Man a King* outlined his plan to end this bleak chapter in the nation's history.

"A chicken in every pot" was the slogan of his Share the Wealth campaign, through which he declared that no one in America should be allowed to make more than $1 million a year and that any amount over that should be put into a fund for the poor. His popularity rose so fast and so wide that he was elected to the U.S. Senate just two years after becoming governor.

Long's biggest driving force seemed to be his ego. His second book was a slightly premature *My First Days in the White House*. And his best-known accomplishment in the Senate was leading a weeklong filibuster against a bill backed by President Franklin Roosevelt. Long himself spoke for more than 15 hours, during which time he supposedly complained that the bill circumvented Mosaic Law by violating the book of Leviticus, chapters 15 and 16. According to the book *Beautiful Crescent,* he also read the U.S. Constitution and Declaration of Independence, parts of Victor Hugo's *The Laughing Man,* other Bible chapters, a monologue on Greek mythology, and a recipe for fried oysters. Alas, the filibuster failed. But soon afterward those in the know began taking his presidential ambitions seriously. Long's political career was ended by an assassin's bullet as he walked through the state capitol in Baton Rouge on September 8, 1935.

To this day, there is much speculation that his bodyguards killed him. However controversial his life and death, the city owes Long a debt of gratitude for the original New Orleans airport, the Huey P. Long Bridge over the Mississippi River, Louisiana State University Medical Center, and free textbooks in public schools.

WAR AND PEACE

In the 1940s New Orleans, like the rest of the country, entered World War II. Along with men donning uniforms and women collecting rubber, the city's major contribution to the war effort took place on City Park Avenue at Higgins Industries. Here, boatbuilder Andrew Jackson Higgins designed and built his ramped landing craft used to ferry soldiers and equipment to shore during the decisive D-Day invasion. President Eisenhower later told biographer Stephen Ambrose that the Higgins landing crafts, the production of which marked the first major influx of women into the New Orleans job market, were the reason the Allies won the war.

After the war, as in most cities, the New Orleans population spread out, creating new suburbs and returning its attention to the place its heart had always been—home. Perhaps in no other town its size do people have less interest in what goes on beyond the city limits. In most parts of the United States, people are commonly asked where they were when they heard President Kennedy had been shot. In New Orleans the question is much more likely to be, "Where were you when Betsy hit?" referring to Hurricane Betsy, whose 145 mph winds and torrential rain devastated the city in 1965 and set a standard by which all future storms would be measured. That was, until August 29, 2005.

KATRINA: WHAT A BLOW HARD

The city reached yet another turning point on that late-summer day when Hurricane Katrina blew into town. Of course, no one could fathom just how bad it would be. Many locals will recall that while preparing to evacuate, their thought process never went beyond, "This one looks bad. I better pack for three days instead of two." And although Katrina was a monster of a storm as it churned through the Gulf of Mexico, measured by multiple sources, it was no more than a Category 2 hurricane by the time it made its way 100 miles upriver to New Orleans. And while its ferocious winds did their share of damage, the majority of the city's destruction came courtesy of floodwaters that washed out federally built levees (supposedly constructed to provide Category 4 protection). Nearly 2,000 people died and tens of thousands more were left homeless with most of the city's housing stock under as much as 11 feet of water.

With such devastation, there were those who deemed it simply a waste of time and effort to rebuild New Orleans. But it was not the locals who made that argument. Most were too busy clearing debris and picking up hammers. Perhaps because being from a historic city, they had a more big-picture view than the average person. They knew that this was certainly not the first time the best efforts of man and nature have conspired against New Orleans and it seems unlikely to be the last. They knew that just because a good punch knocks you down, you don't have to let yourself be counted out. Those are the people who continue to rebuild their homes and their lives (with the very gratefully acknowledged help of thousands of volunteers from across the country and around the world). And their efforts are paying off. The latest Census Bureau data released in July 2009 showed New Orleans to be the fastest-growing large city in America.

So, once again, New Orleans has come close to being destroyed and has survived. The city changes, but the essentials remain the same. The Big Easy and her people continue to laugh, to cook, to make music. As for those who think that is not worth preserving—What do we care?

Laissez les bon temps rouler.

HOTELS

The disarmingly seductive charm of this rollicking port city's historic lusty digs has lit the love lamp of more than a few river kings and steel magnolias over the years. Step into the past inside a 19th-century Greek Revival mansion and former home to generations of Creole gentry. Pass a stormy night on a mahogany four-poster bed, sharing secrets while listening to the hypnotic rain dance on the French double windows. Awaken slowly to the morning light caught in the lace curtains and find that croissants and cafe au lait have been left by room service outside the door along with a spray of flaming-red bougainvillea. Push open the double doors and step out onto a private wrought-iron balcony overlooking a tropical, gas lamp-dotted courtyard garden of Japanese magnolias and sweet olive, with a lovely triple-tiered fountain. The thrum of city life seems worlds away from this Elysian of Creole quietude.

OVERVIEW

For generations of New Orleanians, the city's hotels have been where the action is—from high society chow-downs and brimmed-hat afternoon teas to romantic in-town weekends and after-six elbow bending at a favorite watering hole. Any town can have hotels, but the Big Easy is among the Western Hemisphere's best examples of what it means to be a bona fide hotel city—and to acknowledge it with uncommon grace. Ultra-posh European-style hotels with chandelier-lit marble lobbies and multimillion-dollar artwork collections can boast guest books signed by Hollywood's hottest flavors of the month and European jet-setters who couldn't care less. Boutique hotels offer elegant alternatives to mega-hotels with conventioneer-jammed lobbies, as well as dainty inns long on history but short on amenities. Of course, an accommodating city like New Orleans can be counted on to rescue travel budgets from the brink of disaster by offering a range of mid-priced and family-friendly chain hotels and motels as well. Granted, they may not offer tea and scones or four-star dining, but there are plenty of such accommodations scattered throughout the city (check the Yellow Pages), plus they'll save you enough money to go out and enjoy afternoon tea on your own.

Guests with special needs will find they have not been forgotten. A growing number of hotels both large and quaint offer, for example, non-smoking and/or allergen-free rooms (even floors) and are partially or wholly wheelchair accessible. To be on the safe side, it's strongly recommended that you call ahead to check. Those traveling with pets or very small children should also check ahead. Unless otherwise noted, the hotels in this chapter accept most major credit cards and offer rooms with color TV (most with remote control; many with pay-per-view channels), telephones, private baths, and air-conditioning. Other amenities are listed by individual hotel.

Preferred and convenient locations include Uptown, the Central Business District/Warehouse Arts District, and, of course, the French Quarter. We will focus on accommodations in these areas. Of course, budget chain motels can be found in town as well as in the adjacent Jefferson Parish suburbs of Metairie and Kenner on the east bank of the Mississippi River and in Gretna on the west bank—15 to 20 minutes from New Orleans.

The most expensive times of the year to visit New Orleans include Mardi Gras, the French Quarter Festival, the New Orleans Jazz and Heritage Festival (see Annual Events and Festivals chapter), conventions, and holidays. Expect to pay more—sometimes *much* more—during these times.

Many if not most properties require a two- to five-night minimum stay during these high-traffic times. Peak season is during spring and fall, but summertime (and early Dec) guests can expect widely varying discounts. Hotels also offer specially discounted travel packages throughout the year. Check these out. Also call ahead to find out the reservation and cancellation policy, as this varies depending on hotel and time of year. Now lay your head on a goosedown pillow and think about exciting Big Easy explorations still to come. Sweet dreams.

Price Code

The price in all cases reflects the average rate for high-season, double-occupancy accommodations. Many if not most hotels have a range of price codes as rooms and suites vary in size, amenities, and desirability. Price codes do not include special services provided by the hotel such as babysitting, valet laundry, parking (if charges apply), telephone calls, room service, hotel-motel tax (11 percent if applicable), and per-head room-night taxes ($1 to $3).

$.................. **Less than $85**
$$ .... **$85 to $125**
$$$ .... **$126 to $175**
$$$$ .... **$176 to $225**
$$$$$ .... **$226+**

FRENCH QUARTER

BIENVILLE HOUSE HOTEL $$-$$$$
320 Decatur St.
(504) 529-2345, (800) 535-9603

The white canopy below the iron-trellis balconies and quartet of colorful flags provides shade for guests strolling through the Creole double doors into this French Quarter-style manor. Murals and gracious furnishings offer a taste of Old World charm. A multimillion-dollar lobby-to-rooftop renovation has created new interior and exterior appointments—for example, an elegantly furnished lobby, four sundecks, 83 guest rooms, and a tropical flagstone courtyard and pool. Triple-sheeted beds provide a sumptuous nightly welcome, while a new state-of-the-art "life safety"

and sprinkler system lets guests sleep with confidence. A coffeemaker is on hand to brew that first jolt of java in the morning before heading down to the lobby for a day-starting complimentary continental breakfast. Some rooms have balconies overlooking the courtyard and pool; others have nice views of the Mississippi River. Indoor valet parking and guest access to a nearby fitness center are two perks of this intimate boutique property and one-time riverfront warehouse.

BOURBON ORLEANS $$-$$$$$
717 Orleans St.
(504) 523-2222, (800) 521-5338
www.bourbonorleans.com

Step into the legendary Orleans Ballroom (if it's unoccupied) and try to imagine the 19th-century quadroon balls, where Creole dandies wooed the city's famously bewitching quadroons—women of mixed races. Today the fully restored ballroom built by entrepreneur John Davis is the centerpiece of this hotel accented by a white-columned lobby of crystal chandeliers and Oriental rugs. Step out onto a quiet balcony and listen to the jazz echoing from nearby Bourbon Street. Or sip a Sazerac in the courtyard where pirate Jean Lafitte once strolled and smell the soft jasmine on the warm evening breeze. More than 200 custom-designed guest rooms, including 28 suites including town house suites, offer views of French Quarter street life, picturesque rooftop skylines, or the tranquil inner courtyard overlooking the pool. The property is 2 blocks from Jackson Square in the heart of the French Quarter.

Rooms feature Chippendale and Queen Anne furnishings accented by two-poster canopied king beds, marble-topped wetbars, and antique writing desks. Marble-finished bathrooms feature the modern touch of a second telephone. Other amenities include a morning newspaper, oversize towels, nightly shoe shine, coffeemakers, bedroom and bathroom TVs, concierge, valet parking, and voice mail. All the favorite tastes of New Orleans are served inside Paillard during breakfast. Nightly cocktail hour is held in the elegant lobby bar. Business needs are met by the hotel's secretarial, multilingual translation, photocopying, fax, telex, daily stock market report, and national and international courier services. Cribs and rollaway beds are available at no extra charge.

THE CLAIBORNE MANSION $$$–$$$$$
2111 Dauphine St.
(504) 949-7327
www.claibornemansion.com

Cleo Pelleteri, the congenial owner who bought and renovated this architectural masterpiece in 1993, had no idea that one day her registry would be among the most valuable in the entire city. But, then, who could have fathomed that renowned artist LeRoy Neiman would sign the guest book with a hand-drawn caricature of himself complete with hat, moustache, and dangling cigarette? Pelleteri, however, is mum as to the other luminaries (and there are plenty) who've graced this three-story Greek Revival mansion, built in 1859 by W. C. C. Claiborne II, son of Louisiana's first American governor. Discretion is alive and well at this understated oasis of Creole luxury tucked in the Faubourg Marigny neighborhood 4 blocks from the French Quarter. This three-story mansion with exterior yellow walls is across the street from Washington Square Park, and within easy walking distance of the Marigny's funky bookstores, bric-a-brac shops, and cafes.

Neutral tones, 14-foot ceilings, original pinewood floors, and minimally decorated off-white walls throughout the house provide European-style sophistication for the discerning traveler. Exquisite finishing detail includes a lovely sitting nook at the end of the second-floor hallway and original artwork and framed photography by Julia Sims. Individually decorated rooms and suites feature fresh flowers, oversize marble bathrooms, queen-size beds, telephones with voice mail, and sumptuous breakfasts prepared in the original open-hearth kitchen in the service wing out back. Some rooms have four-poster canopied beds draped with patterned fabric. Modern flourishes include sleek black-metal curving pedestals for the color TV sets and, in some suites, contemporary iron poster beds with white linens. (Another

personal touch includes the crystal chandelier Pelleteri had spray-painted white that hangs in the ultra spacious second-floor hallway.)

Splurge on the Creole-style double-parlor suite (No. 11) just off the foyer, featuring original medallion ceilings and a separate living area with marble mantel, a 19th-century-style writing desk, and a Rohler & Campbell grand piano. The bedroom has two iron-post double beds and a palatial bath complete with dressing area, a bronze chandelier, and plush terry robes. The two-story service wing has additional rooms on the ground and second floors that overlook what is perhaps one of the loveliest courtyards in the city. Other amenities include complimentary continental breakfast and off-street parking.

DAUPHINE ORLEANS $$$$
415 Dauphine St.
(504) 586-1800, (800) 521-7111
www.dauphineorleans.com

Back in the 1850s, May Bailey's girls practiced the world's oldest profession in what is now the hotel bar; Audubon painted his birds in the studio cottage, which today is a meeting room named in his honor. To show off some real New Orleans smarts, though, it won't hurt to know that the romantic Dauphine Patio was once part of the historic Hermann-Grima estate. French double doors open to a tropical palm-filled courtyard accented by the 111-room hotel's exterior yellow walls and lush hanging ferns. The 14 rooms inside the Hermann House Courtyard feature exposed-brick walls, cherry-wood armoires, bronze chandeliers, and other elegant refinements such as fabrics in rich textures and subdued patterns. Baths have marble-finished sunken tubs. Goose-down pillows in the smoke-free Evergreen rooms should help guests sleep like a baby before rising to a complimentary continental breakfast served with the daily newspaper at your door. Noteworthy freebies include afternoon tea. Extra amenities include welcome cocktails, a fitness center, courtyard pool, cable TV, valet parking in an on-site parking garage, and wireless Internet.

THE FRENCHMEN $–$$$$

417 Frenchmen St.
(504) 948-2166, (800) 831-1781
www.frenchmenhotel.com

Each of this hotel's 27 spacious rooms, some with private balconies, has been refurbished and individually decorated with period furnishing reminiscent of the swank Creole homes of the mid-19th century. High ceilings and ceiling fans complete the look. First- and second-floor rooms of this 1850s town house open to a swimming pool and heated spa nestled in a tropical New Orleans courtyard garden. A twenty-four-hour concierge is available to help point guests in the right direction, while the riverfront trolley less than a block away provides a convenient and fun way to get there. Complimentary continental breakfast and limited off-street parking are available. This Faubourg Marigny hotel is a half block from the French Quarter across Esplanade Avenue.

THE HISTORIC FRENCH
MARKET INN $$–$$$$

501 Decatur St.
(504) 561-5621, (888) 538-5651
www.frenchmarketinn.com

Cozy and historic best describe this restored two-story 19th-century inn, built for Baron Joseph Xavier de Pontalba. Today 68 comfortable rooms with original exposed-brick walls and antique furnishings are situated 2 blocks from Jackson Square and 1 block from the Jax Brewery shopping complex. Complimentary cocktails and continental breakfast are part of the package. A pool and hot tub offer relaxation amid the brick courtyard of potted plants, lounge chairs, and table sets.

HOTEL MONTELEONE $$$–$$$$$

214 Royal St.
(504) 523-3341, (800) 535-9595
www.hotelmonteleone.com

In 1886 Antonio Monteleone, a shoemaker from Contessa, Italy, put his name on this hotel across the street from his cobbler shop. More than a century and five major additions later, this opulent and (still) family-owned landmark inspires some people to say, "The French Quarter begins in the lobby of the Monteleone." Just push past the gleaming brass front doors and step into the sparkling lobby. European elegance never enjoyed a better nouveau interpretation, accented by a quartet of gleaming teardrop-shaped crystal chandeliers, polished marble floors, and, of course, the hotel's gorgeous grandfather clock carved in mahogany by Antonio Puccio in 1909, which towers 12 feet and chimes at the quarter hour. The Queen Anne ballroom provides a richly woven flashback to 18th-century drawing rooms with its mix of Wedgwood and Arabesque art forms, Italian chandeliers, and European tapestries.

This is the kind of place where guests can expect to find the longtime bellman affectionately nicknamed "Hotel" Al. He started work here in the 1950s. One of the bartenders began his first shift in the early 1970s when the revolving Carousel Bar, which opened in 1944, was already famous among locals and visitors alike. But barstools, not flying horses, are the mode of transportation within the lounge's cobalt-blue walls. Artwork lighting includes wall-mounted lamps clutched by plaster clown fists. Nightclub-style, high-backed booths and a starlight ceiling in the adjoining room set the stage for nightly entertainment at the grand piano.

Today this landmark is one of the oldest continuously operated hotels in the city. People from Tennessee Williams and Truman Capote to political kingpins and movie stars have called it home. The hotel's 600 guest rooms and 55 suites are elegantly furnished with armoires and king- and queen-size beds; some suites have four-poster canopied beds, separate vanity and dressings areas, and views of the French Quarter. Head rooftop to freshen your tan line, to take a dip in the heated pool, or walk a few miles on one of the fitness center's treadmills. Valet parking is available in the hotel's 350-car garage.

HOTEL ST. MARIE $$-$$$
827 Toulouse St.
(504) 561-8951, (800) 366-2743
www.hotelstmarie.com

This elegantly restored property owned by New Orleans' Valentino family (which also owns the Place d'Armes and Prince Conti Hotels; see below) offers the easy comfort and subtle grace of an authentic European guesthouse. Brick walls with traditional gaslights frame the modest palm- and fern-lined courtyard and pool of this 105 guest room and suite hotel, a half block from Bourbon Street. Many rooms offer balcony views of the French Quarter. Valet parking and complimentary continental breakfast and daily newspaper are included in the tariff.

i Looking for accommodations in all the wrong places? The folks at the Greater New Orleans Hotel-Motel Association, 2020 St. Charles Ave., might be able to help. Give them a call at (504) 525-2264. Or call the New Orleans Metropolitan Convention & Visitors Bureau, Inc., 2020 St. Charles Ave., at (504) 566-5011 or (800) 672-6124.

HOTEL VILLA CONVENTO $$-$$$
616 Ursulines St.
(504) 522-1793, (800) 887-2817
www.villaconvento.com

More than one carriage driver has told wide-eyed visitors the story of the legendary House of the Rising Sun. Some people speculate that it might have been this place once upon a time. No one is sure. What is known is that this four-story Creole town house was built around 1833 on land purchased from the Ursuline nuns (whose convent is nearby; hence the name). The property passed to a succession of owners and even served time as a rooming house. The most famous tenant, Jimmy Buffett, came back with a video crew to film a documentary on his early life in New Orleans. The modern-day owners, the Campo family, bought this historic building in 1981. The family comes with a little history of its own—they are Isleños,

descendents of Canary Islanders who immigrated to New Orleans from Spain in the early 1800s. Today 25 rooms located 2 blocks from the French Market are individually decorated; some have high ceilings, four-poster beds, and balconies overlooking Ursulines Street. Two courtyard rooms feature original brick walls; two fourth-floor suites offer panoramic views of the Mississippi River and Vieux Carré rooftops. Complimentary coffee and tea croissants are served each morning. No children under age 10 allowed.

LE RICHELIEU $$-$$$$$
1234 Chartres St.
(504) 529-2492, (800) 535-9653
www.lerichelieuhotel.com

All things being equal, an "affordable class" hotel such as this—with its history, charm, service, and discretion—should cost a whole lot more. Maybe that's why ex-Beatle Paul McCartney (for whom money is certainly no object) hunkered down here with his brood for two months back in 1975 while recording his Wings album *Venus and Mars* at Sea-Saint Studio during Mardi Gras. McCartney booked an entire floor. When fans asked if the cute former Mop Top was registered at the hotel, they were told "no." It was the truth (the registration was in the name of his company). But how did the Mac avoid being mobbed on the streets while he mingled with revelers? He did what a lot of Carnivalites do—he masked as a clown/jester. On Ash Wednesday, the day after Mardi Gras when things get back to normal, Sir Paul reportedly composed a song called "My Carnival" at the hotel. The tune never made it onto the album. Does it matter? (Guests can stay in the Paul McCartney Suite for $225 and up per night.)

This motor hotel is named for the Armand-Jean du Plessis, Duke and Cardinal de Richelieu, the powerful Prime Minister of Louis XIII and the acknowledged architect of France's 17th-century grandeur. A portrait of Cardinal Richelieu, painted by local artist Carl Cramer, hangs in the lobby. The site was originally part of a 1745 land grant from Louis XV of France to the Ursuline nuns so that they could care for sick French soldiers and establish a school for "young ladies." As a result, a *caserbes*, or lodging, and hospital were built at this location, which housed French, Spanish, and American soldiers for more than a century. A rebellion led by French patriot Nicholas Chauvin de La Freniere broke out when outraged colonists learned that the cash-strapped Louis XV had secretly given Louisiana to his cousin, Charles III of Spain. La Freniere and four of his compatriots were executed by firing squad in the barracks courtyard of what is now the hotel's parking lot. Interestingly, the La Freniere–led "October Rebellion" of 1766 was the first revolution against a foreign power on soil of the Continental United States. The land was divided into lots and sold to citizens in 1824.

Longtime owner Frank Rochefort oversees 86 individually decorated Victorian rooms and suites with quality reproduction furnishings, armoires, brass ceiling fans, desks, hair dryers, ironing boards, and refrigerators. Other amenities include percale sheets and free local calls. Some rooms have balconies overlooking the courtyard and pool or Chartres Street. Additional creature comforts include valet laundry, babysitting, cafe, bar/lounge, and private self-park-and-lock lot (one of the few hotels in the city where guests can park their own cars and keep their keys). The hotel is nearby the Old U.S. Mint and French Market and within walking distance of Jackson Square and Bourbon Street.

MAISON DUPUY HOTEL $$$–$$$$$
1001 Toulouse St.
(504) 586-8000, (800) 535-9177
www.maisondupuy.com

Historic footnotes have never failed to lend charm and nuance to the 300-year-old French Quarter—and this address is no exception. John Pitot, the first elected mayor of New Orleans, built the first U.S. cotton press at this site in the 18th century. During the 19th and 20th centuries, this corner site was home to everything from a blacksmith shop to a sheet metal company. It wasn't until 1973 that Clarence and Milton Dupuy built and opened their hotel (the last allowed in the French

Quarter before a moratorium was enacted in 1975). The brothers sold the property in 1996 to the Thayer Lodging Group, which undertook an extensive $5 million renovation one year later.

Today guests at this residential neighborhood hotel, 2 blocks from Bourbon Street, can count on peace and quiet—a commodity worth its weight in gold to anyone visiting during Mardi Gras or other special events. Two hundred spacious guest rooms each feature imported draperies, signature local art, and marble bathrooms. Balconies overlook the French Quarter or the hotel's lush fountain courtyard accented with gas lamps and potted palms—a best-kept secret perfect for romantic evening dinners. Other amenities include a fitness center and two restaurants.

OLIVIER HOUSE HOTEL $$$–$$$$$
828 Toulouse St.
(504) 525-8456, (866) 525-9748
www.olivierhouse.com

Original exposed-brick walls, hanging ferns, and huge banana trees make the gas lamp–dotted garden courtyard an appealing place in which to savor the hotel's complimentary morning coffee. This trio of town houses was built in 1839 for wealthy plantation owner Marianne Bienvenue Olivier. In 1970 Jim and Kathryn Danner bought and renovated the property, 1 block from Bourbon Street, and still operate it as a 42-room hotel. To the right of the lobby is a spacious chandelier-lit parlor with original brass lighting fixtures and a marble-mantel fireplace. No two guest rooms or suites are alike. Miss Anna's Creole Cottage, for instance, boasts a queen bed, living room and

i   **Have more questions than answers? For visitors and in-town weekenders staying at the city's hotels, the concierge is a font of information and the inside track on everything from the best nights to dine at a particular restaurant to advice on where to locate that hard-to-find voodoo gris-gris. These savvy professionals of the hotel industry are worth their weight in gold (or at least a good tip).**

dining areas, large bath, brick floors, fireplace, antique furnishings, and private courtyard. The Honeymoon Suite features a spacious bedroom with queen four-poster bed, parlor doors, tall ceilings, hardwood floors, a fireplace, and floor-to-ceiling windows, plus a corner balcony over-looking both Toulouse and Dauphine streets.

OMNI ROYAL ORLEANS $$$$–$$$$$
621 St. Louis St.
(504) 529-5333, (800) 843-6664
www.omnihotels.com

If it's views you're after, this 346-room luxury hotel has plenty. For starters there's the seventh-floor pool lounge, La Riviera, open Apr through Oct, which offers a limited lunchtime menu of sand-wiches and salads but serves up one of the best rooftop views of the French Quarter skyline in the city. Head up the concrete steps to the breeze-cooled observation deck for a terrific panorama of St. Louis Cathedral, the Mississippi River, and the Crescent City Connection twin span. Where's the beef? It's downstairs at the ground-level Old English-style Rib Room, an award-winning eatery best known for its mesquite-grill rotisserie. Just as savory are the window-table views of passersby on Royal Street. The Touche Bar meantime is a sidewalk cafe that comes alive when the after-work crowd of French Quarter antiques and art dealers drops by.

Rooms decorated in 19th-century style for the "casual voyager" looking for grace and comfort offer romantic views of lush tropical courtyards, Jackson Square, the Mississippi River, or the rooftops of the Vieux Carré. Amenities include hair dryers, goosedown pillows, minibars, original artwork, complimentary wireless Internet access and computer modem hookups and data-ports, 24-hour room service, same-day valet and laundry services, babysitting, fitness center, and (perhaps most important considering the city's unpredictable weather) umbrellas.

Spanish wrought-iron balconies, a French facade, and interior combination of 19th-century English, French, Spanish, and American antiques and artifacts pay homage to the past. So, too,

does the impressive marble stairway guarded by a pair of priceless Venetian Moors, which leads to the brightly lit lobby of gilt mirrors, freshly cut flowers, polished brass appointments, and crystal chandeliers.

PLACE D'ARMES $$–$$$
625 St. Ann St.
(504) 524-4531, (800) 366-2743
www.placedarmes.com

Sometimes there's a lot to be said for simplicity. And if you want to get far from the madding crowd of megahotels but still be close to the action, this small, casual property with classic old New Orleans architecture may hold the key. Near Jackson Square, this hotel, located between Chartres and Royal Streets, is only a few magic yards from St. Louis Cathedral, Cafe du Monde, the Mississippi River, and many other French Quarter attractions. Or walk 2 blocks in the opposite direc-tion and you're on Bourbon Street. Eight adjoin-ing, beautifully restored 18th-century row houses with 85 guest rooms (warning—some don't have windows) surround a lushly landscaped pool courtyard of magnolia and banana trees, perfect for relaxing at the end of the day before head-ing out to dinner at one of the nearby seafood or Creole dining establishments. Complimentary continental breakfast and in-room Internet access, plus valet parking make up the short list of ame-nities (there is no restaurant or lounge) at this comfortable charmer.

PRINCE CONTI HOTEL $$$
830 Conti St.
(504) 529-4172, (800) 366-2743
www.princecontihotel.com

Discreetly tucked away near the heart of the French Quarter, ½ block off Bourbon Street, is this European-style pension hotel with 76 guest rooms, many with period antiques. Guests can start off the day with complimentary continental breakfast. Other amenities include complimentary in-room Internet access, secured drive-in parking, and valet laundry. Located in the carriageway is The Bombay Club Restaurant & Martini Bistro, a sophisticated lounge featuring nearly 100 different types of martinis.

THE SAINT LOUIS $$-$$$$
730 Bienville St.
(504) 581-7300, (800) 535-9111
www.stlouishotel.com

This site was the 19th-century home of a Spanish family and, later, a brewing company before the present-day hotel was built in 1971. Two of the best features of this gem, a mix of French colonial and Creole architecture, are its quiet brick court-yard and central location in the French Quarter, ½ block from Bourbon and Royal Streets. Secluded privacy in elegant surroundings close to the Quarter's nerve center may seem like a tall order, but this courtly retreat of Creole gentility pulls it off without breaking a sweat. Many of the 97 spacious rooms and suites, each decorated with French Provincial antiques or reproductions, have wrought-iron balconies overlooking the hotel's lush Mediterranean courtyard and stone fountain (except during inclement weather, when it's cov-ered by rain flaps). All rooms feature concierge service, nightly turn-down service, and com-plimentary newspaper; some have beautifully decorated parlors and walk-in closets, or separate vanity areas.

SONIAT HOUSE $$$-$$$$$
1133 Chartres St.
(504) 522-0570, (800) 544-8808
www.soniathouse.com

Talk about grand introductions. We're referring, of course, to the fabulous carriageway entrance to this quintessential romantic hotel, especially at night, when a multitude of candles light the shadowy, lush courtyard. From the open galler-ies framed by lace ironwork to the lovely peach walls accented by white double French doors with romantic fanlights, this scene has been known to breathe the fire of pure Creole passion into more than one couple on their umpteenth "honeymoon." Originally built in 1829 by prosper-ous plantation owner Joseph Soniat Dufossat as a double town house for his large family's city visits, this brick-walled time capsule has played host

to such modern-day guests as Brad Pitt, Jessica Lange, and Robert Duvall. And if they enjoyed the privacy and discreet service, you probably will, too. This place is as peaceful as a country inn (it's next to an 18th-century Ursuline convent) and as intimate as a private home (you'd never know it was 2 blocks from looney-bin Bourbon Street). Of course, a meticulous restoration prior to its open-ing in 1983 didn't hurt.

Proprietor Rodney Smith has furnished each room and suite with all the comforts of a luxury hotel without disturbing the architectural integ-rity of the house. Rooms feature the English, French, and Louisiana antiques Smith and his wife, Frances (who owns an antiques business), have collected during their quarter century of world travel. Their attention to detail at this 33-room-and-suite "best small hotel in New Orleans" makes guests and travel cognoscenti alike nearly pass out with praise. (On a wall of framed testimonials is this one: "These people will spoil you rotten.") Consider: Custom fabrics, antique Oriental rugs, four-poster beds draped with a canopy of linen or century-old crewel embroidery, silk curtains, polished hardwood floors, woodcut prints, and paintings by con-temporary New Orleans artists. The more down-to-earth amenities include bathside telephones, Frette Egyptian cotton bed linens, goosedown pillows, and spa baths in several of the rooms.

W NEW ORLEANS FRENCH
QUARTER $$$-$$$$$
316 Chartres St.
(504) 581-1200, (800) 448-4927
www.whotels.com

The echo of a nearby paddle wheeler's calliope welcomes fans of small European hotels to this intimate property. Many of the 98 deluxe, and traditionally furnished rooms and carriage house suites have balconies overlooking the lushly land-scaped and flower-filled fountain courtyard and pool; others overlook French Quarter streets. Oversize rooms have double, queen, or king beds with 350 thread count sheets, down comforters and pillows, oversize desks, 27-inch TVs with high-speed Internet access, coffeemakers, minibars, and dual-line telephones with voice mail. Room service for breakfast, lunch, and dinner is available from Bacco (see Restaurants chapter). But it would be a shame not to experience in person this highly acclaimed on-site restaurant owned by the Brennan family of Brennan's and Commander's Palace fame. So take a lint brush to the sports coat or slip into that cute little number you bought on Royal Street yesterday afternoon, and head downstairs for lunch or dinner. One block from Royal Street's art galleries and antiques shops, 2 blocks from bustling Bourbon Street, and 4 blocks from Jackson Square, this hotel offers valet parking, complimentary newspaper, and 24-hour coffee and tea service.

CBD/DOWNTOWN AND WAREHOUSE DISTRICT

THE AMBASSADOR $$-$$$$
535 Tchoupitoulas St.
(504) 527-5271, (888) 527-5271
www.ambassadorhotelneworleans.com

Many of the city's hotels possess the requisite charm and elegance to woo visitors "from the moment they enter the lobby doors." And this facility, with its sparkling white porcelain floors, certainly deserves to be in that number. But it's while heading in the opposite direction that guests will come to appreciate one of this hotel's finest attributes—its location, smack in the middle of the Warehouse Arts District. The trendy district is chock-a-block with renovated warehouses now serving as art galleries and studios, restaurants, condos, nightclubs, and even the Louisiana Children's Museum. The district is an imaginative, fun, and leisurely place to stroll, especially after the bustling French Quarter crowds only 3 blocks away have started to work your last good nerve.

Three 19th-century coffee warehouses were renovated to create this property—an intermingling of old and new set against the city's thriving riverfront district. Each of the 165 guest rooms come with four-poster wrought-iron beds, hardwood floors, and 18th-century-style desks; 51 guest rooms also have 13-foot ceilings, nightly turndown, and wrought iron balconies. Amenities include complimentary continental breakfast, in-room safe, coffeemakers, and hair dryers. Telephones with voice mail and fax/modems, plus wireless high-speed Internet access will help captains of commerce get down to business. A tropical courtyard features a flowing fountain and oversize swimming pool.

COURTYARD BY MARRIOTT $$$-$$$$
124 St. Charles Ave.
(504) 581-9005, (800) 321-2211

This 140-room hotel in the Central Business District is only a 10-minute walk to the French Quarter's famed Pat O'Brien's—and, most likely, a 30-minute walk back. (In New Orleans the shortest distance between any two bars is a zigzag.) Spacious, moderately priced lodgings offer guests at this six-story hotel a chance to explore the past: Courtyard worked with a local historical society to re-create the Verandah hotel, which stood on the site from 1839 to 1855. Ornate iron-trellis balconies overlook St. Charles Avenue and provide views of downtown New Orleans; a dramatic atrium inside incorporates original Verandah columns. Attention to the comfort of present-day business and leisure guests can be seen in such amenities as large work desks, complimentary newspaper, "reach-anywhere phones," indoor whirlpool, and exercise room. The hotel is on the St. Charles Avenue streetcar line, which provides easy access to nearby attractions.

HARRAH'S NEW ORLEANS $$$-$$$$$
228 Poydras St.
(504) 533-6000, (800) 847-5299
www.harrahsneworleans.com

Rising 26 stories directly above New Orleans' only casino is this 450-room hotel featuring oversized rooms and suites, all outfitted with two deluxe queen beds with pillow-top mattresses, table and chairs, high-definition flat-screen TVs, coffeemaker, Gilchrist & Soames spa products, lightweight waffle robes, and wireless Internet ($10.95 per day). Premium rooms also feature a mini-refrigerator. But what lures many visitors to this downtown retreat, within walking distance of the French Quarter, are the spectacular views of the Mississippi River and the New Orleans skyline. A fitness center featuring a full complement of treadmills, stationery bikes, free weights, and state-of-the-art exercise machines helps patrons burn off calories after enjoying a meal at one of five dining venues: Bambu (Asian); Cafes on Canal (sandwiches and burgers); Gordon Biersch (bar and grill); Grand Isle (seafood); and, of course, the popular Buffet at Harrah's.

> ℹ️ It's been said that the Sunday brunch was invented in New Orleans. Not surprisingly, many of the best hotels offer Sunday (and even Saturday) brunches. Some offer buffets, others feature courtyard dining and live jazz, while still others tout "bottomless" champagne. A few offer all of the above. Reservations are often required.

HOLIDAY INN DOWNTOWN
SUPERDOME $$–$$$$$
330 Loyola Ave.
(504) 581-1600, (800) 535-7830
www.hi-neworleans.com

It's hard to miss the 150-foot mural of the early 1900s Selmer clarinet painted by local artist Robert Dafford on the Poydras Street exterior side of this downtown hotel. The mural is how this franchise property tips its horn to the birthplace of jazz and the legendary New Orleans musicians like Buddy Bolden and Louis Armstrong who made it all possible. Dafford and Louisiana artists Shirley Messina, Stig Marcussen, and Daniel Breaux were commissioned to create the original series of art seen throughout the property's public areas and guest room floors.

Check out the murals of Carnival parades in the Mardi Gras Lounge as well as those of famous jazz musicians in the lobby. Particularly noteworthy is the depiction of First Man of Jazz Buddy Bolden performing at the Union Sons Hall (nicknamed "Funky Butt Hall") in 1905. Bolden is the cornet player in the middle. Nearly 300 rooms and suites, 2 blocks from the Superdome and

3 blocks from the French Quarter, include telephones with voice mail, hair dryers, irons/ironing boards, and minisafes. Guest rooms on the key-access club level floor also have honor bars and coffeemakers; a club room serves continental breakfast and afternoon hors d'oeuvres. Other amenities include a rooftop pool, ATM service, complimentary morning coffee and evening ice cream in the lobby, and a restaurant, lounge, and gift shop.

HOTEL DE L'EAU VIVE $$–$$$$$
315 Tchoupitoulas St.
(504) 592-0300
www.hotel-deleauvive.com

The hotel name means house of the living waters, a fitting and serene moniker for this four-story all-suite hotel located in a historical landmark on a quiet, tree-lined stretch of the Central Business District. The elegantly furnished lobby tells only part of the story of this 34-suite property, opened in 1988. The rest is to be found in the one-bedrooms suites, each with spacious living room outfitted with private phone, TV, and sofa sleeper; full kitchen (with dishes and small appliances); plush bedroom with armoire; and glistening-tile bathroom featuring whirlpool and shower. Rates include double occupancy up to four persons, making this property a bargain for traveling families looking to splurge a tad on luxury. (Two- and three-bedroom suites are also available.) A pool surrounded by a lush tropical courtyard adds a nice touch of New Orleans-style leisure. Other amenities include complimentary coffee daily and free croissants and Danish Sat through Mon.

HOTEL INTER-CONTINENTAL
NEW ORLEANS $$–$$$
444 St. Charles Ave.
(504) 525-5566, (800) 455-6563
www.ichotelsgroup.com

The Veranda restaurant menu isn't the only reason to stay at this 500-room modern luxury hotel although many people who have sampled the Creole-Continental fare say it's one of the best reasons. This stylish hotel, part of a London-based joint venture by Pan American Life Insurance Co. and Inter-Continental Hotels and Resorts, is on the St. Charles Avenue streetcar line; the Superdome, Convention Center, and the Warehouse Arts District are within easy walking distance.

Comfortably furnished rooms in this 15-story, glass-and-granite downtown high-rise include such amenities as minibars and separate dressing areas; the bath area has a hair dryer, telephone, and mini-TV. Six "environmental" rooms are equipped with special water- and air-filtration systems. Nearly 40 deluxe guest rooms and suites on the Governor's Floor include six executive suites named after some of Louisiana's historic heads of state. Each suite is decorated in the furnishings and paintings of its statesman's time period. Extra amenities include large marble baths, plush bathrobes, Jacuzzis, full kitchens, dual-line dataport telephones, and a lounge offering complimentary cocktails and continental breakfast. A landscaped garden courtyard with original musical sculpture is on the fifth floor; the pool and fitness center (equipped with Lifecycles, treadmills, a Universal weight machine, and free weights) are rooftop.

HOTEL LECIRQUE $–$$
936 St. Charles Ave.
(504) 962-0900, (800) 684-9525
www.hotellecirqueneworleans.com
Travel and Leisure magazine has already given a thumbs-up to this hip 137-room boutique hotel, centrally located on the St. Charles Avenue streetcar line between Uptown and downtown's Central Business and Warehouse Arts Districts. Step inside and see why. Lobby decor is minimalist Asian fusion with an emphasis on clean lines augmented by Art Deco accents, bamboo half-walls, original artwork, and retro chairs in the sunken public sitting area. Guest rooms continue the theme with framed black-and-white art photographs, muted colors, and sconces. Amenities include walk-in showers (but no tubs), hair dryers, iron/ironing boards, coffeemakers, TV, and dataports. A full gym and indoor pool are on-site. The

hotel's Helix Restaurant & Wine Bar consistently earns rave reviews.

INTERNATIONAL HOUSE $$$–$$$$$
221 Camp St.
(504) 553-9550, (800) 633-5770
www.ihhotel.com
In 2007, Los Angeles-based designer L. A. Pagano, a favorite among celebs like Nicolas Cage and Johnny Depp, gave this 12-story, 117-room boutique hotel a makeover. Today the lobby's ornate pilasters and intimate groupings of furniture handcrafted by local artists hint at the "ritual and religiosity" that flavor the city's soulful, sensual, and mysterious character. Each guest room features a spalike bathroom, glass shower or oversized shower along with Aveda bath amenities, ceiling fans, two-line speakerphones, complimentary wireless Internet, plus original black-and-white photos of local jazz legends. Guests looking for the ultimate discreet touch will appreciate the private telephone number direct to each room. Nonsmoking floors are available.

The hotel bar, Loa, named for the divine spirits of voodoo, sets a deliciously sensual mood for casting a love spell thanks to its sumptuous seating, sculpted bar, and candlelight-only illumination. (Order the Flambeau, an equally intoxicating mix of spiced rum, Grand Marnier, and Chambord.) The Spanish-flavored restaurant Rambla is also on-site.

THE LAFAYETTE HOTEL $$$–$$$$$
600 St. Charles Ave.
(504) 524-4441, (800) 733-4754
www.neworleansfinehotels.com
The dignified Old World charm of the polished French mahogany front desk complements a foyer of Italian marble floors, wood moldings, and English carpets. When the Wirth family built this five-story brick hotel in 1918 on fashionable St. Charles Avenue, it was intended to spur the transformation of the neighborhood "from a sleepy line of boardinghouses into a hum of activity," according to a September 3, 1916, article in the *New Orleans Item*. During World War II, however,

the property was used by the Navy as barracks for Waves (Women Accepted for Volunteer Emergency Service) and afterwards fell into disrepair. The hotel reopened for the 1984 World's Fair but closed two years later until 1991, when developers Mickey Palmer and Patrick Quinn pumped $6 million into a major renovation effort.

This historic hotel adjacent to the Warehouse Arts District and 5 blocks from the French Quarter was worth the wait. It has been restored to its former splendor with original French doors and wrought-iron balconies (a perfect spot for catching beads from Mardi Gras parades that roll down The Avenue). Each of the 44 rooms and suites upstairs is individually decorated and furnished with designer fabrics, gilt mirrors, and English botanical prints; the lavish marble baths with elegant brass fittings are matched by such thoughtful touches as thick terry bathrobes and French-milled soaps. Other amenities include minibars, hair dryers, and umbrellas. (Suites feature a wet bar, refrigerator, and VCR; some have four-poster beds and a whirlpool.) Attentive yet unobtrusive service is the name of the game here.

LE PAVILLON HOTEL $$–$$$$$
833 Poydras St.
(504) 581-3111, (800) 535-9095
www.lepavillon.com

It's surprising this hotel one of the city's grandest—doesn't cause traffic accidents. Drive past the white-columned facade of this chip-off-the-Old-World-block property and see if you can resist staring at the antique Czech crystal chandeliers visible in the lobby behind the glass double front doors. Marble railings from the Grand Hotel in Paris and faux marble columns also accent this 1907 hotel's sparkling lobby. This downtown property on the corner of Baronne Street comes with plenty of history. It was built on the site of one of the city's earliest sugarcane plantation homes. The original owners, the Jesuits, purchased it directly from New Orleans founder Sieur de Bienville. By the turn of the 19th century, the area was a forbidding fringe of cypress thickets and cemeteries, described by a writer of the day

as a place of "foul deeds and midnight murders (where) no ordinary courage was required to venture alone." Later it served as the main depot for the New Orleans and Carrollton railroad. In the 1860s it was transformed into the National Theater, often called Werlein Hall after owner Philip Werlein, founder of the famous music store. When construction of the present-day hotel (then called the New Hotel Denechaud) was completed, it featured the first hydraulic elevators in the city.

In 1991 the hotel was placed on the National Register of Historic Places. Today graciousness is the byword of the 226 masterfully appointed guest rooms and suites furnished in European and American antiques. Some of the seven suites feature European-style mahogany canopies, marble bathrooms, and many other elegant touches, each with its own theme. Valet parking, 24-hour room service, and complimentary shoe shine are just some of the extra personal services guests can expect. Work up a sweat at the executive fitness center, relax with a cocktail at Le Gallery Lounge, or take a swim and enjoy the sweeping city views from the rooftop heated pool. Massive gilt columns, ornate woodwork, and a marble fireplace augment the Crystal Room, known for sumptuous dining.

OMNI ROYAL CRESCENT $$$–$$$$$
535 Gravier St.
(504) 527-0006, (800) 843-6664
www.omnihotels.com

In recent years the city's boutique hotels such as this one have offered travelers a cozy and elegant alternative to the tug-of-war between large convention properties and charming little inns. One of the best things about this century-old refurbished building, only a block from Bourbon Street, is the 24-hour room service. Since the first was erected in 1862 during the Civil War, buildings at this site have served as a Junior Achievement office, a drug company warehouse, a local AFL–CIO headquarters and a frozen yogurt store. But the present incarnation, located in the heart of the Financial District, is hard to beat. A

European-style jewel-box lobby features cozy sitting areas decorated with Oriental rugs, 19th-century paintings, and objets d'art. (Libraries on each floor provide quiet reading sanctuaries.) Ninety-seven recently renovated rooms are simply but tastefully decorated and feature marble baths and bathroom floors, Egyptian cotton linens, tropical-weight cotton bathrobes and slippers, bedside cassette players with classical music selections, fax machines, and dual-line phones with computer ports. Other features include a 24-hour fitness center with sauna and whirlpool, rooftop sundeck with Roman-style pool, and French Quarter skyline views.

THE PELHAM $$$–$$$$$
444 Common St.
(504) 522-4444, (800) 272-4583
www.neworleansfinehotels.com

Several years ago a $3 million conversion of this 1850s Financial District property on the site of the Bienville Plantation gave rise to this 64-guest room boutique hotel decorated with chandeliers, Oriental rugs, and iron Corinthian support columns. Two blocks from the French Quarter, each of the guestrooms is luxuriously appointed and features 10-foot windows overlooking Canal Street, exposed-brick walls, four-poster beds, 18-foot ceilings, crown molding, European and antique furnishings, and marble baths. Amenities include plush terry robes, complimentary newspaper (delivered to your room) and shoe shine, hair dryer, and fine English soaps and lotion.

RENAISSANCE PERE MARQUETTE $$–$$$$$
817 Common St.
(504) 525-1111, (800) 372-0482
www.renaissancehotels.com

Joining a growing roster of hotels in the Big Easy keeping a keen eye on cutting-edge decor. is this 272-room hotel, located 2 blocks from the French Quarter, with its ultrasleek lobby of forward-thinking architecture design. Regional artistic influences and different time periods weigh in vis-a-vis furnishings, decorative treatments, and artwork. Guest rooms feature two-line telephones, voice mail, dataport, cordless phones, and large workspaces with reading lamps. Amenities include down-filled comforters and duvets on premium mattresses, bathrobes, minibar, in-room coffee and tea, safe, hair dryer, iron, and ironing board. Added touches include an outdoor pool, complimentary health club, valet laundry, 24-hour in-room dining, concierge services, and on-site MiLa restaurant.

THE RITZ-CARLTON $$$$–$$$$$
921 Canal St.
(504) 524-1331, (800) 241-3333
www.ritzcarlton.com

When the world's preeminent ultraluxury hotel chain opened its New Orleans' property in Maison Blanche, the former Canal Street shopping legend and beloved landmark, officials made sure that restoration preserved the historic 12-story Art Nouveau building's glazed terra-cotta exterior, prismatic glass, and other turn-of-the-20th-century design elements. It seems only fitting that some of the 452 rooms, including club rooms and deluxe suites, decorated in timeless Southern luxury, offer an ideal vantage point from which to view the Carnival parades that roll down Canal Street. Amenities include twice-daily maid service, 24-hour room service, minibar, in-room safe, and marble bath with terry robes. Other features of the property, steps away from the French Quarter, include a lush courtyard, ground-level gallery of boutiques, and an award-winning (and recently renovated) 25,000-square-foot day spa with 22 treatment rooms and spa cafe.

THE ROOSEVELT NEW ORLEANS $$$–$$$$$
123 Baronne St.
(504) 648-1200, (800) 925-3673
www.therooseveltneworleans.com

Walk under this building's canopy and past the bronze front doors into the opulent blocklong lobby. Gilded columns sparkling crystal chandeliers show the way. If by-the-book Art Deco refinement has a name, it's this Big Easy institution—one of the oldest grand hotels in the country. This property has been near to the hearts of generations of New Orleanians since it opened in 1893 as the six-story Grunewald "in full readiness for the Carnival of 1894." An adjacent 400-room, 14-story annex was added and opened in 1908. In 1923 the hotel was renamed the Roosevelt (in honor of Teddy, who had died five years earlier) after the original Grunewald was demolished and the annex's public rooms were refurbished at a cost of $500,000.

Huey P. Long used this well-loved landmark as his campaign headquarters. Eight U.S. presidents from Coolidge to Clinton have stayed under its roof. Haile Selassie and General Charles DeGaulle once enjoyed its extravagance (but not together). It was the model for Arthur Hailey's best-selling novel *Hotel* (staff remembers him taking "copious" notes and can even identify some of the characters in the book). In 1932 radio station WWL–AM set up shop here and has broadcast performances nationwide live from the legendary Blue Room for nearly two decades. And if that's not enough, the Sazerac Bar & Grill is the home of the famous bourbon-and-bitters drink of the same name, invented here more than 140 years ago.

Now a part of the Waldorf Astoria Collection, this historic New Orleans landmark reopened in June 2009 following a two-year, $145 million restoration that today boasts 504 rooms, including 135 luxury suites, with state-of-the-art amenities. Guest rooms feature high-speed Internet access, flat-screen TVs, 24-hour in-room dining. Deluxe guest rooms feature 300-count bed linens, bathrobes and refreshment centers, while Astoria Suites also include complimentary daily newspaper, Guerlain Spa bath products, evening canapés, and in-room bar set-up. A rooftop pool and terrace features the open-air Pool Café and bar, while internationally acclaimed New Orleans chef John Besh has opened his newest restaurant, Domenica, featuring the cuisine of rural Italy, on the ground floor.

W NEW ORLEANS $$$–$$$$$
333 Poydras St.
(504) 525-9444, (877) 946-8357
www.whotels.com

This 423 guest room and suite hotel features standard and king beds, as well as views of the Mississippi River (WOW suites have Jacuzzis). Rooms are fully stocked with Bliss Spa Sinkside Six bath products, plush down comforters, 350 thread-count sheets, and 32-inch TVs with high-speed Internet access. This 23-story Financial District property is conveniently situated at the corner of Tchoupitoulas Street 2 blocks from the Mississippi River and 4 blocks from Canal Street and the French Quarter immediately beyond. The Convention Center, Superdome, and Warehouse Arts District are within easy walking distance. For exercise check out the health club and outdoor pool.

WESTIN NEW ORLEANS
CANAL PLACE $$$$–$$$$$
100 Iberville St.
(504) 566-7006, (866) 527-1381
www.starwoodhotels.com

Oh, the luxuries—and views—you'll encounter here, starting with the Carrera marble lobby full of antiques and jardinières, on the 11th floor of the Canal Place Shopping Centre. Tea is served in the lobby every afternoon—along with round-the-clock panoramic views of the city, Mississippi River, and French Quarter courtesy of the arched two-story windows. The 29th-floor rooftop pool offers similar views for those wishing to swim off the previous night's meal. Head downstairs to the multiscreen cinema at The Shops at Canal Place, or browse the complex's Gucci, Williams-Sonoma, and other upscale stores. Nearly 440 oversized guest rooms and suites feature richly appointed French influences, large marble baths, dataport/voice-mail phones, stocked minibar, coffeemakers, in-room safes, hair dryers, and irons/ironing boards. A complimentary health club is available as well as 24-hour room service from the restaurant River 127, which offers all-day dining with a scenic view 127 feet above the Mississippi River. The megaluxury hotel is only steps away from the city's riverfront trolley and the Aquarium of the Americas.

WINDSOR COURT $$$$-$$$$$
300 Gravier St.
(504) 523-6000, (888) 596-0955
www.windsorcourthotel.com

Bill Gates (who rented the ultralavish 10-room penthouse) and Princess Anne are on the honor roll of luminaries who have unpacked their bags inside this Southern testimony to impeccable British refinement. Pull into the circular brick drive-in courtyard and see for yourself. Inside this 23-story rose-colored granite facade of roof-level terraces, balconies, and bay windows is a marble-and-jardinières lobby of Old World elegance and contemporary design. A $6 million collection of 17th- through 20th-century furnishings and artwork includes paintings by Reynolds and Gainsborough; many lean heavily on depictions of (the real) Windsor Court and the life of the Royal Family.

Of the 324 sumptuous guest accommodations, all of which enjoy a private balcony or bay window overlooking the city or the Mississippi River, 266 are suites with separate living areas, minikitchen or wet bar, in-room safe, three telephones (each with two incoming lines and dataports), and dressing room with marble vanity adjoining the bedroom and spacious Italian marble bathroom. Baby grand pianos and four-poster beds with Oriental canopies accent the 22nd floor's 2,000-square-foot penthouses—pinnacles of the city's hotel establishment.

Relax in the English-style Polo Lounge for a double martini before adjourning to the Grill Room. This award-winning and internationally acclaimed restaurant (see Restaurants chapter) is open for breakfast and dinner as well as weekend brunch. Other hotel amenities include a sundeck with pool, Jacuzzi, and fitness center with sauna, steam room, massage facilities, and showers. This ultraposh hotel in the heart of the financial district, 2 blocks from the French Quarter and the Aquarium of the Americas, is a member of the elite international family of Orient-Express Hotels.

WYNDHAM RIVERFRONT HOTEL $$$$-$$$$$
701 Convention Center Blvd.
(504) 524-8200, (877) 999-3223
www.wyndham.com

Maybe it's the lovely fountain that makes the multicolumned drive-in entrance to this hotel look smart enough to be in the French Quarter. Instead, this luxury 202-room property is conveniently situated on the edge of the Warehouse Arts District, across the street from the Riverwalk shopping and restaurant complex, the Convention Center, and within easy walking distance of Harrah's casino, the French Quarter, and Aquarium of the Americas. A rice mill once occupied the site of the present-day lobby, home to a cozy bar and 7 on Fulton, which serves breakfast, lunch, dinner, and brunch. Weekend guests are treated to the sight of New Orleans-based cruise ships that dock at nearby Julia Street Wharf in between voyages to the western Caribbean.

Globe-trotters familiar with this international chain's reputation for service as well as comfortable, pleasantly furnished accommodations will not be disappointed by its top-to-bottom renovation in 2006. Rooms come with irons/ironing boards, coffeemakers, hair dryers, and telephones with voice mail and dataports. Traveling dealmakers will appreciate the oversize desks (with ergonomic work chairs), phones with extra long cords, Valet parking, complimentary newspaper, valet laundry, and a fully equipped exercise room are among the other amenities. Also complimentary is the New Orleans-style hospitality.

UPTOWN

THE COLUMNS $$-$$$$
3811 St. Charles Ave.
(504) 899-9308, (800) 445-9308
www.thecolumns.com

Imagine a stretch of The Avenue so lush with oak trees that you might actually miss this hotel's four massive white columns. But this three-story Victorian mansion, listed in the National Registry of Historic Places, has earned the allegiance of many a local who has sipped a sunset cocktail on its spacious front porch as the day slip-slides away like the St. Charles Avenue streetcar passing in front. The view is simply unsurpassed. Open the beveled-glass double front doors and step inside. *Pretty Baby* was filmed here, and framed pictures of Brooke Shields—then and now—hang in the Victorian Lounge to the right of the lobby. On weekend nights this dimly lighted British-style watering hole hosts a regular Uptown crowd. Make yourself at home by slipping into one of the dark-wood booths (one especially cozy nook is in back) and order a favorite drink while music plays and the TV behind the bar broadcasts sports. Part of the enduring charm of this hotel is how little it has changed over the years. Owners Claire and Jacques Creppel have decorated the high-ceiling rooms with small armoires and comfortable double beds. Nineteen guest rooms and suites on the second and third floors have private baths and other modern touches. The large second-floor wooden balcony of white wicker chairs offers a wonderful view of St. Charles Avenue. Breakfast is served in a quiet dining area located off the lobby.

PRYTANIA PARK HOTEL $$
1525 Prytania St.
(504) 524-0427, (888) 498-7591
www.prytaniaparkhotel.com
Budget-bound travelers won't have to scrimp on luxury at this renovated 1850s Greek Revival hotel situated in a quiet section of the historic Garden District. Nor will they have to worry that this value hotel is off the beaten path—it's only 1 block from the St. Charles Avenue streetcar line and minutes from the French Quarter and Audubon Zoo. Original fine millwork, tiled baths, spacious marble-and-mirrored dressing areas, and plush carpeting add to the value of staying at this cozy replica of a small European hotel. Guests can enjoy their complimentary breakfast and morning paper in their rooms or head out to the courtyard. Another convenience is the free (and unlimited) use of the hotel's secured and well-lit parking area. Hand-carved period English pine furnishings fill 62 spacious historic and contemporary rooms (13 are located in a Victorian townhome), all of which have high ceilings, ceiling fans, refrigerators, and microwave ovens.

Some of the pastel-colored rooms have armoires as well as airy lofts reached by a circular metal staircase; others feature linen-draped four-poster beds.

i Looking to Mardi Gras mambo? Don't wait until the last minute to reserve a room unless you relish the prospect of driving into the city each day from, say, Mississippi. Book your hotel early—a year in advance isn't a bad idea. During Carnival most, if not all, hotels have minimum-stay requirements (usually two to five nights). Guests can expect room rates to be at yearly highs.

BED-AND-BREAKFAST INNS

Nobody does a better job showcasing New Orleans' timeless charm than the city's bed-and-breakfast inns. Stroll along a romantic flagstone walkway in the shade of ancient oaks and sycamores. Unwind in a Jacuzzi while listening to the hypnotic rustle of banana tree leaves on a secluded tropical courtyard. Enjoy a breakfast of buttery croissants, fresh berries, and strong, hot cafe au lait while watching the city come alive from a private balcony trimmed in wrought-iron lace.

Take your pick of mostly 150-year-old Victorian, Italianate, or Greek Revival homes adorned with 19th-century antiques. Many inns have four-poster beds, footed cast-iron tubs, marble mantels, 13-foot ceilings, and original pine floors. Even a value-oriented, European pensione-style accommodation features a 1,000-book library and a lush pool and patio area. New Orleans has always been a city full of interesting people, and these inns are where many of them lived. One was the lavish home of a wealthy West Indies sugar planter forced to take refuge in the city following an inconvenient insurrection in Santo Domingo. Another belonged to a free man of color who lived there 20 years before the Civil War. Yet another is a former orphanage built by nuns, while New Orleans was occupied by Union soldiers. These inns represent more than simply a place to stay; they give visitors the opportunity to touch the past—to sleep in its bed, sit at its table, and walk in its gardens.

Price Code

All inns accept all major credit cards. Rates are based on double occupancy, high season.

$..................less than $100
$$ ....$100 to $150
$$$ ....$151 to $200
$$$$ ....$201 to $250
$$$$$...................$251+

HOW THE CHAPTER IS ORGANIZED

As every inn is located within 10 or 15 minutes of the French Quarter, they are simply listed in alphabetical order. Several are in the French Quarter, some are in Faubourg Marigny (the neighborhood adjacent to the Quarter to the east), and the rest are Uptown. All Uptown inns, except one, are located in the Garden District area; therefore in this chapter "Garden District" and "Uptown" are used interchangeably. Some

entries mention the Lower Garden District, which is that part closest to Downtown and the French Quarter. Marigny inns are within walking distance of the Vieux Carré, and Uptown accommodations are all close to either the streetcar or Magazine Street bus, both of which get folks Downtown in short order.

Officially, a bed-and-breakfast is supposed to be an owner-occupied home renting out one or more rooms and a guesthouse or inn is not owner-occupied and offers fewer than 15 rooms. In reality, proprietors tend to play rather fast with these rules, so we've simply lumped them all together.

B&W COURTYARDS BED & BREAKFAST $$–$$$
2425 Chartres St.
(504) 945-9418, (800) 585-5731
bandwcourtyards.com
The Courtyards is located in the neighborhood

adjacent to the French Quarter, Faubourg Marigny. It offers a taste of old New Orleans with a Caribbean twist in a collection of three 19th-century buildings connected by courtyards. All rooms are meticulously decorated and feature private baths, cable TV, phones, modem jacks, central air and heat, and fresh flowers. Most rooms open onto a courtyard. Rates include an upscale continental breakfast served 8:30 to 10 a.m. Adults only.

i Remember, the Garden District and the Lower Garden District are both part of Uptown, the area settled by the Americans when they began arriving in the city in the 19th century, following the 1803 Louisiana Purchase. The French Quarter and Faubourg Marigny are both Downtown, most of which was built by the French and Spanish Creoles.

DEGAS HOUSE $–$$$
2306 Esplanade Ave.
(504) 821-5009, (800) 755-6730
www.degashouse.com

Built ca. 1852, the Degas House offers a gateway to the personal side of a legendary painter. Drawn to the city by his two brothers and a host of maternal relatives, French Impressionist Edgar Degas made New Orleans the only American city in which he lived and worked. Though his stay was relatively short, Degas began 22 works while here. A large collection of prints of his paintings adorn the mansion, located in the Esplanade Ridge Historical District. The common spaces of the house are open to guests, including the rooms believed to be Degas's studio. Each guest room is named for a member of the Degas family. The color selections of the rooms were guided by Degas's letters home and by some of his paintings set in the house. All rooms feature period furnishings, cable TV, phones, and private baths; one has a whirlpool. Guided tours of the home are free for guests and available to the public by appointment. Rates include an extended continental breakfast weekdays and Creole breakfast on weekends.

THE GARDEN DISTRICT BED & BREAKFAST $–$$$
2418 Magazine St.
(504) 895-4302

This 1890 Victorian town house restored to its original splendor, from its 12-foot ceilings to its Southern pine floors, is located in the historic Garden District on Magazine Street, not far from quaint antiques shops and boutiques and cafes. The house's four suites feature antique furniture, queen beds, private baths, air-conditioning, ceiling fans, cable TV and wireless. Guests should also take time to enjoy the tropical garden patio.

THE HOUSE ON BAYOU ROAD $$–$$$$$
2275 Bayou Rd.
(504) 945-0992, (800) 882-2968
www.houseonbayouroad.com

This luxury bed-and-breakfast is nestled on two acres of gardens, ponds and patios just 12 blocks from the French Quarter. The main house was built in 1798 for physician-diplomat Domingo Fleitas. Originally a Canary Islander, Fleitas had the home constructed in the West Indies Creole style of the day, with wide galleries and an abundance of French doors opening onto flowering patios. Eight rooms and suites feature private baths, period antiques, and wet bars. The swimming pool and hot tub are available for guest use. Rates include secured off-street parking as well as full plantation breakfast and champagne brunch on weekends. The inn also offers guests classes in traditional Louisiana cooking conducted by experienced local chefs.

i Many inns and hotels offer discounted rates and special package deals during July and Aug, generally the city's slowest period for tourism. There are great deals to be had, but be forewarned—average daily temperatures in the high 90s are common during that time of year.

LAFITTE GUEST HOUSE $$$–$$$$
1003 Bourbon St.
(504) 581-2678, (800) 331-7971
www.lafitteguesthouse.com

In 1849 Paul Joseph Geleises moved to Bourbon Street and raised everybody's property values by building his family a four-story, 14-bedroom mansion at the then-exorbitant price of $11,700. Today guests can sit on one of the home's wrought-iron balconies and toast his foresight with their cafe au lait while enjoying delicate breakfast pastries and watching French Quarter artists on the street below make their way to Jackson Square to set up shop for the day. All 14 rooms of this meticulously restored guest house have private baths and are furnished with antiques and reproductions authentic to the period. Most have fireplaces, and some have private balconies. Each room is luxuriously decorated and distinctly different from the next. A spacious room off the grand parlor, features a queen-size bed with crown canopy and a marble fireplace, while the next room has a draped Victorian half-tester bed and a wet bar. Open a door and the two rooms become an elegant suite, which through French doors opens onto the lush courtyard. Rates include continental breakfast as well as wine and hors d'oeuvres in the parlor at cocktail hour.

LAMOTHE HOUSE $-$$$$$
621 Esplanade Ave.
(504) 947-1161, (800) 367-5858
www.lamothehouse.com
As a wealthy sugar planter in the West Indies, Jean Lamothe developed a taste for the finer things in life. And thanks to a late-18th-century revolution in San Dominique that brought the planter north to New Orleans, modern travelers to New Orleans can also develop a taste for the finer things in life—at the Lamothe House.

Located at the eastern edge of the French Quarter, this Victorian mansion was one of New Orleans' earliest brick-built double town houses. As was the practice at the time, the house was built with a *porte cochere*—a carriageway running through the center of the house to a courtyard paved with flagstones. Originally decorated to suit a family of very good fortune, the home retains the ambience of a bygone era with high formal ceilings, authentic furnishings, cypress floorboards, and original hand-wrought iron fastenings on the doors and windows.

One suite features a pair of canopied four-poster beds, an ornate armoire, marble-top dressers, and decorative plasterwork. All 20 rooms have private baths. Amenities include a continental breakfast featuring coffee served from a 200-year-old Sheffield urn as well as afternoon sherry served in the comfortable parlor. Ten additional rooms are available in a Creole cottage across the street, the Marigny Guest House.

> **i** The House on Bayou Road B&B also offers guests various New Orleans cooking classes. Learn tips on making a perfect "roux" as well as other local "secrets." Bon appétit! (See write-up in this chapter.)

THE MCKENDRICK-BREAUX
HOUSE $$-$$$$
1474 Magazine St.
(504) 586-1700, (888) 570-1700
www.mckendrick-breaux.com
Resident owner Eddie Breaux spent three years painstakingly restoring this house before opening it as a bed-and-breakfast in 1994. Located in the Lower Garden District, the McKendrick-Breaux House consists of two Greek Revival-style structures: a three-story masonry building and two-story frame town house connected by a courtyard and patio. The buildings, constructed in 1865 and 1857, respectively, feature most of the original plasterwork, woodwork, and flooring. Nine guest rooms—with private baths (most with large clawfoot tubs), telephone, voice mail, modem line, and cable TV—are furnished with antiques and decorated with fresh flowers as well as the works of local artists. Some rooms open onto the courtyard and patio outfitted with garden furniture and tropical plants. Rates include an expanded continental breakfast.

PARK VIEW GUEST HOUSE $$-$$$
7004 St. Charles Ave.
(504) 861-7564, (888) 533-0746
www.parkviewguesthouse.com

Location, location, location—the three top things this 21-room antiques-filled guesthouse has going for it. Butter a croissant during your complimentary continental breakfast in the black-and-white-tiled Audubon Room while savoring the be-still-my-heart view of Audubon Park just beyond the wall of tall windows. Or kick back in the funky-chic public area off the lobby and watch the St. Charles Avenue streetcar rumbling past the front window under one of the loveliest tunnels of live oaks in the city. Tulane and Loyola Universities are a diploma's throw away; the Big Easy's wild side is found at the zoo in Audubon Park across the street. Catch the streetcar outside the front door and within minutes you're strolling the French Quarter. The foyer has two admirably stocked bookcases. Most rooms have private baths. The three-story pink Victorian mansion is listed on the National Register of Historic Places.

RATHBONE INN $$-$$$$
1244 Esplanade Ave.
(504) 309-4479, (866) 724-8140
Located 2 blocks from the French Quarter, this elegant guest house encompasses two restored antebellum mansions. The main house was built as a home for the Rathbone family in 1850. Accommodations range from deluxe rooms to large architecturally detailed suites. Most rooms have high ceilings and a distinctive character, complete with antiques from the antebellum period. All have private baths and suites have kitchenettes. The grand parlor, reminiscent of an 1850s plantation ballroom, is where guests meet during breakfast and for nightly wine and cheese reception. Guests are also invited to unwind in the outdoor Jacuzzi beneath banana trees in the secluded tropical patio area. Rates include continental breakfast.

ROYAL STREET COURTYARD $-$$$$
2438 Royal St.
(504) 943-6818, (888) 846-4004
Innkeepers Phillip Lege and David Smith have created an elegant and comfortable home-away-

from home for their guests in this restored 1850s Greek Revival house, located just six blocks from the French Quarter in historic Faubourg Marigny. Stately columns, expansive galleries, and a grand front door of hand-hewn cypress introduce guests to this antebellum gem. Inside, the sophisticated charm of old Creole New Orleans comes alive in the form of soaring 14-foot ceilings, polished hardwood floors and hand-crafted trim. Nine classically appointed guest rooms feature private baths, cable TV and fridge, as well as a four-poster king, queen, or double beds. Guests are also welcome to spend time relaxing in the inn's intimate tropical courtyard and maybe even take a dip in the courtyard spa. Rates include continental breakfast.

ST. CHARLES GUEST HOUSE $-$$
1748 Prytania St.
(504) 523-6556
www.stcharlesguesthouse.com
Located in the Garden District, the St. Charles Guest House may be as close as one can get to finding European pensione-style accommodations in the States. As its owners aptly describe this small hotel, which offers everything from hostel-type "backpacker" rooms for $45 to a room (with private bath) that sleeps four for $105, the St. Charles is simple, cozy, and affordable. Thirty-six rooms are situated in four adjacent buildings constructed between 1890 and 1910.

Owners Dennis and Joanne Hilton (no relation to the megahotel) have hosted visitors for more than 25 years, and their approach is definitely low-tech. Although Wi-Fi is now available, guest rooms have no phones or TVs, though guests are encouraged to choose a book from the inn's library and enjoy it in the shade of the lush banana trees that decorate the secluded pool and patio area. When visitors are ready to venture out, the Hiltons have developed a special guide book to their favorite spots. Guests are invited to make themselves afternoon tea or coffee, and rates include a bakery breakfast served in a sunny poolside breakfast room. You can't beat this with a stick.

ST. PETER HOUSE HOTEL $–$$$
1005 St. Peter St.
(504) 524-9232, (800) 535-7815
www.stpeterhouse.com

Located on "the quiet side" of the French Quarter, this intimate hotel was built as a private residence in the early 1800s. Charming courtyards and broad balconies trimmed in wrought-iron lace welcome visitors who wish to stay near—but not in—the fray of New Orleans nightlife. Rooms, some of which are furnished with antiques, feature private baths, telephones, and cable TV. One- and two-bedroom suites are also available. Rates include a continental breakfast.

ST. VINCENT'S GUEST HOUSE $–$$
1507 Magazine St.
(504) 302-9606
www.stvguesthouse.com

In the mid-19th century there was an acute need for orphanages as yellow fever epidemics decimated the population, leaving numerous children homeless. In 1861, while the city was under Union occupation, the imposing structure of St. Vincent's was built by the Daughters of Charity, an order of Catholic nuns known for social service.

Financial backing for the project chiefly came from Margaret Haughery, an illiterate Irish immigrant who became a successful businesswoman. Orphaned herself and having lost both a husband and baby to disease, Haughery, a baker, vowed to spend her life alleviating the suffering of children. Before her death in 1882, Haughery donated large sums of money generated by her steam-operated bakery to several orphanages without regard to the children's gender, religion, or race.

On the day of her funeral, all New Orleans closed down as scores followed her coffin to St. Louis Cemetery No. 2, where she rests today. A statue of this generous woman, which simply bears the name "Margaret," still stands at Camp and Prytania Streets. It is the first statue ever erected to commemorate a woman in the United States and the only statue built in honor of a baker.

Today the orphanage is a 70-room European-style guesthouse furnished to reflect "Victorian New Orleans"—ceiling fans, wicker furniture, and a large courtyard. The carriage house clock was a gift to the sisters from Haughery upon completion of St. Vincent's. All rooms have private baths, cable, phone and wireless access. and most of the staff speak more than one language. An in-house restaurant is open for breakfast, lunch and dinner.

Separate male and female, as well as co-ed dormitory-style hostel accommodations are also available. The $20 to $25 per night charge includes linens and access to a communal kitchen.

HOSTELS

MARQUETTE HOUSE $
2249 Carondelet St.
(504) 523-3014

This youth hostel is located Uptown in a 100-year-old Greek Revival home, a block off the St. Charles Avenue streetcar line. Men and women are accommodated in separate dormitories for $16 to $25 per night (with special rates for rebuilding volunteer groups). Sheets, blankets, pillows, and towels are included. A kitchen, showers, dining area, lounge, patio-garden, and picnic tables are provided. Day use is permitted and there is no curfew. Visitors are expected to clean up after themselves. There is no age limit. Everyone, including families and senior citizens, is welcome. Private apartments with a bath and kitchen are also available for around $50 to $75.

Also see write-ups on St. Charles and St. Vincent's Guest Houses in this chapter. Each offers some hostel-type accommodations.

RESTAURANTS

The Big Easy is an embarrassment of dishes. From world-class culinary art to down-home bayou cookery, the city has curried the favor of global gourmets and local epicures, as well as the food lover merely passing through town. For more than 150 years local kitchens have been tantalizing palates with culinary pleasures worthy of opium dreams. A mere short list of New Orlean's famous indigenous foods prompts even the seasoned restaurantgoer to marvel at the mélange of local culinary riches: jambalaya, gumbo, pommes soufflé, oysters Bienville and Rockefeller, po-boy and Muffuletta sandwiches, courtbouillon, crawfish étouffée, trout amandine, soft-shell crab meunière, shrimp remoulade, blackened redfish (or blackened anything, for that matter), barbecue shrimp, spicy andouille, boudin sausages, and red beans and rice. The City that Care Forgot never forgets dessert, from classic crème brûlée and bread pudding with whiskey sauce to flaming bananas Foster and chocolate pudding– filled, seven-layer doberge cakes. Just for the record, all of the above were invented here. And many of them are washed down with traditional cafe brûlot, a local potation of coffee flamed with cinnamon sticks, cloves, orange, and lemon rind with brandy and Grand Marnier. Can there be any doubt that in New Orleans, dining is no mere pastime but rather a way of life?

A multiethnic melting pot, the city's dining joie de vivre owes a gustatory debt to the time-honored cooking traditions of its early Native American, French, West African, Spanish, West Indian, and Acadian inhabitants. Almost from the moment the ramparts were built around the colonial swampland settlement, New Orleans seemed destined for great culinary possibilities. Early on, pots full of tasty sustenance simmered with the bounteous harvest of indigenous foodstuffs culled from nearby bayous and rivers—crawfish, oysters, shrimp, crab, finfish, and other southeast Louisiana delicacies. Gumbo, or "gombo," is the West African word for okra—a signature ingredient in one of the region's mainstays. Jambalaya can trace part of its roots to the French and Spanish words for ham, "jambon" and "jamon," respectively. And the legendary trapping and fishing skills of resourceful bayou Cajuns, exiled from Nova Scotia in the 1700s, moved "one-pot" cooking to the front burner with andouille sausage jambalaya and chicken macque choux.

The 19th and early 20th centuries saw the arrival of Americans from the colonies as well as Irish, German, and Italian immigrants. One of the city's oldest grocery stores, Central Grocery Co. (established in 1906) is owned and operated by descendents of the original Italian family that founded this French Quarter landmark. Here visitors sit elbow-to-elbow munching on the New Orleans-born Italian bread feast called the Muffuletta, stuffed with provolone cheese and deli meats and topped with tangy olive salad. Further spicing up the local dining scene of this cosmopolitan city has been the arrival in recent decades of people from Cuba, Central America, Vietnam, the Caribbean, and other regions of the world. Bennachin, on Royal Street, tempts taste buds with the rich flavors of Cameroon and Gambia found in such dishes as *nsouki ioppa*, the traditional West African gumbo with sausage and smoked turkey. Scandinavian cuisine may, in fact, be the only thing missing from New Orleans menus. OK, so maybe it is impossible to find kochanina (pork gelatin) or aggost (egg custard with herring). But stay tuned.

The Big Easy is a hedonist's Valhalla. As such, it seems only fitting that the city should lay claim to a grand choice of places to eat, ranging from sparkling lairs of world-class cuisine to dimly lit nooks serving up down-home grub. Many cities can boast of having "something for everyone in every price range." But competition among Big Easy restaurants for diners' dollars is so fierce that it seems the bad spots are usually forced to shut their doors in about 15 minutes. The best of the bunch meantime enjoy the awards and accolades that pour in with astonishing regularity. In fact, literary pageants of devotion flow from the pens of the nation's food cognoscenti.

The choices of dining spots in this chapter have been restricted to those that have stood the test of time. With few exceptions, each has been on the local scene at least a year or longer, while many can point to long histories inextricably entwined in the cultural fabric of the city. If you dine in the courtyard at the Bistro at Maison deVille Hotel, for example, you may well imagine hearing the clinking of ice in Tennessee Williams's Sazerac glass. The playwright lived in No. 9 and enjoyed the New Orleans-born cocktail as he sat in the courtyard working on *A Streetcar Named Desire*. Antoine's, the city's oldest restaurant, opened in 1840 and since that time has hosted everyone from Mark Twain and Enrico Caruso to five U.S. presidents.

Unless otherwise noted, the restaurants in this chapter accept most major credit cards. Those that accept cash only are so designated. For convenience this chapter is divided by the following neighborhoods: Esplanade, Faubourg Marigny, French Quarter, CBD/Downtown, Warehouse District, Uptown, Carrollton/Riverbend, Mid City, and Lakefront/Bucktown/Lakeview. Restaurants are listed alphabetically under each neighborhood. Keep in mind that virtually everything in the city, including its restaurants, is at most no more than a 15-minute drive or cab ride from where you're staying. So don't let distance be a hindrance to adventurous dining.

Like most cities in subtropical climates, New Orleans tends to run on the casual side in both attitude and dress. Even nighttime attire, weather permitting, is usually no more than jeans, T-shirts, shorts, short-sleeve shirts and blouses, sundresses, walking shoes, and so on. Still, as this is the South, some women wouldn't be caught dead transgressing the unwritten fashion law of no white shoes between Labor Day and Easter. But if you're not from the South, really, don't sweat it. Travelers will want to dress accordingly for the special occasion of breaking bread at some of the city's finer establishments. Jackets and ties for the gents and evening dresses for the ladies will usually suffice. If hitting one of the chic bistros downtown or in the Warehouse District, dress in black (if you want to blend in with the waitstaff), or slip into the stylish threads you packed for such an occasion. But what you'll find in New Orleans, even in some of the better restaurants, is a mostly relaxed and laid-back dress code. As always, if in doubt call ahead.

Price Code

Our price code is based on dinner for two, without appetizers, dessert, alcoholic beverages, tax, or tip. Your own bill at any given restaurant will be higher or lower, depending on what you order and fluctuating restaurant prices. Prices are for dinner; those establishments that offer lunch typically have reduced-price menus.

$	Less than $20
$$	$21 to $35
$$$	$36 to $50
$$$$	More than $50

FRENCH QUARTER

ACME OYSTER HOUSE　　　　　　　$
724 Iberville St.
(504) 522-5973
www.acmeoyster.com

Though it sounds like the place Wyle E. Coyote goes when he's got a hankering for seafood, he's probably about the only one you won't find sucking down raw oysters in this French Quarter landmark. This relaxed, classic oyster bar is the kind of place where you're just as likely to run into locals, foreign visitors, or celebrities such as Matt Dillon, Deion Sanders, and Ellen Degeneres. The folks here must be doing something right—they've been in business since 1910. At the bar or at a table, the raw oysters are always a best bet and are routinely ranked as the city's most popular in local surveys. However, for those who insist on having their food cooked, the oysters are just as good on a po-boy or as part of a seafood platter. Also recommended are the red bean Poopa, and gumbo Poopa consisting of a French bread "bowl" filled with either red beans and rice or sausage-and-shrimp gumbo. And there's a good stock of local beers to wash it all down. Lunch and dinner are served daily.

i So, you're in a hurry? Better not be when you pull up a chair at many neighborhood eateries. In the Big Easy virtually everything save for the New Orleans Hornets moves at a slower pace that reflects the city's laid-back approach to life.

ANTOINE'S $$$$
713-717 St. Louis St.
(504) 581-4422
www.antoines.com
"I didn't have to go around the world," Numa Vinet, the now-retired 53-year veteran waiter once said, "the whole world came here to me at Antoine's." And what a world. This is the city's first restaurant and the sign hanging outside announces modestly, SINCE 1840. Inside, the guest list of notables who have dined at this venerable haute Creole dining institution reads like a who's who. Mark Twain, Groucho Marx, and Enrico Caruso have enjoyed this restaurant's classic ambience, as have Tennessee Williams, five U.S. presidents (including both Roosevelts), Henry Kissinger, Admiral Richard Byrd, and scads of royalty such as the Duke and Duchess of Windsor. And that's just the tip of the iceberg—of the A-list. The library—you heard right—contains

more than 400 volumes on cooking and wine, some of which are more than 250 years old (one cookbook published in Paris dates to 1659). Many members of the waitstaff have worked here for decades, including several who have punched the clock for nearly half a century. Some menu items come with a history every bit as rich as the sauces prepared under the watchful eye of fifth-generation proprietor Bernard Guste. The pompano en papillote was created to honor a French balloonist who entertained here, the paper bag used to retain the flavor of the fish being fashioned to resemble his inflated balloon. And since 1899 more than three million orders of oysters Rockefeller, named for the nation's then-richest family and perhaps the restaurant's most famous original dish, have been served. Buddy Ebsen once observed, "You haven't lived until you've burned your tongue on oysters Rockefeller at Antoine's. Long may you wave."

The exhaustive menu in French may be overwhelming to the uninitiated, but that's what the gentle waitstaff is for. Recommendations include the original filet de truite a la Marguery (speckled trout poached in a white wine sauce with fresh shrimp, mushrooms, and herbs) and the pompano Pontchartrain (grilled pompano filet with sautéed lump crabmeat). Other well-known house signatures include the puffed potatoes and noisettes d'agneau Alciatore—medallions of lamb wrapped in bacon, broiled, and served with a tangy béarnaise sauce on top of a grilled pineapple slice. Save room for dessert, especially the pêche melba (a candied peach half, vanilla ice cream, raspberry sauce, and chopped toasted almonds) and the fraises au kirsch (fresh strawberries and kirsch liqueur).

ARNAUD'S $$$$
813 Bienville St.
(504) 523-5433
www.arnauds.com
"Count" Leon Bertrand Arnaud Cazenave, a French-born wine salesman, raconteur, and gastronome, opened this restaurant in 1918. The quintessential New Orleanian, Count Arnaud

was given to starting his day with a split of champagne before moving onto his cherished half-and-half bourbon and coffee elixirs. By the time of his death in 1948 at age 76, this establishment was already regarded as a grand purveyor of haute-Creole cuisine and one of the country's fine-dining legends. Presidents, princes, movie stars, and other celebs have dined here, and the international award-winning menu still includes favorite dishes created by the founder. Today native-born executive chef Tommy DiGiovanni oversees such menu traditions as smoked pompano Bourgeás, oysters Bienville (baked with shrimp, mushrooms, and bread crumbs and topped with glacage), and shrimp Arnaud (chilled, boiled shrimp marinated in the restaurant's famous homemade remoulade sauce). The trout meunière is still crisply fried and bathed in a velvety sauce of veal stock, lemon, and butter and served with crunchy brabant potatoes. The cafe brûlot (coffee flamed with cinnamon sticks, cloves, orange, and lemon rind with brandy and Grand Marnier) is a New Orleans tradition not to be missed. Dinner is served daily. A Sunday brunch menu includes pain perdu (Creole-style French toast), eggs Fauteux with house-smoked fresh Gulf pompano, and eye-openers such as Absinthe Suissesse, milk punch, and gin fizz. Reservations are suggested.

This massive restaurant is composed of six public and 10 private dining rooms in a blocklong rambling structure of restored 18th- and 19th-century French Quarter buildings connected by hallways. Today a dozen sparkling chandeliers, classic ceiling fans, original mosaic tile floors, and etched-glass windows create a warm and well-dressed environment. Silverware and china patterns resemble the restaurant's original setting.

BACCO $$$
310 Chartres St.
(504) 522-2426
www.bacco.com
A neoclassical decor of Venetian chandeliers, antique French iron gates, and Gothic arches from an old Tuscan church set the mood for a romantic escape into Italian cuisine. From din-

ing booths inscribed with Italian love poems, to the 18th-century French compass-point wood carvings, to the murals handpainted by Jacques Lame, to the hand-blown Venetian glass grapes, this is one of the city's most visually stunning, award-winning restaurants. Kudos from national magazines such as *Bon Appetit, Esquire,* and *Food & Wine* keep pouring in. In a city where Creole cuisine reigns supreme, this Italian trattoria offers a refreshing departure. Homemade pastas, wood-fired pizzas, and fresh regional seafood are artfully prepared by executive chef Chris Montero.

Mouthwatering signature dishes include foie gras pizza (with caramelized Chianti onions, roasted Portobello mushrooms, mozzarella, and seared Hudson Valley foie gras drizzled with white truffle oil); mussels steamed in vermouth; hickory-grilled pork tenderloin (with a sweet and sour prune sauce); roasted shrimp and pasta salad; and chicken cacciatore. Haley's best-known creation, crawfish ravioli with sundried-tomato pesto butter sauce, is a seasonal favorite. Each tabletop is adorned with a bottle of olive oil and roasted garlic for the wonderfully chewy breads.

BAYONA $$$$
430 Dauphine St.
(504) 525-4455
www.bayona.com
Many out-of-towners recognize proprietor-chef Susan Spicer by her trademark bandana. Few however know that the New Orleans native's career is as remarkable as her eggplant caviar and smoked salmon beignets appetizer, and mustard-glazed lamb loin. Spicer began her cooking career in New Orleans in 1979 as an apprentice to chef Daniel Bonnot at the St. Louis Hotel's Louis XVI Restaurant. Three years later she opened the Savoir Faire bistro at the St. Charles Hotel as chef de cuisine. In 1985 she traveled extensively and returned to work as the opening chef at the Bistro at Maison deVille in the Maison deVille Hotel. In 1990 she launched Bayona, offering her "New World cuisine" in a romantic, 200-year-old Creole cottage in the heart of the French Quarter. The three-room main dining area downstairs offers a warm, European-style ambi-

ence, with terra-cotta–colored walls, dark green faux-marble accents, and huge hand-colored photographs of Italian gardens and trompe l'oeil Mediterranean landscapes. The intimate upstairs dining room is ideal for parties of ten or more; in fall and spring the lush fountain courtyard is the place to be. For entrees try the sautéed salmon with Choueroute and Gewürztraminer sauce and boudin-stuffed rabbit loin with Creole mustard cream sauce. Bayona is open for lunch Wed through Sat and dinner Mon through Sat. Reservations are encouraged.

BENNACHIN $
1212 Royal St.
(504) 522-1230

The exciting, traditional tastes of West Africa aren't the only thing awaiting adventurous diners to this casual neighborhood cafe. A linguistics lesson is provided by the menu written in the languages of the Basso people of Cameroon and the Mandinka people of Gambia—native homes of co-owners Alyse Njenge and Fanta Tambajang, respectively. (Don't fret, the English names and descriptions of each dish are also provided.) Lively music from the African continent plays amid a pleasantly Spartan dining room of large colorful paintings of village life. This may be one of the best places in town to appreciate the significant culinary role the African diaspora has played in local cooking traditions. The nsouki ioppa, for example, is the traditional (and original) West African version of gumbo and comes with beef sausage and tasty strips of smoked turkey. Doh-doh (fried ripe plantains) and akara (black-eyed pea fritters) are other hearty appetizers to consider before getting down to the serious business of entree selection: poultry, fish, and lamb dishes, prepared as spicy as guests request. Meals are simple and usually accompanied by a combination of makdowa (fried ripe plantains), mbondo cone (coconut-rice), couscous, steamed mandowa (broccoli), cassava, and jama-jama (sautéed spinach), depending on the dish. The kembel-ioppa (sautéed lamb strips and bell peppers in a curry-accented ginger sauce) and the sisay singho (spiced baked chicken leg and thigh)

are popular. Several of the dishes can be ordered vegetarian style. Lunch and dinner are served daily. Cash only.

THE BISTRO AT MAISON DE VILLE $$$$
727 Toulouse St.
(504) 528-9206
www.maisondeville.com

In New Orleans there are numerous versions of the Parisian-style bistro. Loyalists insist this spot may come the closest to capturing the heart and soul of the real thing, with its sophisticatedly understated decor of red-leather banquettes, ceiling fans, beveled-glass mirrors, Impressionist-style paintings, natural wood floor, and white table linens. But don't discount the courtyard; weather permitting, it is a must for romantics who want to dine where Tennessee Williams worked on *A Streetcar Named Desire* while staying here at the Maison deVille Hotel, whose guest register has also included Mick Jagger and Elizabeth Taylor. A seasonal nouvelle-Creole menu that incorporates local seafood and produce has earned executive chef Greg Picolo a loyal following. Best bets include the venison osso buco, and the roasted pavé of salmon, which arrives stuffed with crab, shrimp, and scallops, alongside a grilled vegetable polenta cake. Your just desserts should include the almond and sundried cranberry bread pudding. The dress is smart, and lunch and dinner are served daily. Reservations are strongly recommended.

BRENNAN'S $$$$
417 Royal St.
(504) 525-9711
www.brennansneworleans.com

NBC–TV's Garrick Utley once said, "You haven't eaten breakfast until you've eaten breakfast at Brennan's." No question, breakfast at this world-famous restaurant is still a hands-down favorite among those eager for a taste of New Orleans history. The unforgettable signature triad of this institution, whose first location opened in 1946, includes the hearty turtle soup, eggs Benedict or Sardou, and, of course, the flaming bananas Foster invented at Brennan's. But breakfast is by no means the only time to partake of this culinary legend. Romance and intimate elegance are also timeless signatures of this landmark founded by Owen E. Brennan Sr. and located in the historic pink-stucco Morphy Mansion. Today Brennan's three sons—Owen Jr. ("Pip"), Jimmy, and Ted—oversee the restaurant's dozen graceful dining rooms, plus a tropically lush courtyard, as well as a 50,000-bottle wine cellar rated by *Wine Spectator* as one of the best in the world. Among the numerous entrees that have stood the test of time are the original redfish Jaime, topped with lump crabmeat in a fresh mushroom and red wine sauce. Breakfast, lunch, and dinner are served daily, and reservations are highly recommended.

BROUSSARD'S $$$$
819 Conti St.
(504) 581-3866
www.broussards.com

Oh, no. Yet another Creole-French grande dame restaurant? This is New Orleans—best get used to it. Over the years, writers from *Travel Holiday, Esquire, National Geographic Traveler,* and other magazines certainly have while dining at this venerable establishment. The smartly appointed dining room of gilt mirrors, bent-wood chairs, and 19th-century furnishings competes for your dining options with a romantic, century-old candlelit fountain courtyard of wisteria and night-blooming jasmine. Even the entryway of this original 1824 family home signals that you're someplace special. Bronze chandeliers with porcelain tulips hang from exposed cypress-beam ceilings above the imported Italian floors and walls of hand-painted tiles festooned with cherubs.

Today the Acadian-French menu is highlighted by crabmeat ravigote (with lemon, onions, capers, and avocado slices), shrimp with two remoulades, and oysters anyway you like them (try the creamy Bienville with tasso, mushroom, bell pepper, onion, and shrimp). Also popular are the pompano Napoleon (with shrimp and scallops in a puff pastry daubed in mustard-caper cream), roasted duck (in a marinated apples currant bourbon demi-glacé), and pork rib chop in a garlic, caraway, and mustard crust). Best

bets include the Louisiana-style bouillabaisse (with oysters, shrimp, and Gulf fish in a saffron-flavored tomato broth topped with crabmeat and rouille croutons) and grilled wild game—quail breast, boar sausage, and venison chop on apple red cabbage with a Grand Veneur pepper corn sauce).

CAFE DU MONDE $
800 Decatur St.
(504) 525-4544, (800) 772-2927
www.cafedumonde.com

Whether it's for a light breakfast or simply an afternoon respite, no trip to New Orleans would be complete without a stop at Cafe du Monde where locals have indulged in hot, creamy cafe au lait (coffee and chicory with steamed milk) and the sweet perfection of beignets (square holeless doughnuts topped with powdered sugar) since 1862. In fact, this French Quarter spot seems to have been destined for that purpose. Even before Cafe du Monde was built, there was a coffee stand here run by a free woman of color who sold coffee to the French Creoles after St. Louis Cathedral Mass. Sitting beneath the open-air canopy, sipping a cup of heaven and listening to the street musicians who play for cafe patrons most of the day and sometimes into the evening, will be the best $3 you ever spent. (But have a heart and throw a couple of bucks into that open instrument case as you leave, OK?) Also, on the way out walk around the back of the cafe where a picture window allows visitors to watch the beignets being made. Open 24 hours a day; many people find themselves beginning and ending their day here. In a city where the drinking never stops, coffee is often the best nightcap. No alcohol is served, and no credit cards are accepted.

CAFE MASPERO'S $
601 Decatur St.
(504) 523-6250
www.pierremasperosrestaurant.com

For locals the biggest challenge here has always been how to beat the lines of people waiting to get in, which can wrap around the corner during peak season. No problem. According to restaurant staff, your best bet for beating the sidewalk blues is to come after 2 p.m. weekdays and 3 p.m. weekends. Even if your timing is bad, it's worth getting in the queue for a chance to sample the famous pastrami sandwich served inside this 1820s building of redbrick archways, across the street from the Jax Brewery shopping complex. The mouthwatering sandwich includes a generous portion of thinly sliced New York-style peppery pastrami, oven-warmed and served (with melted cheese if you're smart) on freshly baked French bread with fries. Forget about leaving home without it, though, as credit cards are not accepted at this casual joint, which opened in 1971.

CLOVER GRILL $
900 Bourbon St.
(504) 598-1010
www.clovergrill.com

Eager to earn your tourist wings? Tumble into this street-corner legend between midnight and 4 a.m. for a post–barhopping chow-down and plop into one of the window booths. "We may not be pretty but we think we are" is the motto of this lively, campy grill open 24–7, which became part of the French Quarter scene in 1950. Food is served with an attitude and house rules include "Please keep your date seated to avoid accidents" and "We don't eat in your bed, so please don't sleep at our tables." Though fun 'round the clock, the witching hours are the best times to soak up this colorful, offbeat, and marvelously funky venue. Characters abound. Triple-egg works of diner art include omelettes "first concocted in a trailer in Chalmette, Louisiana," prepared to order and served with hash browns, grits, or fries. Transform your plain-Jane Geaux Girl waffles into luscious vamps with the optional banana, pecans, and ice cream. Burgers made to order, club and deli sandwiches, as well as chicken-fried steak and grilled chicken breast platters are served.

FELIX'S RESTAURANT AND OYSTER BAR $$
739 Iberville St.
(504) 522-4440
www.felixs.com

The sign over the bar of this half-century-old L-shaped restaurant, which opens onto both Iberville and Bourbon Streets, says it all: OYSTERS ARE IN SEASON. This crowded, informal eatery is where you can smell the crawfish boiling starting at 8 every morning. It's also the setting for many visitors' introduction to the fine art of eating raw oysters. Similar to, but pricier and more touristy than its neighbor Acme Oyster House across the street, Felix's offers an abundance of oyster offerings. There's raw, Bienville, Rockefeller, en brochette, stewed, fried, broiled, or in an omelette. Other good choices include gumbo, crawfish po-boy, seafood platter, and fried or grilled fish of the day. The full bar features more than a dozen varieties of beer. Although the eating is good, the wait can be long in this 220-seat restaurant that, especially when big conventions are in town, often has lines coming out both the Iberville and Bourbon Street entrances. Breakfast, lunch, and dinner are served daily. Open till 1:30 a.m. on Fri and Sat, Felix's is also a popular late-night eating spot.

GALATOIRE'S $$$$
209 Bourbon St.
(504) 525-2021
www.galatoires.com

As longtime customers often said, once you opened the door to Galatoire's, you were in Galatoire's—and that was only after a sometimes long wait in line on the sidewalk if you came on a Fri afternoon. Fortunately, a renovation of the venerable Creole dining den has added not only second-floor seating but also a waiting area for customers, as well as an overall fresh look. What hasn't changed is the fact that Galatoire's is the place to see and be seen on Fri afternoons when the restaurant is filled with fresh-scrubbed debutantes, lawyers in Brooks Brothers suits, politicians, dowagers sporting broad-brimmed hats, and the like. If the walls could talk . . . A longtime regular tells of the time he hosted a reporter who got so inebriated that he had to be poured onto the upstairs couch to sleep it off. When the reporter roused, still thoroughly in his cups, he was spotted by the host's eagle-eyed waiter crawling on

Glossary of New Orleans Food Terms

Andouille—A plump, smoked Cajun sausage made primarily with pork and often used as an ingredient in red beans and rice.

Beignet—A soft, square-shaped doughnut minus the hole sprinkled with powdered sugar and often enjoyed with cafe au lait.

Bisque—Crawfish heads stuffed with crawfish meat are found in the heartier versions of this time-honored thick Cajun soup served over rice.

Boudin—A hotly spiced Cajun sausage of cooked rice and pork.

Bouillabaisse—The New Orleans version of this traditional tomato-based French fish chowder features shellfish and finfish found in local waters.

Cafe au lait—Dark-roasted New Orleans-style chicory coffee and hot milk traditionally mixed in equal measures.

Cafe brûlot—An after-dinner hot coffee drink mixed with spices, orange peel, and liqueurs, mixed in a chafing dish, flamed, and served in special cups.

Chicory—A dried, ground, and roasted herb root used to flavor coffee.

Courtbouillon *(coo-BEE-yon)*—A roux-based fish soup or stew mixed with rice.

Crawfish—A red, shrimp-size "mini-lobster" found in local fresh waters.

En papillote—A fish baked in a paper bag to seal in the natural flavors.

Étouffée *(ay-too-FAY)*—a rouxless sauce (made up of butter and/or natural shellfish fats) used to smother Cajun seafood dishes. Good examples include crawfish or shrimp étouffée.

Filé *(FEE-lay)*—Powdered dried root bark of the sassafras tree used mostly to flavor and/or thicken gumbos—as in filé gumbo.

Gumbo—A roux-thickened soup prepared any number of ways but typi-

---

his hands and knees across the dining room. The waiter, concerned for the guest's safety, called to the host: "Look, he's trying to escape!"

Even if you don't have your own waiter (another Galatoire's tradition), the chatty dining room of this family-owned restaurant, founded in 1905 by French Pyrenees–born Jean Galatoire, has the culinary cure for what ails you: Crabmeat Maison, grilled pompano, escargot bordelaise, oysters en brochette, trout meunière or amandine, crabmeat canapé Lorenzo, and filet béarnaise, for starters. No reservations are accepted at this establishment, which is open for lunch and dinner Tues through Sun (jackets are required after 5 p.m. and all day Sun).

GUMBO SHOP $
630 St. Peter St.
(504) 525-1486
www.gumboshop.com
Part of the fun of sampling longtime New Orleans staples is learning how they got their name. Most New Orleans chefs will tell you that two of the most important ingredients to any successfully prepared traditional gumbo are filé and okra. "Kombo" is the Indian word for filé and "gombo" is the West African word for okra. Hence the name. As for jambalaya, two stories are passed about. One has it that the dish was named for the French and Spanish words for ham—"jambon" and "jamon," respectively. The story we like best though has a more romantic spin: A long-ago

cally with one or more of the following: seafood (oysters, shrimp, and/or crab), sausage (such as andouille), chicken, okra, and z'herbes (mustard greens).

Grillades *(GREE-yads)*—A tomato and gravy-based dish of thinly cut and browned veal or beef round. Grillades and grits is a popular New Orleans breakfast dish.

Jambalaya—A seasoned rice-and-tomato based "sweep-up-the-kitchen" dish prepared with virtually endless combinations of beef, chicken, crawfish, pork, sausage, and shrimp.

Meunière—A New Orleans seafood butter sauce framed by freshly ground black pepper, lemon juice, and finely minced fresh parsley.

Mirliton—A locally popular green squash, called chayote or vegetable pear elsewhere, used both as an accent vegetable and an edible container for stuffing with ham or shrimp.

Po-boy—The classic New Orleans fresh French bread sandwich, which can be found stuffed with virtually everything under the sun—from fried shrimp, oysters, soft-shell crabs, and catfish to roast beef, meatballs, deli meats, rib-eye, pork chops, and even french fries.

Red beans and rice—A New Orleans staple of kidney beans mixed with rice, seasonings, spices, and typically thick slices of sausage.

Remoulade—A tangy, salmon-colored sauce with Creole (and sometimes Dijon) mustard, horseradish, vinegar, and other flavorings, first served in New Orleans with shrimp.

Roux—A reddish-brown base of flour and fat (butter, lard, or oil), plus the so-called holy trinity of chopped onions, bell peppers, and celery, for many New Orleans sauces and food preparations.

famished traveler arriving late at night at a local inn was prepared a rice-based dish created by a cook called Jean who was nicknamed "Balayez," which means "mix good things together." The traveler was so impressed with the result that he called the meal "Jean Balayez," which eventually became "jambalaya." Either way, guests at this establishment, located in a building that dates to 1795, can count on consistently prepared and hearty portions. Start off with an appetizer of blackened fish nuggets or grilled boudin with Creole mustard, and then dive into the signature seafood okra gumbo, mixed with sautéed onions, bell peppers, and celery and blended with shrimp and crab into a thick roux and served over rice. Heartier appetites might want to opt for

the chicken andouille gumbo or the jambalaya, which is served with spicy smoked Cajun sausage and chicken seasoned and simmered in chicken stock. Open daily for lunch and dinner.

K-PAUL'S LOUISIANA KITCHEN $$$$
416 Chartres St.
(504) 524-7394
www.chefpaul.com

Chef Paul Prudhomme, who was born and raised in Louisiana's Cajun country, began cooking with his mother when he was only seven years old. With no electricity and a family of 13 children to feed, Prudhomme learned early the art of using fresh, seasonal ingredients to cook for a crowd. That tradition was carried over to this world-famous chef's French Quarter restaurant, which, he boasts, has no freezer on the premises. The original K-Paul's, which Prudhomme opened in 1979, was a modest 62-seat facility whose biggest feature, besides blackened redfish, was the long line of people who waited hours to get in. In 1996, however, the building was extensively renovated based on the original designs of the 1834 structure, adding a second-floor dining room, a balcony, and a courtyard, bringing the seating capacity to 200. Each dining room features an open kitchen for customers' entertainment. The restaurant also now takes reservations for meals of such signature dishes as blackened Louisiana drum; blackened pork chops stuffed with ricotta, Asiago, mozzarella, and caciocavello cheeses and fresh basil and served with mushroom-Zinfandel sauce; and the sumptuous sweet potato pecan pie served with chantilly cream. Like any of the city's more expensive restaurants, lunchtime at K-Paul's provides the best value for your buck. The intimate yet casual first-floor dining room features exposed-brick walls. Seating is on a first-come, first-served basis. Coats are not required, but "dressy casual" attire is recommended. Lunch and dinner are served Mon through Sat.

MAXIMO'S ITALIAN GRILL $$
1117 Decatur St.
(504) 586-8883
www.maximosgrill.com

This Italian grill has at long last come into its own, say longtime restaurant-goers. Jazz music and a collection of Herman Leonard jazz photographs set the mood in this 1829 building, which bustles on weekends. The wine selection never fails to reap kudos (it's one of the city's few recipients of *Wine Spectator*'s prestigious "Best of Award of Excellence"), and this chic bistro is probably one of the best places in town to sample vintages by the glass. Opt for balcony seating or a place at the lively grill-bar overlooking the open kitchen, which prepares a slew of fire-roasted shrimp and fish, pan-roasted veal T-bones, gourmet antipasto, and grilled portobello mushrooms, as well as lamb and steak dishes. It's hard to go wrong

ordering the fire-roasted chicken and sausage with prosciutto, Fontina cheese, mushrooms, and cream. Dinner only is served nightly.

MR. B'S BISTRO $$$$
201 Royal St.
(504) 523-2078
www.mrbsbistro.com

Former *Gourmet* magazine editor Gail Zweighental, whose dining experiences span the globe, once rated this restaurant's New Orleans-style barbecue shrimp as one of her favorite dishes. In an episode of the NBC-TV sitcom *Naked Truth*, Holland (Camilla) Taylor tells Tom (Jake) Verica: "I just think it is a shame for you to come all this way and yet still not be anywhere at all. It's sort of like making a pilgrimage to Mr. B's in New Orleans and then leaving without ever tasting their gumbo ya ya." Jake replies: "It is legendary!" These are only two examples of how the Creole cuisine created by executive chef Michelle McCraney, a former sous chef at Emeril Lagasse's Nola, has put this restaurant on the map. Mr. B's Bistro is part of the Brennan family restaurant dynasty (hence the "B" in Mr. B's) and run by the brother-and-sister team of Ralph and Cindy Brennan. This establishment has culled raves from patrons who have dined amid its softly lit, club-meets-bistro decor accented by a walllong dark-wood bar that bustles with the after-work crowd. But the dark-roux gumbo ya ya (with chicken and smoky andouille sausage) and barbecue shrimp (served with French bread for dipping into the peppery butter sauce) aren't the only home runs. So too are the duck spring rolls, braised Mississippi rabbit, pasta jambalaya (with Gulf shrimp, andouille sausage, duck, and chicken morsels tossed with spinach fettuccine). Lunch is served Mon through Sat; dinner daily; jazz brunch Sun.

NOLA $$$
534 St. Louis St.
(504) 522-6652
www.emerils.com

Superstar chef Emeril Lagasse's second restaurant, opened in 1992, is found inside a two-story exposed-brick structure, built in 1827 and a former warehouse that evokes a sort of New York Soho funky-chic. The vogue digs host a hip, upscale clientele of movers and shakers from the business, media, and art communities for lunch and dinner daily. Locals nod to one another over distinctive menu items that lean heavily on Louisiana's acclaimed cooking roots; they are created by Lagasse. Try the fresh Louisiana crabcake with smoky eggplant puree, feta cheese, calamata olives, crispy spinach, and citrus butter. For the main course Lagasse kicks out the culinary jams with his slow-roasted duck au jus (prepared in a sweet and spicy glaze and served with buttermilk-cornbread pudding and fire-roasted corn salad). Reservations are recommended.

OLD COFFEE POT $
714 St. Peter St.
(504) 524-3500

Next door to the world-famous Pat O'Brien's bar is this less well-known spot popular with local folk on the prowl for a stick-to-your-ribs Creole breakfast. Established in 1894, this courtyard restaurant (indoor dining is available, too) has long been a secret pleasure of New Orleanians. House specials include lost bread (the Creole version of French toast) and award-winning callas (Creole rice cakes served with grits and Vermont maple syrup). Many opt for one of the egg or omelette dishes. The Benedict-style eggs Jonathan, for instance, arrives at the table stuffed with ham, tomatoes, and oysters, topped with hollandaise sauce and served with grits or home-style potatoes and flaky buttermilk biscuits. The eggs Conti are poached in a white wine sauce with green onions and fresh chicken livers, served over fresh homemade biscuits. For an irresistible taste of local flavors, plunge your fork into the Rockefeller omelette stuffed with fresh creamed spinach, oysters, herbs, spices, and cheese topped with a light cream sauce. For breakfast, a host of wake-up-little-snoozy drinks range from traditional Bloody Marys to meet-me-in-the-70s Harvey Wallbangers. Breakfast (till 3 p.m.), lunch, and dinner are served daily.

THE PELICAN CLUB $$$
312 Exchange Place
(504) 523-1504
www.pelicanclub.com

On Fri and Sat nights, live music greets guests as they enter this bistro-style restaurant's bar and reception area. The mahogany bar against the wall dates to 1919 and provides a courtly spot for cocktails while waiting to be seated. In fact, if the restaurant is overcrowded, you might have to enjoy your memorable meal at one of the four window tables overlooking Exchange Alley. (Yes, the floor is imported hand-painted Italian tile, but you'll just have to manage.) Chances are, though, your reservations included a request for seating in the middle dining room—bright and airy with white walls, leather banquettes, black-wood chairs, and slowly spinning ceiling fans. (As this place can get a tad noisy on weekend nights, the Club Room, with its noise-absorbing dark carpets and oak-paneled walls, would be a good choice if you're looking for a more quiet spot.) But regardless of where guests sit in this vibrant dining establishment, popular with both the blue-jeans and dress-up crowds, the contemporary menu with Louisiana traditions and Asian flair makes for memorable meals. Executive chef Richard Hughes Jr. has concocted some gratifying palate pleasers including such starters as duck and shiitake mushroom spring rolls and scallop-stuffed artichoke with roasted garlic beurre blanc. But the Pelican Club really takes flight when it comes to this venue's sensational spring rolls filled with charred filet mignon, and Louisiana-style cioppino. Dinner is served daily and reservations are recommended.

PORT OF CALL $
838 Esplanade Ave.
(504) 523-0120
www.portofcallneworleans.com

For as long as anyone can remember, this lively, dimly lit corner restaurant has been the place to drop anchor for one of the biggest and juiciest hamburgers in town. These plump, half-pound treasures, ground fresh daily, arrive hot on a toasted sesame seed bun. By the time you've added the lettuce, pickles, and thick slices of onion and tomato served on the side, using a knife and fork makes pretty good sense. The baked potato that comes with the burgers is almost a meal in itself, especially if you order it with the works. Steaks and specialty house drinks such as the Windjammer, a blend of tropical juices mixed with two kinds of rum, and the Bahamian-style Goombay Punch round out the menu. During weekends the bar near the front door is usually crowded with people waiting for tables. The rope fishing nets hanging from the ceiling and an oldies-playing jukebox add to the entertaining atmosphere of this popular eatery. Open daily for lunch and dinner.

RED FISH GRILL $$
115 Bourbon St.
(504) 598-1200
www.redfishgrill.com
Local artist Luis Colmenares's sculpted metal branches transform the wooden columns in the main dining room into encircling palms. All shapes and sizes of seafood are etched into the sea-colored concrete floor. Hanging on the exposed-brick back wall of the cocktail and oyster bar are half a dozen yard-high oyster half shells with mirrors inside; the backs of the artsy metal stools are adorned with alligators and crabs and fish, oh my. The tables are hand-painted in bright seafood designs. And the menu is divided into such categories as Bait (appetizers, soups, and salads), Fin Fish, Shell Fish, Go Fish (meat, pasta, vegetarian), and Overboard (dessert). Leave it to longtime restaurateur and proprietor Ralph Brennan of the Brennan restaurant family to create a comfortable bistro as whimsical to the eye as the Asian-Cajun tapas plate and the wood-grilled Gulf fish taco are as pleasing to the palate. (See Mr. B's Bistro, Bacco, and Palace Café.) What Brennan and executive chef Robert Gregg Collier have concocted inside this renovated 1800s building, once home to D. H. Holmes department store, is a parade of heavenly delights using earthy crawfish, oysters, and pasta. Its Bourbon Street

location draws a lot of walk-in tourists, but locals, too, have embraced this "casual New Orleans seafood" experiment. Other must-tries include: Creole-style sweet potato catfish; sesame-crusted salmon; gumbo with spicy alligator sausage; hickory-grilled redfish; and spring rolls filled with grilled chicken, shrimp, and andouille sausage. Lunch and dinner are served daily; brunch Sun.

REMOULADE $
309 Bourbon St.
(504) 523-0377
www.remoulade.com
Visitors strolling Bourbon Street who are looking for an affordable grazing menu of local flavors and a fun vibe, courtesy of the late Archie Casbarian (the restaurateur who put the famed Arnaud's next door back on the map), should look no farther. Local staples include cafe au lait, beignets, red beans and rice, half-size po-boys dubbed "po-babies," boiled and fried seafood, and oysters on the half shell. Arnaud's famous remoulade sauce (the same kind found atop the celebrated restaurant's filet mignon Charlemond) tops the burgers and franks. Other offerings include smoked boudin, thin-crust 8-inch gourmet pizzas, Nachitoches (NACK-ah-dish) meat pies, and baskets of spare ribs. Mixed drinks, shooters, and a selection of "bayou potions guaranteed to ward off alligators" are served from behind the restored 1870s mahogany bar. Lunch and dinner are served daily until midnight.

THE RIB ROOM $$$$
621 St. Louis St.
(504) 529–5333
Elegant 20-foot ceilings, exposed brick, gracious arches, and cypress barge-board walls from 19th-century keel boats set the stage for fine dining. The heady aromas wafting from the French rotisserie that dominates the back of the dining room are proof you have arrived at a palais du boeuf non pareil. For generations the city's politicians, lawyers, and art dealers have made this French Quarter dining den on the ground floor of the Omni Royal Orleans Hotel a lunchtime favorite.

And chef Anthony Spizale's prime rib and selection of rotisserie classics such as the chateaubriand, roti-assorti (English-cut prime rib, loin pork chop, and grilled lamb sausage), filet mignon, and lamb T-bone steaks seasoned with fresh herbs will tell you why. At night when the lights are turned down, the ambience changes from power-lunch buzz to pure hushed-tone romance. (For best seats—lunch or dinner—reserve a table overlooking Royal Street.) The menu stays the same with the addition of a few noteworthy seafood creations such as the roasted or grilled filet of salmon, crabcakes, and spit-roasted Gulf shrimp sautéed in a light butter with herbs and served with garlic sauce. Reservations are highly suggested for lunch and dinner, which are served daily.

TUJAGUE'S $$$
823 Decatur St.
(504) 525-8676
www.tujagues.com

In 1856 local butcher Guillaume Tujague, a native of Mazzeroles in southern France, opened this restaurant in the old Spanish armory on Decatur Street. He served hearty fare to dockworkers, butchers, and seamen who gave the French Market neighborhood its delightfully saucy character. Since that time U.S. presidents Roosevelt, Truman, and Eisenhower as well as France's Charles de Gaulle have dined at the city's second oldest restaurant. Politicians, artists, and travelers still rub elbows around the 1849 cypress bar—the oldest standing bar in the city and a classic in every sense of the word. The Latter family bought the restaurant in 1982 but the six-course-only dinners for which the establishment is known are still built around such longtime staples as shrimp remoulade and beef brisket. While Tujague's can never be accused of impulsive innovation, patrons today have their choice of four traditional Creole entrees. Reservations are suggested, especially for weekend dining. Lunch at this more-than-200-year-old landmark is a far less fussy way to experience the ambience. Order the chicken and andouille pasta.

i Don't think that Creole and Cajun are the only two cuisines Big Easy restaurants have to offer. New Orleans is a multicultural melting pot, and its numerous ethnic restaurants offer foods of the world ranging from Chinese and Cuban to Senegalese and Vietnamese. In fact, it's been said that the only type of food not available in New Orleans is Scandinavian.

CBD/DOWNTOWN

BON TON CAFÉ $$$
401 Magazine St.
(504) 524-3386
www.thebontoncafe.com

A brace of gaslights flank the canvas-canopied entrance to this popular establishment. Local dining connoisseurs first discovered this leisurely restaurant when it originally opened in the early 1900s. It closed for a spell only to be reopened in the 1950s by Al and Alzine Pierce when they arrived in New Orleans from their bayou home in south Louisiana's Lafourche and Terrebonne Parishes. Like many Acadian restaurateurs who have set up shop in the Big Easy over the decades, they brought their family recipes with them. Today the Pierces' nephew, Wayne, and his wife, Debbie, continue the family tradition of authentic Cajun cookery in the historic 1840s Natchez building. Amid a decor of red-and-white checkered tablecloths, wrought-iron chandeliers, shuttered window blinds, and exposed-brick walls, guests will find many time-honed Bon Ton creations. Crawfish étouffée, crawfish bisque, shrimp and oyster jambalaya, and soft-shell crabs barely scratch the surface. Other considerations are the center-cut filet, shrimp étouffée, and crawfish bisque. The Rum Ramsey cocktail, adapted from a recipe handed down from the early 1900s and known only to the owners, is famous. Lunch and dinner are served Mon through Fri, and reservations are "strongly urged."

THE GRILL ROOM $$$$
300 Gravier St.
(504) 522-1992, (800) 262-2662
www.windsorcourthotel.com

One thing shared by the world's most impeccable dining legends is a liberation of geography. It is a restaurant's seamless savoir faire, say internationalists, that gives it a worldliness that would make it as at home in Istanbul and Paris as Vienna and Hong Kong—or New Orleans. Ranked as one of the finest restaurants in the United States and Europe, the Grill Room is such a place. The Lalique table at the entrance greets guests to this famed culinary enclave on the second floor of the posh Windsor Court Hotel. But the focal point of this highly polished room is a marquetry screen of Windsor Castle commissioned by Viscount Linley, son of the late Princess Margaret, for Windsor Castle. The elegant, softly lit, and unpretentious decor is accented by upholstered, dark-wood, straight-back chairs and light-colored linen tablecloths; an antique painting, Girl on the Seashore, dominates one wall. From people-watching during power lunches to romantic anniversaries celebrated in grand style, this continental oasis of refinement has been luring discriminating gourmets since it opened in 1984.

Executive chef Drew Dzejak's menu features a unique dining concept of four culinary categories: Southern, Unadulterated, Steakhouse, and Indulge. In the first category look for grilled black hog pork chop; Scottish salmon for those who prefer Unadulterated; a 20-ounce Prime Angus rib-eye under Steakhouse; while those wish to Indulge will find the Duo of Veal. Dinner is served nightly as well as a Sat brunch and Sun champagne brunch. Arrive early to allow ample time for a martini at the Polo Lounge, the hotel's swank watering hole. Reservations are required.

LIBORIO CUBAN RESTAURANT $$
321 Magazine St.
(504) 581-9680

Simple and consistently prepared Cuban mainstays served in a Spartan dining room that often buzzes with Latin music and a lively crowd (especially during lunch) has helped this downtown spot earn its stripes. The restaurant moved to its current location from across the street, but hot meals still arrive in generous portions. The unique Spanish- and African-influenced cooking traditions of the Caribbean's largest island have found a fitting home in a city that enjoys centuries-old ties to the region. Order a Honduran Port Royal beer served ice cold (or the nonalcoholic tamarind- and ginger–flavored Tamarindo) and dive into a traditional Cubano fried sandwich (pork, ham, and Swiss cheese on pressed grilled French bread) or the garlic roasted pork. The paella (with shrimp, lobster, crab, chicken, and fish) is mouthwatering and well worth the 45 minutes the kitchen cooks need to prepare this

How to Crack a Crawfish

Some people call the little red crustaceans mudbugs, others crayfish, but by any name this Big Easy mainstay arrives at dining tables boiled, seasoned—and in the shell. Here's the skinny on how to avoid shellshock: First, break off the head. This part of the crawfish is filled with marvelously seasoned fat juices from boiling, and most of us simply put the opening to our lips and suck. Next turn the tail on its back lengthwise between your thumbs and crack open the shell.

Gently squeeze the tip of the tail between your thumb and index finger and—bingo!—the crawfish meat should slide easily out of its shell. Mmmm. Traditionalists keep a cold Dixie longneck within arm's reach for celebratory swigs. By the way, it's correctly pronounced CRAW-fish, just like it's spelled.

Andalusian-inspired version of New Orleans' jambalaya. Many dishes come with rice and peas (the Latin-Caribbean's answer to New Orleans' red beans and rice) and either sweet or green fried plantains, always tender to the fork. If your meal doesn't include the boiled yuca with garlic sauce, do yourself a favor and ask for it as a side order. Lunch is served Mon through Sat; dinner Tues through Sat. Reservations are required.

PALACE CAFÉ $$$
605 Canal St.
(504) 523-1661
www.palacecafe.com

Located in the former Werlein's music store, Palace Café's building has been a local landmark since the turn of the 20th century. Nowadays it's classic and contemporary Creole and Cajun indulgences, not sheet music, that lure people to this lively, upbeat, grand Parisian-style brasserie owned and operated by Dickie Brennan Jr. of the famed New Orleans restaurant family. (This Brennan got his culinary start at Commander's Palace under the tutelage of Paul Prudhomme, now the proprietor-chef of K-Paul's.) Like most of the family's new generation of eateries, which includes Mr. B's Bistro, Bacco, and Red Fish Grill, the accolades for this $2 million Palace coup haven't stopped since it opened its doors in 1991. Brennan and the Palace Café have been on CNN's *On the Menu*, recognizing the restaurant for "being consistently voted some of the best food in the city and in the nation." Make reservations for one of the upstairs window-side tables during Mardi Gras, and enjoy a best-seat-in-the-house view of Canal Street below as a nighttime Carnival parade rolls by. The downstairs dining room offers a view of the open kitchen. Tasty favorites by executive chef Darin Nesbit include oven-roasted duck, crabmeat cheesecake, oyster pan roast, shrimp Tchefuncte, and, of course, the original white-chocolate bread pudding. Reservations recommended. Lunch is served Mon through Sat; dinner is served nightly. Enjoy the Sunday live blues brunch.

> ℹ If you visit this predominantly Catholic city during Lent, be prepared for longer-than-usual waits at seafood restaurants on Friday. During Lent, the 40-day period of fasting and penitence from Ash Wednesday to Easter, the faithful abstain from eating meat on Friday. Locals of all persuasions recognize the day by dining out en masse.

RESTAURANT AUGUST $$$$
301 Tchoupitoulas St.
(504) 299-9777
www.restaurantaugust.com

Among the city's consistently top-ranked restaurants is this gastronome's Vahalla and nationally praised retreat for the gourmand in us all. To set the right gustatory tempo, start off with award-winning executive chef John Besh's creative appetizers, particularly his three-way foie gras. A changing menu of equally admirable entrees may be underscored by the whole-roast rabbit cassoulet (with white beans and andouille), and the sugar and spice duckling (with stone-ground grits). Personal favorites include the crispy veal sweetbreads with grilled lobster and French lentils, and porcini-crusted sea bass with orzo and Crowder pea risotto. Can't decide? Don't fret. Besh has whipped up a don't-miss tasting menu and tour de force of mouth-watering specialties fated to command the attention—and palate—of even hard-to-please culinary critics: handmade potato gnocchi, and crispy-seared sable fish. If this doesn't leave you breathless in New Orleans, nothing will. Lunch is served Fri and dinner nightly.

FAUBOURG MARIGNY/ BYWATER

ADOLFO'S $$
611 Frenchmen St.
(504) 948-3800

This intimate eatery, located above the Apple Barrel bar, is the place to coat your stomach with an early dinner before hitting the Frenchmen Street jazz clubs in Faubourg Marigny. (See music close-up in Nightlife chapter.) This Creole Italian restaurant doesn't take reservations, so show up early for the best service. The atmosphere is casual and friendly; the food is satisfying. Try the escargots, lamb chops, or any of the fish dishes. Note that Adolfo's is located in an old building at the top of a pretty steep set of stairs and is not wheelchair accessible. Open for dinner nightly.

BUFFA'S $-$$
1001 Esplanade Ave.
(504) 949-0038
This is basically a neighborhood corner bar on the Faubourg Marigny side of Esplanade Avenue (a block before Rampart). But it comes into play when someone sends you to Port of Call for great burgers and you arrive to find a line out the door (which there always is). Cross the street and walk down a block to Buffa's where you'll find a welcoming attitude and burgers just as good. Ask to be seated in the back room, if the smokiness of the bar bothers you while you're eating. Open nightly.

CAKE CAFÉ $
2440 Chartres St.
(504) 943-0010
www.nolacakes.com
This cozy little restaurant, officially known as the New Orleans Cake Café and Bakery, can be found three blocks on the downriver side of Elysian Fields Avenue in the Marigny. A breakfast and lunch spot as well as a full bakery, Cake Café serves, hands down, the best bagels in New Orleans. Everything is made fresh here by the friendly staff and owner Steve Himelfarb who is known locally as The Cake Man. Try the shrimp and grits served with a big homemade biscuit or the crab sandwich with fresh locally caught crab, brie and bacon on any of the cafe's house-baked breads. (Although, challah is the best choice for the crab sandwich.) And don't forget dessert. There's always a variety of pastries (such as pear and goat cheese Danish) or try a red velvet cupcake with cream cheese icing, which is only a buck with a meal. There's outdoor dining available and prices are low enough for visitors to eat here everyday. (Many locals do.) Open for breakfast and lunch Tues through Sun.

THE COUNTRY CLUB $-$$
634 Louisa St.
(504) 945-0742
www.thecountryclubneworleans.com
The name of this Bywater facility can be misleading, as can be its façade that looks like a well-preserved historic home with its traditional yellow paint and colonnaded front porch. Although the Country Club's pool area is for annual pass-holders only, the restaurant is open to the public. The casually elegant atmosphere, which includes al fresco dining, is complemented by an interesting American contemporary menu and a short wine list. Try the tasso-stuffed pork loin with thyme beurre-blanc and green bean almondine or the char-broiled oysters with butter and garlic. The mac and cheese made with smoked gouda is a popular side. Open for lunch and dinner daily, brunch Sat and Sun, except during special events. Call ahead.

FEELINGS CAFÉ $$$
2600 Chartres St.
(504) 945-2222
www.feelingscafe.com
The tropically lush, romantic courtyard crumbling with history and serving as the restaurant's bar, has been a favorite among locals for years. For an untouristy spot in which to unwind with pre-dinner cocktails, it has few equals. The courtyard surface features bricks recycled from the massive fireplace of the original D'Aunoy Plantation, built in 1795 and one of the first constructed in the historic Faubourg Marigny neighborhood. Guests can dine downstairs in the main dining room adjacent to the bar. Or, for an extra touch of romance, when making reservations request one of the candlelit tables on the second-floor balcony that overlooks the courtyard. Try the Gulf Fish Nicholas, a fresh grilled filet, brushed with

Dijon mustard, topped with grilled shrimp and served on a bed of creamed spinach or the Seafood Baked Eggplant featuring shrimp, crawfish, sausage, and rice over fried eggplant and topped with hollandaise. Open for dinner Thurs through Sun, as well as for Sun brunch.

THE JOINT $$
801 Poland Ave.
(504) 949-3232
www.alwayssmokin.com

Barbecue just doesn't get much better than it is at this funky Bywater eatery. And locals aren't the only ones who've noticed. The Joint was listed among the Top 10 New Barbecue Restaurants by *Bon Appetit* magazine. There's nothing fancy here where patrons sit on benches and listen to the jukebox. But there is the juiciest slow-cooked ribs, beef brisket, pulled pork, and chicken—all to be finished with either of two types of sauce found on each table. Down-home sides include potato salad, baked beans, coleslaw, and green salad with smoked tomato and onion dressing. Open for lunch Mon through Sat, dinner Wed through Sat.

MIMI'S $-$$
2601 Royal St.
(504) 942-0690
www.mimisinthemarigny.com

Mimi's in the Marigny is divided into two parts. Downstairs is a popular neighborhood bar that stays open 'til the wee hours and upstairs is a hip dancehall where people can be found dancing the night away and eating some pretty good tapas, which is served late into the night. The tapas is $6 or less. Try the herbed grilled shrimp or the calamari with chorizo. For a really good time, enjoy the tapas on Sat or Sun night when DJ Soul Sister spins vinyl and the party really gets going. Tapas served nightly.

MONA'S $-$$
504 Frenchmen St.
(504) 949-4115

If it's traditional Mediterranean fare you're hankering for, this Marigny restaurant is the place to go. Especially good are the falafel, chicken kabob, gyros, and the vegetarian plate. There's no need for reservations and while there, visitors can shop the small store for good prices on jars of capers, bags of chick peas, and even a hookah. Open for lunch and dinner daily.

PRALINE CONNECTION $
542 Frenchmen St.
(504) 943-3934
www.pralineconnection.com

Walk into this intimate Faubourg Marigny restaurant with its stainless-steel ceiling fans, black-and-white tile floor, and a waitstaff adorned in flashy ties and fedoras, and one word comes to mind: slick. No doubt, this Creole soul food restaurant is one of the coolest places you'll ever eat in. And will you be glad you did. The fried chicken is crispy and delicious, and the filé gumbo is hearty and satisfying. Most meals include melt-in-your-mouth corn bread. Other best bets include barbecued ribs, hot chicken wings, and soft-shell crabs in this casual yet bustling setting populated with a mix of locals and tourists. No reservations are accepted, so to avoid the biggest crowds in this small dining room, take in a late lunch or early dinner. On your way out, stop in the adjacent candy shop to stock up on pralines and other goodies for the trip home. Open for lunch and dinner daily.

SUKHO THAI $$$-$$$$
1913 Royal St.
(504) 948-9309
www.sukhothai-nola.com

If the spices in the local Cajun food isn't hot enough for you, step into Sukho Thai. Here patrons can order the spice level of their food as mild, medium, hot, or Thai hot. Try the shrimp with plum dipping sauce or the seafood clay pot, as well as a number of vegetarian dishes. Portions are generous. One appetizer and an entrée can easily feed two people. Open for lunch Tues through Fri and dinner Tues through Sun.

13 MONAGHAN $

517 Frenchmen St.

(504) 942-1345

http://13monaghan.com

This is another good place to grab some food late, when club-hopping on Frenchmen Street. The menu is full of good "drinking" food—eggs, sandwiches, and lots of vegetarian-friendly choices—all very well priced. Especially popular with the late-night crowd is the crispy baked Tater Tots covered in melted cheese, referred to by locals as "tachos." Open late nightly.

WASABI $$

900 Frenchmen St.

(504) 943-9433

http://wasabinola.com

For those who need a sushi fix, Wasabi is a good bet and conveniently located near the Marigny jazz clubs. The decor is tasteful Japanese and the very decently priced menu is full of traditional sushi and sashimi choices. This is also a great place to get takeout, for those who would rather spend the evening in. A second location opened near Lake Pontchartrain in 2009. Open for lunch and dinner daily.

YUKI $$–$$$

525 Frenchmen St.

(504) 943-1122

This modern Japanese izayaka (tavern) is a relative newcomer to the Frenchmen Street scene, but certainly an interesting addition. Here visitors will find a different vibe than most of what surrounds it. The walls of the cozy and mellow tavern are adorned with old Japanese posters and Japanese movies are sometimes silently projected on the wall. A variety of live music can be heard. There's an excellent sake menu, complemented by elegantly prepared Japanese tapas including shumai crab dumplings and shichimi peppered french fries with wasabi mayonnaise. Open dinner hours Tues through Sun, late-night Fri and Sat.

ESPLANADE

CAFE DEGAS $$

3127 Esplanade Ave.

(504) 945-5635

www.cafedegas.com

Particularly in fall and spring, when the weather can be downright blissful, the covered deck of this fashionable bistro-style eatery in historic Esplanade Ridge is a pure delight. Named after the 19th-century French Impressionist Edgar Degas, who lived down the street for a brief time, this restaurant is ideal for lunch or dinner after visiting the nearby New Orleans Museum of Art. Daily specials augment the French-language menu (with English translations). The sometimes breezy venue is popular among hoi polloi and politicians who can be found dining on such creations as crispy veal medallions and broiled escargot. The restaurant is open for lunch Wed through Sat, dinner Wed through Sun, and brunch Sun.

LIUZZA'S BY THE TRACK $

1518 North Lopez St.

(504) 218-7888

Ask any New Orleanian to rattle off the names of their favorite neighborhood joints, and this one invariably shows up in the top five. It's also among the spots New Orleanians who've moved out of state are eager to visit when they drop into town. And for good reason: Liuzza's menu hits the backstretch of cherished local dishes ranging from its acclaimed fried oyster salad and well-seasoned Creole chicken and sausage gumbo to fresh sautéed shrimp and corn chowder with crawfish. Its moniker derived from the restaurant's proximity to New Orleans Fair Grounds Race Track, this homebred winner has proven itself a front-runner when it comes to its plethora of po-boys that include a don't-miss roast beef with "nostril-searing" horseradish so good *Gourmet* magazine once proclaimed it "the reason to come to New Orleans." Open for lunch and early dinner Mon through Sat.

MID CITY

DOOKY CHASE $$
2301 Orleans Ave.
(504) 821-0600

New Orleans' premier Creole soul food restaurant, Dooky Chase is also the place where the movers and shakers of the city's African-American community meet. Edgar "Dooky" Chase and his wife, Emily, opened the restaurant in 1941. Over the years the eatery has grown from the best-kept secret of the black community to a restaurant of international renown, mostly because of chef Leah Chase's talent. Chase, the wife of Dooky Chase Jr., is a home-taught cook who creates such delicacies as breast of chicken a la Dooky, stuffed with oysters, baked in a marchand de vin sauce, and served with sweet potatoes. Locals and tourists alike can be found daily in the casually glamorous Dooky Chase dining room, which features a collection of African-themed art including stained-glass panels depicting life in black New Orleans. Other best bets at this restaurant, which features a full bar and short wine list, are fabulous fried chicken, red beans and rice, Creole gumbo, stuffed shrimp, and the fried seafood platter. Or, if you're really hungry, call ahead and order the Creole Feast. (*Note:* Tourists unfamiliar with the city are advised to take a cab to this restaurant at night.) Lunch and dinner are served daily and reservations are recommended.

FIVE HAPPINESS $
3605 South Carrollton Ave.
(504) 482-3935
http://fivehappiness.com

When Five Happiness owner Peggy Lee first visited the Big Easy in the early 1980s, she found that local Chinese restaurants were serving rather bland food. Knowing New Orleanians' love for spicy food, she decided to relocate to New Orleans her California-based restaurant, which specialized in Szechuan and Hunan fare. Since that time, this Mid City eatery has grown into one of the city's most popular Chinese restaurants.

The dining rooms are comfortable and spacious. Best bets include Szechuan shrimp, pot stickers, hot and sour soup, and the Triple Delight—a combination of chicken, beef, and shrimp sautéed with vegetables in a brown sauce. Combination lunch specials are available Mon through Sat. Lunch and dinner are served daily. Reservations are recommended on weekends.

UPTOWN

CLANCY'S $$
6100 Annunciation St.
(504) 895-1111

Don't let the unassuming exterior fool you. This neighborhood restaurant offers a top-notch fine dining experience from a kitchen that has produced a number of the city's best chefs. The contemporary New Orleans cuisine includes unforgettable smoked soft shell crabs. In fact, any of the crab dishes is a good bet, along with creative daily specials. Open for lunch Thurs and Fri, dinner Mon through Sat. Reservations are recommended.

COMMANDER'S PALACE $$$$
1403 Washington Ave.
(504) 899-8221
www.commanderspalace.com

A local longtime food critic once wrote about the test he gives friends and restaurantgoers who say they've grown tired of this standard-bearer of Creole dining. He asks them simply whether they would prefer to dine at Commander's or (fill in the blank). Guess which one they pick 99 times out of 100? He explains that while some locals may grow tired of hearing about Commander's, no one ever tires of actually putting a napkin on his or her lap inside this legend. A generation of chefs who have gone on to make their own culinary marks in the city have worked the Commander's kitchen. Even the short list is impressive: Emeril Lagasse (see Emeril's and Nola), Paul Prudhomme (see K-Paul's) and Frank Brigtsen (see Brigtsen's). Now helmed by Executive Chef

Tory McPhail, the restaurant offers a menu that still woos even the most hard-to-please palate with starters such as parmesan-crusted oysters or the gumbo du jour. Along with traditional New Orleans favorites (which are all good), try the sea bass or rack of lamb. Lunch and dinner are served daily; a live jazz brunch is offered Sat and Sun. Reservations are required.

DELMONICO'S $$$$
1300 St. Charles Ave.
(504) 525-4937
www.emerils.com

Locals were happy indeed when this 104-year-old restaurant reopened its doors in June 1998 after superstar chef Emeril Lagasse bought the place. Signature dishes include Emeril's barbecued shrimp baked grit cake and shrimp remoulade Creole deviled eggs. Also try the slow-cooked crispy pork over dirty Creole rice, the filet mignon, and traditional bananas foster dessert. Dinner served nightly. Reservations are recommended.

i Foodies and gourmands have several resources for keeping abreast of the local dining scene, including weekly reviews by restaurant critic Brett Anderson in the *Times-Picayune*'s "Friday Lagniappe" section; food writer Lorin Gaudin, Wednesday mornings on ABC26's *Good Morning New Orleans;* and critic Tom Fitzmorris' call-in radio program on WSMB 1350-AM Mon through Fri 4 to 7 p.m.

JAMILA'S CAFE $$
7808 Maple St.
(504) 866-4366

Just when you were beginning to wonder if all Mediterranean restaurants served more or less the same fare, along comes this cozy Maple Street retreat of mouthwatering Tunisian surprises. The appetizers alone will be enough to make even seasoned lovers of traditional Greek, Turkish, and Lebanese fare sit up and take note.

Best bets include the appetizers *ojja* merguez (sautéed homemade seasoned lamb sausage, caraway seeds, tomatoes, and bell peppers mixed with eggs), grilled merguez (with lentils), and leg of lamb. A succinct mix of traditional Mediterranean meat, fish, and vegetarian dishes served with couscous (steamed whole-wheat semolina) is available. Open for dinner Tues through Sun. Reservations recommended.

KYOTO $$
4920 Prytania St.
(504) 891-3644

At this Japanese restaurant, everything from the salmon and yellowtail to the mackerel and eel consistently wins high praise. Lovers of local seafood should try the soft-shell crab and crawfish rolls. Sit at the sushi bar or one of the tables in this uncluttered, well-lit dining establishment to order a la carte or off the full menu, which features a large appetizer section as well as numerous traditional Japanese noodle soups and grilled and fried dinners. Open for lunch and dinner Mon through Sat.

PASCAL'S MANALE $$
1838 Napoleon Ave.
(504) 895-4877

The photographs of guests who have dined here that hang on the wall attest to the lure of this timeless restaurant owned and operated by the same family since 1913. The old-fashioned oyster and cocktail bar is lively and draws a spirited after-work crowd. But one look around the linen-covered tables reveals that this place is still the legendary home of one of the city's most delicious comfort foods—barbecue shrimp. Large fresh Gulf shrimp still in the shell (with heads on, too) are served in a peppery butter sauce. Freshly baked French bread is served on the side, and tradition calls for dunking doughy pieces of it into the warm, buttery nirvana that only seems to taste better the longer the meal lasts. Daily specials as well as traditional Italian, Creole, seafood, and steaks are served. Lunch is served Mon through Fri, dinner Mon through Sat.

CARROLLTON/RIVERBEND

BOUCHERIE $$$

8115 Jeannette St.
(504) 862-5514
www.boucherie-nola.com

Housed in a converted cottage in the Carrollton neighborhood, Boucherie offers an elegant and intimate atmosphere perfect for date night. Chef Nate Zimet offers a sophisticated twist on traditional local ingredients, such as boudin balls with a garlic aioli or steamed mussels with collard greens and crispy grit crackers. The smoked beef brisket with garlicky Parmesan fries as well as the barbecued ribs with grilled broccoli and shoestring shallots hearken to Zimet's roots when he sold his popular barbecue fare from a truck at local night clubs. Open for lunch and dinner Tues through Sat.

BRIGTSEN'S $$$$

723 Dante St.
(504) 861-7610
www.brigtsens.com

Frank Brigtsen, one of the city's heralded chefs, opened the doors to this converted shotgun cottage in a quiet Carrollton neighborhood in 1986 and has been swamped by loud applause ever since. Brigtsen, who still works five nights a week in the kitchen, where he personally prepares the lion's share of dinners, infuses Creole-Acadian cooking traditions with creative and seasoned twists. "Brilliantly creative" is a phrase often found simmering alongside descriptions of Brigtsen's culinary skills. It's hard to disagree after one taste of his rabbit tenderloin, served on an andouille Parmesan grit cake with Creole-mustard sauce or the blackened yellowfin tuna with smoked corn sauce and red bean salsa. Brigtsen says he learned many of his techniques during seven years under chef Paul Prudhomme at K-Paul's restaurant (see K-Paul's). "I was right next to the man watching every move he made, all the nuances, all the timing." Small, cozy rooms with whirring ceiling fans create an intimate yet informal dining experience. Dinner is served Tues through Sat and reservations are suggested.

CAMELLIA GRILL $

626 South Carrollton Ave.
(504) 866-9573
www.camelliagrill.net

Neighborhood families as well as college students from nearby Loyola and Tulane Universities can be found queuing up for the pleasure of snagging one of this tiny diner's 20 counter stools (the place's only seating). So why all the fuss? Because taking one of those seats is like sitting down to an old movie where waiters and cooks in crisp uniforms dispatch orders and service with the kind of aplomb that's so rare these. All food is made to order on grills in plain view, which is also part of the fun. Best bets include the hamburgers and omelettes (served anytime) stuffed with ham and oozing with cheese. And don't forget the fresh pies baked daily. Open daily for breakfast, lunch, and dinner and open till 1 a.m. on weekends, the Camellia Grill is also popular for late-night eating. No alcohol is served, and no credit cards are accepted.

JACQUES-IMO'S CAFÉ $$

8324 Oak St.
(504) 861-0886

This is the little soul-food den you've heard about where customers actually walk past the open kitchen to arrive at the covered-deck dining area out back. And, yes, that's owner-chef Jack Leonardi wearing a chef's jacket and Bermuda shorts. But peccadilloes such as those don't even scratch the surface of what makes a meal at this popular Carrollton neighborhood spot so memorable. What does begin to tell the story of this always bustling den is fried chicken so outstanding devotees have described it as a near religious experience, and a national travel magazine dubbed it the best of its kind anywhere in the United States. But the lengthy regular and specials menu featuring old-school soul food and Creole standards (a must-have is the deep-fried roast beef po-boy) also shares the spotlight with an adventurous shrimp and alligator sausage cheesecake, paneed rabbit with oyster/tasso cream sauce, grilled duck, and pork chop stuffed with ground

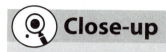

Close-up

Po-Boys in Paradise

There's an old joke that goes: What's a New Orleanian's favorite seven-course meal? A po-boy and a six pack of Dixie beer.

While the highfalutin' may spend hours raving about the latest nouvelle cuisine, the average local knows that there's no dish more satisfying than the sloppy, overstuffed po-boy. In fact, satisfaction was the inspiration for this sandwich's invention. There are a couple versions of the origin of the po-boy sandwich, one of which is that during a streetcar strike financially strapped wives would make long sandwiches on enormous baguettes for their picketing husbands—the "po-boys." According to New Orleans historian Buddy Stall, during the Depression, when a large portion of the population fell on the worst of times, local merchants, brothers Clovis and Denny Martin, decided to concoct a sandwich that could fill an empty stomach for a nickel. They found that a sandwich made with French bread, lots of gravy, and scraps of meat did the trick. However, the pointy ends of the bread were wasted, so they called on baker John Gendusa to create a loaf that was longer and more slender. This came to be known as po-boy bread or New Orleans French bread. Within six months of its creation, the po-boy, or poor boy as outsiders call it, had become the most commonly eaten sandwich in the city.

Today, there are almost unlimited kinds of po-boys. For the novice, here are the basics: First, you have your fried seafood po-boys, the most common of which are shrimp, oyster, or soft-shell crab. For these the French bread is usually buttered and probably toasted. Appropriate condiments are ketchup and/or hot sauce. Next is the ham and cheese, usually with mynaz (that's local lingo for mayonnaise). Tell them you want it hot so that the cheese is melted and ask for a little Creole mustard, too. You'll be glad you did. Then there's the roast beef po-boy, best served hot with enough gravy and mynaz that both drip off the sandwich when you pick it up. And if you want lettuce, tomato, and pickle on your po-boy, ask for it "dressed." Got that, dawlin?

Following is a list of some of the places around town to find the best po-boys and other traditional New Orleans dishes. Bon appétit.

FRENCH QUARTER

Johnny's Po-Boys $
511 St. Louis St.
(504) 524-8129
www.johnnyspoboy.com

A French Quarter institution since 1950, Johnny's is without a doubt the best place to get po-boys in the Vieux Carré. Rated by *Good Housekeeping* magazine as one of the "100 great values for your money" restaurants in the country, the restaurant serves 45 varieties of po-boys as well as breakfast (all day), home-style hot lunches, seafood, gumbo, and salads. Try the hot roast beef po-boy, which is always delicious (and don't forget to ask for lots of gravy) or the seafood

platter. One of the daily specials is a combination plate with red beans, jambalaya, and gumbo—a good introduction to local cuisine. Breakfast and lunch are served daily. No credit cards are accepted.

CENTRAL BUSINESS DISTRICT

Mother's $
401 Poydras St.
(504) 523-9656
www.mothersrestaurant.net

A few blocks from the Convention Center, in the shadow of towering office buildings and hotels, sits an unobtrusive little brick structure with a small white sign reading, MOTHER'S WORLD'S BEST BAKED HAM RESTAURANT, EST. 1938. A time-honored and secret family recipe produces a tender, sweet, crispy, caramelized ham that is the most popular item on the menu. The signature po-boy is the Ferdi Special—a combination of baked ham, roast beef "debris" (the part of the roast that falls into the gravy in the oven), shredded cabbage, and Creole mustard. The dining room, with brick walls and concrete floors, is usually overflowing with diners as well as those standing in line, especially at lunchtime. Breakfast, lunch, and dinner are served daily.

MID CITY

Liuzza's $
3636 Bienville St.
(504) 482-9120
www.liuzzas.com

Opened in 1947, Liuzza's is one of the city's most popular neighborhood restaurants. The Frenchuletta is Liuzza's answer to the Muffuletta (a cheese, ham, salami, and olive salad sandwich served on a large round bun, which was originally the Central Grocery's answer to the po-boy). The Frenchuletta is basically the same thing, except that the meats are grilled and it's served on French bread. The closest thing to low-cal here is the spinach salad, which is topped with half a dozen fried oysters and bacon. Best bets also include the sautéed shrimp remoulade on French bread, roast beef with brown gravy, and the soft-shell crabs. The preferred drink is beer served in a frosty 18-ounce glass goblet. Lunch and dinner are served Tues through Sat. Credit cards are not accepted, but an ATM is located on premises.

Mandina's $
3800 Canal St.
(504) 482-9179
www.mandinasrestaurant.com

Down-home cooking is the name of the game at this locals' hangout. This friendly neighborhood dining den has been serving up daily Creole, Italian, and Cajun specials plus burgers, deli and po-boy sandwiches, seafood, chicken, and steaks since its doors opened in 1932. The place bustles at lunch, and a lively crowd can always be found on weekend nights hunkered around the dinette tables under the whirring ceiling fans. Trout meunière and catfish almandine at half the price charged at upper-crust establishments can be found on the menu, as well as the locally famous "loaf"—a whole loaf of French bread gutted and filled with a choice of fried oysters, shrimp, catfish, or half-and-half (shrimp and oysters). Come as you are. Lunch and dinner are served daily.

OLD METAIRIE

The Galley $$
2535 Metairie Rd.
(504) 832-0955

Homemade corn and crabmeat soup, hot boiled shrimp and crawfish, and a lengthy specials board of home-style Italian and Creole dishes are found at Vicki and Dennis Patania's patio restaurant in the heart of Old Metairie. What really put this casual family eatery on the map, though, are the same plump, soft-shell crab and catfish filet po-boys the husband and wife team have served since 1977 at the New Orleans Jazz and Heritage Festival. The overstuffed po-boys served in freshly baked French bread are among the best in town. Seafood baskets and platters filled with soft-shell crab, stuffed crab, catfish, shrimp, or oysters are popular standbys as well as the roast beef and seafood po-boys. Vicki's soups are famous among regulars, who keep the lively main dining room and patio crowded most nights. Her corn-and-crabmeat, oyster-artichoke, corn-and-crawfish, eggplant-and-shrimp, and three-cheese soups rule the roost. Opened in 1990, The Galley serves lunch and dinner Tues through Sat.

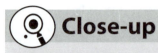 **Close-up**

Olé! The Nuevo Wave of New Orleans Cuisine

The globe-trotter was midway into his first-ever dinner at Laurentino's, savoring forkfuls of simmering seafood fideua and patatas alioli, when he remarked to his companion: "Unbelievable—this is just like dining in Barcelona." Not the Barcelona of the pricy nouvelle cafes found amid the Catalonia capital's chichi dining scene, mind you. But rather the Barcelona of Catalan soul food savvy travelers seek out on the *carrer* less traveled in the ancient Mediterranean seaport's storied Barrio Gothic. Unbelievable, too, was Laurentino's location: the far corner of a stubby strip mall tucked on the fringe of suburban Metairie. Blink and you'll miss it.

What is impossible to miss, however, is the culinary mouth-quake Iberian gastronomy has unleashed in recent years on the East and West Coasts. And this white-hot megatrend is gaining ground in New Orleans, challenging the dining status quo while offering an armada of bona fide, full-bodied tastes of Espana. Though it's been more than 200 years since Spain ruled Louisiana, several restaurants have stepped smartly into the bullring with a full-blown tapas dinner menu (Vega Tapas Cafe, 2051 Metairie Rd., Metairie; 504-836-2007; and Rambla, 217 Camp St., New Orleans; 504-587-7720), and a mixed menu of Spanish and Latin American specialties (Rio-Mar, 800 South Peters St., New Orleans; 504-525-3474).

But it's Barcelona native Xavier Laurentino who oversees the only restaurant in the metropolitan area—and perhaps the entire Third Coast—specializing in the authentic foods of his native Catalonia, Spain's northeasternmost province. A quintessentially Mediterranean cuisine, Catalan recipes reflect a legacy of cross-cultural contact with Greeks, Romans, Arabs, and Sicilians, not to mention plenty of influences from southern France. Laurentino comes by it naturally. The longtime New Orleans resident and seasoned restaurateur opened his establishment (4410 Transcontinental Dr., Metairie; 504-779-9393) armed with family recipes handed down for generations. "My father," he says, "was an honest and humble man who taught me how to cook and instilled in me the love for honest and simple food."

Catalan food may indeed be historically peasant-simple, but under Laurentino's stewardship it becomes a cuisine rich in nuance and subtext. Take, for instance, paella Valenciana, "the flagship of Spain's gastronomy that originated centuries ago on the delta of the Ebro River," he explains. Iberia's best example of one-pan cooking and a sophisticated, Old World predecessor to jambalaya, paella is a deftly seasoned rice dish blended with seafood, chicken, meat, or a combination. But the Catalan version of paella is a country cousin called fideua *(feh-du-AH)* that replaces rice with angel hair pasta for a lighter and subtle alternative that better absorbs the flavors and creates a heavenly twist on Spain's national dish. Swirl in a

beef and shrimp. What this lively dining joint does, it does extremely well—consistently. And that's why visiting travel writers and food critics have joined locals in singing the praises of this humble establishment virtually from the moment it opened its doors. All together now: "Jock-a-mo fee-na-ne!" Open for dinner Mon through Sat.

MAT & NADDIE'S CAFE   **$$**
937 Leonidas St.
(504) 861-9600
www.matandnaddies.com

The tidy menu, at this renovated 1852 cottage with a picket fence, features Creole fine dining cookery. From the appetizer menu try the mushroom, roasted red pepper and hazelnut stuffed artichoke or the crabcakes with cucumber slaw and mango-chipotle chutney. From the entrée menu, there's bronzed Gulf drum over lemon-basil and shrimp risotto, as well as grilled yellowfin tuna with charred tomato coulis. The "It's All Good Creole Buffet" lunch is served Mon through Fri; dinner is served Thursday through Sat and Mon.

dollop of alioli (Spain's version of French aioli, or garlic mayonnaise) for your first bite of fideua, which arrives at your table in an individual *paellera,* or paella pan, and your palate will dance a Sardana.

To be sure, Catalan cuisine is as old—if not older—than many of its European counterparts. Some of the region's cooking traditions can be traced to the 14th century, when Barcelona ruled a mini-empire that stretched from Sicily and Malta to the French regions of Rousillon and Cerdagne and parts of Greece. Hundreds of years ago, tapas were free tidbits on a slice of bread large enough to cover the top of a wine glass as a sort of lid, ostensibly to keep flies out of the wine. (*Tapa* is Spanish for lid or cover.) Some historians say tapas were born when Spanish King Alfonso X was so ill he could only eat small bites of food with wine between meals. Others claim the humble food was the mother of invention that gave sustenance to farmers and laborers so they could work until the job was done and it was time to eat the main meal of the day.

Either way, Laurentino's tapas bear the Catalan stamp of authenticity. The patatas alioli (cubed potatoes slowly fried to a golden brown and drizzled with homemade alioli), as well as the Mediterranean olives and thin slices of robust Manchego cheese, served on Catalan garlic-tomato bread, for instance, are as good as (if not better than) what a traveler might find at a beachside joint in Calella de Palafrugell or a hip tapas bar in Tarragona. Ditto for the savory slices of Serrano (Spain's prosciutto) and pan-seared marinated pork loin medallions. "This is one of the most famous tapas in Spain," says Laurentino. Indeed, if the proprietor were any more true to his school, the restaurant would have to stay open past midnight as is the custom in Barcelona and larger cities throughout Catalonia.

The globe-trotter was by no means the only one singing the praises of Catalan cuisine. In a Sunday *New York Times Magazine* cover story titled: "The Nueva Nouvelle Cuisine: How Spain Became the New France" proclaimed Catalonia the epicenter of nouvelle cuisine. Meantime, *Los Angeles Times* restaurant critic and former *Saveur* magazine editor Coleman Andrews's book, *Catalan Cuisine: Europe's Last Great Culinary Secret,* is a 352-page love-fest celebrating the food traditions of a province settled by ancient Greeks in sixth century B.C. and by the Romans 300 years later.

The globe-trotter warmed a glass of Spanish Grand Duque de Alba brandy in his hands and smiled at the proprietor. "Your food . . . transports me," he said.

Laurentino beamed. "That makes me happy," he said, standing beside a pair of colorful murals depicting the photogenic Costa Brava coastline of his native homeland. "So very happy."

UPPERLINE $$$
1413 Upperline St.
(504) 891-9822
www.upperline.com

Proprietor and longtime restaurateur JoAnn Clevenger is one of the indefatigably charming figures on the local fine-dining scene. She encourages patrons to ask questions and explore her 40-year rotating collection of artwork, which includes paintings, sculpture, and pottery. Some regulars have referred to the establishment as a fun after-hours museum.

A mostly local clientele is found inside this 1877 town house, which offers a classy, warm mood framed by fresh-cut flowers, an Art Deco bar, high ceilings, and lace curtains. The sophisticated, award-winning menu is exciting but never stuffy thanks to executive chef Ken Smith. Winners abound: fried green tomatoes in a zesty shrimp remoulade; spicy shrimp with jalapeño corn bread; duck gumbo; seared salmon with crawfish bouillabaisse and aioli; and braised lamb shank in Burgundy with saffron risotto. Clevenger hosts theme and historical wine dinners throughout the year as well as her famous garlic "festival" June through Aug. Dinner is served Wed through Sun. Reservations are highly recommended.

LAKEFRONT/BUCKTOWN/ LAKEVIEW

DEANIE'S SEAFOOD $$
1713 Lake Ave.
(504) 831-4141
www.deanies.com

For generations Bucktown Harbor at the 17th Street Canal has been the docking point for fishers bringing in the catch of the day. Not surprisingly, several fine seafood restaurants have grown up around the place. This right-off-the-lakefront Bucktown spot doesn't boast a river view, but once you start eating, you won't care. The meal starts off on the right track with hot, steamy new potatoes, which are served instead of bread in this casual, bright, and airy eatery. Try the barbecue shrimp crawfish étouffée, crabmeat au gratin, stuffed flounder, and the broiled stuffed shrimp dinner. Expect to wait in line for dinner, especially on weekends. Lunch is the least crowded time to go. There is now a second location at 841 Iberville St. in the French Quarter. Lunch and dinner served daily.

R&O'S PIZZA PLACE $
216 Old Hammond Hwy.
(504) 831-1248

People always look as though they're having a good time in this crowded, noisy Bucktown restaurant, and no wonder. The mostly local, family crowd knows that they can expect some of the best po-boys and simple specialty dishes in town. The large, airy restaurant has been expanded several times, and each time the customer base has expanded with it. This is not a place for intimate conversation, but if your family wants to go out with a baby who sometimes cries and a brother who talks too loud, no one will even notice. Although it's called a pizza place, the sandwiches are the real star. Try the roast beef po-boy dripping with gravy and mayo, the stuffed crab Parmesan po-boy with lots of red gravy and mozzarella, or the soft-shell crab po-boy that almost melts in your mouth. Lunch daily and dinner are served Wed through Sun.

TONY ANGELLO'S RISTORANTE $$
6262 Fleur de Lis Dr.
(504) 488-0888

Tony Angello's serves Creole Italian cuisine, a tiny bit of heaven created by the marriage of two great cooking styles and found only in New Orleans. At first glance, this signless restaurant could be mistaken for a large house on a corner lot in west Lakeview. But the crowds headed for the door with smiles on their faces give the place away. Inside, a welcoming attitude, subdued lighting, and attentive service make this a popular date spot and always a good experience even before you take the first bite. Sit back and relax with one of the fine Italian wines the restaurant offers by the glass or bottle, and then say the magic words: "Feed me, Mr. Tony." This will be followed by a series of small courses, such as stuffed shells, lobster cup, soft-shell crab, spinach salad, soup, cannelloni, veal with peppers and mushrooms, and eggplant Tina—each more delicious than the last. There are several versions of "feed me" from which to choose, as well as a full a la carte menu. Dinner is served Tues through Sat, and reservations are recommended to avoid a long wait. Jackets are not required, but "dressy casual" attire is suggested.

NIGHTLIFE

New Orleans nightlife is world renowned—so much so that it would be hard to believe that the city could live up to its reputation. However, one thing New Orleans has always been good at is throwing a party. And not just at Mardi Gras. Locals are always up for a good time. In fact, they make it a priority. Therefore, just as it is hard to find a bad meal in the Big Easy, it is equally difficult to find an entertainment venue where people aren't having fun.

Though some are better than others, the following listings should provide a pretty good time. They were chosen for uniqueness or simply being the best at what they do. There's every type of after-dark diversion, from the gentility of sipping martinis on a Victorian porch to the recitations of beat poets and folk singers who seem to have just stepped out of a time machine; the smooth sounds of traditional jazz to the raucous fun of a Cajun fais do do. One thing's for sure: If you can't have fun in New Orleans, you can't have fun anywhere.

Now get out there—and make sure you're back by dawn.

FRENCH QUARTER

BOMBAY CLUB
830 Conti St.
(504) 586-0972
www.thebombayclub.com
People don't meet in this stylish club; they rendezvous. Subdued lighting, intimate booths, and live piano music make this one of the most elegant bars in town. There's a full selection of domestic and French wines as well as 85 different signature martinis including the Breathless, made with Skyy vodka and white crème de cocoa along with a splash of Godiva liqueur and served in a chocolate-rimmed glass; the James Bond 007 features Absolut vodka, Boodles gin with a splash of Dubonnet—shaken, not stirred—and served with a lemon twist; the Cajun King martini has Absolut pepper and citron with dry vermouth and spiced Tabasco olives.

CATS MEOW
701 Bourbon St.
(504) 523-2788
www.catskaraoke.com

Want to know who's playing where when you're in town? Listen to WWOZ 90.7 FM, New Orleans award-winning non-profit jazz radio station. Along with great music, the Livewire Music Calendar is announced at the top of every odd hour. Or read the full calendar at www.wwoz.org, where you can also hear the station's live broadcast. Also check out www.offbeat.com, the Web site of New Orleans' authoritative music magazine.

When the Cats Meow opened its doors in 1989, karaoke was somewhat of a novelty. And believe it or not, 15 years later this place is still packed pretty much every night with guests singing their hearts out. The music is a mix of hits from the '50s to today, including rock, disco, dance, and hip-hop. Happy hour runs 4 to 8 p.m. Mon through Thurs and 2 to 8 p.m. Fri through Sun and features three-for-one drinks. Housed in a structure dating to the 1820s, the bar also features two balconies overlooking Bourbon Street as well as an intimate courtyard.

CHRIS OWENS 500 CLUB
500 Bourbon St.
(504) 523-6400, (504) 495-8383
www.chrisowensclub.net
The show opens at 9:30 p.m. Thurs through Sat when the house band Latin Rhythms and the undisputed Queen of Bourbon Street, Chris Owens, take the stage. What ensues is an energetic and entertaining floor show performed to the hilt by Ms. Owens much as she has for as long as most people can remember. Not to be missed by those who enjoy dancing and a good nightclub act "like in the old days."

i The drinking age in New Orleans is 21, but you can get into the clubs legally at 18. Many places charge a cover for 18 to 21 year olds to make up for the lost drink revenue.

FRITZEL'S EUROPEAN JAZZ PUB
733 Bourbon St.
(504) 586-4800
www.fritzelsjazz.net
An unobtrusive yet historic building constructed in 1831 provides an intimate setting for talented local musicians as well as touring international jazz groups that take the stage nightly at 9 p.m. The eclectic crowd of tourists and locals combined with German beers and well-chilled Schnapps make for a lively European pub atmosphere. No wonder this is an after-hours hang out for "off duty" musicians looking for a late-night jam. There's a one-drink minimum.

HOUSE OF BLUES
225 Decatur St.
(504) 529–BLUE
www.hob.com
This national chain, inspired by the original Dan Aykroyd/John Belushi *Blues Brothers* movie, hit a high note when it opened in the French Quarter—in part because blues music, the club's original focus, has always found a spiritual home here. However, most of the credit for the club's

popularity would have to be given to the big-name acts—Bob Dylan, Eric Clapton, Wynton Marsalis—it has brought into the city. Nightly concerts also feature well-known local groups as well as promising unknowns. A word of warning for those who have been walking around the French Quarter all day and who actually want to sit down to listen to music: Get here when the club's doors open at 8 p.m. to snag one of the few church pew seats on the music hall's balcony. Preshow dinner is also available in the club's restaurant, which is decorated with primitive art as well as the faces of great contemporary musicians in plaster relief. Burgers, pizzas, salads, and specialty sandwiches dominate the menu. The restaurant also offers daily lunch; a Sunday gospel brunch takes place in the hall.

LAFITTE'S BLACKSMITH SHOP
941 Bourbon St.
(504) 593-9761
www.atneworleans.com/body/blacksmith.htm
Dating to the 1770s, this dank and dusky bar is housed in one of the city's oldest buildings that lore tells us once belonged to pirate Jean Lafitte. The place still feels like a pirate could walk in the door any minute. People can find privacy in the quiet, darkened corners created by the crumbling walls and exposed beams. Hours are 10 a.m. to 4 a.m. daily.

MARGARITAVILLE CAFE/ STORYVILLE TAVERN
1104 Decatur St.
(504) 592-2565
www.margaritavilleneworleans.com
Singer Jimmy Buffett developed a love for New Orleans through stories he heard from his grandfather, a steamship captain who frequented the city's port, and later when Buffett started his musical career here. His laid-back Margaritaville Cafe/Storyville Tavern in the French Quarter is the place to find performances by local talents. Live music is offered Fri through Sun (hours vary so call ahead) with no cover charge. The cafe features a varied menu with local delicacies as well

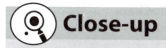

Close-up

Frenchmen Street: Where Locals Go to Hear Music

Just downriver of the French Quarter is an area founded in 1805, called Faubourg Marigny, or simply The Marigny to locals. At the heart of this bohemian neighborhood is Frenchmen Street where those in the know nightly gather to hear the city's best jazz, blues, and world beat music. Anyone who wants to experience the true sound of New Orleans should take their disco nap, then head over to the 500 and 600 blocks of Frenchmen where the music plays all night long. The premier club is Snug Harbor at 626 Frenchmen (see write-up in this chapter) where artists with names like Marsalis and Neville can often be heard. Also check out the following:

The Blue Nile, 532 Frenchmen (504) 948-2583, for jazz, blues, rock, funk, and Latin jazz nightly. There is a second stage upstairs.

Cafe Negril, 606 Frenchmen (504) 944-4744, to hear jazz, funk, blues, reggae, and lots more. Best known for Monday night open mic jams that draw well-known as well as up-and-coming acts. Almost never a cover.

The Apple Barrel, 609 Frenchmen (504) 949-9399, a tiny club with great acoustics featuring jazz or blues every night.

d.b.a., 616 Frenchmen (504) 942-3731, for acts like jazz guitarist Walter "Wolfman" Washington or the Jazz Vipers nightly. The bar also serves a sophisticated menu of beers and liquors.

Jimbeaux's (formerly The Spotted Cat), 623 Frenchmen, also offering nightly jazz or blues. Regular performers include Mike Hood, Snake Greenberg, and the Panorama Klezmer Jazz Band.

as themed specialties such as the "Brown Eyed Girl" Triple Chocolate Pie.

THE NAPOLEON HOUSE
500 Chartres St.
(504) 522-4152
www.napoleanhouse.com
By 1821 Napoleon Bonaparte had seen his empire reduced to the tiny island of St. Helena, where he found himself in exile. His reign over the hearts of French expatriates, however, had remained undiminished. In New Orleans, no less than Mayor Nicholas Girod and pirate Jean Lafitte sipped absinthe and hatched plots to rescue their hero. Ships were readied, the mayor had his home enlarged to properly accommodate an emperor, and who knows what would have happened if Napoleon hadn't had the bad taste to die before the mission could be completed. Today, the mayor's 1797 home, at the corner of St. Louis and Chartres in the French Quarter, is a National Historic Landmark where generations have gathered to practice the art of civilized drinking. A timeworn look, with peeling paint and yellowed oil portraits on the walls, along with the piped-in classical music and subdued lighting, are part of the pub's shadowy charm. Be sure to order a Pimm's Cup, the house specialty. This tangy gin concoction is equally good when sipped sitting next to the open French doors on a rainy afternoon or over a cozy, candlelit table on a hot summer night. For the hungry, there's a reasonably priced menu of salads and sandwiches.

OZ
800 Bourbon St.
(504) 593-9491
www.oznewworleans.com
A gay dance club, Oz often sports a mixed crowd who dance the night away to club music from the '70s to the '90s spun by DJs like Bull and Tim Pflueger. There are manager's drink specials all night, and at 11:30 p.m. the games begin. Wed is drag show night, when the Ladies of Oz take the

stage. Hours are Mon and Tues 4 p.m. to 2 a.m. and Wed 1 p.m. through Mon 4 a.m.

THE PALM COURT JAZZ CAFE
1204 Decatur St.
(504) 525-0200
www.palmcourtcafe.com

Jazz for grown-ups is an appropriate description of this elegant setting featuring exposed-brick walls covered with a collection of music-themed photographs, linen tablecloths, a classic mahogany bar, and mosaic tile floors. The club, located in an old French Market warehouse, offers a variety of Creole dishes and live traditional jazz music five nights a week at 8 p.m. The cover charge is $5. Reservations are highly recommended.

PAT O'BRIEN'S
718 St. Peter St.
(504) 525-4823, (800) 597-4823
www.patobriens.com

Pat O's, as locals call it, is the home of the original Hurricane—first served more than half a century ago. And visitors can begin sipping this taste of New Orleans (a fruit punch and rum powerhouse guaranteed to knock even the most seasoned drinker off his game) when the bar opens at 12 p.m. Mon through Thurs and 10 a.m. Fri through Sun. B. H. Pat O'Brien opened his first drinking establishment a block from the saloon's current location in the early part of the 20th century. Unfortunately, there was a little Constitutional amendment in place at the time called Prohibition. Mr. O'Brien's Club Tipperary was one of New Orleans' many speakeasies that were open only to those who knew the secret password "Storm's Brewin'." With the 1933 repeal of Prohibition, the business turned "legit" and took on the moniker it would retain, Pat O'Brien's—a name that has been synonymous with fun for generations. Whether you want to sit at the piano bar or outside around the courtyard fountain, getting here early is a good idea to avoid waiting in line. Open till the wee hours, Pat O's is also a great last stop of a night on the town.

PRESERVATION HALL
726 St. Peter St.
(504) 522-2841, (504) 523-8939
www.preservationhall.com

There are two universal truths associated with this traditional jazz hall: (1) You will wait in line to get in, and (2) you will be glad that you did. This dilapidated French Quarter landmark is the closest thing you will find to a living museum. Inside the small, dimly lit club, jazz lovers stand or sit on the floor to experience America's only original art form in its purest rendition. A number of the regular musicians are in their 70s or 80s and helped develop jazz during the early part of the last century. Shows are nightly 8 p.m. to 11 p.m. and admission is $10. Be forewarned, this is simply a performance hall. No alcohol is served, but guests are welcome to bring their own and Pat O'Brien's is conveniently located right next door. (Also see the Close-up in this chapter.)

CBD/WAREHOUSE DISTRICT

HOWLIN' WOLF
907 South Peters St.
(504) 522-9653
www.thehowlinwolf.com

The Howlin' Wolf is *the* rock club in New Orleans, booking the top touring groups and lots of underground must-see shows. It's where serious musicians go to hear music ranging from Harry Connick Jr. and The Foo Fighters to Jimmy Page, Dr. John and Jimmy Buffet. The exterior of the new location features a mural, a recreation of a New Orleans neighborhood featuring Louis "Satchmo" Armstrong and the Dirty Dozen Brass Band, created renowned local artist Michalopoulos. Ticket prices vary, depending on the artist but tend to run from $5 to $25.

LE CHAT NOIR
715 St. Charles Ave.
(504) 581-5812
www.cabaretlechatnoir.com

Vintage street lamps on the 700 block of St. Charles Avenue light the way to Le Chat Noir, New Orleans' only European-style cabaret. When

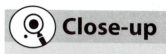 **Close-up**

Preservation Hall

"If there's only one place I go," the American expat visiting from Berlin said wagging his finger, "it's Preservation Hall to hear some authentic New Orleans jazz." Timing is everything. Had the friend blown into town 40 years ago, he would have found that the local traditional jazz scene had nearly played its own funeral. At the time few venues existed for the aging musicians who played the joyous improvisational music born in the wee hours of the 20th century inside the bars and bordellos of the Big Easy's legendary Storyville red-light district.

Fortunately, the late Allen Jaffe, a dyed-in-the-clef jazz lover from Pennsylvania, moved to New Orleans and opened the dilapidated landmark on St. Peter Street known as Preservation Hall in 1961. Traditional New Orleans jazz was given a rebirth. "Those who predicted an end to local jazz at phases from the 1920s, through the 1940s revival, and by the end of the 1960s were simply wrong," writes local musician and jazz historian Dr. Michael White in the Louisiana Endowment for the Arts' *Cultural Vistas* magazine in 1991. "It seems that New Orleans jazz as a living tradition will have a future."

Today that future meets the past inside Preservation Hall, a dusky, dimly lighted enclave crowded nightly with jazz lovers happy to sit on a hard wooden bench or the floor for a chance to experience what is perhaps the Crescent City's most enduring legacy. And we're not talking only about music. Many of the regular musicians are in their 70s and 80s. As performers they stand—and sit—as living proof that the city's venerated cool cats of improvisation, playing elbow to elbow with jazz heirs half their age on the cramped stage, still make the "roof shake and the walls come a-crumblin' down." The intergenerational ensemble that is the Preservation Hall Jazz Band carries the torch of this century-old legacy nightly from 8 p.m. until 11 p.m. Sets last about 35 minutes with a brief intermission. Admission is $10.

Traditional New Orleans music was handcrafted by the city's African-American jazz pioneers, such as Buddy Bolden, Jelly Roll Morton, Kid Ory, Joe "King" Oliver, and Louis Armstrong, to name only a few. Today the city's jazz bands—the outgrowth of New Orleans' post-Civil War brass bands—still feature a front line of trumpet, clarinet, and trombone backed by a drums-bass-banjo rhythm section. For visitors who have never heard songs like "St. Louis Blues," "Closer Walk with Thee," "St. James Infirmary," or "Mood Indigo" performed live, it can be a near-transcendental experience.

Be forewarned: Preservation Hall is not a nightclub or bar. Few, though, are likely to lament the absence of booze and food. The real attraction is center stage when this no-frills, near-mythical landmark's changing roster of leading local jazz musicians honors the roots of what historians have called America's only truly original art form.

Don't let long lines stretching down the block hit a sour note. Jazz has been around 100 years—it's not going anywhere. And neither should you. Grab a rum-and-punch Hurricane at Pat O'Brien's next door and strike up a conversation with other like-minded music fans in the queue. Before long the friend visiting from Berlin was exchanging addresses with the backpacking college kids from France and the white-haired retired couple from Ohio. Once inside, visitors are invited to listen to as many sets as they wish. And it's worth the wait.

After all, the city's sultans of swing—then and now—remind the listener what it means to hear New Orleans.

guests enter this restored turn-of-the-20th-century building they first find Bar Noir, which fronts the Cabaret Room. With its top-drawer liquor menu, striking black-and-white mosaic tile floor, and expansive windows that offer a view of the St. Charles Streetcar, the Bar Noir is a sophisticated place to enjoy a drink, listen to live piano music, or peruse the pictures of past performers on the Wall of Fame. House specialty drinks include Cosmopolitans and the Black Cat. The bar generally opens one hour before showtime.

The Cabaret Room is reminiscent of elegant 1940s nightclubs with candles flickering atop linen-draped tables. The room is venue for a wide variety of interesting theater, cabaret acts, and music with the performance schedule changing weekly. Table reservations are suggested for all shows with doors opening half an hour before showtime. Dress code is casual dressy. Park in the adjoining lot.

LEPHARE
529 Gravier St.
(504) 636-1890
www.lapharenola.com

As hip a place as you'd likely find anywhere in Manhattan, LaPhare aesthetically and architecturally is a Vahalla of cool offering an eclectic mix of old exposed-brick walls, slightly crooked raw wood columns, and cushiony contemporary furniture groupings designed to get youngish professionals to let down their hair. Enjoy cocktail hour perched by the large windows facing the street—perfect for watching the local and visiting glitterati pass by. Theme nights keep the joint interesting—there's free salsa lessons and dancing on Tuesday (starting at 7 p.m.), Thursday Rock Night (9 p.m.), Friday's Beauty and the Beat (9 p.m.), and Saturday night's Stellar starring DJ Jive starting at 10 p.m.

i At some point in the night you are bound to come across a kid in the French Quarter who wants to bet you that he knows where you got your shoes. Don't be a sucker. Instead of taking the bet, just tell him the proper answer, which is: "I got 'em on my feet."

LOA INTERNATIONAL HOTEL
221 Camp St.
(504) 553-9550
www.ihhotel.com

Located in the International House boutique hotel, Loa is just a couple of blocks from the French Quarter but light-years away from Bourbon Street. Lit only by candles set on old plaster shelves and furnished with sumptuously upholstered sofas, Loa exudes the glamour of an upscale martini bar slightly softened by New Orleans' signature laissez-faire. Dress is always stylish. Open daily 4 p.m. until whenever.

LUCY'S RETIRED SURFERS BAR
701 Tchoupitoulas St.
(504) 523-8995
www.lucysretiredsurfers.com

Bra', where's my 'board? Even if you can't tell the difference between a Gordon & Smith longboard or a Morey Boogie, you'll have no problem, dude, fitting right in with the laidback nightcrawlers who frequent this perennially popular watering hole. Best known for its easygoing, come-as-you-are beach vibe and street-corner sidewalk tables offering patrons a view of the nocturnal ebb and flow of the trendy Warehouse District scene, this venue morphs into party central come weekends. Specialty drinks include the Mexican Martini (with jalapeno-stuffed olives and cranberry), and the Shark Attack (lemonade, rum, and "the blood of one innocent victim"). A modest menu of tasty bar food runs the gamut from Jamaican jerk chicken and the oh-so-succulent Juicy Lucy burger to fish tacos worthy of their Southern California ancestry. Open daily 11 a.m.

MULATE'S
201 Julia St.
(504) 522-1492
www.mulates.com

If you don't have time to make your way out to Acadiana, Mulate's is the closest thing in town to an authentic Cajun dance hall. That's probably because the original Mulate's in Breaux Bridge, Louisiana, is one. This spacious club offers lots of dancing room and tons of friendly people to make sure you get that two-step right. This fun place also serves good spicy Cajun food.

WHISKEY BLUE
W Hotel
333 Poydras St.
(504) 525-9444
www.whotels.com
Dim lights, black-and-white photos of old jazz greats, and low-slung leather stools—all the stylish brainchild of upscale bar designer Rande Gerber. And all set the cool mood of this upscale nightspot in the oh-so-hip W Hotel. The drinks are a bit pricey, but the company is worth it if sophistication does it for you. Sit at a short table or try out the queen-size bed that sits in the center of the room. Dress is casual to dressy but always chic. Hours are Mon through Sat 5 p.m. to 3 a.m. Valet parking available.

FAUBOURG MARIGNY

SNUG HARBOR
626 Frenchmen St.
(504) 949-0696
www.snugjazz.com
With performers such as jazz pianist (and father of Wynton) Ellis Marsalis and singer Charmaine Neville, as well as talented, lesser known musicians, Snug Harbor is one of the city's premier jazz clubs. Arrive early to snag a good view in the rustic, two-tiered seating area. Hungry or just want to avoid the cover charge? Then sit in the dining room that serves juicy burgers and fried seafood, or hoist a few at the bar. The show is piped into both. This is also a favorite after-hours place for musicians. Shows begin nightly at 8 and 10 p.m. Cover charge varies.

MID CITY

MID CITY LANES ROCK 'N BOWL
3000 South Carrollton Ave.
(504) 861-1700
Caution: This is not your father's bowling alley. Mick Jagger, Nicole Kidman, Tom Cruise, Brad Pitt, and Susan Sarandon have partied here—or at least they did at the old location before this one-of-a-kind New Orleans cultural institution, opened in 1941, recently moved to its current digs. And why not? How many places on earth can you listen to down-and-dirty blues, finger-snapping zydeco, or alternative grunge while sipping brewskies, tripping the light fantastic, and trying to keep the bowling ball out of the gutters for a change?

The dance floor and bowling lanes are filled with a typical New Orleans mix of nightcrawlers ranging from middle-aged professionals to college students with just enough pocket change for a few bottles of beer. Weekends, live music keeps the place jumping and the eardrums ringing till the wee hours. The best time to arrive is after 11 p.m. or later when the place is buzzing with fun.

Mid City Lanes Rock 'N Bowl is open Tues through Sat nights from 5 p.m. till. The weekend cover charge depends on which band is performing. Bowling is extra.

UPTOWN

THE COLUMNS
3811 St. Charles Ave.
(504) 899-9308
www.thecolumns.com
There is no more civilized activity than sipping a martini or other cocktail of choice while sitting on the Victorian porch of the elegant Columns Hotel, feeling the gentle night breeze on your face, and watching the streetcars clank down oak-lined St. Charles Avenue. As many locals (if not more) as hotel guests can be found any given night passing a trés genteel time on the porch or in the ornate Victorian lounge of this charming 19-room hotel, housed in one of the last remaining examples of turn-of-the-20th-century Louisiana plantation architecture.

DOS JEFES UPTOWN CIGAR BAR
5535 Tchoupitoulas St.
(504) 891-8500
www.dosjefescigarbar.com

As may be expected, the crowd here is mostly young and male. They come to enjoy the 50 brands of stogies on hand, the rustle of the banana trees on the patio, and the live music nightly.

F&M PATIO BAR
4841 Tchoupitoulas St.
(504) 895-6784
www.fandmpatiobar.com

It may not look like much from the outside, but this Uptown bar is a popular place for locals who are staying up late. It's got the perfect combination of ingredients for a middle-of-the-night outing: a terrific jukebox, F&M's "famous" cheese fries, and an open attitude toward tabletop dancing. The main portion of the bar is living-room comfortable, and the tropical patio fluctuates between tranquil and bustling, depending on the time of night and the crowd. There's also a photo booth to record your New Orleans all-nighter for posterity.

Tchoupitoulas Street, which runs along the river, is not the best place to be late at night. Park close to the bar or, better yet, cab it. You'll be in no condition to drive when you leave there anyway. Open pretty much all night, every night.

MAPLE LEAF
8316 Oak St.
(504) 866-9359

This music scene staple features top talent and a narrow dance floor that tends to become even more so as the night progresses—generally until the crowd spills out into the street or onto the patio. A broad range of bands can be heard here, including those that play Cajun, zydeco, R&B and Latin. This is a popular spot for the drinking and dancing Uptown college crowd who don't seem to mind the lack of personal space and who apparently don't have to get up in the morning.

THE NEUTRAL GROUND
5100 Daneel St.
(504) 891-3381
www.neutralground.org

Claiming the title of New Orleans' oldest coffeehouse, this time warp and cleverly named spot definitely marches to the beat of its own drummer—who can some nights be found at the microphone spouting original poetry about a romance gone wrong while accompanying himself on the bongos. Serving good strong coffee, teas, and pastries, the Neutral Ground also features nightly entertainment, whether poetry or a variety of music. Sunday is open mic night. Take time to check out the paintings and sculpture that abound. Play a game of chess or just relax on one of the lumpy old couches and enjoy the retro feel of this fun, offbeat place. Open nightly.

TIPITINA'S
501 Napoleon Ave.
(504) 895-8477
www.tipitinas.com

One of New Orleans' oldest music clubs and today among its most beloved (and coolest) music venues, Tipitina's was formed as a home stage for Professor Longhair near the end of his career. From there it had grown to be one of the city's premier musical venues until the House of Blues began providing competition. Still, it's the place to hear good local and occasionally touring rock and R&B bands. And don't miss the sweaty good time of the Sunday fais do do (traditional Cajun dancing) with Bruce Daigrepont and his band starting at 5:30 p.m.

SHOPPING

In the Big Easy the next closest rival for your money after dining is likely the city's A to Z of eclectic retail shops. Collectors of fine antiques, vintage and upscale clothing buffs, nostalgia fiends, dyed-in-the-wool craft nuts, and single-minded hobbyists alike could not ask for better hunting grounds. From custom-made perfumes and hand-stitched European-style finery to rare 18th-century books and imported Balinese bamboo furnishings, New Orleans seems to offer a little bit of everything under the subtropical sun.

Anyone who has traveled abroad knows of shopkeepers in some cities, which shall remain nameless, who have elevated to high art the ill treatment of customers—even those who speak fluent French. Fortunately, the prevailing warm winds of bona fide Creole hospitality that sweep through New Orleans have a way of making the easily intimidated out-of-town shopper feel right at home, even in the city's haute retail enclaves like Saks Fifth Avenue and Gucci. Visitors likewise can duck into a third-generation antiques shop just to admire a Tiffany tea service and expect to be accorded the same treatment as a major collector. Or step into one of this waterfront's funky bric-a-brac shops; if you're lucky you might meet one of the colorful characters—and there are plenty—for which the city is known.

And fun? Just as the Crescent City's hot dining spots and even hotter nightclubs are the stuff of legend, so too are the myriad shops every bit as diverse and unique as the people who own them. Shop owners in this heavily touristed town are accustomed to the ways of travelers from all over the world. And they enjoy breaking the ice with newcomers and putting them at ease, usually with a polite "Where y'all from?" It's all part of this port city's more than 300-year-old tradition of commerce and trade.

Unlike most other sections in this book, this chapter is organized by three main shopping districts—the French Quarter, Warehouse District, and Uptown—followed by some of the city's better known shopping complexes located in the French Quarter and riverfront. While additional retail clusters exist throughout the metropolitan area, those selected for this chapter were chosen, among other reasons, for their ease of accessibility and diversity. We'll start in the French Quarter and wind our way leisurely down the Quarter's main shopping streets (Royal, Decatur, and St. Peter, to name a few). You're going to meet some interesting locals along the way, people who help make a New Orleans shopping spree unlike anything you've experienced. Let's burn some plastic.

FRENCH QUARTER

ARCADIAN BOOKS AND PRINTS
714 Orleans St.
(504) 523-4138
Desmond Russell opened this funky trove of Francophile tomes half a block off Royal Street in 1981 and today carries thousands of rare and secondhand French-language volumes in philosophy, science, religion, drama, and history. In the fine tradition of secondhand bookstores, a couch near the stacks has seen better days and invites an angle of repose for anyone eager to peruse Balzac, *The Confessions of Jean Jacques Rousseau,* and other rediscovered literary gems. Floor-to-ceiling shelves stock a wide array of books in

English on local subjects, including Louisiana, the South, horticulture, art, and regional cooking.

ARIUS ART TILES
504 St. Peter St.
(504) 529-1665
www.ariustile.com
Lovely ceramic tiles handcrafted by artists in Santa Fe, New Mexico, are the specialty of this tidy Jackson Square shop. Collectors and browsers alike should check out the hand-painted artworks incorporating Latin, Hebrew, Southwestern, Mayan, mystical, jazz, and Native American themes. A line of New Orleans-themed tiles includes fun scenes of the French Quarter and Bourbon Street, Cafe du Monde, crawfish boils, and Mardi Gras. One wall features several multitile murals, including a brilliantly colored Amazon rain forest teeming with red and gold macaws in flight.

CENTRAL GROCERY CO.
923 Decatur St.
(504) 523-1620
Sitting elbow to elbow with locals and tourists alike at one of the two narrow counters in the back of this Italian market while munching on a Muffuletta sandwich has been a tradition almost from the day this place opened in 1906. Several establishments (including this one) lay claim to being the originator of the popular Italian-bread feast overstuffed with provolone cheese and deli meats and topped with tangy olive salad. Sidestepping the controversy, it's safe to say the mighty Muffuletta certainly helped put this enterprise on the map as well as in the hearts of New Orleanians.

Don't stop at the sandwiches though. Floor-to-ceiling shelves are stocked with gallon-size containers of imported extra-virgin olive oil, balsamic vinegars, Agostino Recca anchovy fillets, tins of mackerel and codfish, grape leaves, and other cooking essentials from the Mediterranean. Hanging from a small wooden beam above the deli counter near the front door are Sicilian Filzette- and Citterio-brand salami, prosciutto, mortadella, panchetta, hot or sweet coppacola, and boneless baccala. Cajun-style andouille and boudin sausage and tasso ham abound.

CIVIL WAR STORE
212 Chartres St.
(504) 522-3328
Pop quiz: Who, besides the Confederacy, printed currency during the Civil War to distinguish itself from the North? If you correctly answer, "Loyal Southern states such as Texas, Louisiana, Mississippi, and Alabama, and even many cities," step up to the glass counter display of 1860s moolah. Talk about inflation, though: A $5 bill printed by the Confederacy or a Southern state during the Civil War today can fetch up to $2,000 (though most of what's for sale is quite affordable). Other history can be learned—and purchased—at this one-room shop specializing in rare Civil War-era collectibles.

Gleaming sharpshooter pistols (they still work) compete for attention with Confederate-era bonds and stamps, diaries, and scribbled autographs, as well as a wall of gallant swords. Owner Hardie Maloney also sells ancient Roman coins dating to the reign of Gordian III in A.D. 238, U.S.-minted coins from the 1880s to the present, and silver dollar-size Spanish pieces of eight (worth less than a buck back then and $50 today). You don't have to be a die-hard Civil War buff to appreciate the irony of a box full of battlefield shrapnel found at a place called Bloody Angle.

CRESCENT CITY BOOKS INC.
204 Chartres St.
(504) 524-4997
www.crescentcitybooks.com
Upstairs, not one but six ghosts reportedly haunt the fiction racks. But don't count on the specter of trashy beach novels anytime soon at this bastion of scholarly used and antiquarian books. Unless, of course, your idea of skimpy summer reading is *William Harborne and the Trade with Turkey: 1578-1582.*

Since 1992 art and history lovers, gallery owners, and academicians alike have found a friend at this pleasantly crowded two-story bookseller. Joe Jackson stopped in once and within seconds had scooped up an entire collection of Robertson Davie's works. Ceiling fans whir over shelves stocked with an A to Z of world history (organized by era as well as by country), the body politic of Latin America and Caribbean cultures, ancient and modern architecture, contemporary and 19th-century criticism, and many other topics. The War Room is dedicated to books on all the major 20th-century conflicts fought by the United States.

Museum curators and scholars routinely shop here for classical and academic monographs as well as the kind of rare, backbreaking tomes that cost a bit more than last year's best-selling hardback. But that, too, is available in the fiction section on the second floor. Just watch out for things that go bump in the night.

i Looking for a unique shopping experience? Perhaps it's time to pick up a paddle. Neal Auction Co. (4038 Magazine St., 504-899-5329) and New Orleans Auction Galleries (801 Magazine St., 504-566-1849) host auctions throughout the year as well as previews—a great place to mingle while checking out that collection of rare stereoscopic viewing cards. Both auction houses offer catalogs upon request.

DASHKA ROTH
332 Chartres St.
(504) 523-0805
www.dashkaroth.com
This two-story shop specializes in an exclusive line of originally designed, handcrafted Judaica in eye-catching mixed metals and thousand-year-old fused glass from Israel. Jewelry and objets d'art crafted by two dozen local and national Judaica artists include menorahs, chais, wedding dreidels, Shabbat candle holders, mezuzah pendants, tzedakah (charitable donation) boxes, Stars of David, and Seder cups hand-painted with the ancient ketubah, or marriage contract. One of the menorahs is a replica of the one presented to Bill Clinton for Hanukkah in 1993 at a White House ceremony by the children of Washington, D.C.'s Jewish Community Center. The shop opened at its current location in 1994 and features a fine selection of non-Judaica, mixed-metal jewelry and earrings by more than 50 artists, plus owner Dashka Roth's own creations.

i "If you grow it, they will come" is still the philosophy behind the perennially popular Crescent City Farmers' Market Days and locations. Tues 10 a.m. to 1 p.m. (Uptown Square parking lot, 200 Broadway); Thurs 3 to 7 p.m. (3700 Orleans Ave.); Sat 8 a.m. to noon (700 Magazine St.). For more information call (504) 861-5898.

ESOTERICA
541 Dumaine St.
(504) 581-7711, (866) 581-7711
www.onewitch.com
Some occultists appreciate household gadgets that are both handy and macabre. This probably explains the skeleton beer bottle openers stashed behind the counter, just looking to pop the top on a cold bottle of Voodoo beer. Handy and macabre also describes the bookrack. Browsers will find a large selection of tomes for the Wiccan on their gift list, such as *The Complete Book of Witchcraft*, *The Pagan Book of Days*, *Aleister Crowley's Magick*, and Tarot dictionaries. Brass chalice sets and earthy handmade brooms with cypress handles are found alongside chicken-foot necklaces, herbs, camphor candles, incense, and a selection of pentagram-shaped jewelry and earrings.

FAULKNER HOUSE BOOKS
624 Pirate's Alley
(504) 524-2940
www.faulknerhousebooks.net
William Faulkner lived in this 1840 four-story Creole house while writing his first novel, *Sol-*

diers' Pay. The main room features original brick walls, 16-foot ceilings, and double French doors with fanlight. Upstairs is the private residence of owner and attorney Joseph DeSalvo Jr., who opened their business in 1990 on Faulkner's birthday, September 25.

Specialties include used and rare books, with a focus on local authors, poetry, first editions, and, of course, the entire collection of Faulkner's works. This bookseller's homage to the man DeSalvo calls "the dean" of Southern literature shares shelf space with Tennessee Williams, Ernest Hemingway, George Bernard Shaw, Oscar Wilde, and many others. The few, the proud, the waggish might want to consider a copy of the *Algonquin Literary Quiz Book* as a cocktail party icebreaker.

FLEUR DE PARIS
523 Royal St.
(504) 525-1899, (800) 229-1859
www.fleurdeparis.net

From silk and linen to cotton and lace, elegant finery fit for the Southern belle in any woman are specialties of this corner shop known for its chic, eye-catching window displays. Beaded evening gowns and bridalwear fashioned by in-house designers overlook cocktail dresses, separates, and antique-style lingerie. Check out the unique custom-made hats with European-style ribbons, flowers from Paris, and South American feathers and other stylish accessories for the modern woman who thinks locally and dresses globally.

THE FRAME SHOP AND GALLERY
1041 Bourbon St.
(504) 581-1229

This funky street-corner shop keeps alive the fading art of museum-quality custom framing. The same staff that has worked here since the establishment first opened its doors in 1970 is well known for meticulous craftsmanship when putting the finishing touches on an original painting or sketch, photograph, poster, or print. Imaginative framing concepts are a specialty. Not long ago a woman's Flamenco fan (a trea-

sured family relic salvaged from the attic during spring cleaning) was given new life with an eye-catching shadow-box display. Another artful solution for a small Turkish tribal rug from Istanbul: Hold the textile between two panes of glass (trimmed with a faux-gilt wood frame) to create the effect of the hand-woven kilim "floating" in mid-frame. Inventory includes black-and-white art photography, Jazzfest and Mardi Gras posters, original works by notable local artists, and one of the French Quarter's largest selections of quality antique European prints from the 1500s through the Art Deco 1920s. The no-frills ambience of the French Quarter venue is pure Bohemian rhapsody—right down to the back-shop buzz of a rotary saw creating new frames and the earthy scent of freshly cut wood mingling in the air.

FRENCH ANTIQUE SHOP INC.
225 Royal St.
(504) 524-9861
www.gofrenchantiques.com

As the name implies, this shop specializes primarily in 19th-century and later treasures from France. And, as discriminating antique collectors will attest, the timelessness of handcrafted works of art from this era has rarely been matched. Start with the stately collection of Baccarat crystal and French bronze chandeliers for some irrefutable elegance. Then work your eyes down to the gorgeous hand-carved cherry-wood and mahogany armoires, marble mantels, and provincial gold-leaf mirrors, fine porcelains, and marble statuary.

GEM DE FRANCE
729 Royal St.
(504) 571-6305
www.gemdefrance.com

Whether you're a dyed-in-the-wool Francophile or searching for mementoes that remind of your recent trip to Avignon, this is the place for you. Lyon-born Sonia Cohen helps oversee what may be among the city's best spots for decorative items, household wares and collectibles from the country that put ooh-la-la on the map for globetrotters worldwide. From milled soaps from

Marseilles and Provençal-hued tablecloths and napkins to artwork, clocks, posters and hand-made pewter items, everything inside this well-lighted French Quarter venue bears the signature look of something French. "Everything the person needs to add a touch of France to their home," says Cohen.

HOVÉ PARFUMEUR LTD.
824 Royal St.
(504) 525-7827
www.hoveparfumeur.com

Mrs. Alvin Hovey-King, who turned a lifetime of perfume and ingredient collecting into an exclusive enterprise, founded the oldest perfume manufacturer in the city in 1931. Today the present owner oversees what may well be the best smelling place in the French Quarter, offering 52 proprietary fragrances and scented oils for men and women, all under a 150-year-old bronze hanging light fixture from the Quadroon Ballroom of the Bourbon Orleans Hotel. Fragrances sold inside this historic Creole house, built in 1813, are available in both perfume and cologne, and each comes in a lovely Williamsburg pink box. Popular scents have been formulated into creamy solid perfumes, rich bath and body oils, soaps, and body powders. Hové-made soaps come in magnolia, vetivert, and tea-olive aromas. Sachets, gift baskets, potpourris, and a fine selection of antique straight razors are available.

JACK GALLERY
709 Royal St.
(504) 588-1777
www.s2art.com

For anyone who has ever lamented that they just don't make 'em like they used to, the Entertainment Gallery has an answer: "We do." Recreations, not "compromised reproductions and tattered antiques," of hundred-year-old Parisian street advertisement posters in exquisitely vibrant colors on crisp, fresh paper is the specialty of this well-lighted shop. Here the Golden Age of Posters (1865–1939) lives again in hand-drawn, limited edition lithographs produced by expert chromists. So, too, do the original artists' beguiling Art Nouveau beauties and stunning Art Deco vamps, stylized avatars of the Belle Epoque and the emerging Industrial Age.

In the final production stages, a team of artisans slowly "pulls" each lithograph, one color at a time, in perfect registration, on rare 19th-century French-made Marinoni Voirin lithography presses at New York's prestigious S2 Atelier. These are the same presses used to produce the subtly blended and richly textured original Golden Age posters. Each lithograph contains the date and signature in the place of the contemporary artist and bears the S2 Atelier and Entertainment Gallery symbols.

THE KITE SHOP
542 St. Peter St.
(504) 524-0028

From beautifully hand-painted Balinese silk creations to those emblazoned with Charlie Brown's face, the second oldest shop of its kind in the United States features perhaps the most intriguing selection of kites anywhere in the city. Duffers accustomed to tree magnets will want to check out the line of windless kites (it's about time), 6-foot graphite Prism Ions, box-shaped numbers called The Cube (designed to dart and tumble in the wind), and the Delta wing–shaped squadron ready for stealth action. The shop, on the Canal Street side of Jackson Square, offers decorated minikites as well as New Orleans–themed fly-by-days with Mardi Gras masks and crawfish.

LA MAISON D'ABSINTHE
823 Royal St.
(504) 523-0903, (877) 737-2772
www.lamaisondabsinthe.com

Long-time Francophile and absinthe paraphernalia collector Cary Bonnecaze opened what may be the country's most impressive—and obsessive—tribute to infamous "green fairy." Enthusiasts looking to get their absinthe groove on need look no further. Everything is here—from absinthe spoons, glasses, fountains (original and reproductions) and brouilleurs (drippers), to T-shirts, bumper stickers ("Got Absinthe?"), books (*Hideous Absinthe: A History of the Devil in the Bottle*) and even huge, reproduction art nouveau prints—all promoting and celebrating the infamous anise-flavored spirit. Everything, that is, except for absinthe itself (you'll have to buy that at a liquor store or other outlet).

Originated in the Swiss town of Couvet in 1789 by French physician Pierre Ordinaire and the favored cocktail among 19th century Parisians, the drink banned in Europe and the United States in the early 1900s was legalized in May 2007 and lately has enjoyed a renewed popularity among trendsetters and hip bar crowds on the East and West coasts.

For a $5 admission fee patrons can visit the stop's Absinthe Museum of America, billed as "the first and only absinthe museum in America," which is chockablock with pre- and post-ban absinthe propaganda of the day, scores of old absinthe bottles and a display case featuring hundreds of antique absinthe spoons.

LOUISIANA LOOM WORKS
616 Chartres St.
(504) 566-7788, (800) 889-8281
www.customragrugs.com

It's hard to find another shop in the French Quarter where passersby are treated to the sight of an 1893 Amish jack loom in warp drive. The easygoing husband-and-wife team of Walt and Rhonda Rose say it takes about four hours to set up the loom. Walt handles the thread patterns while Rhonda shreds the half-size bolts of fabric for making the hand-loomed rag rugs that decorate the shop's walls and hardwood floors. The tradition has its roots in Scandinavia, say the owners, but it's the shop's second loom that keeps modern-day custom orders flying out the front door.

Custom-made rugs take two weeks from ordering to delivery and cost about 5 cents per square inch. Feel free to ask questions—the Roses never blush when it comes to sharing their passion for their time-honored craft.

LUCULLUS
610 Chartres St.
(504) 528-9620

Lucullus was the Roman general who returned from battle in order to take up feasting (a man after every New Orleanian's own heart, if one ever existed). He became famous as much for the style with which he celebrated his banquets as for the food. Today, Lucullus has been reborn in his spiritual home, New Orleans, in this shop carrying culinary antiques, artworks, and objets d'art. English and other continental antiques from the 17th, 18th, and 19th centuries depict or complement the grand pursuit of gastronomy. One room centers on an open-hearth kitchen that displays cooking equipment and utensils from the last 200 years. An interesting display of glassware, silver, and porcelain can be found arranged on antique tables and sideboards. Even the paintings on the walls carry out the food motif. The Chartres Street location occupies a charming 19th-century French Quarter building, which retains much of its original architectural detail.

MOSS ANTIQUES
411 Royal St.
(504) 522-3981
www.mossantiques.com

This quiet and understated antiques shop offers truly elegant visions in the form of Napoleonic-style mahogany armoires and 19th-century drop-front secretaries. Other items include burled-walnut and crystal inkwells, stately Provençal oak desks and cabinets, and oil paintings and decorative artworks. Imagine a spirited game played on an oak-and-brass Victorian cribbage board while sipping tea served in a five-piece Sheffield silver service. Perhaps a French-walnut grandfather clock handcrafted in Europe at the turn of last century would keep players from tarrying while one of the shop's century-old crystal chandeliers helped shed some light on the game.

M. S. RAU ANTIQUES
630 Royal St.
(504) 523-5660, (866) 349-0705
www.rauantiques.com

To step into this institution, opened in 1912, is to understand the art of how best to present one of the finest collections of antique European and American treasures in the city. Third-generation proprietor Bill Rau's grandparents started the business, and today serious art buyers and collectors from around the world patronize this establishment. Wedgwood, rare pink diamonds and other highly select jewelry, English and French furnishings, porcelains, whiskey flasks, and objets d'art like Fabergé enamel bell pushers are specialties. Renowned craftsman Paul DeLamerie produced the silver candlestick holders in the locked glass case in 1713.

A collection of rare antique canes includes one French number used to hold a camera high above crowds. The photographer meantime looked into a tiny mirror in the staff, which reflected what the camera saw overhead. In one room are exquisitely handcrafted German, Swiss, and American music boxes. Another room features some top contenders from Europe's golden age of furniture; another, Russian and British sterling tea sets and 19th-century macro-mosaic table plaques.

NEW ORLEANS FAMOUS PRALINE CO.
300 Royal St.
(504) 525-3370
www.neworleanspralines.com
Hope springs eternal for nonchefs when food essentials like boxed mixes for jambalaya, étouffée, and gumbo are near at hand. This brightly lit and well-organized outlet for Creole and Cajun cooking lore features recipe books, hot sauces (and gator-emblazoned oven mitts ideal for wrestling even hotter dishes), a wide selection of utensils, assorted local condiments, and Louisiana coffee.

THE QUARTER STITCH NEEDLEPOINT
630 Chartres St.
(504) 522-4451
Whether it's Christmas stockings, pillows, throw rugs, Beatrix Potter animals, or something in between, this shop carries entire kits needed to save—and make—a stitch in time. Needlepoint fans can select from designs crafted by local artists such as Clementine Hunter, featuring New Orleans and Mardi Gras scenes, plantation homes, Creole cottages, magnolias, even festive crawfish boils. Then choose from a selection of custom-dyed yarns in cotton, wool, rayon, and acrylic. It couldn't be easier. Starter kits for youngsters are available as well as gift sets, complete sweater and angel kits, and six-strand embroidery floss.

RENDEZVOUS INC.
522 St. Peter St.
(504) 522-0225
Unless you're a Munchkin, you'll have to stoop over to open the double French doors of this chandelier-lit shop: The doorknob is 15 inches from the ground. Don't ask. Once inside this agreeable shop, visitors quickly learn that elegant linens and lace—not stature—are the name of the game. Specialties include lace window suncatchers with artful designs ranging from hearts and wedding chapels to tulips and butterflies. Fans of finery will also discover an A to Z of Battenburg and cotton goods: tablecloths, runners, doilies, aprons, placemats and napkins, pillow covers, christening dresses, vests, and women's collars and shawls. Pragmatists shopping on a sweltering day might do well to beat a path to the shop's parasols or men's linen handkerchiefs. Shirts for boys and sundresses for girls are alongside baby booties, ruffle bonnets, lace-and-glass picture frames, and wedding accessories such as ring bearer pillows and garters.

ROTHSCHILD'S ANTIQUES
321 Royal St.
(504) 523-2281
www.rothschildsantiques.com
This fourth-generation family-owned business, presided over by Michael D. Greenblatt, prides itself on representing, with integrity, elegant chandeliers made from 1880 to 1920. Greenblatt even sheds some light on the subject: Any chan-

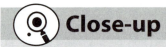 **Close-up**

French Market

It had been raining and it seemed doubtful the sparse Saturday afternoon crowd at the French Market would hit typically elbow-to-elbow density any time soon. At least that's what we thought until we tried to sweep into Loretta's, a praline confectioner tucked near the Ursuline Street entrance of the 5-block-long historic covered market. Instead we found ourselves pulling up the rear of a line that stretched from the glass counter all the way to the front door. But French Market connoisseurs know even long waits are aptly rewarded when they leave with a little white paper bag filled with New Orleans' ubiquitous solution for a sweet tooth in need of sustenance: pralines.

But these weren't just any pralines, mind you. The traditional Southern candy likely made fresh that morning beckoned from tidy trays behind the counter in a quintet of flavors—coconut, rum, chocolate, peanut butter, and regular. We opted for the peanut butter and rum versions before setting off to explore this beloved landmark and venue for conducting commerce since 1791.

Completion of a three-phase revitalization project for the country's oldest open-air marketplace has resulted in the upgrading of buildings and public facilities, constructed in the 1930s during the Works Progress Administration, and opened the market to the riverfront streetcars that operate just on the other side of a nearby dividing concrete wall. Despite its lengthy past, none of the original French Market structures built during 18th-century Spanish colonial rule exist due to centuries of conflagrations, hurricanes, and floods.

Even so, the French Market (1100 North Peters St., 504-522-2621) is still among top spots locals playing tour guide love to bring out-of-town guests. This simple act of hospitality hasn't hurt the reputation of this sprawling smorgasbord anchored by a community flea market and farmers' market, plus dozens of specialty retail shops, restaurants, and cafes. Consider: Tourism-related Web sites are rife with "expert reviews" and visitor testimonials giving above-average to high marks for the popular attraction's local color ("Does the chayote vendor singing opera take requests?" the friend asked) and bargains, notably on jewelry, leather, sunglasses, folk art, and Carnival and jazz-themed souvenirs. Others applaud the bounty of andouille sausage and pre-packaged Louisiana foodstuffs that help more than a few out-of-state tourists whip up jambalaya and gumbo back home for their Mardi Gras parties.

delier with down-turned lighting fixtures was made in the 1880s or later, after the invention of electricity. Why? Anyone who unknowingly suggests that people in their otherwise right mind would burn candles upside down, he says, has more than a few wires crossed. Greenblatt also oversees a handsome selection of 18th- and 19th-century French and English handcrafted furnishings as well as on-site custom work.

ROYAL ANTIQUES LTD.
309 Royal St.
(504) 524-7033
www.royalantiques.com

Walk through the stately rooms of 18th- and 19th-century antique masterworks and notice the contrast of a 250-year-old, ceiling-topping Louis XV armoire next to a French country farm table. Other worldly footnotes of handcrafted grace inside this nearly century-old institution include English riding crops, French brass-bound cider jugs, Rococo gold-leaf mirrors with distressed glass, and early-19th-century Chinese red-lacquer cabinets with secret drawers. An 1896 Russian samovar is limited these days to serving illumination in its new assignment as an elegant lamp, perfect for shining light on a reading of Anna Karenina.

Also in abundance are shelves of Cajun and Creole cookbooks and numerous kiosks hawking more different brands and varieties of hot sauce than one might imagine possible in a free market governed by supply and demand. Many bottles bear names sufficiently off-color that you'd be hard-pressed to find a polite New Orleanian who would subject dinner guests to indelicate sobriquets such as Red Ass and Butt Blaster. But at these same kiosks is where eagle-eye shoppers can snare Louisiana's Tabasco and Melinda line of peppery condiments, jars of Arnaud's Original Remoulade Sauce (from the legendary French Quarter restaurant of the same name), and noteworthy imports such as Jamaica's Busha Brown line of jerk seasoning. Shrimp, crawfish, and crab boil seasonings are in abundance. Elsewhere, martini lovers will find the perfect accoutrements for the classic cocktail thanks to the local Boscoli family's Creole marinated cocktail onions and jalapeno-stuffed jumbo olives. The Louisiana Creole Tomato Festival is held at the market each June to pay homage to the tart and juicy tomato grown chiefly in the parishes surrounding New Orleans.

Hands down, the cultural crowning glory of this outdoor commercial strip in the lower French Quarter is Café du Monde (1039 Decatur St., 800-772-2927; www.cafedumonde.com). The city's oldest coffee shop, established 1862, is open 24/7 and serves two New Orleans mainstays: cafe au lait, a rich brew made with chicory-laced dark-roasted coffee; and the square, French-style donut known as beignet, best enjoyed heavily dusted with powered sugar (for this reason it's best to leave your black threads at home). The menu's only concession to modernity seems to be the introduction of iced coffee in 1988. Pray you get a table near the sidewalk. For here is among locals' (and certainly tourists') favorite places to watch the whirl go by. Just beyond is the French Quarter "theater" of horse-drawn carriages, street performers, sidewalk musicians, and artists, not to mention views of Jackson Square and St. Louis Cathedral, all punctuated by the occasional sound of a paddle wheeler horn blowing off steam. Nearby is Latrobe Park, a people-watching greenspace accented by sunken seating, a fountain, and a statue honoring the man who designed the city's first waterworks.

Whether your explorations find you standing in line for a rum-flavored praline or hunkered with friends around a table at Café du Monde, the French Market is a generous serving of New Orleans. And indisputable proof why America's most European city has long been a place best savored by the senses.

SOUTHERN CANDYMAKERS

334 Decatur St.
(504) 523-5544, (800) 344-9773
1010 Decatur St.
(504) 525-6170
www.southerncandymakers.com

The heavenly aroma of warm, mouthwatering pralines will tempt even the most strident Sugar Busters® devotee to break with the pack and run with the diet devil. This candymaker understands that variety is the spice of life when it comes to satisfying a sweet tooth. Five kinds of yummy pralines (original creamy, chocolate, peanut butter, cinnamon, and rum and coconut) are fresh-made daily, along with 18 varieties of chocolate-covered clusters and a dozen kinds of fudge and heavenly hash—all cooked from scratch.

Up the sin ante with white-chocolate peanut butter cups so good that *Bon Appetit* magazine requested the recipe. Or try the Mississippi Mud (dark and milk chocolates swirled with fresh caramel) and dark chocolate-covered almond toffee. Not to be outdone are the white chocolate–dipped dried apricots and triple-dipped Oreos (in white and dark chocolates and caramel). A selection of traditionally prepared saltwater taffy

Malls

Whether you love 'em or hate 'em, the American mall has endured over the decades to become one of the most convenient ways to shop since the invention of the catalog—and it's certainly faster. In New Orleans two venues of distinction are a far cry from the sprawling complexes typically found in the suburbs: Jackson Brewery and the Riverwalk Marketplace. These are designed with imagination and offer a level of fun—and location right on the Mississippi River—worthy of praise from even the most discriminating international visitor with plastic to burn.

Jackson Brewery
620–624 Decatur St.
(504) 566-7245
www.jacksonbrewery.com

Not many malls can boast of a strolling jazz band that serenades shoppers as they sample a mall version of Louisiana culture, from Creole cooking and zydeco CDs to Mardi Gras memorabilia and locally handcrafted art and jewelry. This former brewery and proud home to Jax Beer from 1891 to 1974 stands tall on the Mississippi River, reborn in 1984 as a French Quarter shopping complex across from Jackson Square and between Toulouse and St. Peter Streets.

Affectionately known as Jax Brewery, this four-story complex today is home to specialty shops, restaurants, and cafes. Attractions include Gumbo Kids (custom-painted T-shirts and accessories for the little ones), Victoria's Creations (vintage-style clothing, jewelry, hats, and accessories), Street Scene (hand-painted "woodgraphs," reproductions of wood carvings depicting historic New Orleans and French Quarter scenery), and It's About Time (diverse collection of unique time pieces such as watches, clocks and more).

And what New Orleans shopping experience is complete without—you guessed it—food? Peckish shoppers should head to the food court for Hotsey's Grill for burgers and hot dogs, and New Orleans Fried Chicken (both the Southern-fried and rotisserie-style chicken is worthy of any lunch). Every store in The Shops at Jax Brewery offers tax-free shopping for international guests.

Riverwalk Marketplace
Poydras Street at the Mississippi River
(504) 522-1555
www.riverwalkmarketplace.com

Here's a good example of the inherent wisdom of converting a former riverfront land-sore into a breezy enterprise where the Mississippi River and the nearby docks, when lined with cruise ships, seem like the best view in town. In fact, the nearly half-mile-long wall of floor-to-ceiling windows offers one of the best panoramas of the Mississippi in town. Three levels and more than 100 shops and one-of-a-kind pushcart vendors later, you can catch yourself coming and going at the food court on Level C. Buy a daiquiri to go and step outside onto the promenade to recharge your battery. Popular shops include Fleur D'Orleans, Chico's, House of Masks and Gifts, Mardi Paws and Nola T's.

includes a most nontraditional flavor and hands-down favorite: Jamaican rum.

FAUBOURG MARIGNY

AMERICAN AQUATIC GARDENS
621 Elysian Fields Ave.
(504) 944-0410
www.americanaquaticgardens.com
Stressed-out police officers and firefighters occasionally visit to spend a few minutes strolling the peaceful horticultural vignettes created by owners Rich Sacher and Bill Dailey. "It's a quiet place," Sacher says of his magnificent water gardening complex. Even those with boring jobs and brown thumbs will dig this upscale "gardener's garden," a city block-size outdoor Eden of exquisite display ponds (with full kits available), limited-edition sculpture fountains and statuary, Oriental statues and pagodas, and classic English arbors, archways, and trellises. No pink flamingos need apply.

Sacher and Dailey opened their business in 1991 with no idea it would turn into such a success. It was "a hobby that ran amok," says Sacher, who has spent more than 40 years growing water lilies. He used to sell them out of his home until too many customers started banging on his front door. Today he grows and sells his exotic water lilies in a dozen aboveground ponds in the greenhouse out back, along with enchanting ponytail palms and rare Louisiana irises and potato vines.

Elsewhere are elegant handmade teak benches and spirit houses from Thailand and pottery from Vietnam and Italy.

A red, cathedral-shaped corrugated tin building designed by Tulane University architecture professor Gene Sisek houses accessories such as wrestling cherubs (though they look like they're kissing), books on gardening and horticulture, Buddha busts, hand-painted ceramic light fixtures for wall mounting, crystal, dinnerware, and even oil paintings. Ample on-site parking is available, as is shipping of most items anywhere in the United States.

UPTOWN

AESTHETICS & ANTIQUES
3122 Magazine St.
(504) 895-7011
Ever wonder where some of those "I Like Ike" campaign flyers and "I've Contributed to Goldwater" bumper stickers went to die? Look no further. This offbeat repository of bric-a-brac from the early to mid-20th century also pays homage to more than just the politics of the day. Just in time for that 19th-hole cocktail is a golf ball the diameter of an LP, which opens on hinges to reveal a decanter and six shot glasses just waiting for a bartender. Make it a double. The shop's wicker picnic baskets are tailor made for splendor in the grass. Just add a petite pair of glass salt-and-pepper shakers from the 1940s and rose-tinted Depression glasses for the wine. Better get some film for the Brownie.

AIDAN GILL FOR MEN
2026 Magazine St.
(504) 587-9090
www.aidangillformen.com
At Aidan Gill for Men, discerning gentlemen will discover stylish shaving and toiletry accessories and for-the-modern-man items ranging from passport covers and silver cufflinks to decorative champagne bottle stoppers. A selection of old-fashioned shaving implements include silver-handled whisks and razors, mildly scented shaving creams, skin care lotions, and other men's personal care and bath products. In the back, customers can enjoy a haircut and hot-towel shave while sipping complimentary single-malt scotch and reading the latest issue of *Maxim*. Here Gill displays his obelisk *Monument to the Unknown Barber,* which bears the inscription AL BARBERO DESCONOCIDO.

Behind the glass counters is where the Dublin native keeps the large collection of old electric shavers, metal hair dryers, and straight razors he began amassing long before his move from Ireland to the Big Easy in the 1990s. On the wall is a framed print of Irish writers, turn-of-the-20th-century newspaper articles about shaving, and sketches of hairstyles that haven't seen the light of day since the 1950s. The outdoor sitting area is where Gill and his clientele "hatch our revolutions" while smoking cigars and admiring the towering St. Alphonsus Church next door. "There are two 'dead' words in here—unisex and PC," Gill says only half-jokingly. Make no mistake—men behaving gladly (like men) will find this venue a guilty pleasure.

ANNE PRATT
3937 Magazine St.
(504) 891-6532

Since 1995 this artist's eclectic gallery of ethnic art has featured hand-beaded Haitian banners in exquisitely rich colors and funky little painted chairs full of balanced whimsy. The award-winning Pratt has spent mucho time in Mexico and was so enchanted by the beauty of its artists' crucifixes that she had to bring some home. Other Spanish colonial artistic expressions imported from Mexico include a headboard made from a wrought-iron balcony. Custom-designed and handcrafted silver and gold jewelry as well as Old World-style iron-and-wood decorations for the home, loft, or office round out Pratt's devotion to the art of following one's personal compass.

AS YOU LIKE IT SILVER SHOP
3033 Magazine St.
(504) 897-6915, (800) 828-2311
www.asyoulikeitsilvershop.com

Hundreds of active and inactive silver patterns fill elegant dark-wood cabinets and gleaming shelves, such as ornate 1854 Imperial Chrysanthemum by Gorham Co. and 18th-century Francis I by Reed & Barton. This 34-year-old business features a fine selection of tea sets, champagne goblets, salt and pepper shakers, candelabra, and trays.

AUX BELLES CHOSES
3912 Magazine St.
(504) 891-1009
www.abcneworleans.com

Owners Bettye Barrios's and Anne Gauthier's love of European flourish and elegant pragmatism has given this shop all the warmth of a French country kitchen in springtime. And just in case you're having one of those wish-I-were-in-the-south-of-France kind of days, the blue-and-white Provençal-print kitchen napkins are stored in the drawers of the antique French cabinet near the front of the store. Other homey touches include old-fashioned scales, notepaper, linens, pottery, tin watering pitchers for the garden, European soaps, and biscuit cutters. Dried-flower arrangements are offered in the back.

THE BEAD SHOP
4612 Magazine St.
(504) 895-6161

Glass beads and bead jewelry of all types from around the world are tucked inside this attractive green cottage. A feast of color in the round is found in Venetian glass and crystal from Austria and the Bohemian region of the Czech Republic. In addition to a selection of loose beads are "Tin Cup" necklaces (popularized by the movie of the same name), Russian and Baltic amber jewelry (look in the glass-top wooden box), sequin-and-bead art from Haiti, craft books, and handwoven baskets, rugs, and throw pillows. Customers are encouraged to custom design and make their own bead jewelry on the spot. Those with more time on their hands might want to enroll in one of the design classes offered by owner Nancy Campbell.

BELLADONNA
2900 Magazine St.
(504) 891-4393
www.belladonnadayspa.com

Walk into this unisex day spa and head upstairs to check out the quiet hallway of opaque Japanese shoji doors that open to softly lighted tiled rooms used for facials, massages, aromatherapy, and other pamperings. The late New Orleans designer Roy Fairman created the second-floor respite from the workaday world for owner Kim Dudek, who opened the full-service facility in 1995. Jacuzzis, Vichy showers, and 120-jet hydro-tubs augment salt rubs, seaweed wraps, and aromatherapy. The first floor is where personal, bath, and beauty products are found alongside stylish sleepwear and booths for pedicures and manicures. An outdoor Zen tea garden features a gurgling fountain, low-slung table, and floor cushions tailor made for the urban escapist. Sexu-ally segregated lockers, saunas, and steam show-ers are available, as are complimentary kimono, flip-flops, towel, and shampoo.

BLUE FROG CHOCOLATES
5707 Magazine St.
(504) 269-5707
www.bluefrogchocolates.com
Lifelong students of chocology will nearly swoon from that first rush of oh-so-yummy aroma that greets visitors to this tidy emporium dedicated to confections created from the cocoa bean. Spe-cializing in domestic and imported chocolates from around the world, this venue, opened in August 2000, offers a bounty of dark, semi dark, and milk-chocolate sweets in nearly every shape and size under the sun––including a chocolate gavel for that barrister with a sweet tooth.

CAMERON JONES
2127 Magazine St.
(504) 524-3119
The Manhattan vibe of the avant-garde, forward-looking, and simply cool furnishings and acces-sories today's design—not designer—conscious urban dweller will make anyone wish they owned an Upper East Side loft to decorate from the ground up. This longtime Magazine Street fixture is among the best places in town to check out all those sleek and drool-worthy *articles essentials* found between the pages of hip shelter zines such as *Architectural Digest* and *Dwell*. From spe-cialty room dividers, hip lighting, trendy mirrors, and retro occasional chairs and end tables to a

polished metal entertainment bar from which to prepare the hottest cocktails raising expectations at Big Apple nightclubs, this establishment is a sure-fire cure for the aesthetic blues.

i The least crowded time to cruise the shopping corridors of Uptown's Maga-zine Street and Royal Street in the French Quarter is weekdays before noon. This is a time when tourists are sleeping off the pre-vious night's excesses and the city is yawn-ing awake over its second cup of coffee. The mercury is at its lowest point of the day.

IMPORTICOS
5523 Magazine St.
(504) 891-6141
Look no further if you ever wondered how a modern-day Balinese chieftain might decorate his jungle abode before *Architectural Digest* arrives for a cover shoot. Indonesian chic at this Uptown gallery is defined by stately and sturdy bamboo furnishings for adults (even kiddy furni-ture is available), bronze art and candle holders, statuary, silver jewelry, batik clothing, vases, and framed indigenous paintings and pictures. Music lovers can listen before they buy from a selection of world beat, Latin, and Caribbean music CDs.

LA BOULANGERIE
4600 Magazine St.
(504) 269-3777
Oft-voted the city's best bakery, this traditional French-style venue sticks to what it does best and offers no apologies. This, a recent visitor quickly learned when he expressed dismay that the establishment didn't sell espresso. "I'm sorry but this is a proper bakery," the counter person said in a decidedly French accent. "You'll find cof-fee shops down the street." Opened in 1999, this Franco-flavored venue offers a tour de force of flans, cheesecakes, sandwiches, fruit tarts, scones and Danishes—but, most importantly, a variety of breads baked daily (beginning at 3 a.m.) that

includes La Boulangerie's signature blue-cheese bread loaves. Patrons can take-out or hunker down at one of the cheery establishment's handful of tables near the sidewalk window.

MAPLE STREET BOOK SHOP
7523 Maple St.
(504) 866-4916

Discerning local and national authors as well as dyed-in-the-wool bookhounds say this privately owned pocket of literary paradise is one major reason New Orleans is "a great bookstore city." Walk past the azalea-twined wrought-iron fence and up the front steps, and notice the photographs of Martin Luther King Jr., Paul Prudhomme, and Walker Percy on the exterior wall. Open the cabinlike screen door and be greeted again—this time by the entire collection of Louisiana literary legend Walker Percy, who gave posthumous life to the New Orleans-set classic, *A Confederacy of Dunces,* following the death of author John Kennedy Toole. A photograph of a smiling Percy holding a bulging Maple Leaf-logo paper bag is testament to the close relationship this popular establishment enjoyed with the late author.

Cozy, well-lit rooms with floor-to-ceiling shelves offer everything from Eudora Welty and Alice Walker to photography, spirituality, music, limited-edition volumes, and self-help (BEFORE IT'S TOO LATE, the sign reads). Visitors will know they are in the travel section when they see the Russian-language map of the Moscow subway system. Ancient and Renaissance classics are well represented, as are local cookbooks, fiction and nonfiction, mysteries, criticism, women's issues, and essays.

MAPLE STREET CHILDREN'S BOOK SHOP
7529 Maple St.
(504) 861-2105
www.maplestreetbookshop.com

Next door to the Maple Street Book Shop is this counterpart for youthful readers of all ages. Be sure to check out the section of imaginative New Orleans-themed books such as *Haunted Louisiana* by Christy L. Vivano, *The Cajun Night Before Christ-* *mas* talking book (with Gaston the green-nosed alligator), and *The Jazz of Our Streets* by Fatima Shaik and E. B. Lewis, which tells the story of the birthplace of jazz with watercolors and poems. *If Only I Had a Horn,* by Roxane Orgill teaches youngsters about jazz pioneer Louis Armstrong; Angela Shelf Medearis's *Rum-A-Tum-Tum* tells of the excitement of a second-line parade through the eyes of a child. The up-and-coming musician in the family will find inspiring high notes in the book *Wynton Marsalis: Gifted Trumpet Player,* the only artist to ever win Grammys for best classical and jazz recordings in the same year. If all else fails, there's always Dakota Lane's *Johnny Voodoo.* According to the back cover: "Johnny is so mysterious, and so beautiful. People say all sorts of things about him. Which things are true and which are lies?" Best let a pint-size reader be the judge.

MARTIN WINE CELLAR
3500 Magazine St.
(504) 899-7411
714 Elmeer St., Metairie
(504) 896-7300
www.martinwine.com

If your favorite martini leaves you shaken and stirred, you must have discovered the jalapeño-stuffed jumbo Spanish olives and Creole marinated onions sold at this popular store. Join the crowd. There is always a buzz inside this Uptown shop on Saturday afternoon, when loyal locals browse aisles full of domestic and international wines and liquors, gourmet food items and hot sauces, Jamaican jerk seasoning, Brazilian mustard glazes, Creole coffees, and local seasonings and dressings (try the mango or passion fruit vinaigrettes by Consorzio).

Weekend cooking demonstrations, informal wine tastings, and microbrewed beer samplings create an upscale atmosphere accented by a pleasant selection of cheeses ranging from double-cream havarti to crumbly Spanish cabrales. Gourmet cookies, biscotti, and shortbreads target the sweet tooth, while a crowded deli section offers to-go or dine-in specialty pastas, salads, and sandwiches. The Nova Delight—Norwegian smoked salmon and cream cheese with onion and capers on pumpernickel or a bagel—is particularly good.

MAYAN IMPORT CO.
3000 Magazine St.
(504) 269-9000, (888) 372-2100
www.mayanimport.com

Honduras takes a bow at this emporium specializing in cigars and handcrafts from the Central American country that gave the world the great Mayan city of Copan. Sixty percent of the shop's cigars are imported from Honduras and include such well-known labels as Santa Rosa, Don Fortunato, Valle de Maya, Punch, and Indios. Also from Honduras are mahogany room dividers and decorative boxes, leather handbags, and colorful baskets and tortilla warmers woven from shredded palm leaves called junca. Looking to customize your favorite smokes? The shop uses state of the art computer software to convert business logos, photographic images, and/or monograms into custom cigar labels for advertising and personal use (minimum 10 labels per order).

MIGNON FAGET LTD.
3801 Magazine St.
(504) 891-2005
www.mignonfaget.com

Native artisan Mignon Faget's brilliantly crafted jewelry, which includes those designs on architecture and nature (such as marine life and horticulture), has won her nationwide critical acclaim and megasales in boutiques from coast to coast. Her upstairs studio and workshop produce the downstairs creations, which include the Louisiana Collection of locally familiar icons ranging from Creole cottages to streetcars.

MON COEUR
3952 Magazine St.
(504) 899-0064
www.moncoeurfinejewelry.com

Artist and jewelry designer Janet Bruno-Small has assembled within the cozy confines of her browse-worthy, European-style boutique a don't-miss collection of custom and estate jewelry the likes of which have impressed more than one discerning visitor. But even this venue's eye-catching array of vintage and antique jewelry, rings, necklaces, bracelets, pearls and pins must take a backseat to Janet's own one-of-a-kind creations. For proof check out her Victorian shoe buckles, which she backs with a peyote stitch of beads and then adds draping pearls to create a unique—and uniquely sophisticated—necklace, choker or bracelet. Janet's newest creation is a 400-piece jewelry collection she handcrafted from 200-year-old, plaster-of-Paris Intaglios depicting mythological characters. Janet also specializes in custom-designed jewelry for clients who walk into her shop with little more than a notion—or a gemstone.

MUSICA LATINA
4714 Magazine St.
(504) 895-4227

Don't expect to find cushy high-tech listening booths or a froufrou coffee bar at this tiny (and blessedly unfettered) music shop. It opened in 1969 and is located on an oft-overlooked-by-tourists downscale stretch of this Uptown street. What you will find, pure and simple, is one of the largest selections of Latin music cassettes and CDs as well as hard-to-find LPs anywhere in the city. The Honduran-born husband-and-wife team of Juan Suarez and Yolanda Estrada Suarez carry virtually every Latin music style under the tropical sun: salsa from Puerto Rico; meringue from the Dominican Republic; bossa nova from Brazil; Garifuna dancehall punta from Honduras; tango from Argentina; folk music from the Peruvian Andes; sardana and flamenco from Spain; and much more. Spanish-language newspapers and periodicals are available.

ON THE OTHER HAND
8204 Oak St.
(504) 861-0159

It's worth a stop at this haute couture consignment boutique just for the chance to meet owner Kay Danné, whose unflinching Southern grace and hospitality have been charming shoppers since 1987. Looking for a stylish number by Chanel, Donna Karan, or Yves St. Laurent (to name but a few of the designer brands) but at a to-die-for price? Chances are you'll find it here among the more than 3,500 dresses, Mardi Gras ball gowns, prom and evening dresses, fur coats, hats, scarves, and shoes that overfill six rooms in Danné's Victorian shotgun house, located in Riverbend. Wedding gowns and vintage clothing complete the mix. "There's a story behind every dress," Danné says of her inventory. For an elegant shopping treat, stop by on Saturday afternoon when the owner hosts one of her patio wine-and-cheese soirees, with a guest pianist.

THE PRIVATE CONNECTION/PIECES
3927 Magazine St.
(504) 899-4944
If the New York Times calls it "the most cheerful shop on the street," it's almost worth dropping by just to see if the newspaper is wrong. But we'll save you some time—go. This is the kind of place where art feels good—and there's a reason why. In 1988 owner Clifford Henrotin opened this import shop to combine his passion for adventure travel to Indonesia with the region's fine and folk arts. (If Santa's listening, one of the 6-foot plastic banana trees posing as a cartoon jungle dream would look smashing in the studio of one writer who has been very good this year.) Handcrafted Balinese teakwood and Burmese rosewood furniture and architectural pieces include century-old regal beds; animal-shaped tables; and intricate, brightly colored old wooden panel doors. Batiks, copper stamps, and hand-painted mobiles also are sold.

SCRIPTURA
5423 Magazine St.
(504) 897-1555
What globe-trotter wouldn't appreciate an elegant leather-bound journal in which to jot down the vagaries of travel? Or perhaps a specialty book for scribbling impressions of memorable

(and not-so-memorable) wines, restaurants, and cigars enjoyed along the way? (A limited-edition copy of The Hand Made Cigars Collector's Guide and Journal might help the novice get the lingo down.) This well-lit shop also specializes in custom monogrammed stationery seals and sealing wax. "Essential papers" run the gamut from beautifully boxed stationery from France, Italy, and Japan to lovely cards for "notes and queries." Other treasures include fountain pens in Venetian glass and carved wood, hand-bound scrapbooks in rich textured fabrics, and archival quality photo albums with recycled acid-free paper.

ST. JAMES CHEESE COMPANY
5004 Prytania St.
(504) 899-4737
www.stjamescheese.com
Travelers who had once bemoaned the absence of a true cheese monger in this city did backflips when New Orleans natives and former London residents Danielle and Richard Sutton opened this formidable fortress of fromage in June 2006. With its clear focus on domestic and international artisanal cheeses, visitors will find everything from a French Pont L'Eveque Failaisiens and Italian Pecorino Pienza to a Spanish Garrotxa and Welsh Gorwydd Caerphilly. And that's saying a mouthful. Spanish and Italian specialty meats, French pâtés and foie gras, and local andouille and duck pastrami can also be found behind the counter, as well as a slew of gourmet sandwiches and specialty olives, spreads, sauces and condiments. Visitors can opt for takeout or enjoy a meal in the shop's courtyard or street-front porch.

THOMAS MANN GALLERY
1812 Magazine St.
(504) 581-2113
www.thomasmann.com
Thomas Mann's "techno-romantic" jewelry has earned him coast-to-coast kudos from fans that include Robert DeNiro. Sterling, nickel, copper, and brass are transformed into striking Mann-made museum-quality sculpture, amulets, tabletop art, earrings and pendants, teapots d'art,

and eye-shaped mirrors, as well as art based on nature. Works by other artists include a selection of handcrafted Studio Inferno martini glasses with blue Greek torsos, which are really something to shake a swizzle stick at.

VILLA VICI
2930 Magazine St.
(504) 899-2931

Anyone eager to add the contemporary lines of cotton and linen slipcover furnishings to their bedroom and home will want to run their hands over the stylish (and washable) couches and chairs of this upscale "two-of-a-kind" shop. Breezy canopy beds and living space ensembles from North Carolina and California share floor space with locally crafted art lamps and imported Italian and French reproductions of Mediterranean urns and vases. If you see something you like, buy it—this window-front shop's inventory changes regularly.

WHOLE FOODS MARKET
5600 Magazine St.
(504) 899-9119
www.wholefoods.com

Despite this mega-grocer's motto of "Whole foods, whole people, whole planet," it's the eye-popping selection of international cheese that drew raves from one recent first-time shopper. With an estimated 225 varieties of domestic and international cheese that run the gamut from Swiss Emmenthaler and Spanish Manchego and Zamorano to hard-to-find Basque Idiazabal and more than two dozen French varieties of the fermented curd, it's like stumbling upon a European cheese monger's shop in the middle of a modern supermarket. Plus, the white-jacketed staff not only knows their fromage but also offers a free bite to those curious about the flavor of an unfamiliar cheese. But cheese is by no means the only staple shoppers will find at this 40,000-square-foot emporium, which opened in 2003 at the site of the completely restored old bus barn on Magazine Street.

Meticulously arranged displays of gorgeous fresh seafood and meat are reminiscent of the Rialto Bridge outdoor market in Venice. Elsewhere a cornucopia of natural food includes a nice selection of organic juices and the city's hands-down largest selection of whole grains, ranging from bulgur wheat, pearled barley, and millet to nearly 50 kinds of bulk granola (the pumpkin seed version might make for a good Halloween breakfast). A coffee bar and gourmet food-to-go section give this Austin, Texas-based international company's Uptown location a trendy vibe, along with a licensed message therapist offering 10- to 30-minute neck and shoulder massages—no appointment necessary—for about $1 per minute. Especially on Sat the tables and chairs out front offer a pleasant venue for enjoying coffee or a meal while soaking in the buzz of Magazine Street.

WINKY'S/UPSTAIRS
2038 Magazine St.
(504) 568-1020

This is two shops in one. Downstairs is Winky's, a swing kid's paradise featuring spats, porkpie hats, '40s-style retro dresses, and other clothing and accessories for those who like to kick dance the Charleston to "Take the A-train." Upstairs is UPstairs, a decidedly funky and quirky mélange of retro bric-a-brac cleverly converted into wall clocks. Name the item and chances are it's been pressed into service as an electrical timekeeper—old bingo cards, green olive cans, ham tins, Chinese Checker boards, old purses, and more.

WIRTHMORE ANTIQUES
3727 Magazine St.
(504) 269-0660
www.wirthmoreantiques.com

A 19th-century hand-painted Swedish tall-case clock near the front door greets visitors to this "accidental" store. As owner Gay Wirth explains it, curious shoppers kept sticking their noses into this former warehouse, where she used to store furniture for her other shop on Magazine

Street. Before long she converted the warehouse into the second Wirthmore retail outlet. French Provincial furnishings from the 18th and 19th centuries include armoires with double-sculpted moldings, beautiful walnut panetieres (awaiting fresh loaves of French bread), and grille doors with chapeau gendarme bonnets. Wirth scours the highways and byways of France's Normandy and Burgundy regions for treasures that range from a Louis XV-style bibliotheque with coquillage feet to blue-and-white dinner plates ca. 1920 from a Provence restaurant.

YVONNE LA FLEUR
8131 Hampson St.
(504) 866-9666
www.yvonnelafleur.com

The black stretch limousine parked at the curb and the uniformed chauffeur standing at the front door spoke volumes about the kind of clientele seduced by this chandelier-lit dreamscape of femininity. A cozy interior of Victorian-style salons, each decorated according to the creative whim of owner Yvonne La Fleur, would make even the snobbiest European on a shopping spree feel right at home. Chandeliers, antique baby carriages, an Art Deco settee, and a mirrored wet bar serve as the backdrop for La Fleur's custom millinery. Most of it is fashioned from her collection of veilings and turn-of-the-20th-century flowers from France, silk ribbons from Switzerland, antique feathers from Germany, "and other elegant touches from around the world." The Yvonne La Fleur Private Collection features silk dresses, sportswear, suede, one-of-a-kind evening gowns, and exclusive wedding dresses and bridesmaid's gowns. Other specialties are hand-tailored hats, lingerie, fragrances, bath products, jewelry, and linen apparel.

ATTRACTIONS AND ACTIVITIES

For a city its size, New Orleans nearly breaks the mold when it comes to ways to have a good time that don't require Bill Gates's bank account or spending two hours in gridlock. Museums and historic homes? We got 'em coming out of our crawfish tails. Riverboat cruises and a world-class zoo and aquarium? Ditto. Plantation homes? Fiddle-dee-dee. Historic cemeteries? Pshaw. Add to that loads of recreational activities, camping opportunities, and spectator sports, and you've got all you need to "pass a good time," as our Cajun cousins would say. Also, if you're traveling with little ones, check the following Kidstuff chapter for the city's most family-friendly fare.

If New Orleans doesn't have it all, it certainly has most of it. While the following list of attractions is by no means complete, it is nevertheless comprehensive and reflects the scope of activities that has made and kept New Orleans one of the nation's premier and laudable tourism cities. Always call ahead to verify times and admission costs, but be patient as many New Orleanians are unaccustomed to the harried tempo of out-of-towners, even those on vacation.

Price Code

Our price is based on admission for one adult.

$	$0 to $10
$$	$11 to $20
$$$	$21 to $50
$$$$	More than $50

i Spring and fall months are the best time to enjoy the city's multitude of outdoor attractions and activities. So don't let summer sneak up on you—start planning now by making a list of things you want to do when New Orleans' weather is at its year-round best.

BLAINE KERN'S MARDI GRAS WORLD $$
1380 Port of New Orleans Place
(504) 362-8211, (800) 362-8213
www.mardigrasworld.com
This is a fun, don't-miss attraction. Go behind the scenes of Mardi Gras to see the world's largest fleet of Carnival floats and the artists who create them. Enormous Carnival "dens" are the working studios of international artists and sculptors who form the largest float-building company in the world. Tours allow guests to try on authentic Mardi Gras costumes, eat king cake (the official pastry of Mardi Gras), visit the prop shop where artists create the giant papier-mâché sculptures that adorn floats, watch floats being constructed (get there by 3:30 to see this), and catch a glance at real Mardi Gras floats including those that roll in the Orpheus parade, founded by crooner Harry Connick Jr. Mardi Gras World is open daily 9:30 a.m. to 5 p.m. with 45- to 60-minute tours starting every half hour. Last tour begins at 4:30 p.m. There is a free shuttle bus that picks up at most major downtown hotels. Call for schedule.

CANAL STREET FERRY $
Canal St. at the Mississippi
One of the most romantic views of the city is the one from the Canal Street ferry at night. During the day it's the simplest way to experience the Mighty Mississippi, especially if you don't have 1.5 hours for a steamboat ride. Drive or walk

(Q) Close-up

National World War II Museum

This attraction opened its doors as the National D–Day Museum in June 2000 to national fanfare worthy of the heroes who fought what many historians believe to be the one of the most important battles ever. Operation Neptune sent the largest armada in history—5,333 ships and landing craft carrying 175,000 troops—across 100 miles of the churning English Channel to assault Hitler's Atlantic Wall at Normandy, leading eventually to allied victory in Europe. Later designated by Congress as the official museum of the Second World War, the museum (www.nationalww2museum.org), at 945 Magazine St. in the Warehouse Arts District, boasts state-of-the-art interactive exhibits intermixed with oral histories from veterans worldwide, photographs, hands-on activities, and films.

A room-size diorama of the air and sea armada conveys the size and complexity of the invasion force. This exhibit-rich repository leaves visitors with a better idea of what it was like to ride aboard a Higgins Boat, storm the beaches of Normandy, fly an Allied glider into France, and fight your way through hedgerow country. The museum also presents a collection of personal stories through recorded oral histories of war workers, air raid wardens, and other ordinary Americans who contributed to the war effort at home.

Other exhibit highlights include:

- A reproduction Higgins landing craft built by volunteers, many of whom worked on these boats, designed and crafted in New Orleans, during the war.
- Aircraft, vehicles, weapons, uniforms, home-front materials, and other significant artifacts.
- Interactive galleries featuring electronic maps, minitheaters, photomurals, text panels, and original.
- *Price for Peace* a movie coproduced by Steven Spielberg and museum founder and historian, the late Stephen E. Ambrose.

The museum is open daily 9 a.m. to 5 p.m. Call (504) 527-6012.

aboard and get a panoramic view of the city during the short ride to Algiers Point. Once across, spend some time strolling around this historic neighborhood. Directions for a self-guided tour can be found at http://algierspoint.org/AHS. The ferry leaves Canal Street every 30 minutes on the quarter hour. Cost is $1 per car round-trip and is free for pedestrians.

HARRAH'S CASINO
512 South Peters St.
(504) 533-6000
www.harrahs.com
Opened in October 1999, Harrah's Casino offers the usual gambling fare, within a setting that is

uniquely New Orleans. From the towering artificial oak tree and statue of a jazz trumpeter in the Jazz Court reminiscent of a French Quarter courtyard, to nightly Carnival parades, as well as live entertainment, including vintage jazz and Dixieland. Recent Harrah's additions include a 450-room hotel and a Besh Steak restaurant. Harrah's is located on the edge of the French Quarter, near the foot of Canal Street and bordered by Convention Center Boulevard and Poydras and South Peters Streets. Open 24/7, Harrah's has a 1,550-space parking garage across from the casino at Convention Center Boulevard and Poydras Street.

IMAX THEATER $
1 Canal St.
(504) 581-4629, (800) 774-7394
www.auduboninstitute.org

Put yourself right in the middle of the action while watching one of IMAX Theater's swear-you-were-there movies. The French Quarter theater, adjacent to the Audubon Aquarium of the Americas, opened in 1995 and features 354 "front row" seats for viewing its 5.5-story screen—three times the size of a regular movie screen. Several seats provide a rear-view, closed-captioned system for the hearing impaired. Current larger-than-life flicks include *Dinosaurs Alive 3D, Wild Ocean 3D,* and *Hurricane on the Bayou.* IMAX shows begin daily at 10 a.m. Call ahead, though, because they are subject to change without notice. Advance purchase is recommended but not required. The Audubon Institute offers discounts to individuals who wish to visit more than one of its four attractions—Audubon Zoo, Aquarium of the Americas, IMAX Theater, and the new Audubon Insectarium. (See Kidstuff chapter for information on these other sites.)

KLIEBERT'S ALLIGATOR AND
TURTLE FARM $
41083 West Yellow Water Rd.
Hammond
(985) 345-3617, (800) 854-9164
www.klieberttours.com

This working farm, dotted with duckweed and clove-covered ponds, was opened to the public in 1984 and is worth finding nine friends who will visit with you. (Tours are now by reservation only for groups of 10 or more.) The Klieberts have been raising alligators and turtles for nearly 50 years and have thousands of the beasts living on-site. The most popular attraction of the guided tour is the alligator-breeding pond, where visitors can gawk at gators lounging at the water's edge. The largest can be more than 15 feet long and weigh more than 1,200 pounds. Around June 1 every year the females begin building nests by piling dirt and grass in mounds 2 feet high. They lay eggs only once between June 15 and July 1.

After hatching, the gators are sold for their meat and hides or to breeders in Florida. "By raising them and finding ways to market them," say the Klieberts, "we contribute to their ultimate survival."

More than 17,000 of the farm's turtles produce more than one million eggs each year. Hatchlings are exported and sold for aquariums, children's pets, and food. Special times to visit are Apr to July during turtle egg-laying season and June 15 to July 1 during alligator egg-laying time. The gift shop sells gator heads, teeth, feet, jewelry, back scratchers, and just about any gift you can imagine made out of alligator or turtle parts. The farm is open daily noon till dark, Mar 1 through Oct 31. To get to Kliebert's, take I-55 north to the Springfield exit. Cross over LA 22 west, turn right onto the Interstate Service Road north, go one mile to Hoffman Road on left, then follow the sign.

NEW ORLEANS MULTICULTURAL
TOURISM NETWORK
2020 St. Charles Ave.
(504) 523-5652
www.soulofneworleans.com

Looking for New Orleans soul in all the right places? A call to the New Orleans Multicultural Tourism Network can help. The mission of the NOMTN is to promote the diversity of the city and region through its ethnic cultures, heritage, products, and services within the hospitality, travel, and tourism industries. Whether your interest lies in exploring the historic Faubourg Treme (America's oldest African-American neighborhood), the city's best soul food spots, jazz, the heritage of Mardi Gras Indians, or the tradition of second lines, the tourism network can help steer you in the right direction.

NEW ORLEANS SCHOOL OF COOKING $$$
524 St. Louis St.
(504) 525-2665, (800) 237-4841
www.neworleansschoolofcooking.com

Entertaining cooking classes and the Louisiana General Store are located in a renovated 19th-century molasses warehouse during a 2.5-hour demonstration, learn the ins and outs of cooking gumbo, shrimp Creole or crawfish étouffée in the time-honored Creole tradition that mixes French, Spanish and African food cultures. Everyone leaves the class with a full belly and recipes. Classes are held daily at 10 a.m. Reservations are required.

OLD URSULINE CONVENT $
1100 Chartres St.
(504) 529-3040
Constructed in 1745, the Old Ursuline Convent, the oldest building in the Mississippi River Valley and the only one to survive French colonial times, is 25 years younger than New Orleans but 25 years older than the United States. Its history is a microcosm of early life here. The Ursuline nuns were both saints and pioneers when they opened the doors of their convent to the orphaned children of the French colonists slaughtered at Fort Rosalie, a pitifully long list of names still visible in the convent's yellowing archives. Here the nuns conducted an academy for the daughters of wealthy plantation owners and the city's Creole aristocracy. But the sisters also extended their generosity to the less fortunate by teaching young black and Indian.

The great fire of 1788, which swept away the St. Louis Cathedral and 856 homes in the French Quarter, also threatened the convent, but Pere Antoine with the aid of a "bucket brigade" saved not only this building but also the adjoining Royal Hospital and barracks. It was inside the chapel in 1815 that the nuns and relatives of the men fighting with Andrew Jackson's forces at the Battle of New Orleans spent the night in prayer before the statue of Our Lady of Prompt Succor. Guided tours are offered Tues through Fri 10 and 11 a.m. and 1, 2, and 3 p.m., Sat and Sun 11:15 a.m., 1 and 2 p.m.

ST. CHARLES AVENUE STREETCAR $
2817 Canal St.
(504) 242-2600
www.norta.com
If you've never ridden a streetcar, New Orleans is a good place to start. You haven't lived till you've sat on wood-slat seats, feeling the breeze blow on your face through the huge open windows while this electric-powered green giant shakes and rattles as it rolls down St. Charles Avenue. Just think, you're traveling around the city the same way New Orleanians have done since before the Civil War. Best times to ride are late morning and early afternoon when it's least crowded. For more information, see the Getting Here, Getting Around chapter. Catch the streetcar at Canal and Carondelet Streets. It costs $1.25 per person each way, and exact change is required.

HOME SWEET HOMES

New Orleans' elegant old homes are time-honored barometers of architecture, culture, and taste, each of which contributes a chapter to the 300-year-old story of the city's mostly well-heeled Creole and American families. How any of these relics survived the seemingly nonstop calamity of fires, hurricanes, wars, and economic downturns is almost anyone's guess.

But survive they did. Historic preservation in New Orleans is an ongoing, time-consuming, dollar-sapping endeavor that brings together concerned citizens for a common cause. Following are some of the most painstakingly restored, preserved, and attended-to homes in the city. Don't miss them.

BEAUREGARD-KEYES HOUSE $
1113 Chartres St.
(504) 523-7257
This excellent example of a raised Creole cottage, located opposite the Old Ursuline Convent, was built in 1826 by French auctioneer Joseph Le Carpentier and designed by Spanish architect Francois Correjolles. The house is named for two of its inhabitants, Confederate General P. G. T. Beauregard, who lived here after the War Between the States, and novelist Frances Parkinson Keyes who in the mid-20th century wrote a number of her 51 books here, including *Dinner at Antoine's*, *The Chess Players*, and *Madame Castel's Lodger*.

Featuring twin curved staircases, a Tuscan portico, and a brick-walled garden designed to the home's original plans, the house exhibits an extensive collection of antique dolls, teapots, and folk costumes having belonged to Keyes, as well as the Beauregard Chamber, decorated with original furniture used by the general. Docents in period costumes lead guided tours on the hour Mon through Sat 10 a.m. to 3 p.m.

GALLIER HOUSE MUSEUM $
1118–1132 Royal St.
(504) 525-5661
www.hgghh.org

Noted New Orleans architect James Gallier Jr. built this elegant French Quarter town house for his wife and four small daughters in 1857, a time when the young designer was eager to execute his innovative ideas about residential comfort and convenience. For example, because ventilation was important for comfort during New Orleans' long hot summers, Gallier incorporated a skylight and ceiling vents into his 19th-century design, which can still be seen in this completely restored house-museum.

The exterior has typical Creole cast-iron work, while the interior blends a traditional town house floor plan with Gallier's own ingenuity, such as the composite columns and the unusual plaster cornice work of the double parlor. The collection includes a complete bedroom suite by master cabinetmaker Prudent Mallard and parlor chairs by John Henry Belter.

Gallier's eclectic and stylish design reflects the latest of Victorian taste, with fine New Orleans-made mahogany and rosewood furniture, colorful wool carpets woven on antique looms in England, period French wallpaper, and hand-painted window shades. Utilitarian items such as a cypress icebox, ironing equipment, and a fly-catch also.

A National Historic Landmark and hailed by the New York Times as "one of the best small museums in the country," Gallier House offers unique insights into the lifestyle of a bygone era. The museum complex includes two adjacent 1830s commercial buildings converted into exhibit space for Victorian art and a museum shop.

Gallier was also the designer of one of the city's most elaborate facilities, the famous French Opera House, which was destroyed by fire in 1919, as well as the Bank of America building, built in 1866 on Exchange Place and probably the first in New Orleans to have a structural cast-iron front, and the Florence A. Luling House, built in 1865 and later used as the Jockey Club. Docents lead 45- to 60-minute tours Mon and Fri 10 a.m. to 3 p.m., and Sat noon to 3 p.m.

HERMANN-GRIMA HOUSE $
820 St. Louis St.
(504) 525-5661
www.hgghh.org

This handsome two-story brick mansion, designed by Virginia architect William Brand for Samuel Hermann in 1831, is generally considered to be the best example in the Vieux Carré of American influence on New Orleans architecture—and one of the most elegant residences in the Crescent City. The complex includes a working 1831 French kitchen complete with oven, potagers, and open hearth, an unusual cast-iron cistern, the last private stable in the French Quarter, and original parterre beds filled with fragrant flowering plants. Some of the amenities include marble mantels, faux bois doors, and hand-carved wooden friezes in the parlor and dining room.

Samuel Hermann came to Louisiana from Germany the year after the Louisiana Purchase and settled in New Orleans in 1815. Fifteen years later he had amassed a substantial fortune as an entrepreneur, banker, and broker, and his newfound wealth was amply expressed in his splendid mansion. Hermann's successes were not immune to the Panic of 1837, and he was forced to sell his home in 1844 to prominent New Orleans judge Felix Grima. The house remained in the Grima family until 1921. After restoration, the house opened to the public in 1971 and today depicts the lifestyle of a prosperous Creole family in the years from 1830 to 1860. Elegant furnishings include family portraits, fine American and Rococo Revival pieces, English loom-woven wool carpets, and silk damask draperies reproduced by Scalamandre from an 1830s pattern.

This National Historic Landmark is open for tours Docents lead 45- to 60-minute tours Mon, Tues, Thurs, and Fri 10 a.m. to 3 p.m., and Sat noon to 3 p.m.

PITOT HOUSE MUSEUM $
1440 Moss St.
(504) 482-0312
www.pitothouse.org

It's easy to miss this plantation house, the only one in New Orleans open to the public on a regular basis, because of the distractingly pretty scenery of nearby Bayou St. John. So double back and take a peek inside one of the few West Indies-style houses that lined the bayou in the 1700s—you won't be disappointed. With its stucco-covered, brick-between-post construction and double-pitched hipped roof, the Pitot House was restored to its original 18th-century condition by the Louisiana Landmarks Society in the 1960s and is furnished with Louisiana and American antiques from the period. James Pitot, the first American mayor of New Orleans, bought the house in 1810. Within easy walking distance of the New Orleans Museum of Art in City Park, the house is open for tours Wed through Sat 10 a.m. to 3 p.m. Last tour at 2 p.m.

MUSEUMS: THE "OTHER" HOUSES OF WORSHIP

LOUISIANA STATE MUSEUM $
751 Chartres St.
(504) 568-6968, (800) 568-6968
http://lsm.crt.state.la.us

To enter into the Louisiana State Museum and its historic structures is to venture through a gateway to Louisiana's past. One of New Orleans' top attractions, the state museum is actually a collection of nine structures throughout Louisiana, five of which are located near Jackson Square in the heart of the French Quarter: the Cabildo, the Pres-

bytere, the Old U.S. Mint, the 1850 House, and the Arsenal. We will focus on these.

The Louisiana State Museum is one of the region's best values. In New Orleans visitors may purchase single building tickets or purchase tickets to two or more properties and receive a 20 percent discount. Visitor guides are available to each of the buildings. Plan on at least 45 minutes per building. Optional guided tours, at no extra cost, take about the same time and require at least 24 hours' advance notice.

All buildings are open Tues through Sun 9 a.m. to 5 p.m. All state museums are wheelchair accessible except for the 1850 House. Special accommodations for viewing the house are offered to individuals who request them. All visitors who have other special needs are asked to call in advance to allow museum staff to make arrangements.

THE 1850 HOUSE $
523 St. Ann St.
(504) 568-6968
http://lsm.crt.state.la.us

It was in 1850 that the Baroness Micaela Almonaster de Pontalba first opened the doors of the two magnificent row houses, patterned after stately French architecture of the period, that she had designed and built.

They flank Jackson Square on St. Ann and St. Peters Streets. She inherited the land from her father, Don Andres Almonaster y Roxas, a wealthy Spaniard who rebuilt the Cabildo, Presbytere, and St. Louis Cathedral after the fire of 1788 destroyed those buildings along with most of the old city.

The baroness hired noted local architect James Gallier Sr. to design the row houses (though she dismissed him shortly before construction began and finished it herself), Henry Howard to work on the architectural drawings, and Samuel Stewart as the builder. When the Pontalba buildings, constructed to stop the increasing deterioration of the old part of the city that had begun in the 1840s, were completed, each contained 16 separate apartments on the upper floors and self-contained shops on the ground floors. The cartouches that decorate the cast-iron railings were designed by her and signify the Almonaster and Pontalba families.

The matching blocklong structures added style and dimension to the Place d'Armes (later renamed Jackson Square at the urging of the baroness to commemorate General Andrew Jackson, hero of the Battle of New Orleans). After the Civil War the Pontalba buildings fell into disrepair and, by the turn of the century, had become tenements. New Orleans philanthropist William Ratcliffe Irby bought the Lower Pontalba building from the Pontalba heirs in 1921 for $68,000 and willed it to the Louisiana State Museum in 1927. The City of New Orleans ultimately acquired the Upper Pontalba building on the opposite side of Jackson Square. Extensive restoration of the buildings took place under the Works Progress Administration in the 1930s while renovation of the interiors occurred in 1955. The museum has re-created what one of these residences might have looked like during the antebellum era and depicts family life during the most prosperous period in the city's history. See the Louisiana State Museum write-up above for hours and ticket information.

THE ARSENAL $

600 St. Peter St.
(504) 568-6968
http://lsm.crt.state.la.us
Looking to earn extra points toward your New Orleans coffee merit badge? The best place for field research (after Cafe du Monde, of course) may be the Arsenal, home to the exhibit "Freshly Brewed: The Coffee Trade and the Port of New Orleans." Entry to the museum, built in 1839, is through the Cabildo. The Arsenal, which occupies the original 1769 site of the Spanish arsenal, also presents special and short-term exhibitions, lectures, seminars, and interactive programs for both adults and children. See the Louisiana State Museum write-up above for hours and ticket information.

THE CABILDO
701 Chartres St.
Jackson Square
(504) 568-6968
http://lsm.crt.state.la.us
The Cabildo, built between 1795 and 1799 as the seat of Spanish colonial government in New Orleans, was the site of the Louisiana Purchase Transfer, which brought the territory into America's. Besides doubling its land mass, America also got a cosmopolitan city in the deal, on December 20, 1803, when the transfer was officially signed in the Cabildo's Sala Capitular, or counsel chamber. Because no artifacts of the event exist, the museum has re-created what the chamber might have looked like. The chamber was also home to the State Supreme Court from 1868 to 1910 and the site of several nationally important rulings, such as those in the cases of *Plessy vs. Ferguson* and the Slaughterhouse Cases, post-Civil War decisions with far-reaching civil rights implications.

Beginning with European settlers' encounters with Native Americans and progressing through the Civil War and Reconstruction, exhibits ranging from Napoleon's death mask, one of only four in existence, to colonial era domestic items incorporate a charismatic "people" perspective. For example, the "Iberville Stone," located on the first floor, was recovered from Ft. Maurepas, the first permanent French site in Louisiana, settled by Pierre LeMoyne Sieur d'Iberville not long after he reached the mouth of the Mississippi River on Shrove Tuesday (Louisiana's first Mardi Gras) in 1699.

Battle of New Orleans buffs will want to check out the second-floor exhibit of battle relics, weapons, authentic uniforms, a lock of Andrew Jackson's hair, and even the drum of Jordan Noble, a free black man who helped lead Jackson's ragtag army into battle. (Historical note: Free people of color composed about 40 percent of New Orleans' pre-Civil War population, contributing significantly to the city's skilled labor force. Many owned businesses, engaged in professions, and amassed estates.) Adding historical dimension are objects recalling an infamous facet of this era: the proliferation of piracy and smuggling spearheaded by Jean Lafitte and his Baratarian profiteers. A video and fiber-optic map help visitors navigate the complex history. See the Louisiana State Museum write-up above for hours and ticket information.

CONFEDERATE MUSEUM $
929 Camp St.
(504) 523-4522
www.confederatemuseum.com
This memorial to Confederate veterans opened its doors on Jan. 8, 1891, and is the oldest museum in the state. Louisiana philanthropist Frank T. Howard constructed the hall as a meeting place for Confederate veterans to reflect on their Civil War stories and to house and protect their relics. He wished that the building and its collection might forever proclaim "how a brave people and their descendants hold the name and the fame of their heroes and martyrs with the admiration undiminished by disaster or defeat and with love unquenched by time."

Located just off Lee Circle near Howard Avenue not far from the French Quarter, the museum houses the largest collection of Civil War artifacts in the nation with more than 100 Confederate battle flags, a large array of uniforms, and numerous rare Louisiana-made swords. On display are personal items of such famous figures as Jefferson Davis, Robert E. Lee, P. G. T. Beauregard, Brazton Bragg, and Frank Gardener. Hours are Wed through Sat 10 a.m. to 4 p.m.

i **Among the most beautiful—and free—attractions/activities in a city surrounded by water is watching a sunset. Whether it's from the steps of the French Quarter's Moonwalk or along The Point at West End, you'll have the best seat in the house for enjoying nature's daily taps.**

THE HISTORIC NEW ORLEANS COLLECTION $
533 Royal St.
(504) 523-4662
www.hnoc.org
Visitors step through the patio of this French Quarter town house from the late 1800s and into the house-museum of the collection's founders, General and Mrs. L. Kemper Williams. Remodeled for 20th-century living, the house is filled with antique furniture and Chinese porcelains arranged in harmony with contemporary pieces, all of which reflect the gracious 1940s lifestyle of its owners.

This museum and research-exhibit complex includes the Merieult House, built in 1792—one of the few in the French Quarter to have escaped the conflagration of 1794. Beautiful high-ceilinged rooms showcase rare archival photographs, books, and documents from the Williams's collection; other exhibits include documents from the Louisiana Transfer of 1803, maps that show the growth of the city from the original "old square," and an 18th-century self-portrait of Bienville, cofounder of the city of New Orleans. Rooms are organized to provide a chronological history of the city.

Not to be missed is the nearby Williams Research Center at 410 Chartres St., owned and managed by the same private nonprofit foundation that oversees the Historic New Orleans Collection. The reading room offers access to the bulk of the Williams's collection of books, maps, manuscripts, paintings, prints, drawings, photographs, and artifacts on the history of New Orleans and Louisiana.

The Historic New Orleans Collection and the Williams Research Center are open, free of charge, Tues through Sat 10 a.m. to 4:30 p.m. Guided tours for a small fee are given during the same days at 10 and 11 a.m. and 2 and 3 p.m. Children under 12 are not admitted.

LONGUE VUE HOUSE AND GARDENS $
7 Bamboo Rd.
(504) 488-5488
www.longuevue.com

Locals are immensely proud of this historic Greek Revival city-estate, former home of the late cotton broker, businessman, and philanthropist Edgar Bloom Stern and his wife, Edith, daughter of Julius Rosenwald, the Sears magnate. Designed by architects William and Geoffrey Platt, the house is surrounded by eight acres of simply superb gardens created by Ellen Biddle Shipman, referred to in her green-thumb circle as the dean of American women landscape architects.

The magnificent twin hearts of Longue Vue gardens are the Spanish Court and its Moorish flourish inspired by the 14th-century Generalife Gardens of the Alhambra in Spain, and somewhat less formal Wild Garden with its "forest walk," both of which are framed by horticultural displays and lyrical fountains. A Discovery Garden for children, featuring a walk-through bamboo tunnel, opened in 1998. Beautiful manicured lawns feature a who's who of New Orleans horticulture: live oaks, magnolias, camellias, azaleas, roses, sweet olives, crape myrtles, and oleanders.

The house itself is an elegant nod to Shipman, who had more than a hand in the interior design, which relies heavily on American and English antiques, needlework, French and Oriental carpets, and a notable British and continental cream ware pottery collection. Longue Vue's Tuscan columns, circular spaces, and classical molding and friezes are a strong reminder of late-18th-century country houses. Visitors are welcomed by a circular vestibule with turn-of-the-19th century Chinese bamboo and cane chairs, the same kind seen at the Brighton Pavilion in England, bottom-lit niches (a mid-20th-century architectural conceit), and classically inspired circular spaces.

Many of the architectural elements that characterize the exterior of the house are displayed in the center hall, including Doric columns flanking the steps leading down from the circular vestibule into the hall, which serve as introductions to the major rooms. The oak and elm sideboard ca. 1750 belonged to Mrs. Stern's mother and came from England.

Some of the more notable rooms also reflect the owners' tastes and include Mrs. Stern's flower arranging room, a library of Norwegian spruce paneling from an 18th-century house in Surrey, England, and a dining room with 19th-century Chinese rice paper, Georgian millwork, Turkish Oushak rugs, and a color scheme of aquamarine, rose, and ecru that reflects the fashionable colors of the late 1930s. Setting the table are examples of the Sterns' Wedgwood "Queen's Ware" collection, one of the largest in the United States.

Not to be outdone is the second-floor drawing room overlooking the gardens, where the Sterns entertained distinguished visitors that included Eleanor Roosevelt, John and Bobby Kennedy, and Pablo Casals. The mantelpiece was carved ca. 1800 as a memorial to George Washington. Visiting hours are Mon through Sat 10 a.m. to 4:30 p.m. (last tour 4 p.m.), and Sun 1 to 5 p.m. (last tour 4:15 p.m.). Building on the tradition of community service established by the family, Longue Vue has programs for school children and older and disabled adults. Ongoing educational programs for both adults and children include those on the decorative arts and horticulture, summer gardening classes, workshops, seminars, and lectures.

NEW ORLEANS HISTORIC VOODOO MUSEUM $
724 Dumaine St.
(504) 523-7685
www.voodoomuseum.com
Cynics may take one look around inside the dusky foyer, where voodoo dolls in little cardboard coffins are sold alongside good-luck herbs, wealth candles, and love potions, and wonder when the zombies are going to show up moaning for blood. But anyone who has read John Tallant's book *Voodoo in New Orleans* or Harvard ethnobotanist Wade Davis's accounts of his scientific exploration of voodoo in Haiti, *The Serpent and the Rainbow,* simply knows better.

Voodoo is a bona fide religion practiced seriously in New Orleans even to this day. And owner-curator Charles Gandolfo's museum offers the curious and skeptic alike one of the best places to discover the history and modern-day practices of this ancient and deeply spiritual African belief system. Memorial prayer altars, displays of occult

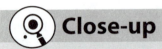

Close-up

New Orleans Historic Voodoo Museum

Years ago a close friend living in Florida was gripped by a downturn in economic circumstances. After deliberating the dilemma a few days, the guiding light of reason revealed a uniquely Big Easy solution: gris-gris. Traditionally, gris-gris (pronounced GREE-GREE) is a red felt bag filled with secret scented herbs, briefly flamed, blessed by a priestess, then tied with a black ribbon. The individual needing help in matters of love, health, court cases, or, in this instance, finances, carries it. But how does even the most sympathetic of friends come by one of these time-honored, "protective" voodoo charms?

In this city that place is the New Orleans Historic Voodoo Museum at 724 Dumaine St. (504-680-0128; http://voodoomuseum.com), which is open daily 10 a.m. to 6 p.m. This dusky French Quarter museum, opened in 1972, keeps alive the flickering flame of ancient voodoo traditions while promoting the understanding and modern teachings of this oft-maligned mystical religion. Newcomers take note: Don't refer to it as "spooky."

Voodoo—or, voudou, as the Louisiana-French spell it—was brought to New Orleans in the 1700s by shackled slaves from West Africa, Haiti, and Santo Domingo stripped of virtually everything save for their deeply rooted spiritual beliefs. The religion has been practiced in New Orleans for nearly 300 years but reached its zenith in the late 19th century when Creole hairdresser Marie Laveau's secret nighttime rituals on the banks of Bayou St. John earned her the reputation as the city's voodoo queen—and someone not to be trifled with.

"Voodoo is such an important part of New Orleans history," John T. Martin, a voodoo priest and tour guide in charge of the museum's special rituals, said, adding, "We aren't here to recruit, we're here to enlighten."

Far from the laughable and even racist stereotypes presented in Hollywood B-movies, voodoo, at its heart, is a deeply spiritual and rich belief system that for centuries was passed down by African elders to youth in the oral tradition. When voodoo-practicing slaves in the New World were forced to convert to Christianity, they incorporated some Catholic traditions, initially for the sake of appearances lest they be punished or even put to death. One tradition that took hold, though, was the use of altars to pray to saints to intercede to God for favors. This practice closely paralleled the ancient voodoo custom of praying to the spirits of nature—

objects including African and Caribbean masks as well as gris-gris and ju-ju from around the world, "spirit boxes," a live python, and, of course, a portrait of voodoo queen Marie Laveau tell the story of voodoo in New Orleans. Guided tours of the museum are conducted daily 10 a.m. to dusk.

NEW ORLEANS MUSEUM OF ART

See The Arts chapter.

NEW ORLEANS PHARMACY MUSEUM $
514 Chartres St.
(504) 565-8027
www.pharmacymuseum.org

In 1823 Louis J. Dufilho Jr., America's first licensed pharmacist, built his apothecary on Chartres Street in the French Quarter. The walled courtyard contained a botanical garden, which supplied medicinal herbs for the pharmacy. As was common, Dufilho worked as both a pharmacist and a doctor. In fact, in those days the pharmacist was sort of a chemist-of-all-trades who also blended perfumes, cosmetics, and house paint available only at the apothecary. The museum still has Dufilho's curved glass cosmetics case filled with century-old face paint and perfume bottles. The museum also displays hand-blown antique glass wind and rain, lightning and thunder, rivers and oceans, animals and trees—for the same reason. It was a match made in heaven.

Consider: Laveau, a devout Roman Catholic who died in 1881, often would conduct her rituals after Mass in the gardens behind St. Louis Cathedral, said Martin. Controversy has always surrounded her exact place of burial. But it is widely believed that St. Louis Cemetery No. 1 is the final resting place of one of New Orleans' most intriguing and, according to accounts of the day, bewitchingly beautiful historical characters.

Today people from all over the world seek out the museum and its owner-curator Jerry Gandolfo, an artist and historian, to learn about the religion's animism-meets-Catholicism roots in New Orleans. In one room of the museum is the "wishing stump," a carved totem reportedly used by Laveau for her rituals at Bayou St. John to attract ancestors and repel evil spirits. Visitors bring offerings as well as pictures of friends and family who have petitioned the spirits, or loas, for health, wealth, love, and reconciliation. Nearby is the same kind of altar used by practitioners of the Spanish-Caribbean version of voodoo, called Santeria.

Other rooms feature an 1850s-style parlor where gris-gris bags are meticulously prepared and Haitian paintings, Gandolfo's original artworks, occult masks, and a "witchstand" incense burner dating to the 1600s are displayed among other artifacts. While general admission is $7, visitors who pay $15 can observe and participate in one of the two-hour public rituals occasionally hosted by Martin. During the hypnotic, drum-fueled damballah dance, a live python is passed among willing participants.

"It's a full-blown ritual for healing or for reconciliation," says Martin. "The drumming becomes very sensuous and driving, and it's amazing what it does to people—it's mesmerizing." On the night of June 23, St. John's Eve, visitors meet at the museum and are escorted to a secret courtyard destination for an ancient ritual commemorating the growing season of the planting cycle.

"I don't think there is anything wrong about being skeptical," Martin said when asked what he tells voodoo cynics, "but I think people need to make themselves aware of other religions and practices and views."

As for the fate of the Florida friend who received the gris-gris? Life couldn't be better. Call it a coincidence.

jars containing crude drugs and herbs as well as voodoo powders and gris-gris potions.

Mayor Robert Maestri bought the building in 1937 and donated it to the city to be converted into a Napoleonic museum honoring Napoleon. Why? Maestri had heard the legend that the structure had been built by pirate Jean Lafitte and his brother, Alexandre, as the future home for the French emperor after they rescued him from his prison on St. Helena. But the legend was false. Once city officials discovered the truth, the place was instead turned into a pharmacy museum. The building, located on Chartres Street between St. Louis and Toulouse Streets, is open Tues and Thurs 10 a.m. to 2 p.m.; Wed, Fri, and Sat 10 a.m. to 5 p.m.

THE OLD U.S. MINT $
400 Esplanade Ave.
(504) 568-6968
http://lsm.crt.state.la.us
Temporarily closed for renovations, this national historic landmark constructed in 1835 (during the presidency of Andrew Jackson), is the only building in the United States to have served both as a U.S. and a Confederate Mint. President Jackson,

hero of the Battle of New Orleans, advocated the establishment of a mint in New Orleans to provide much-needed hard currency for Western expansion, as well as to wrest power from Eastern bankers who wanted to consolidate their resources in that part of the country.

The Greek Revival-style Mint and its Ionic porticos and simple classic lines were designed by renowned architect William Strickland and its construction supervised by two New Orleanians—Benjamin F. Cox, a master carpenter, and John Mitchell, a master mason and builder.

The Mint's originally hand-powered coining machinery was replaced in 1845 with steam power, a sign of the ever-widening influence of the Industrial Revolution. Interestingly, when structural flaws began to show in the mid-1850s, officials hired P. G. T. Beauregard, a recent West Point engineering graduate, to fireproof the building and add masonry flooring and iron beams to the edifice. Beauregard is best known as the commander of the Confederate forces who fired upon Fort Sumter on April 12, 1861, igniting the Civil War.

Louisiana had already seceded from the Union, and the Mint was transferred to the Confederate States Army for its own coinage operations. Later it was used to house Confederate troops. In 1879, following Reconstruction, the Mint reopened and its labor force of coiners, melters, pressers, cutters, and rollers set to work. Conditions were harsh, as windows were kept shut to prevent even the slightest draft from disturbing the delicate balances that weighed money. The Mint ceased operations in 1909 and its machinery moved to Philadelphia after the federal government decided that facilities in San Francisco and Denver were more than adequate to meet demands. In 1966 Uncle Sam transferred the property to the State of Louisiana, and between 1974 and 1981 the Mint was transformed into a museum and research center devoted to Louisiana history.

Today the Mint is home to a notable "New Orleans Jazz" exhibit, which tells the story of this Big Easy–born art form from its humble street origins to current world renown through vintage photographs, authentic recordings, and the lovingly worn instruments of such musical legends as Louis Armstrong and Sidney Bechet. The Old U.S. Mint is within easy walking distance of Jackson Square and is located across the street from the French Market at the Mississippi River.

THE PRESBYTERE $
751 Chartres St.
Jackson Square
(504) 568-6968
http://lsm.crt.state.la.us

Capuchin monks of St. Louis Cathedral were supposed to be (but never were) the first residents of the Presbytere, built in 1791 to match the Cabildo (Town Hall). The lower floor, completed in 1797 by philanthropist Don Andres Almonester y Roxas, was rented for shops. Under the administration of Baron de Carondelet, it was used for governmental purposes.

It wasn't until 1813 that the second floor was added by the wardens of St. Louis Cathedral and the Presbytere was completed, the result of a lawsuit between the church and Almonester's widow. The matter was settled in 1801 when King Carlos of Spain relieved the Almonester family from any obligation to complete the Presbytere. Rear wings were added in 1840, and seven years later the mansard roof and cupola were added to complement the scale of the newly rebuilt cathedral and the proposed new Pontalba buildings. The City of New Orleans purchased the building in 1853 and used it as a courthouse until 1911. The cupola was destroyed in a hurricane four years later and was not rebuilt.

The Presbytere today is home to eclectic exhibits of Louisiana's quixotic heritage past and present. If men's and women's evening wear from the turn of the last century to the present doesn't grab your attention, you will certainly be interested in the collection of rare and historic maps, colonial era paintings, and an exhibit called "In the Eye of the Beholder," which features medical instruments, folk art, mourning jewelry, and World War I weapons. They also have an exhibit called "Carnival Time: Mardi Gras in Louisiana." See the Louisiana State Museum write-up above for hours and ticket information. For information on family-friendly museums, see the following Kidstuff chapter.

TOURS: IF IT'S TUESDAY, THIS MUST BE BARATARIA

Not surprisingly, in a tourism-based city like New Orleans, the variety of tours is nearly endless. Stroll the French Quarter at sunset and admire its shadowy architecture. Head up River Road into Plantation Country for a glimpse back at antebellum life. Explore the vast contributions of African Americans to the city's diverse social and cultural fabric. Take a paddle wheel cruise from the French Quarter upriver to the zoo. Or paddle a canoe through a Barataria bayou, scanning the cypress-covered banks for graceful, long-legged egrets and sunbathing box turtles, as well as hungry gators patrolling for both, as you go.

Whether it's on foot, in a bus coach, an old-fashioned carriage, or aboard an authentic paddle, there are almost as many ways to tour New Orleans as there are things to see. Here are but a few suggestions—a complete list would be exhaustive and redundant. Many more can be found at your hotel's lobby brochure rack or by asking at the front desk or by contacting the Metropolitan Convention and Visitors Bureau at (504) 566-5011.

LE MONDE CREOLE $$
624 Royal St.
(504) 568-1801, (504) 232-8559
www.mondecreole.com
This Secret Courtyards of the French Quarter and Cemetery Tour provides an intimate glimpse of private French Quarter tropical courtyards, as well as the New Orleans Pharmacy Museum and its 19th century medicinal garden, and St. Louis Cemetery #1—recalling the 200-year history of one of New Orleans' oldest Creole families. Tickets for the two-hour tour, departing Mon through Sat at 10:30 a.m., Sun at 10 a.m. must be purchased in advance. Call the above numbers for reservations.

MAGIC TOURS $$
French Quarter
(504) 588-9693
magictoursnola.com
Dubbed "Alternative tours for the intelligent traveler," this tour company delivers lively, historically accurate tours conducted by professors, historians, and journalists equipped to keep things entertaining and handle questions from the crowd. Available tours include daily Garden District/Cemeteries, French Quarter and popular nightly ghost tours. Most tours last approximately two hours and all require advance reservations.

NEW ORLEANS TOURS $$$
4220 Howard Ave.
(504) 592–1991
www.bigeasytours.com
One of the largest motorcoach tour operators in the city, this company offers several comprehensive daily tours to suit nearly any taste, budget, and schedule. Offerings include tours of the Garden District, French Quarter, plantation, and swamp, as well as harbor cruises. Check with your hotel for exact pickup times.

ROYAL CARRIAGES $$
1824 North Rampart St.
(504) 943-8820
www.neworleanscarriages.com
Established in 1941, this is probably the oldest carriage tour operator in the city and definitely one of the most romantic ways to take in the French Quarter. All those honeymooners can't be wrong. The half-hour open-air ride in an authentic carriage drawn by a clip-clopping mule, starts at the riverside entrance to Jackson Square, across the street from Cafe du Monde, and winds through the French Quarter at a leisurely pace. Simply walk right up and sit right down. Tip: The charge is per carriage (which can hold up to four people), so the more riders, the less cost per person.

SOUTHERN SEAPLANE INC. $$$$
1 Coquille Dr., Belle Chasse
(504) 394-5633
southernseaplane.com

For a real Louisiana high, try a flight-seeing trip aboard a seaplane that takes passengers on a fly-by over the city's French Quarter and Superdome before heading south to the bayous and marshes of pirate Jean Lafitte's Barataria. If the 30-minute flight seems too brief, a two-hour trip flies to Kraemer for a 60-minute ground tour of this Cajun town and surrounding wildlife. There are also plantation and wetlands tours.

TOURS BY ISABELLE $$$–$$$$
P.O. Box 740972, 70174
(504) 398-0365, (877) 665-8687
www.toursbyisabelle.com

This company prides itself on small but highly personalized explorations of the city (including Hurricane Katrina damage), plantations, and swamps aboard a 13-passenger van staffed by knowledgeable and licensed guides who speak various languages, depending on the group. The company promises to "make you fall in love with Louisiana," but even if you don't, the tour still provides an intimate alternative to large bus tours. Advance reservations are required and because the company accommodates such small groups not all tours are available every day.

OL' MAN RIVER

**NEW ORLEANS STEAMBOAT
COMPANY** $$–$$$
2 Canal St.
(504) 586-8777, (800) 233-2628
www.steamboatnatchez.com

Sure, it's a Twain thing, but it would be more than a small shame not to get swept away at least once by the mighty Mississippi during a visit to the Big Easy. And one of the safest and most comfortable ways to do this, while savoring some of the beauty and romance of New Orleans, is by taking a short trip aboard the steamboat.

The 265-foot, three-deck steam stern-wheeler *Natchez* holds 1,600 passengers and takes visitors on two-hour cruises twice daily, departing from the Toulouse Street Wharf across from Jackson Square. The harbor/jazz cruise departs 11:30 a.m. (returning 1:30 p.m.) and 2:30 p.m. (returning 4:30 p.m.) and includes a narration of the highlights, music from the boat's calliope, a museum-quality engine room open to visitors and optional lunch.

A dinner/jazz cruise boards passengers at 6 p.m., leaves at 7 p.m., and returns at 9 p.m., and features music by the Dukes of Dixieland and casual buffet-style dining. Some cruise offerings are seasonal and reservations are required for all.

**THE PADDLEWHEELER CREOLE
QUEEN** $$$–$$$$
2004 World Trade Center
#2 Canal St.
(504) 529-4567, (800) 445-4109
www.creolequeen.com

The paddlewheeler Creole Queen also offers a jazz dinner cruise, four to five nights a week, including every Fri and Sat. Boarding is at 7 p.m. on the Riverwalk/Canal Street Dock. The two-hour cruise leaves at 8 p.m. and includes music, a Creole buffet, and a cash bar.

Boarding is at 1:30 p.m. for the daily harbor cruise, which stops for a tour of Blaine Kern's Mardi Gras World (see write-up, this chapter). The 2.5-hour tour leaves at 2 p.m. and is narrated by the ship's captain while cruising past the French quarter and historic Algiers Point. Reservations are highly recommended for both cruises.

SWAMP THINGS

AIRBOAT TOURS BY ARTHUR $$–$$$
4262 Highway 90 East
Des Allemands
(800) 975-9345
www.airboattours.com

Just 45 minutes (if you're boogying—coming out of Downtown can be slow) west of New Orleans in St. Charles Parish, Capt. Arthur Matherne waits to take you on a thrilling airboat ride through the swamps from a small fishing village that will make you feel like you've gone back in time. Matherne guides passengers deep into the marsh while sharing tales of his lifelong experiences of fishing for alligators, crab, shrimp, and frogs in Bayou Gauche.

This leisurely and educational experience can turn into a ride on the wild side when Matherne revs up his 400-horsepower engine and turns the bayou into a raceway. Matherne, a U.S. Coast Guard-licensed captain, will also customize tours for hunting, fishing, or just to enjoy the sunset. Tours are by appointment only with a maximum of 32 passengers. Half-hour, one-hour, and custom tours are available.

HONEY ISLAND SWAMP TOUR $$–$$$
106 Holly Ridge Dr., Slidell
(985) 641-1769
www.honeyislandswamp.com
Located on the Pearl River boundary between Louisiana and Mississippi, the Honey Island Swamp is one of the wildest and most pristine river swamps in the United States; nearly 70,000 acres are designated as a permanently protected wildlife area. See alligators, bald eagles, waterfowl, herons, egrets, raccoons, nutria, mink, otters, and a host of other marsh wildlife on the area's most popular swamp tour. Explore the deeper, harder-to-reach bayous and sloughs of the swamp interior known so well by highly trained guides who have studied the Honey Island area (named for a small island within the swamp known for its swarming bees).

Don't forget to take your camera on this two-hour narrated adventure offered year-round every morning and afternoon. Customized tours for birding, duck hunting, nighttime, or special occasions are available. Call for departure times and to make required reservations. If you'd rather let them do the driving, New Orleans hotel pickup is available for an extra charge. Call Cukie at (504) 242-5877. A gift shop, Cajun food, and restrooms are available at the dock. To get to the swamp take I–10 east across Lake Pontchartrain

to Gause Boulevard at exit 266. Head east for 2 miles to the traffic light at the intersection of LA 190 and LA 1090 (Military Road). Turn left and drive 1 mile north on Louisiana. Highway 1090 to the I–10 Service Road. Turn right and follow the service road 1.5 miles to where it ends at Pearl River. Parking is on the left.

JEAN LAFITTE SWAMP TOUR $$–$$$
Route 1, Box 3131, Marrero
(504) 689-4186, (800) 445-4109
www.jeanlafitteswamptour.com
A native tour guide spins tales of the legends and lore of Louisiana's still untamed wilderness while a covered 60-passenger flatboat glides beneath a canopy of moss-draped cypress trees. Named for the famous buccaneer who helped the Americans beat the British at the Battle of New Orleans, this ecotour takes visitors into the heart of southeast Louisiana's swamplands, billed as the "home of the white nutria." Swamp boats depart daily at 10 a.m. and 2 p.m. for a one-hour and 45-minute tour. Hotel pickups (for an extra fee) begin at 8:45 a.m. Airboat tours are also available. Call (504) 587-1719 for reservations. To get here cross the Crescent City Connection (Mississippi River Bridge) and continue on the Westbank Expressway 7.5 miles to the Barataria Boulevard exit. Turn left and continue down Barataria 3.5 miles to LA 3134 (the Lafitte-Larose Highway), turn left and drive 5 miles. The swamp tour site is on the left.

SPECTATOR SPORTS

Baseball

NEW ORLEANS ZEPHYRS
6000 Airline Dr., Metairie
(504) 734-5155
www.zephyrsbaseball.com
The New Orleans Zephyrs baseball team played its inaugural season at Zephyr Field in 1997, which then-team president Rob Couhig called "the crown jewel of minor league baseball."

Fans of this Florida Marlins AAA affiliate watch minor league ball in style Apr through September. The $20 million, 10,000-seat (with chair-backs) ballpark features the largest scoreboard in all of minor league baseball, 16 VIP suites, a covered party area adjacent to seating, and a fan swimming pool with two hot tubs.

Spectators are also treated to a variety of theme nights that include fireworks shows, dollar beer, and hat and T-shirt giveaways. And whether or not the team's a contender, the entertainment value of the games has attracted more than half a million fans during a regular season. This breaks the city's last baseball attendance record, set in 1947 when the now-defunct New Orleans Pelicans (named after the state bird) drew 400,036 fans at Pelican Stadium.

Gates open 90 minutes before game time. All Zephyrs games are broadcast on WIST AM 690. Tickets range from $6 to $10. Call Mon through Fri 9 a.m. to 5 p.m., on any game day or visit the box office at the ballpark.

To get to Zephyr Field from New Orleans: Take I-10 west toward Baton Rouge. Exit at Clearview Parkway and head south. Turn right on Airline Drive and after two stoplights you will see the stadium's two big signs on the left. Turn at the first one.

Basketball

NEW ORLEANS HORNETS
New Orleans Arena
(504) 525–Hoop, (800) HORNETS
www.nba.com/hornets
Offering virtually everything except someone's firstborn, the City of New Orleans finally snagged a new National Basketball Association team in 2002 (to replace the one Utah snagged from us a couple of decades earlier). October 30, 2002, marked the inaugural tip-off of the New Orleans (formerly Charlotte) Hornets in their new home, the New Orleans Arena. Ironically, they hosted the Utah Jazz.

The arena is the green stadium at the rear of the Superdome on Poydras Street Tickets start at around $15.

Equestrian

FAIR GROUNDS RACE COURSE
1751 Gentilly Blvd.
(504) 944-5515, (800) 262-7983
www.fgno.com
The Fair Grounds, America's third-oldest Thoroughbred race course, offers horse racing from Nov through Mar. In operation since 1872, the Racetrack, as locals call it, also operates a slot-machine gaming facility onsite, as well as nine off-track betting parlors throughout southeast Louisiana.

The Fair Grounds Race Course is located near City Park. To get there from downtown, take Esplanade Avenue (which runs along the northwest border of the French Quarter) away from the Mississippi River to Broad Street, turn right, then left at Gentilly. The racetrack is on the left.

i Want to get out to Zephyr Park but I-10 is backed up? Just take Airline Drive. Go down Tulane Avenue (which runs parallel to Canal Street, a few blocks upriver). Tulane Avenue turns into Airline Drive immediately after crossing Carrollton Avenue. Keep going. The field is right past Clearview Parkway, on the left.

Football

NEW ORLEANS SAINTS
Louisiana Superdome
Sugar Bowl Drive
(504) 731-1700
www.neworleanssaints.com
The National Football League awarded its 16th franchise to New Orleans on All Saints Day, November 1, 1966. And the team's been in need of a prayer practically ever since. The squad has seen its highs (Tom Dempsey's 1970 league record-setting 63-yard field goal on the last play of the game to defeat Detroit 19–17; the 2006 comeback from disaster dream season) and lows (their dismal 1980, 1–15 record).

But the real story of the Saints has always been the fans who have stuck by the team through the worst of times and, well, the worst of times. Although pulling for perennial losers certainly has developed the fans' sense of humor. In the early '80s, when it seemed that things couldn't get any worse, fans still showed up but wore paper bags over their heads and nicknamed the team "The Aints."

Following the great 2006 season highlighted by the Saints triumphant post-Hurricane Katrina return to the Superdome and the second post-season win in the club's history, the Saints turned in two mediocre seasons with no post-season play. At the same time, the fans, God love 'em, have produced season ticket sell-outs.

All together now: "Our Father, who art in heaven . . ."

Call the Saints ticket office at (504) 731-1700 or Ticketmaster at (800) 488-5252 for possible ticket availability. If you don't have tickets, you can hear sportscaster Jim Henderson give play-by-play and former Saints running back Hokie Gajan provide color commentary on WWL–AM 870. The Superdome is located on Poydras Street at the foot of the Central Business District. It's 27 stories high with a dome-shaped roof measuring more than nine acres. It's pretty hard to miss.

SUGAR BOWL
Louisiana Superdome
1500 Sugar Bowl Dr.
(504) 525-8573
www.allstatesugarbowl.com
The idea of a New Year's Day college football game in New Orleans was hatched by *New Orleans Item* newspaper publisher Colonel James M. Thomson and sports editor Fred Digby in 1927. It took eight years to develop public and financial support for the project.

Then on January 1, 1935, in the depths of the Depression, the first Sugar Bowl Football Classic was held in Tulane Stadium. Tulane's Green Wave, who were undefeated in the South,

were pitted against the only undefeated Northern team, Pop Warner's Temple University Owls. Tulane prevailed, 20–14, before a crowd of 22,026 fans who had paid $1.50 to $3.50 each to get in. A tradition was born.

The Sugar Bowl was the subject of the first live television program in New Orleans, in 1953, which was broadcast coast to coast. Seven years later it was the first game televised in color across the United States.

Over the years, the Sugar Bowl has hosted several national champions and a virtual who's who of legendary football coaches, including Frank Broyles, "Bear" Bryant, Bobby Bowden, Bob Devaney, Vince Dooley, Woody Hayes, "Shug" Jordan, Johnny Majors, Joe Paterno, and Bud Wilkinson.

The Dome, home of the Sugar Bowl, seats around 77,000 in its expanded football configuration. Tickets for the Sugar Bowl usually go on sale in Aug and are sold through Ticketmaster. Tickets generally start around $150. Call Ticketmaster at (504) 522-5555 and (800) 488-5252.

Sports Venues

THE LOUISIANA SUPERDOME
1500 Sugar Bowl Dr.
www.superdome.com
The Louisiana Superdome is located on Poydras Street at the foot of the Central Business District. For more information on the Dome, see the Close-up in this chapter.

NEW ORLEANS ARENA
1501 Girod St.
www.neworleansarena.com
Adjacent to its towering big brother the Louisiana Superdome, the New Orleans Arena (affectionately dubbed the Dome's Mini Me) opened with much fanfare in October 1999. The state-of-the-art 19,000-seat arena is home to the New Orleans Hornets. (The venue is also designed for concerts.)

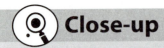

Close-up

Louisiana Superdome

It was November 1965 and New Orleans Mayor Vic Schiro, a one-time Hollywood bit player known for telling his staff, "Just give me my lines and I'll go out there and ham it up," was behind in his race for reelection. He was running against former police chief and popular city councilman Jimmy Fitzmorris. Public sentiment held that Schiro had botched citywide emergency preparations during Hurricane Betsy less than four weeks before Election Day, a major political misstep that also proved devastating to the city. To make matters worse, Schiro had to stop campaigning to have his appendix removed.

Something had to be done.

Political consultant David Kleck stepped in with a campaign promise to beat all others: If there's anything New Orleanians love as much as food, it's sports. So why not promise to build a domed stadium? Businessman and civic promoter Dave Dixon had been talking about it for years, but he'd never received any backing.

Thus was hatched "A Fireside Chat with Sunny [Schiro's wife] and Vic," a live half-hour broadcast from the mayor's Lakefront home, featuring hizzoner clad in his sick-bed pajamas and robe. Schiro went before the cameras and made his grand declaration to build a domed stadium. He was followed by Dave Dixon showing drawings of the proposed structure and, finally, eastern New Orleans real estate developer Marvin Kratter, who agreed to give the city a tract of suburban land on which to erect this monument to the mayor's imagination. (The Schiro campaign had convinced Kratter to donate the land in order to increase the value of his adjoining property.)

The program aired two days before the election. Next-morning headlines blazed the announcement and, according to former *Times-Picayune* political columnist Iris Kelso, one broadcaster even went so far as to state, "New Orleans will have the greatest stadium in the world, thanks to Mayor Vic Schiro." In a case of Louisiana politics-as-usual, Schiro's big promise got him reelected, but he never made any attempts to push forward the Superdome project. Gov.

RECREATION

Price Code

Our price is based on admission for one adult.

$.......................$0 to $10
$$ .... $11 to $20
$$$ .... $21 to $50
$$$$ .... More than $50

Bike Rentals

BICYCLE MICHAEL'S $
622 Frenchmen St.
(504) 945-9505
www.bicyclemichaels.com
This neighborhood bike shop in the Faubourg Marigny, across Esplanade Avenue from the French Quarter, rents city hybrid and mountain bikes, as well as road bikes, off-road mountain bikes, and tandems. Rates start at $10 per hour. The owners suggest BYOH—bring your own helmet—to guarantee a comfortable fit, although helmets can be rented. Hours are Sun 10 a.m. to 5 p.m. and 10 a.m. to 7 p.m. all other days, except Wed when the shop is closed. Rentals include locks. A major credit card is a must.

Boating/Instruction

**JEAN LAFITTE NATIONAL HISTORICAL
PARK AND PRESERVE** $
Barataria Unit
LA 45 Crown Point
(504) 589-2330
www.nps.gov/jela

John McKeithen picked up the ball, and with his backing the Superdome was finally built in downtown New Orleans in the early '70s.

Completed in 1975 at a cost of $163 million, the Louisiana Superdome is the world's largest indoor arena. The stadium sits on 13 acres with the entire facility encompassing 52 acres. It stands 27 stories high, and the roof (the largest of its kind) covers 9.7 acres. The stadium is the home of the New Orleans Saints, the Sugar Bowl, and Tulane University football. It's where the Pope addressed 80,000 schoolchildren, a president (George H. W. Bush) was nominated, and the largest indoor concert audience in history (87,500) saw the Rolling Stones perform in 1981.

The Dome has played host to nine Super Bowls (with the 10th to be Super Bowl XLVII in 2013), four NCAA Final Four tournaments (all off which set attendance records), and was the site of Walt Disney Studios' world premiere of *The Hunchback of Notre Dame.*

The structure is so big that seats were designed to be different colors so that to a television camera the stadium would look full, even if some of the stands were empty. The stadium is also credited with spurring the development of the lower Poydras Street corridor and, consequently, the expansion of the city's Central Business District.

In his book *Superdome: Thirteen Acres that Changed New Orleans,* author Marty Mule points out: "Until the Louisiana Superdome was built, urban renewal was rarely associated with the construction of sports arenas. Now Baltimore, Cleveland, and others have made new stadiums the centerpiece of a refurbished downtown, the magnet for attracting visitors and suburbanites into the city center."

Though the $163 million expenditure to build the Dome was widely criticized at the time, a study of the facility's 20-year economic impact concluded that nearly $4.6 billion has found its way into state coffers via the stadium. "It is hard to imagine a better return on an investment," said University of New Orleans economist Dr. Timothy Ryan, the study's author.

If only Vic Schiro could see it now.

Nine miles of canoe trails, closed to motorized boats, and accessible by three canoe launch docks, allow up close and personal exploration of the swamps and marshes. Guided canoe treks take place some Saturday mornings, and moonlight canoeing is offered monthly on the night before and the night of the full moon, both by reservation only. Another nine miles of waterways are open to all boats. Canoe rentals are available just outside the park, and a number of public and private boat launches provide access for motor boats.

Fishing

Watching the sun rise above the coastal marshlands of southeast Louisiana on a cloudless morning while heading out on a flat-bottom boat to some of the world's best fishing waters is a surefire way to heal an achy-breaky hook. The good news is this Sportsman's Paradise earned its state moniker, as well as a secure place in hearts of novice and experienced fishers alike, in part because of the region's plentiful lakes, bays, bayous, and marshes, not to mention the nearby Gulf of Mexico, all blessed with an abundance of finfish.

Year-round warm temperatures keep local inland-water and deep-sea fishing charters, many located within a 35-mile radius of New Orleans, operating during all four seasons. Inland-water fishing in particular offers a unique glimpse of marsh coastal wildlife—alligators, otters, nutrias, minks, egrets, blue herons, ospreys, pelicans, and raccoons.

The cost for many but not all charters includes rod and reel, fishing license, soft drinks, bait, ice and gas, filleting and bagging, and instruction. Some charters provide transportation to and from hotels.

BOURGEOIS CHARTERS $$$$
2783 Privateer Blvd., Barataria
(504) 341-5614
www.neworleansfishing.com

This fishing charter 30 minutes from New Orleans on the West Bank of Jefferson Parish offers the chance to fish the same wildlife-filled bayous that pirate Jean Lafitte roamed almost 200 years ago. Groups of two to 100 people depart the Sea-Way Marina in Lafitte aboard Capt. Theophile Bourgeois's 24-foot boats, specially designed for shallow-water draft, and head deep into the bayou for fly- and spin-fishing for speckled trout, drum, and flounder. Charters depart at 5 a.m. (returning 11:30 a.m.) and 1 p.m. (returning at dark).

Overnight accommodations in a two-bedroom bed-and-breakfast Cajun cabin complete with optional personal chef and fishing trips are available.

CAPT. PHIL ROBICHAUX'S $$$$
Saltwater Guide Service
1842 Jean Lafitte Blvd., Lafitte
(504) 689-2006
www.rodnreel.com/captphil

Not far from the town of Lafitte, 30 minutes south of New Orleans, is the Barataria-Terrebonne Estuarine Complex, which contains 34 percent of the state's marshlands and is one of the largest, most dynamic estuary systems in the United States. Capt. Robichaux or one of his trained guides leads charter groups to find some of the best redfishing and speckled trout fishing around. Charters usually leave the dock between 6 and 6:30 am, and return between 1:30 and 2:30 pm. Price includes tackle, artificial baits, gas, oil, ice, fish cleaning, and rods & reels.

CITY PARK FISHING $
City Park, 1 Palm Dr.
(504) 482-4888
www.neworleanscitypark.com

Bass, catfish, and perch make their homes in the lagoons of City Park. A state freshwater fishing license is required. City Park's Big Bass Fishing Rodeo, the oldest freshwater fishing contest in the country, is held each spring. This popular event features Cajun music, barbecue, and trophies for the catch of the day.

FISHING GUIDE SERVICES $$$$
7301 Downman Rd.
(504) 243-2100
www.fishing-boating.com/fishingguide services

Anyone who promises a 10-fish minimum catch must be on to something good. Capt. A. D. "Dee" Geoghegan has more than 40 years' experience fishing the waters of southeast Louisiana and specializes in light-tackle saltwater fishing in Breton Sound, Chandelur Isle, and the Louisiana marsh aboard his 26-foot Privateer open-hull *Fish Stalker*. Cost is $350 for up to three persons, plus $40 each for gas, live bait, fish cleaning, and rental rods. Overnight accommodations with private baths and central heat/AC for up to eight are available.

FISHUNTER GUIDE SERVICE INC. $$$$
1905 Edenborn Ave., Metairie
(504) 837-0703, (800) 887-1385
www.fishunterguideservice.com

The father-son team of Capt. Nash Roberts III and Capt. Nash Roberts IV, both biologists, take anglers year-round for light-tackle fishing in the shallow (1 to 1.5 feet depth) interior marshes and bays that border New Orleans. The 21-foot Neumann Custom Marsh Max boat departs at safe light from Port Sulphur (on the West Bank of Jefferson Parish), returning at 2:30 p.m. Two three-bedroom/two-bath fishing camps, with complete kitchens and outside decks overlooking the marsh are available for overnight accommodations.

TEASER FISHING TEAM $$$$
2625 Fawnwood Dr., Marrero
(504) 341-4245
www.rodnreel.com/teaser

Capt. Mike Frenette, a three-decade fishing vet-eran, steers his new 36-foot *Contender* from Venice on the west bank of Jefferson Parish to the mouthwaters of the Mississippi River for blue marlin, blackfin, and big eye tuna, grouper, barracuda, trigger fish, and jack crevalle. Anglers with more domestic tastes can fish the inland marshes and passes for largemouth and striped bass, flounder, and speckled trout.

Daylong charters can accommodate up to six passengers. Overnight accommodations at the Teaser Clubhouse include snacks, nonalco-holic beverages, dinner buffet, breakfast, and in-house chef. Three-, five-, and seven-day pack-ages are available.

Golf

AUDUBON PARK GOLF COURSE
Audubon Park
6500 Magazine St.
(504) 212-5290
www.auduboninstitute.org/golf.html

This Uptown golf course combines more than a century of history with the latest in golf course design. The Denis Griffiths design features con-toured fairways, manicured Tif Eagle greens, four lagoons, and exquisite landscaping on a par 62, 4,220-yard layout set among 100-year-old oak trees.

The course is located just minutes from downtown New Orleans. Audubon Park is on the St. Charles Avenue streetcar line. Hours of opera-tion are Wed through Mon 11 a.m. until dusk, 7 a.m. until dusk the rest of the week.

BAYOU OAKS DRIVING RANGE
City Park, 1 Palm Dr.
(504) 483-9394
www.neworleanscitypark.com

This 74-stall driving range is open Mon noon to 8 p.m., Tues through Sun 7 a.m. to 8 p.m. Private lessons are available by appointment.

BAYOU OAKS GOLF COURSES
City Park, 1 Palm Dr.
(504) 483-9396
www.neworleanscitypark.com

Once the largest municipal golf facility in the South, City Park suffered major losses in Hurricane Katrina. Reopened in Sept. 13, 2008 after Katrina, City Park currently offers one 18-hole facility, the park's north course. Plans are in the works to eventually restore the other three courses.

LAKEWOOD COUNTRY CLUB
4801 General DeGaulle Dr.
(504) 373-5926
www.lakewoodgolf.com

"Lakewood is a great driving golf course—very tight [and] demands accuracy off the tee," Tom Watson is quoted as saying. Anyone eager to play in the footsteps of the legends—Watson, Jack Nicklaus, Seve Ballesteros, and Lee Trevino, among others—will want to check out this 7,000-yard Ron Garl-renovated course (originally designed by Robert Bruce Harris), which has hosted 26 PGA tour events. The championship 18-hole par 72 golf course, nestled between century-old oak and cypress trees, offers tight fairways and smooth, quick greens.

OAK HARBOR GOLF CLUB
201 Oak Harbor Blvd., Slidell
(985) 646-0110
oakharborgolf.com

The 6,885-yard layout of this "beauty and the beast," situated 2 miles from scenic Lake Pontchar-train and built in the tradition of PGA West, Oak Tree, and Kiawah Island courses, earned *Golf Digest*'s nomination for best new course when it opened in 1992. The Pete Dye-inspired Lee Schmitt design makes use of railroad ties and bulkheads around the many bayou waterways that intersect the layout, a worthy adversary to even scratch golfers, but plays a manageable 6,261 yards from the regular men's tees. Sound strategy is always a premium on this champion-ship course 20 minutes east of downtown New Orleans off I-10, as danger lurks in the form of water that comes into play on 12 of the holes.

Horseback Riding

EQUEST FARM
City Park, 1001 Filmore Ave.
(504) 483-9398
www.equestfarm.com
Hop into the saddle amid the oak trees of New Orleans' favorite park and learn the ropes of handling a horse. One-hour guided trail rides through the park cost $30. Horseback riding lessons are available as well at the stable on Filmore Street near the golf course. Classes are held year-round. Riding camps for children during holidays and evening lessons are available.

Tennis

CITY PARK TENNIS CENTER
City Park, 1 Palm Dr.
(504) 483-9383
www.neworleanscitypark.com
The largest public tennis facility in the South, the City Park Tennis Center has been named one of the top 25 municipal tennis facilities in the nation by *Tennis* magazine. As many as 70,000 people play tennis yearly on the center's 21 lighted hard and clay courts. The facility offers a number of programs for children and adults. Court rentals range from $7 to $10 per hour.

PARKS

Whether you find yourself sitting in front of the fireplace of a waterfront cabin, paddling a canoe down a moonlit swamp, or lounging in the limbs of an ancient oak tree, New Orleans area parks will make you feel like you've discovered where the South's natural charm originated.

A State of Bliss—State Parks

LOUISIANA STATE PARKS
Office of State Parks, P.O. Box 44426,
Baton Rouge 70804
(888) 677-1400
(877) 226-7652, reservations
www.lastateparks.com
Louisiana State Parks offer travelers the opportunity for overnight camping, hiking, and swimming. Five such sites—St. Bernard State Park in Violet, Bayou Segnette State Park in Westwego, Fairview-Riverside State Park in Madisonville, Fort Pike State Commemorative Area in the Rigolets, and Fontainebleau State Park in Mandeville—are located within an hour's drive of New Orleans.

All parks are open daily, year-round with staff members on call 24 hours. Improved campsites feature electricity and water; unimproved sites do not. Certain on-site facilities are closed seasonally, so call ahead. The number for the central system for making reservations for any state park facility is listed above.

i For a romantic rendezvous, why not make a date to meet under the thousand-year-old McDonogh Oak at City Park? It's easy to find. Just park at the Timken Center concessions building, cross the arcing stone bridge over the lagoon, take a left, and follow the path a short ways. The McDonogh Oak is on the right side of the path and identified by a small plaque.

BAYOU SEGNETTE STATE PARK
7777 Westbank Expressway
Westwego
(504) 736-7140, (888) 677-2296
Thirty minutes across the Mississippi River from New Orleans is an unusual blend of natural recreation and urban comfort. Swampland meets marsh, and nature enthusiasts can observe wildlife while children play in the wave pool. Facilities include 98 premium campsites, a massive group camp, playgrounds, picnic tables, pavilions, and a wave pool. A conference room rounds out the facility. Boat launches provide access to both fresh- and saltwater fishing with catches of bass, catfish, bream, redfish, and speckled trout.

Admission to the park is $1 per person. Camping is $18 per night. To get here, cross the Mississippi River Bridge to the Westbank Expressway, and continue west on US 90 to Westwego.

FAIRVIEW-RIVERSIDE STATE PARK
Off LA 22, Madisonville
(985) 845-3318, (888) 677-3247

North of New Orleans on the other side of Lake Pontchartrain, this park is a tranquil setting on the banks of the Tchefuncte River. The waterfront park is surrounded by mossy live oaks, piney woods, a cypress swamp, and the historic Otis House. Catches of bass, bluegill, bream, and white perch can be landed by boat or along the banks of the Tchefuncte. However, channel catfish, speckled trout, and crabs are more abundantly found where the river meets Lake Pontchartrain. Upstream the river is wide and free of obstacles for water-skiing. Accommodations include 81 improved campsites as well as 20 tent sites. For boaters, there is a public launch in Madisonville, less than 2 miles away and only a few minutes from the park by boat. For landlubbers there are picnic tables, grills, pavilions, and a playground.

Admission to the park is $1 per person. Camping is $16 to $18 per night for improved sites and $12 for tent sites.

FONTAINEBLEAU STATE PARK
LA 190, Mandeville
(985) 624-4443, (888) 677-3668

Just across Lake Pontchartrain from New Orleans is this 2,809-acre park, which has provided a much-needed urban escape for 50 years. The entry drive, with its stately live oaks, leads visitors past ruins of an old sugar mill, historic plantation, and brickyard. This lovely park is bordered on three sides by Lake Pontchartrain as well as the wetlands and woods of bayous Cane and Castine.

Located near the tail-end of the famed Mississippi Flyway, part of the North American continent's immense migratory corridor, the park's trails offer outstanding bird-watching. Facilities include 126 improved campsites, 200 unimproved sites, a primitive group camping area, three group camps, lodge, swimming pool, beach, picnic tables, grills, pavilions, sailboat ramp, playground, and restrooms. Cycle, hike, or horseback ride down 9 miles of the 31-mile Tammany Trace—an old railroad track converted into a paved trail which passes through the park. Fontainebleau also features a 1.25 mile nature trail for hiking.

Admission to the park is $1 per person. Camping is $12 per night for unimproved sites, $16 to $18 per night for improved sites.

ST. BERNARD STATE PARK
501 St. Bernard Hwy.
Braithwaite
(504) 682-2101, (888) 677-7823

Just 19 miles south the French Quarter in St. Bernard Parish, this is the only state park located next to the Mississippi River. The woods, surrounding wetlands, and man-made lagoon system give visitors the chance to get back to nature without venturing too far from the city. The park offers 51 improved campsites, a pool, a covered pavilion, a large grill, picnic tables, and restrooms. A clearly marked (but rather short) nature trail takes the hiker across rustic bridges and throughout the park.

There is no charge for admission to the park. Swimming is available May through Aug and costs $2. Campsites are $16 per night. To get here: Take I-10 east to LA 47 south, turn left on LA 46 through Violet and Poydras, then right on LA 39 South. Or, from the French Quarter, take North Rampart Street (LA 46) south through Violet and Poydras and then right on LA 39 south.

Look Out, It's the Feds— National Parks

JEAN LAFITTE NATIONAL HISTORICAL PARK AND PRESERVE
419 Decatur St.
(504) 589-2133
www.nps.gov/jela

There's only one national park in the New Orleans area, but it's everywhere. Jean Lafitte National Historical Park and Preserve, named after that rascally pirate-turned-patriot-turned-pirate, is composed of three parts: the Barataria Preserve on the West Bank near Crown Point, dedicated to the natural and cultural history of the region's uplands, swamps, and marshlands; the Chalmette

Battlefield, 6 miles southeast of New Orleans and the site of the 1815 Battle of New Orleans; and the New Orleans Visitor Center in the French Quarter's French Market, which interprets the history of New Orleans and Louisiana's Mississippi Delta region. Sit back, relax, and enjoy your federal tax dollars at work.

i Don't miss City Park's new five-acre sculpture garden featuring 60 works by major 20th-century European, American, Israeli, and Japanese artists, gifts from the Besthoff Foundation, combined with works from the New Orleans Museum of Arts permanent collection. The sculptures are among meandering footpaths, pedestrian bridges, lagoons, and Spanish moss-laden 200-year-old trees. Open Wed through Sun for free.

BARATARIA PRESERVE
LA 45, Crown Point
(504) 589-2330

The Barataria Preserve is dedicated to the culture of the people, past and present, who have made the delta their home, as well as the unique ecosystem that sustained them. It preserves a portion of that environment containing natural levee forests, bayous, swamps, and marshes. Though wild and teeming with wildlife, this wilderness is not pristine. Evidence of prehistoric human settlement, colonial farming, plantation agriculture, logging, commercial trapping, fishing, hunting, and oil and gas exploration overlay much of this former wilderness.

The preserve encompasses 20,000 acres of hardwood forest, cypress swamp, and freshwater marsh. Eight miles of hard-surface trails include a 2.5-mile boardwalk that winds through three distinct ecosystems—a cypress swamp, palmetto forest, and marsh. Natural history walks are conducted Sun through Fri at 1:30 p.m.; group tours of the park are available.

Nine miles of canoe trails, closed to motorized boats and accessible only by three canoe launch docks, will give you an up close and personal view of the swamps and marshes. Guided canoe treks take place some Saturdays, and moonlight canoeing is offered monthly on the night before and the night of the full moon, both by reservation only. Another nine miles of waterways are open to all boats. Canoe rentals are available just outside the park, and a number of public and private boat launches provide access for motorboats.

To get to the park: Cross the Mississippi River Bridge to the Westbank Expressway and exit at Barataria Boulevard (LA 45). Turn left and drive approximately 8 miles to reach the park.

CHALMETTE BATTLEFIELD
8606 St. Bernard Highway, Chalmette
(504) 281-0510

The Chalmette unit preserves one of the country's most significant battle sites, which saw a decisive American victory over the British at the end of the War of 1812. Adjacent to the battlefield is the Chalmette National Cemetery. Take a self-guided tour, which begins at the visitor center, where exhibits and an audiovisual program explains the importance of the battle. Next, follow the 1.5-mile tour road that features six stops incorporating various features of the battlefield. A free brochure tells about the significance of each stop.

Two additional structures in the park worth noting are the Chalmette Monument and Beauregard House. The cornerstone of the monument, dedicated to the American victory, was laid in January 1840 shortly after Andrew Jackson visited here to commemorate the 25th anniversary of the battle. Construction did not begin until 1855 and was completed in 1908. The Beauregard House, built 18 years after the battle, is a beautiful example of French-Louisiana architecture and is named for its last private owner, Judge René Beauregard.

KIDSTUFF

*R*iddle: What do you call a place where you can pet a stingray, visit a haunted dungeon, and have exotic animals eat out of your hand? *Answer:* New Orleans.

The Big Easy truly has earned the reputation of "sin city." (Yes, they even sell beer at kids' baseball games here, but only to adults.) For the most part, though, this is a town of close-knit families. And when we're not at one another's backyard crawfish boils and barbecues, we like to go out and have fun. Luckily, the city boasts an almost endless supply of natural wonders and even fun museums to capture any young person's—and parent's—imagination. The following is a list of interesting ways for kids to spend time in the Big Easy. But remember, in New Orleans, fun is like chocolate—even a little is still pretty delicious. And away we go. . .

(*Note:* A number of listings in the Attractions chapter may also be of interest for families.)

Price Code

Our price is based on admission for one adult.

$	$0 to $10
$$	$11 to $20
$$$	$21 to $50
$$$$	more than $50

MUSEUMS THAT AREN'T A DRAG

LOUISIANA CHILDREN'S MUSEUM $
420 Julia St.
(504) 523-1357
www.lcm.org

Strike a pose, then walk away and watch your shadow remain on the wall. "Make groceries" (local jargon for grocery shopping) in a pint-size supermarket with carts, produce, and a cash register. Dine in a five-star pretend restaurant. It's all everyday fare at this "please touch" imagination station in the Warehouse District, rated among the nation's top 10 children's museums by both *Parenting* and *Your Family* magazines. Discover more than 100 hands-on exhibits, daily art activities, and educational as well as entertainment programs for all ages.

Kids learn about the physics of simple machines by lifting their own weight with the help of a pulley, or discover the importance of fitness by climbing the Rock Wall or riding a bike with Mr. Bones in Body Works. Even toddlers get to climb, crawl, and explore in a playscape expressly for 1- to 3-year-olds.

This place is so much fun, they rent it out for grown-up parties at night. Really. Museum hours are Tues through Sat 9:30 a.m. to 4:30 p.m., Sun noon to 4:30 p.m. During summer months, the museum is open until 5 p.m. and also on Mon 9:30 a.m. to 5 p.m. All kids under 16 must be accompanied by an adult. To get there from Canal Street, take Magazine Street toward Uptown to Julia Street (about 9 blocks). Take a left on Julia Street, and the museum is up on the right.

MUSÉE CONTI (THE WAX MUSEUM) $
917 Conti St.
(504) 525-2605, (800) 233-5405
www.get-waxed.com

New Orleans has been called the most European city in America, and the Musée Conti is proof. Not because of its name, but its contents. Other cities tout wax museums whose biggest draw is a figure of George Burns. The Musée Conti, on the other hand, tells the tale of New Orleans and depicts everything from the city's founding to the legendary Battle of New Orleans, to the mysterious world of voodoo. Just for fun there's also the Haunted Dungeon, with more than 20 monsters.

The painstaking, European-style craftsmanship that went into creating this French Quarter facility is unparalleled in the United States. Ordinary beeswax was combined with a secret chemical compound and infused coloring to create the remarkably lifelike figures; each strand of human hair, imported from Italy, was individually attached with a special needle. All male figures were given full beards. Look closely and notice that even the clean-shaven ones have faint stubble. Only the most natural-looking, medical glass eyes were used. Note also the size of the figures. They may appear smaller than life-size, but they are accurately portrayed. The tradition of wax figures dates back to ancient Babylon and has continued throughout the ages. The Musée Conti is located on Conti Street in the French Quarter between Burgundy and Dauphine Streets. Don't miss it. The museum is open Mon, Fri and Sat 10 a.m. to 4 p.m. and for private appointments.

NEW ORLEANS FIRE DEPARTMENT MUSEUM AND EDUCATIONAL CENTER $
1135 Washington Ave.
(504) 658-4713
www.cityofno.com/pg-51-10-museum.aspx
Fighting fires was quite a challenge before the invention of the automobile and the telephone. Learn how they did it at the Fire Department Museum, housed in an authentic firehouse built in the 1850s. See a pre-Civil War hand-drawn ladder truck and fire alarm telegraph, as well as an authentic collection of firefighting equipment used over the last 150 years, all while picking up important pointers on fire safety.

The firefighters' valiant steeds once galloped through Uptown streets (then called the City of Lafayette) pulling a steam-driven pump made of gleaming brass atop a shiny red wooden chassis. Later known as Chalmette #23, the station in the Roaring '20s was the city's last to trade in its horses for motorized transport and remained a viable firehouse for another 50 years.

Admission is free (donations are accepted) but tours are by appointment only. Call ahead. To get to the museum take the St. Charles Avenue streetcar to Washington Avenue and walk up Washington toward the Mississippi River past Commander's Palace Restaurant, about 5 blocks.

RIVERTOWN MUSEUMS

A 4-block riverside stretch of Williams Boulevard in Kenner, 25 minutes from downtown New Orleans, is home to an impressive cluster of modest-size family-friendly museums: the Toy Train Museum; the Mardi Gras Museum; the Science Center; the Planetarium and Mega Dome Cinema and the Cannes Brulee Native American Center. The Children's Castle and the Rivertown Repertory Theatre are also located here.

Spend a half day exploring some or all of Rivertown's museums and Children's Castle (www.rivertownkenner.com). Most of the museums are open Tues through Sat 9 a.m. to 5 p.m. The Children's Castle is open only on Saturday mornings and the Planetarium's hours vary. If you plan to visit all the Rivertown museums, purchase a budget-stretching pay-one-price pass, available at the Rivertown Welcome Center (415 Williams Blvd.). To get here take I–10 west to the Williams Boulevard exit. Turn left (south) on Williams Boulevard and follow the street all the way down until you cross the railroad tracks. Free parking is available.

CANNES BRULEE NATIVE AMERICAN CENTER $
415 Williams Blvd., Kenner
(504) 468-7231
Cannes Brulee is Rivertown's most distinctive museum featuring traditional artwork and crafts created by Native Americans from Louisiana and the Southeastern region of the United States. On exhibit are jewelry, tools, weapons, basketry, clay pottery, woodcarvings, musical instruments, children's toys, dreamcatchers, paintings, moccasins, and a dugout cypress pirogue.

On some Saturdays, these artists give demonstrations of the traditional methods used to create these items. Call for a schedule. Cannes Brulee was the name given to the area by early European explorers. Meaning "burnt cane," the Europeans so dubbed the area after coming

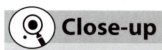 **Close-up**

Bugging Out: The New Insectarium

Did you know that bugs are the largest group of animals on earth? Learn that and a lot more at the new Audubon Insectarium, which has received the industry's highest honor, the Thea Award for Outstanding Achievement in a Science Center. Housed in the historic U.S. Customs House near the foot of Canal Street, this interactive museum offers the chance to see things from a bug's eye view in the Life Underground exhibit. Here visitors are "shrunk" to insect size, courtesy of an over-sized setting and giant animatronic bugs.

See hundreds of beautiful butterflies flit about in the Japanese butterfly garden, Watch the fun high-definition film *Awards Night* (featuring the voices of Joan Rivers and Brad Garrett) about the outstanding achievements of certain insect superstars. In the museum's working husbandry lab, visitors can see a butterfly emerge from its chrysalis and learn all about how insects grow and reproduce. In the Field Camp, an entomologist guides kids and adults through up-close live insect encounters.

And if all that isn't enough, in the Tiny Termite Café, visitors can snack on various bugs (really!), such as a fried cricket with apple and a dab of cream cheese on a cracker.

The museum's Flea Market gift shop is choke full of insect-themed items, many unique to the insectarium.

The insectarium is at 423 Canal St. Hours are Tues through Sun 10 a.m. to 5 p.m. (Last tickets are sold at 4 p.m. and advance ticket purchases are recommended. Call (504) 410-BUGS (2847) or (800) 774-7394. For more information, visit www.auduboninstitute.org.

---

across Native Americans who would cut and burn river cane to help drive out small game.

CHILDREN'S CASTLE $
503 Williams Blvd., Kenner
(504) 468-7231
Opened in 1995, the Children's Castle is one of several attractions in Kenner's historic Rivertown district. The area is mostly made up of museums (all of which are worth visiting), but the Children's Castle is where the art of live performance reigns supreme. Shows featuring musicians, magicians, puppets, and storytelling are presented every Sat morning. Shows are at 11:30 a.m. Call for reservations.

THE MARDI GRAS MUSEUM $
415 Williams Blvd., Kenner
(504) 468-7231
Miniature float replicas, elaborate costumes, giant walking figures, and a huge papier-mâché king cake make a great introduction to Mardi Gras, dubbed the biggest free show on earth. The Mardi Gras Museum brings Carnival to life year-round with an extensive array of memorabilia, photographs, videos, and costumes. Visitors step into Mardi Gras in a street-scene reproduction complete with all the sights and sounds of New Orleans' most popular party. Self-guided tours include the 20-minute Richard Dreyfus-narrated video *Farewell to the Flesh*, as well as 13 other videos shown throughout the museum that highlight the traditions of Mardi Gras. Live costume-making and float-building demonstrations are scheduled periodically.

i If you're planning to take the kids to the Rivertown museums listed in this chapter (and you should), visit their Web site, www.rivertownkenner.com, to find out about special events taking place while you're here. The site also offers games for the kids!

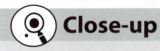 **Close-up**

City Park

Mention City Park to locals and watch their eyes light up as they recall childhood thrills atop the flying horses, teenage revelry in Tad Gormley Stadium, or, perhaps, a lover's first kiss beneath a thousand-year-old oak tree. The French Quarter may be this town's center, but City Park is its heart.

New Orleanians have gathered beneath its canopy of live oaks—so named because the species stays green year-round—since the area was part of the Allard Sugar Plantation in the 1700s. Actually it was even before that, when the Accolapissa and Biloxi Indians, who traded along the banks of adjacent Bayou St. John, made their homes in the then-swampy oak-filled forest.

The park served as the focal point of Creole passions in the 18th and 19th centuries and was the site of many gentlemen's affairs d'honneur, or duels. The practice of defending one's (or a loved one's) honor with swords was so common among Creoles that duel listings appeared in local newspapers, much like today's sports matchups. Though the practice may seem barbaric, it was considered quite civilized. The pair fenced, and when blood was drawn the matter was settled. The most popular dueling spot was beneath what was appropriately dubbed the Dueling Oaks.

Americans began arriving in droves in the early 1800s following the Louisiana Purchase. Like the ostentatious designs of their Garden District homes, the Americans' contribution to dueling—the use of pistols—seemed simply over the top to Creole sensibilities. By 1890 dueling in the park was outlawed.

Women today might be hard-pressed to find a man willing, much less able, to draw a sword for their honor, but they can still find the Dueling Oaks. They're located northeast of the park's New Orleans Museum of Art on Dueling Oak Drive, among one of the largest collections of mature live oaks in the world, 250 of which are registered with the Live Oak Society. The eldest of these ancient trees is the McDonogh Oak, named for the philanthropist who bequeathed the park's original 100-acre tract to the city in 1850. The tree is approximately 1,000 years old.

PLANETARIUM AND MEGA DOME CINEMA
2020 4th St., Kenner
(504) 468-7231
This state-of-the-art planetarium and observatory features narrated sky shows and laser light extravaganzas. Hours and shows vary. The Mega Dome Cinema is where dinosaurs and safari animals come to life on a giant screen. Shows change periodically. Call for times.

SCIENCE CENTER $
409 Williams Blvd., Kenner
(504) 468-7231
The center is geared to kids age six and older and offers hands-on exhibits centered on science as it

is used in daily living, such as hurricane tracking (which qualifies as a daily living situation in New Orleans), human physiology, and the "secret science" found inside walls.

TOY TRAIN MUSEUM $
519 Williams Blvd., Kenner
(504) 468-7231
Adjacent to the Illinois Central Gulf railroad tracks is this turn-of-the-20th-century building chock-full of hundreds of model trains, some dating to the 1800s. There's even a train playscape for the little ones, featuring a half-scale caboose playhouse, a make-believe circus, a train engine,

Over the last 150 years, this tract of land has evolved into the fifth-largest urban park in the United States, encompassing 1,500 acres and boasting magnificent architecture and gardens, delightful play areas for the city's children, and topflight recreation facilities, including impressive golf, tennis, and track centers, plus two football stadiums, softball diamonds, soccer fields, and riding stables. All the while, this almost magical place has never ceased to spark people's imaginations.

In 1907 the Peristyle, an elegant open-air dance floor, was built. This Greek-style colonnade was designed to frame the view of the moonlit lagoon while graceful Creole couples waltzed the night away.

If botanical gardens are to plants what museums are to art, then City Park's version of horticulture is a masterpiece. When it opened in 1936 during the Depression, the botanical gardens became the city's first public garden featuring a classical combination of art and nature. Art Deco-inspired fountains, ponds, and sculpture with both mythological and natural themes punctuate the seasonal splashes of color produced by native botanical favorites. Exotic imports in this lush 10-acre site were set aside for "the indulgence of man and nature." Much of the garden was created by Works Progress Administration workers following the artistic vision of architect Richard Koch, landscape architect William Wiedorn, and sculptor Enrique Alferez.

One of the park's most popular draws is the Carousel Gardens amusement area, home to one of the few remaining wooden carousels in the country. The masterwork of famed carousel carvers Looff and Carmel, this turn-of-the-20th-century wonder is listed on the National Register of Historic Places, and its extensive 1988 restoration garnered nationwide attention and praise from the National Trust for Historic Preservation. But to locals it's simply the flying horses, a part of childhood for so many. When the carousel is not being rented out for kids' birthday parties, it's often the site of grown-ups-only cocktail socials.

But why in a city that has so many places to party would adults choose a child's merry-go-round? Perhaps it has to do with the memory of a time when they were so little they had to be lifted into the saddle. Then the music would play and they'd feel the breeze on their faces while flying high through the air on their beautiful wooden steeds, as City Park taught yet another generation what it feels like to be alive.

and the Dixie Diner, where youngsters can enjoy a pretend meal.

THE GREAT OUTDOORS

AUDUBON AQUARIUM OF
THE AMERICAS $$
1 Canal St.
(504) 581-4629, (800) 774-7394
www.auduboninstitute.org

Enter the riverfront aquarium's underwater world that includes more than one million gallons of fresh- and saltwater exhibits.

Stroll through a sunlit tunnel surrounded on three sides by a Caribbean reef (sort of like snorkeling without getting wet), where the colors of the coral are reflected in a dazzling collection of tropical fish. Check out two of the aquarium's celebrities, Southern sea otters Buck and Emma, and watch them get fed at 2 p.m. daily. Visit the Rockhopper penguins waddling around on their big orange feet. And, if you dare, touch a cownose stingray in the Adventure Island exhibit.

The aquarium is open Tues through Sun 10 a.m. to 5 p.m. The Audubon Institute offers discounts to individuals who wish to visit more than one of its four attractions—Audubon Zoo, Aquarium of the Americas, IMAX Theater, and the new Insectarium.

ℹ For those traveling with the newly potty trained, who sometimes can't wait: The only public restrooms in the French Quarter (not inside a "customers only" business) are conveniently found at the back of the building that houses the Café du Monde on Decatur Street and on the second floor of Jax Brewery.

AUDUBON PARK $

6500 St. Charles Ave.
(504) 861-2537, (800) 774-7394
www.auduboninstitute.org

Originally a plantation, this 400-acre park has been a part of New Orleanians' lives since it was the site of the 1884 World's Fair. It features shimmering lagoons, fragrant gardens, recreation areas, an array of local wildlife, and 4,000 live oaks and other majestic trees. Cross Magazine Street and discover the Audubon Zoo.

AUDUBON ZOO $–$$

6500 Magazine St.
(504) 581-4629, (800) 774-7394
www.auduboninstitute.org

Check out the tree house and rope bridge on Monkey Hill, the city's highest point, built by WPA workers to show local kids what a hill looks like. Or walk past an ancient Meso-American bas-relief glyph of a jaguar while spider monkeys swing on vines overhead and a jabiru stork clicks its beak looking for a mate—all in the shadow of a Mayan temple pyramid. No, you're not in an Indiana Jones movie, but rather Audubon Zoo's Jaguar Jungle. The 1.5-acre exhibit uses a mix of zoology and history to tell the story of Central America's exotic animals and Mayan civilization.

Then visit the 58-acre zoo's popular Louisiana Swamp Exhibit, which showcases the state's indigenous wildlife, including a rare white alligator, as well as human life on the bayou. Both exhibits underscore a trend among the nation's progressive zoos to focus on education in addition to entertainment.

Audubon is consistently rated among the nation's best zoos and features 1,500 animals representing 360 species—many of them rare or endangered—in natural habitat exhibits. Exhibits include the Komodo Dragon, Reptile Encounter, Tropical Bird House, World of Primates, and Butterflies in Flight, as well as those devoted to animals of North and South America, Africa, and Asia.

The zoo opens Tues through Sun 10 a.m. to 5 p.m. The Audubon Institute offers discounts to individuals who wish to visit more than one of its four attractions—Audubon Zoo, Aquarium of the Americas, IMAX Theater, and the Insectarium.

CITY PARK $

1 Palm Dr.
(504) 482-4888
www.neworleanscitypark.com

More than a century ago, philanthropist John McDonogh bestowed to the City of New Orleans a 100-acre tract of land in Mid-City, which has evolved into the fifth-largest municipal park in the country. Today the park encompasses 1,500 acres and accommodates 10 million annual visitors. Enjoy City Park by just sitting under beautiful moss-draped live oak trees, eating an ice-cream cone, and feeding the ducks. Or check out the Carousel Gardens amusement area and Storyland play area, two of the best reasons for visiting the park with children.

Since the turn of the last century, children have enjoyed the "flying horses" of the amusement area's antique carousel. One of only 100 wooden merry-go-rounds left in the United States and the last in Louisiana, the carousel is listed on the National Register of Historic Places. Other rides include two miniature antique trains, a Ferris wheel, bumper cars, a 40-foot fun slide, the Lady Bug roller coaster, tilt-a-whirl, the toy helicopter ride, and antique cars. Open Thurs through Sun, hours vary. Ride tickets are purchased separately in addition to admission, or visitors can purchase a wristband good for unlimited rides all day.

Storyland, a fairy tale theme park rated one of the top 10 playgrounds in the country by *Child* magazine, gives kids the chance to climb into the mouth of Pinocchio's whale, have a pretend sword fight aboard Captain Hook's ship, or fish in the Little Mermaid's Pond, all beneath the approving gaze of Mother Goose as she flies amid the limbs of ancient oaks.

Storyland is open Tues through Sun. Call or check the Web site for varying seasonal hours. The park also offers recreational activities such as canoeing, fishing, tennis, and horseback riding. (See Attractions and Activities chapter for details.)

GLOBAL WILDLIFE CENTER $-$$
26389 Louisiana Hwy. 40, Folsom
(985) 796-3585
www.globalwildlife.com

Where else can you feed a giraffe? The Global Wildlife Center is a 900-acre nonprofit home to more than 3,000 free-roaming animals from all over the world. It's the largest free-range facility in the country. Zebras, antelope, camels, bison, and other animals have the lay of the land while visitors are "contained" in covered wagons pulled by tractors. During the 90-minute tour, a guide entertains and educates visitors about the different species as well as wildlife preservation. The really fun part, though, comes when the wagon stops and you get to feed the animals.

Global Wildlife Center is open daily year-round; always call ahead for wagon tour times and availability. The center is located about one hour north of New Orleans. To get here take I-10 west to the Causeway exit. Take Causeway north and proceed over the Causeway toll bridge to St.

Tammany Parish and I-12. Go West on I-12 to exit 47 (Robert exit). Turn right on Highway 445 (north) and proceed for approximately 11 miles to Highway 40 east. Turn right, and the park entrance is 1.5 miles down on the left.

WOLDENBERG RIVERFRONT PARK
Riverfront

It's always good to know where the wide-open spaces are when traveling with kids. Adjacent to the aquarium and IMAX Theater, these 17 acres of urban green space, public artwork, and brick pathways offer an up-close view of the Mississippi River and, perhaps more importantly, a place to relax while the kids run around when visiting the French Quarter. Festivals and open-air concerts are held here throughout the year.

Note that some parts of the park may still be under construction, call first to see what areas are open. To get to the park: Take I-10 east to the Chalmette exit (LA 47). Head south to St. Bernard Highway and turn right.

i Definitely take the kids out for beignets and cafe au lait (or chocolate milk) at Café du Monde on Decatur Street in the French Quarter. Then duck around back to watch those deep-fried taste treats being made through the cafe's display window.

THE ARTS

New Orleans abounds with great artists surrounded by a population that truly understands and appreciates their work. However, unlike other communities of artists, these probably never come in contact with a bow, a leotard, or a period costume. Instead they take food and with inspired levels of cunning and craft create the magic of barbecue shrimp, bread pudding, or a hot roast beef po-boy.

And that's just the folk art.

Among the most accomplished of these truly brilliant artists whose work touches millions of waistlines each year would be such luminaries as Paul Prudhomme, Susan Spicer, and just about everybody's mama. As a result, the Big Greasy may not have quite as developed a fine arts scene as, say, cities where people think that eating is something you do just to survive.

If you are looking for the New Orleans arts scene, you will find that it is small. However, it is full of artists who have been forced to find ways to reach and cultivate an audience of people who would just as soon go out to dinner. Often performances are accompanied by open discussions between musicians or dancers and audience members about the opera or ballet that they've both just experienced.

Professional artists regularly bring their work to schools, facing, perhaps for the first time, the challenge of figuring out how to move a child. The city's orchestra, which is owned and operated by its musicians, regularly performs under less than ideal circumstances when it could just as easily never leave the comfort of the Mahalia Jackson Theater. But then it would never reach that audience who will only hear music played out in the suburbs or in a park. Yes, the New Orleans art scene is small—but it's full of inspiration.

DANCE

DELTA FESTIVAL BALLET
3351 Severn Ave., Suite 304A
Metairie
(504) 888-0931

Delta Festival Ballet is Louisiana's only resident professional dance company, with a school and a junior company. The company performs at various venues from its New Orleans home to Reserve, Louisiana, and Biloxi, Mississippi. With more than 50 ballets and divertissements in its repertoire, ranging from 19th-century classics to rock ballets, Delta Festival is also the official dance company of the New Orleans Opera Association. The company's annual Christmas presentation of *The Nutcracker* in conjunction with the Louisiana

Philharmonic Orchestra is a local favorite. Ticket prices are approximately $10 to $40, depending on performance. The box office is open Mon through Fri 10 a.m. to 4 p.m. Call for the performance schedule.

NEW ORLEANS BALLET ASSOCIATION
1 Lee Circle
(504) 522-0996
www.nobadance.com

The core of the ballet association's programs at the Mahalia Jackson Theater of the Performing Arts in Armstrong Park is the performance series called Mainstage Season—the presentation of professional guest companies showcasing a diverse range of dance from classical to modern. Past performers include the Jose Limon Dance

Company, the Pittsburgh Ballet Theatre, Maria Benitez Teatro Flamenco, the Twyla Tharp Dance Company, and the Urban Bush Women. The association offers a full season of performances and a series of one-hour lecture/demonstrations for students. Each performance is followed by the popular INFORMance, a free dialogue with artistic directors or company members, open to all ticket holders. Tickets start around $28. Students and seniors get a $7 discount. The box office is open Mon through Thurs 8:30 a.m. to 5 p.m. and Fri 8:30 a.m. to 2:30 p.m.

FILM

THE NEW ORLEANS FILM FESTIVAL
900 Camp St.
(504) 309-6633
www.neworleansfilmfest.com
The NOFF is best known for its annual film festival (see Annual Events and Festivals), which exhibits more than 130 movies and videos, many of which are produced by regional artists. Throughout the year the society also presents multi-cultural film and video screenings, industry workshops, and lectures by guest speakers. Screenings, held at various venues around town, include a French Film festival each summer and an Italian film festival each spring. Call for dates and times.

THE PRYTANIA THEATRE
5339 Prytania St.
(504) 891-2787
www.theprytania.com
The Prytania is the only single-screen neighborhood movie theater left in the state; it's the kind of place where a person (not a machine) often answers the phone and movie times out front are written with a marker on posterboard. The original Prytania Theatre was built on this Uptown corner in 1915, and before that movies were shown here under a tent. Reel old-timers remember the early days of talkies, when the streetcar would pass in front and make the sound record skip. The movie house went through various incarnations until a new local owner saved it from the wrecking ball

in 1997. Today, the theater shows "Hollywood movies with an art flair," which generally means those predicted to be big at the box office. This recently renovated landmark, which boasts new seating, a renovated lobby, a new huge screen with state-of-the-art sound and projection, also cohosts the New Orleans Film Festival, the French Film Festival, and the Jewish Film Festival.

ZEITGEIST THEATRE EXPERIMENTS
1618 Oretha Castle Haley Blvd.
(504) 827-5858, (504) 352-1150
www.zietgeistinc.net
Zeitgeist Theatre Experiments is a volunteer, nonprofit, cultural arts organization offering alternative art exhibits in a variety of disciplines as well as an odd assortment of independent films in an intimate 100-seat theater. From *The Girl Next Door*, about the trials and tribulations of a rising porn star, to a documentary on a jazz great, *Louis Prima: The Wildest!*, this is the place to find offbeat cinema.

GALLERIES

French Quarter

ANGELA KING GALLERY
241 Royal St.
(504) 524-8211
www.angelakinggallery.com
Angela King's airy track-lit, antique marble-floored gallery stands out from the pack with its remarkable range of contemporary art. The works of at least 20 American, English, and European artists can be found on exhibit at any given time. Visitors could find the vivid renderings of Peter Max, who regularly shows his pop-culture acrylics, or the extraordinary surrealist paintings of Raymond Douillet. There's beautiful human-form Lucite sculptures by Frederick Hart, as well as the abstract expressionist sports impressions of LeRoy Neiman, and M. L. Snowden's meditations on nature in bronze. Angela King Gallery is open Mon through Sat 10 a.m. to 5 p.m. and Sun 11 a.m. to 5 p.m.

BEE GALLERIES FEATURING MARTIN LABORDE
319 Chartres St.
(504) 587-7117
www.beegalleries.com

Years ago artist Martin Laborde stood at the top of an ancient Mayan pyramid in Mexico and had what he describes as a "mystical experience." The result was Bodo, a cartoonish, pointy-hatted character in wizard's robes who flies, floats, and glides across midnight canvases, like a child on a dream journey. Sometimes he takes along a dog. "Bodo is what I want to be," says this longtime favorite New Orleans artist who enjoys a deeply loyal following (his murals adorn the exterior wall of the Upperline restaurant Uptown). LaBorde's international following is matched only by the many awards he has garnered, including the prestigious Pushkin Medal of Honor from the Hermitage Museum in Leningrad.

BRYANT GALLERIES
316 Royal St.
(504) 525-5584, (800) 844-1994
www.bryantgalleries.com

"Art is the pouring of all your knowledge, your culture, your religion, and your moral philosophy into building aesthetic pleasure," says renowned artist Juan Medina. "The more universal your culture, so it will be with your art."

For years collectors throughout the United States and Europe have been mesmerized by the complexity of Medina's graphics, based on his interests in philosophy, science, and religion. And a visit to this gallery is good chance to view the artist's work.

Upstairs, visitors can explore one of the numerous rotating exhibits of guest artists hosted by the gallery. Ed Dwight's negative-space sculpture of jazz legends makes it look as though seemingly disconnected parts of Satchmo's hand, trumpet, and face are floating in air. Glass artist Martha Wolf meantime offers a menagerie of fanciful animals—mostly lions and gators and elks, oh my!—she created by using heat (and a bit of imagination) to melt pieces of colored glass.

FREDERICK GUESS STUDIOS
910 Royal St.
(504) 581-4596
www.fredrickguessstudio.com

What a nice flip of the coin it is to walk past a Royal Street gallery and see an artist through a pair of open French doors, sitting at his easel, brushes in hand, working on his newest creation. Artist/owner Fredrick Guess doesn't mind the ebb and flow of people while he works in his sunny gallery of brilliantly colorful New Orleans mindscapes—his favorite subject. In fact, the inquisitive interruptions help bring the New Orleans newcomer back down to earth and helps him see new possibilities in whichever canvas happens to be propped on the wooden easel. Ask him about how he chooses his expressive colors. Guess is likely to answer by mixing a few acrylics on his palette with a fingertip, then smudging it on a piece of paper to show off the results. Concentration indeed seems the least of this artist's concerns as you marvel at the contemporary impressionism Guess lends his Creole cottages, Carnival balls, Mardi Gras Indians, voodoo altars, and French Quarter moments.

i Want to know what's going on this week? Check the critics' picks and pans, not to mention the weekly arts and entertainment calendar, in the "Lagniappe" section of Friday's *Times-Picayune* and in *Gambit Weekly* on Monday.

A GALLERY FOR FINE PHOTOGRAPHY
241 Chartres St.
(504) 563-1313
www.agallery.com

Joshua Mann Pailet's paradise for photography lovers moved in 2003 to this softly lighted location, but the venue remains a favorite haunt for collectors searching for a rare print by lens pioneers such as Henri Cartier-Bresson, Robert Doisneau, and Eduard Steichen. (In case you were wondering, Cartier-Bresson's classic 1932 photo-

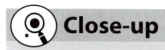 **Close-up**

Artist Gets Fired Up

The furnace at Studio Inferno blazes at 2,300 degrees to melt the recycled glass artist Mitchell Gaudet uses to create his colorful New Orleans-inspired art pieces. Red hot pepper necklaces, cobalt-colored representations of New Orleans art deco water meter covers, fleurs de lis in a rich orange hue. They can be found among other pieces that reflect the city more in attitude, such as the whimsical curly-armed monkeys hanging in a chain from the ceiling of the studio's gallery, or the sensual male and female human forms.

"New Orleans' cultural gumbo of people and customs, music and Carnival, has always been a strong inspiration," said Gaudet, who founded his hot glass studio and artist space in the old World Bottling Company warehouse in 1991. "Each piece reflects the distinct flavor of our city and is designed to bring a little bit of Southern elegance and decadence into your home."

This is an excellent place for visitors to find affordable pieces of art to bring home, especially if they are in town right before Christmas or Mother's Day when the studio runs its two big sales of the year.

The studio also features work space of a number of other artists who create and sell their work there, including paintings, ceramics and custom lamps.

If planning to visit, call ahead and find out when Gaudet will be working with glass, as visitors are welcome to watch the process.

Studio Inferno is at 3000 Royal St. in the Bywater neighborhood, just downriver from Faubourg Marigny. Hours are Mon through Sat 10 a.m. to 4 p.m. and by appointment. Call (888) 875-1882.

graph titled "Behind the Gare, St.-Lazare, Paris" today fetches a cool $175,000. By comparison, Steichen's 1906 "The Flatiron" seems almost a steal at $12,500.) Here Herman Leonard's timeless takes on jazz legends like Louis Armstrong, Billie Holiday, Duke Ellington, and Dexter Gordon can be found alongside Yousuf Karsh's 1958 photograph of Robert Frost.

More than 5,000 photographs including museum-quality salt prints, daguerreotypes, and panoramas join rotating exhibits, such as E. J. Bellocq's "Storyville Portraits: 1911–1913" and Sandra Russell Clark's tour de force of old New Orleans cemeteries. Vintage photogravures include those from the legendary Harriman Alaska Expedition of 1899, as well as 19th-century North American Indians. The first floor also features a selection of art photography books covering the American and French styles, jazz, the South, even truck stops found on the hard road of life.

Upstairs is a second-floor gallery of exhibits of contemporary photographers including signed-and-numbered prints by Annie Leibowitz and the late Helmut Newton. Josephine Sacabo's "Ophelia's Garden" offers an ethereal collection of dreamscapes writer Stephanie Mallarme has described as "an inner mural to protect herself from the brilliant indiscretions of the afternoon." The works of other photography legends found throughout the 4,000-square-foot establishment include Gordon Parks, Scavullo, and Eisenstaedt. The gallery also has a user-friendly Web site that enables visitors to check its complete inventory by artist, medium, subject, and price (after registering with your e-mail address and a password).

KURT E. SCHON, LTD.
510 St. Louis St.
(504) 524-5462
There isn't a blue dog or red cat to be found in

this showcase of 17th, 18th, and 19th-century artwork. For four decades the Schon gallery has specialized in Victorian art—paintings that reflect the high standards of quality, strength, and professionalism upheld by the influential Royal Academy, which flourished during the reign of Queen Victoria from 1837 to 1901. In 1966 the gallery began collecting Barbizon paintings, which originated in a small village in the Fountainbleau forest. There, in 1825, a small group of artists broke with 300 years of tradition and began painting landscapes in a new way. Examples of Schon's original collection can now be found in museums around the world. In case you hadn't guessed, this gallery is no place for dilettantes.

LA BELLE GALERIE & THE BLACK ART COLLECTION
309 Chartres St.
(504) 529-3080
This 9,000-square-foot building is purportedly the largest gallery in the United States featuring African-American art. Permanent displays include paintings and limited-edition prints by local and national artists, antique African artifacts, music-related photographs, and official Mardi Gras posters and Jazz Festival prints. The gallery also offers custom framing and shipping worldwide. A 3,000-square-foot exhibition space upstairs is available for social or business gatherings.

i Can't figure out what that artist is trying to say? Free (with admission) tours of the New Orleans Museum of Art's permanent collection and special exhibitions are conducted by knowledgeable docents at 11 a.m. and 2 p.m. daily except on Thurs.

MICHALOPOULOS
617 Bienville St.
(504) 558-0505
www.michalopoulos.com
The almost psychedelically distorted depictions of French Quarter and Uptown architecture seen in James Michalopoulos's acrylics, oils, and serigraphs in bright primary colors can put a discerning smile on the face of even the most jaded been-there-seen-that collector of unique contemporary art. His expressionistic and "gestural' style seem to make his houses breathe and move like the people who inhabit them. Over the years many have tried to emulate his style, but none have succeeded in nailing the essence of New Orleans as captured by Michalopoulos's linear-defying brush. In addition to architectural renderings, his subjects include landscapes, automobiles, and figures. Michalopoulos, thrice commissioned to create the official poster for the New Orleans Jazz and Heritage Festival, also has prints and posters available of his works.

RODRIGUE STUDIO
721 Royal St.
(504) 581-4244, (800) 899-4244
www.georgerodrigue.com
The Blue Dog is everywhere at this gallery, the New Orleans home of artist George Rodrigue's yellow-eyed, cobalt-blue-with-white-snout canine. She appears in all of his paintings, sitting in the same position and with the same expression. *People* magazine described it as "the stunned look of Wile E. Coyote." The been-there-done-that Blue Dog is the Cajun artist's humorous canvas mascot and appears in the foreground of Acadian shacks (Tee George's Cabin), draped in an American flag cape (*My Security Blanket*), and decked out in a tuxedo and shoulder-to-shoulder with a woman with long flowing hair (*Wendy and Me*). The 65-year-old New Iberia native also folds New Orleans into his paintings. Sometimes the pooch du jour fronts a trio of felines in Carnival purple, green, and gold (*Mardi Gras Cats*) or is adorned in Rexlike regal red velvet (*Mardi Gras '96*).

In his newest collection of landscapes, Rodrigue uses intense oils and vivid acrylics (some without Blue Dog!).

Warehouse District

ARTHUR ROGER GALLERY
432 Julia St.
(504) 522-1999
www.arthurrogergallery.com

Combining the works of established local artists such as Elemore Morgan, George Dureau, and Francis Pavy with a show by New York artist Peter Halley was original enough to make this one of the Warehouse District's most prominent galleries. It also earned Arthur Roger numerous awards and recognitions, including one from the Art Market Guide, as "a relatively new hybrid: a gallery that retains its regional flavor while showing enough established artists to have a national identity."

CONTEMPORARY ARTS CENTER
900 Camp St.
(504) 528-3805
www.cacno.org

Anchoring the Warehouse Arts District is the CAC, established in 1976 by a group of artists who recognized the city's desperate need for space in which to showcase alternative and experimental works. The center has no permanent collection; five rotating exhibits each year by local and international artists present a wide range of genres. The main Lupin Foundation Gallery on the second floor and three smaller first-floor galleries provide the 10,000-square-foot center with ample show space, especially for its multiple exhibits.

HERIARD-CIMINO GALLERY
440 Julia St.
(504) 525-7300
www.heriardcimino.com

Mid-career and nationally established Louisiana, Miami, and New York artists have found a home away from home at this hip Warehouse District venue specializing in mostly abstract and conceptual painting and photography. Opened in 1997 by Robert Heriard and Jeanne Cimino, this gallery represents such well-known artists as Carlos Betancourt, Michel Alexis, Brian Borrello, and Paul Campbell.

JONATHAN FERRERA GALLERY
400 Julia St.
(504) 522-5471
www.jonathanferreragallery.com

During a recent visit, a Dan Tague exhibit titled "Cost of War/Price of Freedom" featured super-sized, thought-provoking Giclée prints of battlefield soldiers and tanks created out of U.S. currency, and Skylar Fein's opened metal briefcase full of identical little sheep all facing the same direction. If you like your art edgy and rife with subtle (or not-so-subtle) political and social commentary, you'll likely find this gallery a contemporary breath of avant-garde air. Elsewhere the gallery's well-known "No Dead Artists" exhibit each year in September is a showcase for mostly local, up-and-coming photographers, painters, sculptors, and mixed-media artists to strut their stuff while leaving little doubt that even in a traditional city like New Orleans there is ample room for "the shock of the new."

LEMIEUX GALLERIES
332 Julia St.
(504) 522-5988
www.lemieuxgalleries.com

Years ago during a first-ever visit, it was Honduran artist Luz Maria Lopez's bold, colorful canvases bursting with ancient Mayan symbolism which beckoned this art lover to this intimate gallery specializing in contemporary Louisiana and Third Coast artists. Besides Lopez, other artists represented by LeMeiux include self-taught painter Leslie Staub and her whimsical, plaster-icon framed drawings from her children's book, *Whoever You Are,* and Shirley Rabe Masinter's realistic urban landscapes in watercolors and oils. LeMieux also represents sculptors Kim Bernadas, Kinzey Branham, Mark Derby, Sara Moczygemba, and Sybille Reretti.

i Most French Quarter and Warehouse District galleries take part in coordinated openings the first Saturday of each month from 6 to 9 p.m.

Uptown

CAROL ROBINSON GALLERY

840 Napoleon Ave.

(504) 895-6130

www.carolrobinsongallery.com

Take a streetcar ride down St. Charles Avenue to Napoleon Avenue. Then walk to this restored turn-of-the-20th-century, two-story house on the corner of Napoleon and Magazine Streets. Established in 1980, this gallery represents the works of regional, national, and international artists with ties to New Orleans in oil and watercolor paintings, ceramics, sculpture, photography, and glass. The gallery's goal is to showcase diversity in art in a relaxed and friendly atmosphere. Visitors are encouraged to take their time viewing the sizable collection.

THE DARKROOM

1927 Sophie Wright Place

(504) 522-3211

www.neworleansdarkroom.com

What Charles Megnin has fashioned within the walls of this one-time poolhall is a New York-cool Valhalla of rotating shows (four to five each year) highlighting the works of local and international exhibiting photographers. Since it opened in 2004, The Darkroom has scheduled workshops and seminars hosted by some of the country's leading fine-art photographers on topics ranging from portfolio building to post-production digital workflow. This venue also offers exhibit-quality and custom photographic printing and framing, as well as a selection of professional portfolios and a small, rotating roster of photography-related coffee table books.

THOMAS MANN GALLERY I/O

1812 Magazine St.

(504) 581-2113

www.thomasmann.com

Contemporary American craft leader Thomas Mann's "techno-romantic" jewelry and eclectic furnishings have been igniting the imagination of serious collectors and lovers of forward design for 40 years and today his jewelry and sculpture can be found in more than 250 galleries in the United States and around the world. And the largest selection of the internationally acclaimed artist's award-winning works is found at his Magazine Street gallery in Uptown's Lower Garden District. Brilliant examples of Mann's sculptural—and highly wearable—objets d'art include his "space frame" brooches and one-of-a-kind "caged necklaces" combining "technical ephemera" such as quartz and nonprecious metals like nickel, brass, and copper. The gallery also showcases the works of more than 40 U.S. and international artists and hosts numerous exhibits throughout the year.

MUSEUMS

NEW ORLEANS MUSEUM OF ART

City Park, 1 Collins Diboil

(504) 488-2631, (504) 658-4100

www.noma.org

Maybe size really doesn't matter. But a $23.5-million expansion project that added 55,000 square feet years back to City Park's largest structure sure has given locals something to crow about—and more room to roam. Founded in 1910 with a gift to the city from philanthropist Isaac Delgado, NOMA, the city's oldest fine art organization, has a permanent world-class collection of more than 35,000 objects valued in excess of $200 million. And with its expansion, the museum's strong suits—French and American art, photography, glass, African works, and Japanese paintings from the 17th- to 18th-century Edo period—only continue to grow.

The facility's comprehensive study of French art includes such treasures as groups of work by French Impressionist Edgar Degas, who visited maternal relatives in New Orleans in 1871 and painted in a house on Esplanade Avenue just 12 blocks from the museum. Works by the masters of the School of Paris include paintings and sculptures by Picasso, Braque, Dufy, and Miró.

A unique Arts of the Americas collection surveys the cultural heritage of North, Central, and South America from the pre-Columbian through the Spanish colonial periods, with special emphasis on objects from the Mayan civilization of Mexico and Central America and paintings and sculpture from Cuzco, the Spanish Viceregal capital of Peru. A display of American art is found in a suite of period rooms featuring 18th- and 19th-century furniture and decorative arts.

One of the more popular collections in this 130,000-square-foot gem is the work of Peter Carl Fabergé (1846–1920), master jeweler to the last czars of Russia, on loan from the Matilda Geddings Gray Foundation. Three Imperial Easter eggs, as well as the famous jeweled Imperial lilies-of-the-valley basket, crafted in 1896 for the Empress Alexandra Feodorovna, highlight this exhibit.

Besides enhancing New Orleans' reputation as a major tourist and convention center, NOMA also plays an important role as an educational resource. Each year the museum opens its doors to more than 25,000 schoolchildren for free guided tours. NOMA's museum-on-wheels, "Van Go," serves as an educational liaison between the museum and the New Orleans area.

Hours are Wed 12 to 8 p.m. and Thurs through Sun 10 a.m. to 5 p.m. Admission for non-Louisiana residents is $8 for adults, $7 for seniors (aged 65+) and students with ID, and $4 for children (aged three to 17). Admission is free to NOMA members and Louisiana residents with ID. On occasion there may be an additional charge for major international exhibits. NOMA is located in City Park, convenient to the City Park/Metairie Road exit of I–10. The museum may be reached by public bus via the Carrollton Avenue or Esplanade bus lines of the RTA. Ample free parking is available, and the museum is fully wheelchair accessible.

OGDEN MUSEUM OF SOUTHERN ART
925 Camp St.
(504) 539-9600
www.ogdenmuseum.org
The arts district's newest museum offers rotating exhibits of Southern-themed art from the 18th through 21st centuries, which includes paintings, prints, watercolors, photographs, ceramics, and

sculpture. The museum is set in a renovated 1888 building designed by renowned local architect Henry Hobson Richardson and a newly constructed connecting five-story gallery. The Warehouse District museum is open Wed through Sun 10 a.m. to 5 p.m. Admission is $10 for adults, $8 for seniors (aged 65+) and students with ID, and $5 for children (ages five to 17). Admission is free to Louisiana residents (with proper ID) on Thurss from 10 a.m. to 5 p.m.

MUSIC

CATHEDRAL CONCERTS
Christ Church Cathedral
2919 St. Charles Ave.
(504) 895-6602
Begun in 1974 as part of this Episcopal church's outreach effort, the Cathedral Concerts encompass a wide variety of musical offerings performed by talented local musicians, including baroque, classical, jazz, and contemporary. An interesting aspect of the series is the post-concert reception during which audience members have the opportunity to talk with performers. The hourlong concerts are generally held on Sun at 4 p.m. There is a church nursery provided for younger children. Cathedral Concerts are free, although donations are appreciated. For more information, call the church office Mon through Fri 9 a.m. to 5 p.m.

i The city's orchestra, ballet association, and other groups of performers often sponsor talks between the audience and artists either before or after a show. They are educational and fun. Ask if one is scheduled for the show you're attending.

LOUISIANA PHILHARMONIC ORCHESTRA
1010 Common St., Suite 2120
(504) 523-6530
www.lpomusic.com
As the only full-time professional orchestra in the Gulf South (and the only musician-owned profes-

sional symphony in the United States), the LPO goes out of its way to serve and develop its audience. A 14-concert classical series is performed in venues throughout town including Loyola University's Roussel Hall, First Baptist New Orleans and Mahalia Jackson Theater. Ditto for its similarly popular "Casual Classics" and "Park" series. The box office is open Mon through Fri 9 a.m. to 5 p.m. Call for program and performance dates.

THE NEW ORLEANS OPERA ASSOCIATION
1010 Common St., Suite 1820
(504) 529-2278, (504) 529-3000
www.neworleansopera.org
North America's first grand opera was staged in the Big Easy, and New Orleanians enjoyed the highest quality performances until the old French Opera House burned down in 1919. In 1943 a group of local music lovers, bent on reestablishing opera in the city, created the New Orleans Opera Association. Today the association presents a quartet of professional offerings each season. Operas not in English are accompanied by projected supertitles. Ticket prices are $30 to $125. The box office at 305 Baronne St. is open Mon through Fri 9 a.m. to 4:30 p.m. Performances are held at the Mahalia Jackson Theater of the Performing Arts.

THE TRINITY ARTIST SERIES
Trinity Episcopal Church
1329 Jackson Ave.
(504) 522-0276
www.trinitynola.com
The Trinity concerts are performed by local as well as touring musicians. Programs have included performances by such notables as jazz artists Ellis Marsalis and the Moses Hogan Chorale; blues musicians Earl King and Marva Wright; and touring shows by the Paris Opera Boys Choir and the Tibetan Monks. A season highlight is always the Bach-a-Thon, a 24-hour concert celebrating the music of J. S. Bach, performed from midnight to midnight on or around his birthday, March 21. The church's classic pipe organ is also a mainstay of the series. Trinity performances take place

every Sun at 5 p.m. and last about an hour. The programs are free; however, donations are gladly accepted. For more information, call the church office during regular business hours.

i In New Orleans, it's hard to find a bad meal and easy to find a good show for free. The Cathedral Concerts and the Trinity Artists Series often showcase topflight talent; the Louisiana Philharmonic Orchestra periodically performs in City Park and at Zephyr Field.

THEATER

CONTEMPORARY ARTS CENTER
900 Camp St.
(504) 523-1216
www.cacno.org
In the heart of the Warehouse Arts District, the CAC offers a modest yet well-received roster of stage performances, including the Music of New Orleans Concert Series, with its emphasis on the city's diverse musical traditions, and the NEA Jazz Masters on Tour Series. Ticket prices vary. Box office hours are Mon through Sat 10 a.m. to 5 p.m., Sun 11 a.m. to 5 p.m.

LE PETIT THEATRE
616 St. Peter St.
(504) 522-2081
www.lepetittheatre.com
Founded in 1916 when a group of amateur theater-lovers began putting on plays in one of the group's drawing rooms, Le Petit is the oldest continuously operating community theater in the United States. Housed in an 1822 Spanish colonial-style building, just down the street from St. Louis Cathedral, the little theater offers a full season of plays and musicals performed by an all-volunteer cast as well as productions associated with the Tennessee Williams Festival in March. Acting legend Helen Hayes said, "Le Petit Theatre is not just good community theater—it is magnificent community theater." (Coincidentally, the

theater's 460-seat auditorium is named for the celebrated actress.) Ticket prices vary, depending on the show.

RIVERTOWN REPERTORY THEATRE
325 Minor St., Kenner
(504) 468-7221
www.rivertownkenner.com/theatre.html
Located in the historical Rivertown museum district, this 300-seat theater presents mostly traditional favorites such as Cole Porter's *Anything Goes, Miss Saigon,* and *Guys and Dolls,* September through May. Ticket prices are $22 to $25 for adults; $20 to $22 for seniors and students age 13 to 21; $10 to $12 for children age six to 12. Group rates are available. Box office hours are Tues through Fri 10:30 a.m. to 2:30 p.m.

SOUTHERN REPERTORY THEATRE
333 Canal St.
(504) 522-6545
www.southernrep.com
"Dedicated to the Southern mystique," Southern Rep seeks to "capture the legend of Southern life and display it on stage." This Actors' Equity house founded in 1986 by Loyola University professor Rosary O'Neill produces regional as well as classic works in an intimate setting. Ticket prices vary depending on performance. Box office hours are Wed through Fri 12 p.m. to 6 p.m. and Sats during performance weeks.

ARTS SUPPORT AND CLASSES

NEW ORLEANS SCHOOL OF GLASSWORKS AND PRINTMAKING STUDIO
727 Magazine St.
(504) 529-7277
www.neworleansglassworks.com
Since its opening in 1990, GlassWorks has been the site of exhibitions highlighting the works of prominent as well as emerging artists. Past exhibits include the luminous vitrography of Dale Chihuly, the delicate botanical works of Paul Stankard, and the sensual designs of Richard Royal. Free demonstrations are held Mon through Sat (call ahead for times) of Venetian-style glassblowing in the South's largest contemporary facility feature glass sculpture, glass casting, lampworking, stained glass, printmaking, and bookbinding—all housed in a restored 19th-century storefront. Have your hand cast in glass; pick out a piece of colorful glass artwork to take home; chat with an artist. Then get in on the act by signing up for one of the weekend beginner classes. Donations to this nonprofit organization are welcome.

ANNUAL EVENTS AND FESTIVALS

Is it any wonder that a sassy, freewheeling city forever checking its pulse against the meter of some eternally offbeat, funky tempo would have found so many jubilant ways to ritualize its heartfelt love of life, music, and food? New Orleans has festivals and events to celebrate everything under the sun and stars. In fact, the city denies itself nothing for the sake of a good time, and the Big Easy will even offer a warm smile and breezy nod of understanding for those who might arch their brow in judgment of our characteristically carefree ways.

Ironically, we can chalk up at least part of our Big Easy heritage to religion. As a city settled by predominantly French and Spanish Catholics, New Orleans never quite grasped the Protestant work ethic like the rest of the country did. This, no doubt, explains why this unabashedly flamboyant and Europeanlike enclave possesses such a seductive and masterful flair when it comes to letting the good times roll at the drop of a crab. This ethos was ingrained in the city's psyche early on, and by the time those somewhat stuffy, style-starved Americans from the Colonies began arriving here in the early 1800s following the Louisiana Purchase, New Orleans simply twirled its parasol over its shoulder and continued along its merry Creole way.

Many outsiders think of the Big Easy as an oversize frat party that uses the Superdome as a beer keg. Without a doubt the city can parade, dance, and eat up a storm like nobody's business. In fact, it takes a full calendar year for the City that Care Forgot to pack in with near-spiritual devotion all the best life has to offer, set against a backdrop of trombone-sliding brass band funk, spicy sausage jambalaya, and sunny days. But New Orleans more than anything else is a city of celebrations. If it offers hot eats, cool tunes, and just the right spin of lighthearted fun, chances are someone has built a festival around it. Outsiders wonder how we manage to get any work done. We wonder why we bother.

Not one but two parades, spaced a weekend apart and held in the Irish Channel and Old Metairie, respectively, celebrate the patron saint of Ireland with kisses and cabbages. In the French Quarter, dog lovers and their costumed canines in the Krewe of Barkus as well as the Bourbon Street Awards' drag-and-leather contest keep the campish possibilities of Mardi Gras on a long leash indeed. Enjoy sweet Creole tomatoes?

The Great French Market Tomato Festival offers a weekendlong tribute to the region's heralded accept-no-substitutes cooking mainstay. Or join locals at the Greek Festival to pay tribute to the culture that gave the world philosophy—and the ouzo needed to understand it—all while munching on stuffed grape leaves and dancing to bouzouki music. The Essence Music Festival, which draws some of the nation's top entertainers from the worlds of rhythm and blues, soul, and hip-hop, has already earned its stripes as a major attraction and tourist draw.

You can't miss locals at the New Orleans Jazz and Heritage Festival. We're the ones dressed more casually than Californians at a surf wedding, dancing our heinies off or striking up friendly conversations with out-of-towners while waiting in line at a food booth for some shrimp remoulade or alligator-on-a-stick. When Carnival season officially kicks off on January 6, it doesn't stop until midnight on Mardi Gras after more than 70 parades, thousands of king cakes, high-society balls, and downscale street parties later. During this time the Big Easy turns fantasy into reality and reveals to the world the true colors of its beautifully adulterated, quixotic soul: purple, green, and gold.

New Orleanians also make room on the social calendar for special occasions a little more serious but truly just as fun. A shining example is the Tennessee Williams Literary Festival, a tour de plume of the life and times of the author who gave the world *Night of the Iguana* and *A Streetcar Named Desire,* the famous play set in New Orleans about that always-shouting-about-something couple next door, Stanley and Stella Kowalski. The annual 10K Crescent City Classic helps locals burn off calories, while Art for Arts' Sake opens the art season with a nighttime "Artwalk" of more than 60 Uptown, French Quarter, and Warehouse District galleries hosting open houses. Celebration in the Oaks trumpets the arrival of the holiday season with a dazzling display of one million lights decorating City Park's centuries-old live oaks. And on December 31 the city kisses another year good-bye with its New Year's Eve countdown in the French Quarter outside Jackson Brewery on the Mississippi River. And then we start all over again. Got aspirin?

JANUARY

ALLSTATE SUGAR BOWL
Louisiana Superdome
1500 Sugar Bowl Dr.
(504) 838-2440
www.allstatesugarbowl.com
New Orleans Item newspaper publisher Colonel James M. Thomson and sports editor Fred Digby hatched the idea for a New Year's Day college football game in New Orleans in 1927. It took eight years to develop public and financial support for the project. On January 1, 1935, in the depths of the Depression, the first Sugar Bowl Football Classic was held at Tulane Stadium. Tulane's Green Wave, which were undefeated in the South, were pitted against the only undefeated Northern team, Pop Warner's Temple University Owls. Tulane prevailed, 20-14, before a crowd of 22,026 who had paid $1.50 to $3.50 per person admission. A tradition was born. The Sugar

Bowl was the subject of the first live TV program in New Orleans, in 1953, which was broadcast coast to coast. Seven years later it was the first game televised in color across the United States.

Over the years the Sugar Bowl has hosted several national champions and a virtual who's who of legendary football coaches including Frank Broyles, "Bear" Bryant, Bobby Bowden, Bob Devaney, Vince Dooley, Woody Hayes, "Shug" Jordan, Johnny Majors, Joe Paterno, and Bud Wilkinson.

The Dome, home of the Sugar Bowl, seats around 77,000 in its expanded football configuration. Tickets for the Sugar Bowl usually go on sale in Aug and are sold through Ticketmaster at (504) 522-5555 or (800) 488-5252.

FEBRUARY

LUNDI GRAS
Woldenberg Park/Spanish Plaza
(504) 522-1555
www.auduboninstitute.org
As a city famous for cherishing tradition, and no more so than during Carnival season, it seemed only a matter of time before the celebration of Lundi Gras, which lasted from 1872 until the beginning of World War I in 1917, was reborn in high style. Today Lundi Gras, or Fat Monday, the day always preceding Mardi Gras, is sort of a minifestival within a festival. Revitalized in 1986, it features the city's two premier Carnival organizations—Rex and Zulu.

Thousands of locals and tourists alike are lured to the daylong outdoor festivities starting at 10 a.m. at Woldenberg Park on the banks of the Mississippi River and including music, food, and, of course, some Carnival ceremony. Traditional New Orleans brass bands, Mardi Gras Indians, and local rhythm and blues singers lay down the soundtrack for dancing Lundi-goers, while boiled crawfish, po-boys, filé gumbo, alligator-sausage-on-a-stick, and other local foodstuffs provide another taste of what Carnival is all about. Characters such as the Witch Doctor and Mr. Big Stuff from the Zulu Aid and Pleasure Club, the city's oldest African-American Carnival krewe, second-line through the festival every hour. At 5 p.m., make way for the ceremonial arrival of King and Queen Zulu by way of the Mississippi River.

After the arrival of Zulu, the second phase of Lundi Gras moves upriver to Spanish Plaza for the 6 p.m. arrival of Rex, or King of Carnival, by Coast Guard cutter and a flotilla of riverboats to an official welcome from the Mayor of New Orleans, the consular corps, and other officials and dignitaries. Hizzoner reads a proclamation that officially turns the City that Care Forgot over to Carnival's Main Man, Rex, for 24 hours until the equally official end of Mardi Gras, which occurs at midnight on Fat Tuesday.

MARCH

NEW ORLEANS SPRING FIESTA ASSOCIATION
826 St. Ann St.
(504) 581-1367, (800) 550-8450
www.springfiesta.com

To glimpse the procession of horse-drawn carriages with the Spring Fiesta Queen and her court as it makes its way through the French Quarter under an azalea-filled afternoon is to experience the genteel, small-town side of New Orleans pageantry. For more than six decades this spring event has welcomed the graciousness of spring with four days of guided tours of select, highly historic, and architecturally significant homes in the French Quarter, Garden District, and Plantation Country. Mind your manners.

The centuries have seen passions kindled and passing fancies dwindle inside the city's mercilessly romantic Victorian-style Creole homes, Garden District mansions of Italianate grandeur, and former slave quarters renovated with tasteful Greek Revival flourishes. And this festival is a unique way to explore the history and romance always in fashion behind the curtains of New Orleans' architectural legacy. Tickets for the various tours as well as the gala that follows Saturday's presentation of the queen's court in Jackson Square and "Night in Old New Orleans" parade of carriages through the French Quarter are available through the New Orleans Spring Fiesta Association.

ST. PATRICK'S DAY
Irish Channel and Old Metairie
www.irishchannel.org

Nobody begs, steals, or borrows any excuse to have a parade like the Irish, and where else but in New Orleans would they have mustered the blarney to hold two processions a week apart for the same occasion? Equally important, how many places can paradegoers count on catching cabbages, carrots, and potatoes for an Irish stew from float-riding Hibernians as part of an annual bash held in the name of Celtic pride?

Everyone is a leprechaun for the day as a convoy of floats and trucks festively decorated with all manner of lucky charms and four-leaf clovers rumble down city streets. Walking club members twirl white and emerald-green umbrellas and hand out paper roses in exchange for a peck on the cheek and an "Erin Go Braugh!" Wear a "Kiss me, I'm Irish" button and try to catch the eye of a green-vested float rider scanning the crowd and maybe you'll catch enough plastic cups, doubloons, and beads to make even your non-Irish friends green with envy.

The first shamrock-festooned event is probably the larger of the city's Irish parades and falls on the Saturday before St. Patrick's Day. It rolls aptly enough through the Irish Channel, where many of the city's Irish immigrants settled in the 1800s, looking like one of those old-fashioned, waving-from-atop-the-back-of-the-convertible kind of neighborhood parades from a bygone era. The Irish Channel is bordered by Jackson and Louisiana Avenues, Magazine Street, and the Mississippi River. The parade usually starts at 2 p.m. Sat at the corner of Race and Annunciation Streets, rolls up Magazine Street to Louisiana Avenue, heads down Louisiana to Prytania Street, where it makes a U-turn back to Annunciation, down Annunciation to Washington Avenue, and ending at the corner of Washington and Tchoupitoulas Street.

Old Metairie weighs in with its own high-stepping, beer-sippin'-guys-handing-out-flowers-for-kisses parade the following Sun at noon. The route of this popular 35-year-old Jefferson Parish parade is crowded but no more so than on Metairie Road. Green spaces and parking places are jammed with RVs and pickups parked door handle to door handle overnight as well as families out for a day of fun with their charcoal grills, coolers, lawn chairs, and sun umbrellas.

Arrive early and count on spending three hours to see the entire parade, which includes nearly two dozen floats, more than 30 trucks, seven minifloats, and a dozen marching bands. This spectacle enjoys a reputation for thumbing its collective nose at the silly notion of sobriety. In the past it wasn't uncommon for some paraders to duck into each bar on the route for a not-so-quick glass of kelly-green cheer. By the time they had reached Metairie Road, the procession had turned into a highly unsteady state of affairs. Some members of the Jefferson Parish City Council have even proposed a ban on alcohol consumption by parade participants as a result of reports of excessive drinking. One council member said the message of the parade should not be "getting dead drunk."

Old Metairie's parade begins near Archbishop Rummel High School on Severn Avenue and 41st Street in Metairie, rolls south on Severn, and turns east when it gets to Metairie Road. It continues down Metairie Road, turns left onto Focis Street, and proceeds up Focis to the intersection of Focis and Canal Streets, where it disbands.

TENNESSEE WILLIAMS/NEW ORLEANS LITERARY FESTIVAL
938 Lafayette St.
(504) 581-1144
www.tennesseewilliams.net

The name sounds highbrow, but by the time you've finished screaming your brains out in the Stella and Stanley Shouting Contest, you're far wiser to the ways of our little corner of the world. And that world likes to honor its own—in this case America's legendary playwright and the literary heritage of the city he called his "spiritual home." This weeklong March festival is a lightning rod for high-typing literary figures as well as those of us whose favorite Tennessee moment

is the Natalie Wood skinny-dipping scene in the screen adaptation of *This Property Is Condemned*.

Highlights include nearly three dozen literary panels, theatrical productions, poetry readings, musical events, and an expansive book fair, as well as literary walking tours of the French Quarter, jazz and New Orleans movie sites, St. Louis Cemetery No. 1, and Anne Rice's haunts. Nearly a dozen master classes have been combined into the three-day French Quarter Literary Conference, where aspiring writers and avid readers alike can glean writing tips firsthand from some of their favorite authors.

Most events take place at Le Petit Theatre du Vieux Carré, 616 St. Peter St., which serves as festival headquarters. Neighboring French Quarter venues (check the Web site for locations) also host various events. A Literary Panel Pass for admission to all weekend discussions as well as one-day passes are available. Individuals can register for one or more 90-minute master classes or for the entire French Quarter Literary Conference, which includes all master classes, a Festival Panel Pass, and two evening receptions. Tickets to other theater events are available.

The festival ends on a thunderous note during the popular Stella and Stanley Shouting Contest, better known as the "Stell-Off," with prizes awarded to the best interpretation of the warring mates in *Streetcar*. A bevy of wannabe Stanleys bellow to the lovelorn Stella who stands on a balcony at the historic Pontalba Apartments in Jackson Square.

APRIL

CRESCENT CITY CLASSIC
8200 Hampson St.
(504) 861-8686
www.ccc10K.com

Even a city renowned for its unbridled indulgence of sensual and gastronomic pleasures can muster the discipline to host what has become a major spectacle of endurance drawing top runners from all over the world. As one might expect in New Orleans, this 10K road race, which begins on Decatur Street at Jackson Square and ends at the entrance to City Park, also draws its share of walkers and others in costume who prefer to take their time and get nowhere fast. An estimated 20,000 persons participate in this mid-Apr race. Live music, food booths, and sporting gear tents await contestants at the end of the race. Come out and watch someone set a world record—either for best time or for the amount of jambalaya and beer consumed at the finish line.

FRENCH QUARTER FESTIVAL
400 North Peter St.
(504) 522-5730, (800) 673-5725
www.frenchquarterfestivals.org
Didn't the city just celebrate Mardi Gras less than two months ago? Yes, Virginia, but by April we're in major party withdrawal. And for many New Orleanians the annual French Quarter Festival is the perfect sort of post-Lenten fete between Carnival's end and when Jazzfest pumps up the jam in late Apr. Far from being merely some warmed-over affair, though, this highly popular festival's breezy blend of outdoor springtime fun in the city's most historic district lasts only a weekend, but it serves up what we cherish most about our Big Easy good times—food, music, and still more food.

Since 1983 this festival, consistently ranked among the best in Louisiana by *Offbeat* magazine readers, has earned its gold-cluster crawfish tails as a major event offering more than 250 hours of free musical entertainment, "the world's largest jazz brunch" (with more than 70 booths serving up specialties from the city's best restaurants), tours of private French Quarter courtyards, and fireworks over the Mississippi River. Concerts, a battle of the jazz bands, a bartender's competition, the Pirate's Alley Art Show, and second-line parading take place throughout the Vieux Carré and Woldenberg Riverfront Park.

Kick back on the grass in Jackson Square with some crawfish-stuffed bread, red beans and rice, or grilled chicken livers with hot-pepper jelly—or all three, no one's watching—while listening to live jazz, gospel, zydeco, and classical music on one of several music stages. Amble over to the International Stage on Dutch Alley at the French Market and catch a German oompah band or Irish folk group, then head to the Esplanade in the Shade Stage (at the Louisiana State Museum's Old Ming), where the Louisiana Philharmonic Orchestra trumpets the classics. Grab some cafe au lait and mosey over to the French Market along Decatur Street to hear some live Cajun and zydeco groups. Other venues include the Abita Veer Stage and Harrah's Louis-Louis Pavilion at Wolderberg Riverfront Park.

Whatever you do, though, you'll be doing it in good company: More than 450,000 people attend the three-day Fri-to-Sun event each year.

NEW ORLEANS JAZZ AND HERITAGE FESTIVAL
Fair Grounds Race Course
(504) 522-4786
www.nojazzfest.com
A friend takes no small amount of pride in the fact that he has yet to miss a single day, much less a nanosecond, of this two-weekend food-and music-drenched blowout since it started in 1970. Come rain or career, the poster child for New Orleans' mother of all festivals each year dons his straw hat, sunglasses, T-shirt, and suspendered jeans and heads out to the Fair Grounds armed with his meticulously color-coded performance schedule of what acts he's going to see and when.

Devotees of this festival, which draws jazz lovers and die-hard foodies alike from all over the world, understand completely. Munching on spicy crawfish bisque, catfish amandine, stuffed artichokes, Creole-stuffed crabs, sweet potato pie, boudin sausage, blackened redfish, or a barbecued alligator po-boy while shaking your booty to an A-list of music powerhouses is enough to knock the flip-flops off just about anybody.

Dress in your favorite boppin' attire. In recent years Jazzfest's heavyweight muscle has been buffed by an ever-widening roster of both cutting-edge and venerated local and international performers from the worlds of gospel, jazz,

Latin, blues, reggae, Afro-Caribbean, ragtime, salsa, bluegrass, zydeco, rock, hip-hop, and alternative music. Nonstop performances presented simultaneously on 12 stages throughout the Fair Grounds Race Track keep the joint jumping from 11 a.m. to 7 p.m. Whether it's the likes of B. B. King and the Neville Brothers or community gospel choirs and African-inspired dance collectives, the event was recently named the country's best music festival by Pollstar and is all but guaranteed to crease the face of even the most hard-to-please fest snob.

A multitiered, air-conditioned grandstand features the Music Heritage Stage as well as the Food Heritage Stage and the Cajun Cabin, spotlighting the diversity of Louisiana's culture with contemporary arts-and-crafts exhibits, video presentations, cooking demonstrations, a variety of music performances, and "intimate interviews." Brass bands and marching clubs begin and end their parades in this area.

Souvenir hounds should head to the Louisiana Heritage Fair on the racecourse infield for one-of-a-kind hand-painted silk clothing, fanciful leather masks, jewelry, photographs, and sculptures. The Congo Square African Marketplace highlights the vibrancy of indigenous African culture through original artwork, crafts, and music performances.

Jazzfest is held Fri through Sun in the last week in Apr and Thurs through Sun in the first week in May. Jazzfest producer/director Quint Davis gives the event an added educational spin with a series of free music and cultural workshops open to the public and held at local schools and colleges as well as the Mahalia Jackson Theater for the Performing Arts.

Jazzfest began in 1970 when 300 musicians entertained a crowd half that number at New Orleans' historic Congo Square. Music legends Mahalia Jackson, Duke Ellington, Pete Fountain, and Al Hirt performed—all brought together by producer George Wein, founder of the Newport Jazz Festival. Today over 10,000 musicians, cooks, and craftspeople entertain more than 400,000 persons each year during the rollicking, fun-filled 10-day event.

Parking is available. Grayline Tours operates a continuous round-trip Jazz- fest Express bus service from the downtown Sheraton New Orleans, French Quarter, and City Park to the Fair Grounds Race Course during festival days 10:30 a.m. to 7:30 p.m. Call (800) 535-7786 for cost. The Regional Transit authority operates public bus routes to the Fair Grounds. For information call (504) 827-7970. Taxis also offer convenient transportation at a special-events rate, which varies year to year, or the meter reading, whichever is higher. Festival tickets are available through Ticketmaster or by mail. Browse the Web site for up-to-the-minute information, photographs, online chats, and much more. Better yet, meet you at the Gospel Tent.

i The internationally renowned Jazzfest held the last weekend in April and first weekend in May is one of the hottest tickets in town—and not just because of the music. The weather this time of year can include rain and/or scorching heat. So come prepared—bring an umbrella (a disposable plastic raincoat isn't a bad idea either) as well as sunblock, sunglasses, and bottled water.

MAY

GREEK FESTIVAL
1200 Robert E. Lee Blvd.
(504) 282-0259
www.greekfestnola.com
If Greek folk dancing mixed with shouts of "opa!" and seasoned with tasty dishes of spring lamb, souvlaki, and Athenian salad sound like fun, this fund-raising festival may be your cup of ouzo. Just phyllo the crowds. Each year since 1973 more than 15,000 festivalgoers have sampled the alpha-to-omega roster of fun, which includes gourmet foodstuffs like pastitsio (pasta and ground meat), spanakopita (spinach pie), tiropita (cheese pie), dolmades (rice-stuffed grape leaves), gyro and baklava sundaes, as well as all

manner of Hellenic imports, from clothing and Greek vases to gold and silver jewelry.

This community festival is held during Memorial Day weekend at the Hellenic Cultural Center at Holy Trinity Cathedral. Built in 1864 and reconstructed in 1985 after a fire, Holy Trinity Cathedral is the oldest Greek Orthodox Church in the United States and is located on Robert E. Lee Boulevard at St. Bernard Avenue. The festival also offers tours of the Holy Trinity Cathedral and features both a 1 mile and 5K Olympic Run to benefit the cathedral. (For registration information call 504-467-8626.) Admission is $5 at the gate, children under 12 are free. Hours are Fri 5 to 11 p.m., Sat 11 a.m. to 11 p.m., and Sun 11 a.m. to 9 p.m.

NEW ORLEANS WINE AND FOOD EXPERIENCE
P.O. Box 4248, 70185
(504) 529-9463
www.nowfe.com
Since 1991 gourmands and gourmets alike have united for five days under the banner of nonprofit culinary good deeds called the New Orleans Wine and Food Experience. Full registration is $695, but what participants get in return is well worth the hassle of digging up a pair of elastic-waist pants: two grand tastings with more than 1,000 vintages (from 175 wineries) and specialties of more than 75 of the city's best-known restaurants Sat and Sun at the Louisiana Superdome; six food and wine seminars; and the "Royal Street Stroll," during which French Quarter antiques shops and art galleries hold open house with yet more wine tastings and food.

Local palates got a first taste of this event in 1991 when a group of food and wine enthusiasts (of which the city has plenty) got together with some of the great chefs of New Orleans as well as some of the top vintners and wineries in the country. The "experience" begins with a Premium Fine Wine Dinner at more than 30 restaurants, which include multiple wines from a particular vineyard with a principal, often the winemaker, on hand to explain the wine before each course. Vintner dinners cost $75 to $125, and reservations and pay-

ment are made directly to the restaurant. Typically, more than 5,000 people from almost every state and several foreign countries are in attendance.

JUNE

THE GREAT FRENCH MARKET CREOLE TOMATO FESTIVAL
1008 North Peters St.
(504) 522-2621
www.frenchmarket.org
It may sound small-town to say, but Louisiana's luscious, sweet, and unbelievably tasty home-grown Creole tomatoes are worth biting home about. If this festival holds high its namesake, it's only because the state's tomatoes form the backbone of so much local cooking. Like its luminary counterparts, the Florida orange and California avocado, the Mississippi Delta soilgrown Creole tomato is heralded by virtually everyone who has ever enjoyed the good fortune of its company. And the idea of throwing a free outdoor party at the French Market in June to celebrate the sacred vegetable-fruit with live music, cooking demonstrations, crafts, and face painting, with a few clowns tossed in to boot, seems as good a reason as any to duck chores for the day.

JULY

ESSENCE MUSIC FESTIVAL
Sugar Bowl Drive
(504) 208-4010
www.essencemusicfestival.com
This three-day celebration and tour de force of African-American culture and music has become a powerhouse draw for locals and travelers alike during one of the city's traditionally slow tourism months. Consider: An estimated 270,000 attendees pump a reported over $100 million into the local economy during this major early-July event, which started in 1995. Holding this event in the home of the African-American jazz legacy made a lot of sense to festival organizers, the New York-based Essence Communications Inc., publisher of *Essence* magazine. But they went a step farther: In addition to standing-room-only performances

by leading blues, jazz, soul, and hip-hop artists at the Louisiana Superdome, the festival also offers a roster of empowerment seminars at the Ernest N. Morial Convention Center. Tickets are available through Ticketmaster at the number listed above.

AUGUST

SATCHMO SUMMERFEST
400 North Peters St.
(504) 522-5730, (800) 673-5725
www.satchmosummerfest.com
The most famous trumpet player in the history of modern music is feted as only he could be celebrated in the city of his birth. This five-day Aug event offers music lovers and jazz fans the chance to experience and explore the life and times of Louis "Satchmo" Armstrong, who helped put jazz on the map nearly a century ago. Most of the events take place in and around the Louisiana State Museum's Old U.S. Mint at 400 Esplanade Avenue in the French Quarter. This food and free-music festival also features seminars on Armstrong's music and legacy, a club crawl, art and photo exhibits, a jazz Mass, and second-line parades. From brass bands to big bands, continuous live music on three stages will keep the joint jumpin' when the city's newest festival, launched in 2001, reminds us what a wonderful world it is.

i The newest reason to brave the August heat is the Satchmo SummerFest, a weekendlong celebration of New Orleans native and jazz pioneer Louis "Satchmo" Armstrong through food, free music, and special events. The event is held early in the month in the French Quarter in and around the Old U.S. Mint. See ya there!

SEPTEMBER

SOUTHERN DECADENCE
French Quarter
(504) 522-8047
www.southerndecadence.com
For some cities family barbecues and last-minute trips to the beach mark the end of summer. In New Orleans, however, Sept 2–7 is the time when hundreds of castanet-playing, whistle-blowing drag queens parade through the French Quarter serving up a silver platter full of attitude, all in the name of fun. This always colorful and highly anticipated parade kicks up its heels—literally—at 2 p.m. the Sun before Labor Day when the grand marshal arrives with his entourage and begins leading the rowdy boys and girls of summer on a secret route through the French Quarter. One year this outrageous group's walk on the wild side took them through St. Louis Cathedral—during Mass. Another year they teased tourists in the lobby of the Fairmont Hotel.

What began as an informal march back in 1973 from Matassa's Bar to 2110 Barracks St. has become one of the city's favorite expressions of lifestyle freedom, one which draws an estimated 125,000 revelers and contributes a reported $96 million to the local economy. People looking for more information are encouraged to contact *AmBush Magazine* at the number listed above or visit the Southern Decadence Web site.

i New Orleans festivals are renowned for good times, great food, and, as one might expect in the Big Easy, lots of booze. If you enjoy alcohol, do so responsibly. And if you've had too much to drink, do yourself and everyone else a favor: Don't drive; call a cab. This may be a freewheeling city, but that doesn't mean the police won't bust drunken drivers.

OCTOBER

ART FOR ARTS' SAKE
900 Camp St.
(504) 523-1216
Time to dry-clean the spaghetti-strap black Halston or give that special Armani suit a once-over with the lint brush. The art season is officially opening, and we don't want to be seen looking, um, unstylish while browsing the wine-and-cheese open house hosted by local art galleries,

do we? No matter how you dress to paint the town, though, this annual citywide extravaganza, started in 1980 to benefit the Contemporary Arts Center, has become one of the year's best excuses to explore what New Orleans' visual artists are creating for, well, arts' sake. Participating in the "Artwalk," held on the first Sat in Oct, are more than 50 commercial galleries on Magazine Street in Uptown, Julia Street in the Warehouse District, and Royal Street in the French Quarter, open from 6 to 9 p.m. Sidewalks are pleasantly crowded with everyone from window-shoppers to serious patrons. A free bus shuttle provided by the Magazine Street Merchant Association runs a continuous loop from Race Street in the Lower Garden District to Joseph Street Uptown and is designed to alleviate some of the gridlock of drivers cruising Magazine Street for a parking space. Riders can disembark at any corner.

GUMBO FESTIVAL
1701 Bridge City Ave.
Bridge City
(504) 436-4712
www.hgaparish.org/gumbofestival.htm
For every food there is a season, and the murky, densely flavored valedictorian of Louisiana's down-home school of cooking is no exception to the roux. The annual Gumbo Festival, held the second weekend in Oct in Bridge City, proclaimed in 1973 by then-Gov. Edwin Edwards as the Gumbo Capital of the World, offers the chance to pay homage to 2,000 gallons of this stewy, roux-based heaven out of Africa cooked fresh daily. Gumbo, or "gombo," is a native name for okra, a popular ingredient in the dish, among the Bantu tribes of Africa.

The festival, started in 1972 by the Rev. Monsignor J. Anthony Luminais and parishioners of Our Lady of Prompt Succor Church and the Holy Guardian Angels Mission, is a small-town tour de force of gumbo served a variety of ways, including with okra, seafood/sausage, chicken/sausage, duck, poule d'eau, and z'herbs. New Orleans-style red beans and rice with sausage, jambalaya, and hamburgers, hot dogs, and homemade cakes and candy round off the food booth menus. Live

entertainment includes the usual complement of Cajun/zydeco, country, jazz, blues, and rock music, a midway, craft booths, souvenirs, and carnival rides. Don't be bashful, the Beautiful Child Contest is now open to all age groups.

The Gumbo Festival is held in Bridge City on the west bank of Jefferson Parish across the Huey P. Long Bridge. To reach the bridge take I-10 west from downtown New Orleans 15 to 20 minutes to the Clearview Parkway exit. Follow the clearview parkway south sign at the off-ramp, which will loop around onto Clearview Parkway heading toward the Mississippi River. Take Clearview Parkway all the way to the end and enter the bridge when you see the well-marked sign. The narrow-enough-to-be-one-lane two-lane divided bridge was built in 1935 and shakes a little, especially when tractor-trailer rigs whiz past at perilous speeds. But it's a short drive over the Mississippi River and into Bridge City and well worth the effort for this festival. Admission is $1 per person, per day. Parking and onstage entertainment are free.

NEW ORLEANS FILM FESTIVAL
900 Camp St.
(504) 309-6633
www.neworleansfilmfest.com
As a film festival city, it may not be that long before New Orleans starts nudging its way into the spotlight dominated by Cannes, Sundance, Toronto, and Telluride. Until then, the 20-year-old New Orleans Film Festival quietly dims the lights in mid-Oct, flips on the projector, and rolls the global gamut of celluloid culture, from high-flung, full-length independent features to fast, cheap, out-of-control art-house flicks. But no matter how you like your popcorn buttered, this volunteer-driven labor of love sponsored by the nonprofit New Orleans Film Society, founded in 1989, is a cinematic feast for the devotee of experimental film as well as the merely curious moviegoer who couldn't care less that Igmar and Ingrid Bergman weren't related.

More than 30 major feature-length regional premiers are held at the Canal Street Landmark Cinema (dubbed the "Big House" during the festival) at 333 Canal Place at the edge of the French Quarter. Screenings of nearly 90 independent and low-budget movies from around the region and the world that people are not likely to see anywhere else are held at the Contemporary Arts Center at 900 Camp St., and Prytania Theater at 5339 Prytania St. in the Garden District. Cinema 16's Independent Filmmakers' Showcase is the competitive part of the festival and presents features, shorts, documentaries, animation, music videos, and experimental films of all lengths in 16mm, Super-8, and video formats.

Special events include galas, cocktail parties, and gatherings for local and visiting filmmakers and industry guests as well as late-night events with live music from local bands. Directors and other industry pros hold panel discussions on everything from funding and producing to distributing the independent film, documentary filmmaking, and how to obtain an agent. The closing-night party is a chichi celebration typically held at a Warehouse District nightclub. Tickets for movies are available at Canal Place Cinema and the Prytania Theater box office, and a cover charge is required for the Sat and Thurs closing-night parties held at locations announced at least a week before the festival begins. The cost for weekend workshops varies, so call ahead.

i The city looks magical during the holidays. Special holiday events beloved by locals include candlelight caroling in Jackson Square, driving or walking through "Celebration in the Oaks," where City Park's centuries-old oaks are decorated with thousands of lights and ornaments, and strolling the Roosevelt Hotel's marvelously decorated blocklong lobby. Bring the kids!

NOVEMBER/DECEMBER

CELEBRATION IN THE OAKS
1 Palm Dr.
(504) 483-9415
If any part of New Orleans looks like a fairy-tale wonderland during the holidays, it's City Park

when the greenspace's centuries-old live oaks are bedecked, adorned, and otherwise strung branch to trunk with more than one million twinkling Christmas lights, fanciful ornaments, and mirrored objets d'art. Each year an estimated 500,000 people visit Celebration in the Oaks. Visitors can park their cars and take a walking tour, which should include a stop at the Christmas tree-lined and festively decorated Botanical Gardens and Storyland. Here kids and grown-ups alike can enjoy a cup of hot chocolate and other refreshments in between rides on the park's historic carousel of antique wooden horses, tilt-a-whirl, giant slide, and roller coaster. Santa, of course, visits nightly to hear youngsters' holiday wish lists. Caroling, a live Nativity, real snow, and fireworks on various nights (always call for dates) round off the events, which run from the day after Thanksgiving. The park is open for nighttime driving and walking tours from 5:30 to 10:30 p.m. Call after Thanksgiving for the entrance fee.

CHRISTMAS NEW ORLEANS STYLE
400 North Peters St.
(504) 522-5730, (800) 673-5725
www.christmasneworleans.com
During the holidays the city rolls out the red holly berries with a Santa sack full of fun under the banner "Christmas, New Orleans Style," from decorated hotel lobbies and old New Orleans homes and traditional Creole reveillon dinners to a night of candlelight caroling in romantic Jackson Square. Festivities kick off in early Dec with tree-lighting ceremonies held at the French Market at the corner of St. Philip and Decatur Streets and at Lee Circle and continue throughout the month with holiday tours of old New Orleans homes Uptown and in the French Quarter, hosted by the Preservation Resource Center at (504) 636-3040 and French Quarter Festivals at (504) 522-5730, respectively. For other holiday walking tours call Friends of the Cabildo at (504) 523-3939, St. Louis Cathedral at (504) 525-9585, and St. Catherine of Siena in Old Metairie at (504) 835-2445. Or see how the Creoles decorated their Victorian homes during Christmas in the 19th century with tours of the Gallier House Museum,

1118 Royal St., and Hermann-Grima, 820 St. Louis St. Call (504) 525-5661.

Peckish? Try one of the four- or five-course, fixed-price reveillon lunches or dinners offered by a growing number of restaurants citywide through Christmas Eve. This French tradition, revitalized locally in 1987, lasts three weeks and hearkens back to the mid-1800s when Creole families would follow Christmas Eve Midnight Mass at St. Louis Cathedral with a simple, breakfast-till-dawn feast of eggs, sweetbreads, daube glacé, and filled cakes. Today, in theory, the reveillon menu should feature once-a-year or otherwise unique dishes not normally available at the restaurant. Unfortunately, in reality some, but certainly not all, participating restaurants simply choose to repackage their regular menus.

Duck into the Roosevelt Hotel and stroll this venerated hotel's blocklong lobby of manger scenes, flocked Christmas trees, and an angel hair "snow tunnel" decorated with more than 30,000 lights. Then head into the Roosevelt's famed Sazarac Bar for a little holiday cheer. Elsewhere the city's churches, universities, and performing arts organizations host productions of The Nutcracker, Messiah, and holiday music programs.

i Among the most unique holiday celebrations anywhere in the country is the Festival of the Bonfires held in the River Parishes 34 minutes from New Orleans. During Christmastime up to 100 towering tepee-shaped bonfires constructed along the Mississippi River levee are lighted to help guide the way for Papa Noel following a centuries-old tradition.

CHRISTMAS EVE BONFIRES
River Parishes
(800) 367-7852
www.festivalofthebonfires.org

Legend has it that the early Cajuns who settled upriver from New Orleans in a region called the River Parishes burned huge Christmas Eve bonfires along the riverbanks to light the way for Papa Noël and his sled team of alligators. Another version says the bonfires were lit for people returning from Mass on the opposite side of the Mississippi River. Either way, the tradition continues today each Christmas Eve night as an estimated 100 towering infernos burn for hours on the west side of the levee along the Mississippi River in Vacherie, Lutcher, and Gramercy at LA 44, a one-hour drive west of New Orleans on I-10. Residents of St. John the Baptist and St. James parishes spend weeks building the huge wooden structures, which can be counted on for warmth on a cold Christmas Eve night. Ample street parking is available, and there is no charge to walk along the levee and enjoy mingling with the locals and tourists who turn out for this special event. A Festival of the Bonfires is usually held the second weekend in Dec at the Lutcher/Gramercy Knights of Columbus Home on LA 51 in Lutcher.

NEW YEAR'S EVE
Jackson Brewery
620–624 Decatur St.
(504) 566-7245
www.jacksonbrewery.com
Seriously, could a street-party city like New Orleans end the year on anything but a bang? (And, no, we're not referring to those shameful few who choose to discharge firearms into the sky at midnight.) The countdown action takes place in the French Quarter, where a lighted ball drops from the top of Jackson Brewery to the whoops and hollers of cheering midnight revelers. This Third Coast celebration may not be as well known as its Time Square counterpart, but at least in New Orleans partygoers can count on being surrounded by tons of places in which to grab—what else?—the first meal of the New Year. Pop the bubbly and pass the crawfish.

MARDI GRAS

Following a traditional breakfast of eggs Sardou and Bloody Marys in the palm-flanged court-yard of the French Quarter's Louis XVI Restaurant, we ambled outside to greet the beckoning cloudless day and outrageous revelry. Our tight-knit, costumed coterie featured a Sultan of Schwing, a French maid, a tigress, and a pair of regally attired faux royalty—Hapsburgs, no doubt. We mamboed toward Bourbon Street as The Meters' impossibly funky version of "New Suit" blared from a stereo perched on a fern-framed, bead-bedecked balcony overhead. *"Every year at Carnival time we make a new suit . . ."* Then we turned the corner and came face to face with ground zero of the greatest free show on earth: Mardi Gras.

Comically ribald, kaleidoscopic extravagances were everywhere: gorillas in surgical greens; bikini-clad women (and men); wizards and princesses; multicolored Styrofoam dinosaurs; drag queens in stunningly beautiful costumes; and leather-and-bondage entourages. A 16-person, group-themed entourage sporting identical red "Obama Mia!" T-shirts paused in the middle of the street to sing a tune from the Broadway show hit "Mamma Mia!"—and quite well, actually—but with the lyrics cleverly altered to address the political climate of the moment.

OK, so maybe your mama never told you there'd be days like these, but any celebration that results in the official daylong closing of local city, state, and—gasp!—federal offices is bound to be, well, different.

In Carnival tradition, hooch-addled, hormone-crazed college guys shouted "Show your t*ts!" to women on balconies, who were all too happy to oblige before tossing plastic beads to the depths of fratlike depravity. Such are the microeconomics of Carnival. And it wasn't even noon yet. We swam the sea of elbow-to-elbow humanity—note to claustrophobics: stay at home—to the Bourbon Street Awards, a fancifully staged theatrical presentation of elaborate, elegant, and erstwhile campy drag costumes. On Judy, on Liza, on Joan, on Bette! *"Every year at Carnival time we make a new suit . . ."*

But the out-of-town sibling visiting from Southern California had seen it all before. During Carnivals past she has been lured into an impromptu dance with a New Orleans police officer, greeted by whoops and hollers inside Pat O'Brien's courtyard bar while removing her

sweater (only) to beat the heat, and playfully strewn with Silly String on Canal Street while trying to catch a prized gilded coconut from a Zulu float rider. She has joined in spontaneous second-line dancing and once snuck in behind a marching band during a parade, accompanied by a local who knew better than to engage in this strictly illegal activity. She had gorged on time-honored Carnival mainstays like Popeye's fried chicken and Café du Monde beignets and has quaffed a cistern's worth of rum-and-fruit-juice Hurricanes from Pat O'Brien's. Along the way she learned the finer points of scooping up the choice beads at a Bacchus parade float tossed out on to the sidewalk, but not before nearly being rushed to the hospital with a badly sprained finger after confronting the competition––youths less than half her age who had the same idea. And she's a soccer mom.

For one day each year New Orleans is the hot dog the rest of the country wants to run wild with through the streets. During Carnival the Big Easy takes no prisoners—except, of course, those who flagrantly break the law. Unless someone urinates on public streets or gets into a fight, two of the most common violations, the city lets its hair down and encourages revelers to do likewise. For example, drinking alcohol is allowed on the streets of the French Quarter (year-round, not just during Mardi Gras), so long as partygoers have a plastic "go cup." Bars provide these free of charge. Boozing it up while behind the wheel of a car, though, is a Carnival no-no.

Truth is, Carnival's orderly chaos is a virtually seamless event for the vast majority of millions of visitors, thanks largely to the heightened presence of local police working round the clock. For more information, consult your common sense or watch the episode of Cops filmed in New Orleans during Mardi Gras.

Note that if your travel plans include coming to New Orleans for Carnival, you'd best plan on booking a hotel reservation no later than six months before Mardi Gras. Many hotels, especially in the French Quarter, require a minimum four-night stay—usually the Fri or Sat night before Fat Tuesday through Mardi Gras night. Less-restrictive reservation policies can usually be found in smaller hotels and motels located in surrounding suburbs.

HISTORY

It was New Orleans' founders—the Lemoyne brothers, Iberville and Bienville—who brought Mardi Gras from France to the New World in 1699. Historians tell us that Mardi Gras was a raucous affair even during the early 1700s. In fact, the celebration had become so mired in danger by 1817 that city officials were forced to ban masking altogether. No one is entirely sure as to the year of the first formal parade, but most people put it around 1835 or 1838. The most widely cited of the earliest reports of the time, which appeared in the *Daily Picayune* in 1838, refers to "a procession of masked figures through the public streets with every variety of costumes from Harlequin to the somber Turk and wild Indian. Yesterday was a jolly day in our city."

The Song of Mardi Gras

In 1872 His Imperial Highness, Grand Duke Alexis Romanoff Alexandrovitch, was touring the United States on a buffalo hunt when he spied a young musical-comedy actress named Lydia Thompson in a New York performance, according to Robert Tallant in his book *Mardi Gras*. The elegant Grand Duke, as renowned a lover as he was a sportsman, was smitten. Thompson was headed to New Orleans for a performance days before Mardi Gras, and Alexis was hot on her heels. Buffalo? Pshaw!

In New Orleans, meantime, a group of prominent citizens quickly formed a Carnival organization called the School of Design and chose a King of Carnival to welcome the Duke. Little did Alexis and Thompson know that the local grapevine had been burning with word of their reported romance and that plans had been hatched to celebrate their love during the parade.

During the first Rex parade, an estimated 10,000 maskers lined a route that stretched more than a mile, according to Tallant. Each marching band that passed the City Hall reviewing stand, where the Duke sat with city officials, performed the song "If Ever I Cease to Love." It was the same song Thompson had sung during her New York stage performance seen by the Duke—and, also, later privately during her rendezvous with him. While the romance between the pair faded, "If Ever I Cease to Love" did not; today it remains the song of Mardi Gras.

i Despite what you think you know about Carnival in the French Quarter, stronger enforcement of laws prohibiting public sex (and even total public nudity), especially on Bourbon Street, has made such Fat Tuesday indulgences a far riskier venture for hookup-seeking revelers. A word to the wise: Get a room—if you can find one!

The Krewe

By mid-century the frivolity became somewhat more organized with the formation of the first formal Carnival organization, the Mistick Krewe of Comus. For the record, the word "krewe," the name for Carnival organizations that stage the parades, now appears in *Webster's Dictionary* and is defined as "a fanciful spelling of crew, generalized from the Mistick Krewe of Comus. . ." Surely no more fitting tribute to Carnival's enduring contribution to the international language of fun can be found anywhere.

Krewes are private social organizations. Membership in krewes is by invitation only, and membership criteria depends on those established by each krewe. The number of members in each krewe varies widely, ranging from fewer than 300 for smaller new krewes to longtime Carnival groups like Endymion that boasts more than 5,000 members.

ℹ Carnival season commences January 6, the 12th night after Christmas, also known as the Feast of the Epiphany, when the three Wise Men are said to have visited the Christ Child. Festivities end at midnight on Fat Tuesday. The fluctuating dates of Easter and, as a result, the preceding Lent season mean that Mardi Gras can take place anytime between Feb 3 and Mar 9.

Many krewes do not exist simply to put on a parade one evening during Carnival season—they're year-round social clubs. Krewes hold dances, crawfish boils, and other social gatherings through the summer and fall. These events usually bring in a little extra profit, which helps fill the krewe's coffers while giving members and their families an opportunity to socialize. Many krewes hold a coronation dance in the fall, where the Queen and Maids for the coming year are presented and the King is chosen. Krewes that hold such a dance often choose their king by lot from the members of a more exclusive "King's Club."

Several krewes have also gone into the "ball business" in the off-season. New Orleans attracts many large conventions. These folks want to get a taste of what Mardi Gras is all about, so the organization holding the convention will contract with a krewe to present their ball one evening at a hotel. This is great fun for the krewe, since the King, Queen, and Court get a chance to wear their costumes once again. It's also a good fund-raising opportunity for the krewe, since they can charge the organization holding the convention a good bit of money for staging the ball.

The early 20th century saw the creation of the premiere African-American Carnival krewe—the Zulu Social Aid and Pleasure Club. In 1910 Zulu presented its first parade, and its king, William Story, spoofed the traditional all-white Uptown Carnival organizations by carrying a banana stalk scepter and wearing a lard-can crown. The organization began the tradition of celebrity krewe kings in 1949 when Louis Armstrong rode as King Zulu. Zulu's tongue-in-cheek take on Mardi Gras has made it one of the most popular and enduring of all Mardi Gras parades. In fact, the most highly prized throw is still—and will likely always be—one of the Zulu's gilded coconuts. Ironically, the Zulu Social Aid and Pleasure Club, once forbidden to parade down Canal Street in segregated New Orleans, is now the first krewe to hit the streets Mardi Gras morning, preceding Rex, the very kind of old guard Carnival organization Zulu set out to mock.

By the 1980s the roster of krewes had exploded following the addition of suburban, women's, and neighborhood Carnival organizations, plus the appearance of the first "superparades"—Endymion and Bacchus. New Orleans' contribution to revelry rolls very tall indeed, especially when the streets are filled with triple-decker and superfloats, such as the 120-foot-long and 18-foot-high "Leviathan" of the Krewe of Orpheus, founded by entertainer and New Orleans native Harry Connick Jr. in 1993. Today more than four dozen krewes parade in the New Orleans metropolitan area during the

Carnival season, with as many as nine rolling on a single night. For the most up-to-date schedule of parade dates and times, check out the *Times-Picayune*'s annual Mardi Gras supplement, published typically two weeks prior to Fat Tuesday.

i For the most up-to-date schedule of parade dates and times, check out the *Times-Picayune* annual Mardi Gras section, typically published two weeks prior to Fat Tuesday.

Krewes are not the only organized tribute to the season, as half a dozen walking clubs hit the streets on Mardi Gras. The most well-known group is Pete Fountain's Half Fast Walking Club, a tradition since 1961. Dubbed "the Prince of Mardi Gras," the clarinet-wielding jazz musician and his rollicking entourage start off at Commander's Palace at 7:45 a.m.—or thereabouts, depending on how long breakfast lasts—and wind their way through the French Quarter. The Krewe of Barkus, a French Quarter extravaganza of costumed canines, has become one of the season's paw-ticularly popular parades. Junior and senior high school marching bands are also a parade mainstay of this $800 million annual party known as Mardi Gras. The perennially popular and national award-winning St. Augustine High School band is among the best and certainly the most popular.

Likewise, the Mardi Gras Indians contribute their own special flair to the season, one every bit as rich in Carnival tradition as krewes. For more than a century many in the city's African-American community have dressed like Native Americans, singing and dancing down neighborhood streets while playing tambourines and bells. Members of various "tribes," including the well-known Wild Magnolias and Creole Wild Wests, work throughout the year creating their gorgeous ostrich- and peacock-plumed headdresses and costumes of sequins, beads, satins, velvet, and metallic cloth. These painstakingly handcrafted costumes are

startlingly beautiful and exquisitely elaborate in detail. These neighborhood marching organizations commemorate that time when local African slaves seeking freedom found refuge and safety with neighboring Native American tribes such as the Choctaws.

Today during their parades, youths known as spy boys run ahead of the group, on the lookout for an "enemy" tribe, which dates to a time when competing tribes literally warred in the streets. Next in rank are the "flag boys" who carry the tribe's banner. Remember the song "Iko Iko," popularized by New Orleans' Dixie Cups? "My flag boy and your flag boy are sitting by the fire/my flag boy told your flag boy, 'I'm gonna set your flag on fire.'" The head of the tribe, naturally, is the "Big Chief."

Segregation

Like many other old-line Southern institutions, segregation was an accepted way of life when it came to membership in Carnival organizations. But in 1988 segregation of Carnival krewes officially came to a screeching halt when the New Orleans City Council issued its historic and then highly controversial antidiscrimination ordinance. The ordinance forbade any parading organization from restricting its membership on the basis of race. (It was—and still is—permissible to exclude individuals on the basis of gender.) The ordinance was based on a ruling by the U.S. Supreme Court, which upheld the rights of cities to ban racial discrimination in clubs where business contacts are made.

i Arrived in town for Mardi Gras but forgot to bring a costume? No problem. The city has several shops that sell Carnival costumes and paraphernalia, including masks and beads, to help visitors hit the streets in grand style. Check the Yellow Pages or ask someone at the hotel or inn for the location of the nearest store.

CARNIVAL BASICS

When to Find Mardi Gras

During Mardi Gras, historians and morning-after revelers alike may look around and ask the same question: How did we get here? The roots of pre-Lent feasting and frolicking that grew up to become Mardi Gras can be found in ancient Christendom's attempts to fold the ceremonies of Europe's pagans into a new religion observing the passion and crucifixion of Christ. Mardi Gras, or Fat Tuesday, is the last big party of the Carnival season and takes places the day before Lent begins on Ash Wednesday.

Throws

Masked float riders dress in themed costumes and toss what are known as "throws" to the eagerly outstretched hands of revelers who fill the parade route. The most traditional—and, by far, the most numerous—throws are plastic bead necklaces and colored aluminum coins called doubloons. Over the decades more throws were added to the roster that now boasts plastic krewe-themed cups, Moon Pies, panties, giant cigars—you name it.

If a throw has fallen to the ground, the safest way to pick it up while avoiding having your fingers stomped—we're not kidding—is to first step on it to stake your claim. When the crowd clears and the dust settles, bend down and pick it up. Remember, everything is fair game at a parade, and the most prudent way to catch a throw is to get the attention of a float rider, preferably with the traditional Carnival cry, "Throw me something, Mister!" It also doesn't hurt if you can jump like Michael Jordan. And just in case you want to show off your doubloon smarts, New Orleans artist H. Alvin Sharpe and Rex member Ford Thomas Hardy invented the wildly popular aluminum doubloon back in 1960.

Die-hard legends of St. Charles Avenue paradegoers often stake out a spot on the neutral ground (median to the rest of the country) with chairs and coolers the night before Fat Tuesday, all but guaranteeing a secured prime location for catching beads. Be forewarned: Police in recent years have taken a dim view of the ubiquitous wooden ladder, retrofitted with safety seats for youngsters, hogging public space hours before the parade even rolls.

Mardi Gras is not just about the ribald and not-so-subtle innuendo found along the flagstones of the French Quarter. Family-oriented fun is best found along the parade routes of St. Charles Avenue in Uptown, Canal Street in Mid City, Veterans Boulevard in Metairie, and elsewhere in the suburbs of the west bank of Jefferson and Orleans Parishes and the north shore of St. Tammany Parish. Here, lawn chairs, homemade ladder-seats for tykes, and coolers full of fried chicken and soda pop are the norm. Rarely does anything rise above a PG rating. What does rise to excruciating levels is the noise from the rolling, music-blaring vans fronting local dance school groups who march in between the floats.

The King Cake

The king cake is Carnival's food du jour—a round Danish or coffee-cake pastry traditionally covered in icing in the Mardi Gras colors of purple (for justice), green (faith), and gold (power). Nowadays the once-simple pastry can be found filled with everything from pralines to cream cheese to raspberry jam—sometimes all three. A king cake can also be found in virtually every office during Carnival season. And the co-worker who winds up with the little plastic baby (another bastion of this baked goodie) inside his or her slice is obliged to bring the next cake to work. By the end of Mardi Gras, many locals would rather not have to even look at another king cake until the following year.

Many believe that the first king cakes were served on the Feast of the Epiphany, January 6, as part of a religious celebration, and the trinkets inside represented the gifts of the Magi. In Louisiana the first king cakes were baked by early French settlers as part of private family customs.

On the Epiphany in 1870, a king cake was served to eligible single girls at the first Ball of the Twelfth Night Carnival Club. Presumably, the young lady who found the golden bean inside her slice of cake was crowned the Queen of the Carnival.

Bakeries in the 1930s began making the cakes at the request of some krewes, yet king cakes weren't made for general consumption. Mass production of king cakes began after World War II, and the cake has retained a venerable position in Carnival tradition ever since.

Today king cake sales gross millions of dollars annually, and visitors can send them as gifts.

i Among the smartest ideas for Bourbon Street–bound tipplers Fat Tuesday is taking a cab between your hotel (or house) and the French Quarter. This way you know that you and your entourage will have a safe ride home. You'll save a little on the cost of parking and a lot on the time and headache spent finding a parking space.

Queen of the Carnival

For New Orleanians, January 6 is typically when a former debutante finds a small gold bean—in lieu of a small plastic baby—in her slice of king cake at the Twelfth Night Revelers Ball, which ends the mystery as to who will be Queen of Carnival that year.

While the men of the Twelfth Night Revelers Ball are still getting dressed for their ball, which begins promptly at 9 p.m., The Phunny Phorty Phellows, a group of primarily 30- and 40-something folks, are already rolling on their streetcar ride announcing that the carnival season has begun.

The Twelfth Night Revelers Ball is a private invitation-only affair; The Phunny Phorty Phellows ride the streetcar hollering at those they meet along the way. Of course, there's no rule that says one cannot imbibe a bit of the grape while riding along the streetcar route, so the Phellows do indeed have a merry time.

By the time the streetcar is parked back in the Barn, the Phellows (there's lots of women Phellows by the way—no sexist organization, this one) have disembarked, and the Twelfth Night Revelers have chosen their Queen, the rest of us are counting the days to our krewe's functions, the first king cake someone brings to the office, or the first parade in our neighborhood. By day, New Orleans is more or less a normal place to live, but by night the city won't be calm and quiet until Ash Wednesday.

i In contrast to New Orleans, Carnival events on the north shore of Lake Pontchartrain offer a downsized change of pace thanks to a roster of family-oriented rural parades and even a couple of boat parades featuring theme-decorated vessels with costumed riders (yes, they still toss beads and doubloons!) that ply the local rivers and bayous.

Each year most Carnival organizations, or krewes, select a queen. And the Twelfth Night Revelers, the second-oldest Carnival organization in New Orleans, is no exception. Where the Twelfth Night Revelers differ from the vast majority of their Carnival counterparts is the fact that each year's maids of honor are all college juniors and, equally important, former debutantes with pedigree. No one in the Carnival social club known as the Twelfth Night Revelers knows ahead of time which maid of honor from the elite ranks of New Orleans high society will be the lucky woman who finds the gold bean and thus be crowned queen. Of this everyone is certain, though: Regardless of who gets the bean, the woman who is hailed as queen at the Twelfth Night Revelers Ball is not likely to soon forget the spectacular, once-in-a-lifetime evening of royal pomp and pageantry dedicated in her honor.

ALL GOOD THINGS MUST COME TO AN END

And the end of Mardi Gras tolls at midnight on Fat Tuesday, when a patrol of the city's finest, linked arm to arm, front a Pattonlike division of slow-moving street sweepers, rumbling down Bourbon Street and sucking up tons of garbage, while admonishing good-till-the-last-drop revelers to call it a night. By the next morning, Ash Wednesday, the city is nearly perfectly still (and unbelievably pretty clean). Bleary-eyed tourists, many with beads still around their necks, crawl into hotel cabs to be whisked to the airport to catch planes back home. The city's faithful Catholics meantime head off to church before work for their traditional ashes, which marks the solemn beginning of the 40-day season of Lent. For many New Orleanians this time of religious sacrifice is celebrated each Friday with a traditional feast of succulent seafood at local restaurants.

But that's getting ahead of the story. As the tigress-attired sibling from Southern California emerged from Lafitte's Landing bar on Bourbon Street, she surveyed the crazy kebab of pierced drag queens and the trio of men dressed like cherubs-gone-S&M who were clinging to a corner lamppost, posing for pictures with their cute little bows and arrows. "Oh, we're definitely not in Kansas anymore," the soccer mom said as a grin creased the black whiskers painted on her cheeks.

And it wasn't even noon yet. *"Every year at Carnival time we make a new suit..."*

DAY TRIPS

New Orleanians love their city—to a fault. But when the travel bug hits there's nothing we like better than hitting the road for day trips to explore the region's fun and always historic surroundings. For this chapter we have included five favorites: the Isleños region of lower St. Bernard Parish; St. Tammany Parish; Plantation Country; Cajun Country; and the Mississippi Gulf Coast.

QUE PASA, ISLEÑOS? THE SPANISH DESCENDANTS OF LOWER ST. BERNARD PARISH

St. Bernard Parish, named for Gov. Bernardo de Galvez, has been dubbed "Louisiana's Spanish Treasure" due to the legacy of its earliest colonial settlers from the Canary Islands—the Isleños. While French settlers inhabited the upper regions of the parish in the early 1700s, it was these Spanish immigrants from the Canary Islands who arrived nearly 80 years later to help stave off British invasion, carving a community out of a swamp wilderness in the lower part of the parish along Bayou Terre-aux-Boeuf. The land was harsh and inhospitable. Still, these poor yet resourceful settlers soon earned reputations as expert trappers, fishers, farmers, ranchers, and boat builders, according to parish historian William Hyland. Lower St. Bernard, flanked by deltas and bayous, Lake Borgne, the Mississippi River, and Breton Sound, provided the Isleños with a cash crop of oyster, shrimp, crab, and other seafood. Many modern-day Isleños living in fishing communities such as Delacroix, Reggio, Shell Beach, and Yscloskey can point with pride to the local multimillion-dollar commercial fishing industry, no less a tribute to the legacy of their 18th-century ancestors.

By the 1830s local Isleño farmers were supplying the new colony of New Orleans upriver with sweet potatoes, onions, pumpkins, and other food staples. During the 19th century many Isleños, such as the Nunez, Estopinal, and Marrero families, became prosperous large-scale sugar planters and built beautiful homes in the area, some of which can still be seen today. Only about 200 Isleños, mostly elders, still speak Spanish, and many fear that the heritage and folkways of their close-knit communities are being lost to the passage of time. Efforts to preserve Isleño culture for generations to come is underscored by the lively annual Isleño Festival (see below), held on the grounds of the modest museum of the same name and coordinated by the Los Isleños Heritage and Cultural Society. Besides Isleño culture and untouristed fishing villages, visitors to lower St. Bernard Parish will also discover scenic oak alleys and picturesque plantation homes (though all are private and not open for public tours), as well as the Chalmette National Historical Park—site of the Battle of New Orleans. Because most of the historic homes do not have identifying plaques or visible addresses, it's highly advisable to get a free copy of the *Discover St. Bernard* tourism brochure, which includes full-color pictures of the homes and other historic points of interest as well as a map of where to find them. For a copy of the map call the St. Bernard Tourism Commission at (504) 278-4242.

Getting There

The best way to explore the Isleños community of lower St. Bernard Parish, 20 miles from downtown New Orleans, is on a driving tour. Getting to lower St. Bernard Parish is a snap. Take I–10 east toward Slidell to the I–510 on-ramp. Take I–510 to Chalmette (the only direction you can go). The interstate turns into Paris Road; follow Paris Road all the way to where it ends in Chalmette at the intersection of St. Bernard Highway, also known as LA 46. (You'll see the signs for the Chalmette Ferry Terminal and the St. Bernard Parish Prison.) Turn right and head west.

i **The St. Bernard Parish Tourist Commission (www.visitstbernard.com) is a good place for additional information on points of interest and special events, such as fishing rodeos, throughout the parish. Call (504) 278-4242.**

Attractions

One of the most striking aspects of the redbrick ruins of the **De La Ronde Plantation** house may be its location—on the neutral ground of St. Bernard Highway just west of Paris Road, near the entrance to Chalmette National Historical Park. (In New Orleans we refer to medians as neutral grounds, after those on Canal Street that once served as a "neutral" space between the French Quarter and the new American section of the city.) Col. Pierre Denis de la Ronde, a leader of the Louisiana militia, built the plantation in 1805 and 16 years later planted the alley of oaks that stretches from the house to the Mississippi River. The plantation home was used by the British as a temporary hospital and headquarters during the Battle of New Orleans; the remains of British General Pakenham were carried here after the battle.

The Chalmette National Historical Park and Chalmette National Cemetery (8606 West St. Bernard Hwy.; 504-589-3382; www.nps .gov/jela) is the site of the 1815 Battle of New Orleans—the final battle of the War of 1812. (See the Parks and Recreation section in the Attractions and Activities chapter.) The park was established in 1939 after a 45-year effort waged by the Chalmette chapter of the United States Daughters of 1812. They were also responsible

for construction of the Chalmette Monument in 1909. (The obelisk had been designed 55 years earlier by Newton Richards, but construction was interrupted by the Civil War.) Museum exhibits and audiovisual programs at the visitor center tell the story of the battle. Park rangers present talks on the area's history while an annual reenactment illustrates American soldier life during the War of 1812. On the grounds is the antebellum Beauregard House, built in 1812 and once owned by René Beauregard, son of General P. G. T. Beauregard.

A local landmark and culinary tribute to home-cooked gluttony called **Rocky and Carlo's** can be found on dry land at 613 West St. Bernard Hwy. in Chalmette (504-279-8323). Check your heart-healthy diet at the door and prepare to binge—you won't be alone. Take a seat, dawlin'. Families pack the joint especially on Sun afternoon for Sicilian and New Orleans house specialties like the Wop Salad, fried chicken, roast beef po-boys, and the eatery's famous fresh-baked macaroni and cheese. Just as famous are the king-size portions prepared by kitchen cooks behind the order counter, which are guaranteed to satisfy the heartiest of appetites. Order a Barq's root beer—another tradition—with your smothered pork chops, and enjoy the down-home ambience of this local landmark, which opened in 1965.

Turn around and head in the opposite direction, east down St. Bernard Highway, past the Kaiser smokestack to the right, and soon you'll be in Meraux and driving under a picturesque alley of live oaks (on the south side) and pecan trees (on the north side) known as Docville Oaks. Photo hounds with a yen for sun-dappled country roads will most likely want to stop for pictures. Just be careful—rumbling tanker trucks travel the highway between the area's oil refineries. The trees were planted in the 1930s by Dr. Louis A. Meraux, for whom the town and oaks are named. He had them transported via Model A wreckers from nearby Olivier Plantation. Meraux, who was also parish sheriff from 1924 until his death in 1938, is regarded as the father of modern-day St. Bernard for the many new schools and roads built under his guidance.

If you packed a picnic, you'll want to take LA 39 off St. Bernard Highway in Violet and head to **St. Bernard State Park** (www.crt.state.la.us/crt/parks/stbernard/stbernard.htm). On your immediate right after crossing the railroad tracks is the Mississippi River Crevasse, a small but deep, tree-lined body of water formed in 1922 when the river broke through the levee. The crevasse is on the site of the former Poydras Plantation, once owned by 19th-century philanthropist Julian Poydras. Continue down LA 49 till you see the sign on your left for the entrance to the state park (see the Parks and Recreation section in the Attractions and Activities chapter).

As you continue your journey down St. Bernard Highway, you'll come to a fork in the road. Keep to your left, as this is where St. Bernard Highway turns into Old Bayou Road. The first historic home, **Sebastopol,** will be on your left. This plantation home was built in 1830 by Pierre Marin, a native of Spain, and Evariste Wagan. While the single-story frame house is not overwhelming as far plantation homes go, it was used as the St. Bernard branch of the Citizen's Bank of Louisiana in 1836. Two decades later Ignatius Szymanski, a Polish refugee and Confederate Army colonel, named it Sebastopol in honor of the stunning Russian defeat in a battle of the Crimean War. Today it is a private home and not open for tours.

Large tracts of land on which thriving sugarcane plantation homes like Sebastopol were built were sold by Isleño families, who later retreated to the lower reaches of the parish to Shell Beach and other fishing communities.

Beauregard Middle School will always have jurisprudence on its side—namely because the school is housed in the **Old Courthouse,** a stately three-story Federal-style building designed by the Freret brothers and constructed in 1915 for the sum of $64,893. The structure served as the parish courthouse until 1938. Vicente Nunez, the son of Canary Island native Esteban Nunez de Villavicencio, originally donated the property to the

parish in 1848. Esteban Nunez was the progenitor of the politically influential Nunez family of St. Bernard Parish.

Farther down Old Bayou Road to the left are the **Ducros Historical Museum and Library** and its next-door neighbor, the Museo de Los Isleños—better known as the **Los Isleños Heritage and Multicultural Park** (www.losislenos.org), both destroyed in Hurricane Katrina.

A sign in front of the museum displays the names of the eight ships—including the *Sacramento,* the *Sagrado Corazon de Jesus,* the *Santa Faz,* and the *Trinidad*—that transported an estimated 2,000 Canary Islanders to Spanish Louisiana. The immigration was part of a grand colonization scheme by King Charles II of Spain and headed by Pierre Phillippe de Marigny. He donated to Spain a huge parcel of land bisected by Bayou Terre-aux-Boeuf ("land of oxen") from Poydras to Lake Borgne and the Mississippi Sound. By 1780, when the region was renamed San Bernardo in honor of Gov. Bernardo de Galvez, more than 700 Isleños were living here. By the 1840s, Italian immigrants began arriving, followed by Germans and Filipinos.

Just behind the site of the new Islenos museum are old board-and-batten structures, including the Coconut Island Store, the first of several old structures from the area relocated onto the grounds as part of the re-created village. A bar and grocery built in the 1920s (and vacant since the '50s), the Coconut Island was dubbed the "Bucket of Blood" for the weekend-night fistfights that broke out inside. The Isleños were nothing if not passionate.

Other historic local structures relocated to the museum grounds include the Estopinal House (and separate kitchen building), constructed of hand-hewn cypress posts and bousillage, a mud-and-moss mixture originally used by Native Americans. The bousillage was placed between posts and used as insulation. The Estopinal House, ca. 1800, is identical in floor plan to the original homes built by the Spanish government for Isleño colonists in St. Bernard in the 1780s. The structure will be restored as a house museum, depicting life in the earliest days of Isleño colonization in Louisiana. Future plans call for additional historic structures as they become available.

For a real treat visit the grounds of the museums during the annual **Isleño Festival** held during the third weekend in March. Modern-day descendants of Canary Islanders roll out the welcome mat with traditional taste treats like caldo (Spanish soup), oyster fritters, and potatoes en salsa verde. Folk musicians from the Canary Islands are usually on hand to perform while volunteers in period costumes hold living-history demonstrations on palmetto-thatch hut building and hand-carved model boat construction. Also on display are traditional home remedies. Don't miss it.

It wasn't until 1842 that sugarcane plantation owner Laurent Millaudon built **Creedmore,** a Greek Revival plantation home on Old Bayou Road and today a well-shaded private residence. The structure, including several outbuildings such as the overseer's house, stables, and privy, is visible from the road. The private residence of **Magnolia Plantation** (reportedly the oldest home in the parish) is easy to miss because in some ways it barely resembles a plantation. Today the original French windows and gallery are hidden behind a spacious redbrick- and window-enclosed front porch. Towering magnolias flank this private home, built in 1794 by Antonio Mendez not long after he and Manuel Solis developed new sugarcane cultivation techniques.

Not too far down Old Bayou Road on the right side is the **St. Bernard Cemetery** and its cluster of bleach-white aboveground tombs dating to 1787. To read the family names chiseled into the smooth granite tombs is to learn the roll call of the proud Isleños immigrants from the Canary Islands who settled lower St. Bernard Parish south of New Orleans in the 18th century—names like Melerine, Alfonso, Molero, Nunez, Estopinal, and others. In fact, Gran Canaria native Joseph Messa, a farmer, was the first to be interred at the St. Bernard Cemetery, one of the oldest in Louisiana. St. Bernard's first sheriff, Francois Garic, a veteran

of the Battle of New Orleans and a sugar planter, is buried here, as well as the family of General P. G. T. Beauregard and a Revolutionary War soldier who died in 1815.

The privately owned **Kenilworth Plantation,** with its six truncated square columns (a design originating in colonial French Haiti), double-hip pitched roof, and brick-between-post construction, stands as one of the area's most enduring examples of antebellum architecture. Set at the back of a grassy oak-dotted lot, the French- and Spanish-colonial mansion was built between 1816 and 1819, fastened together by mortising and wooden pegs—and without a single nail.

Yet another fork in the road leads travelers either to the fishing community of **Delacroix Island** or those of **Shell Beach, Yscloskey,** and **Hopedale.** Explore both byways (Delacroix and Shell Beach are only 10 minutes away in either direction) as they each run alongside scenic Bayou Terre-aux-Boeuf and fleets of skiffs and private shrimp and oyster boats. Arrive in the afternoon and watch deckhands off-load the day's catch. On a sunny day you're likely to pass a family or two, perched atop ice coolers on the grassy road shoulder with fishing poles in hands. Take time to enjoy the bayou view before turning around and heading to Shell Beach and Yscloskey. Usually by late afternoon the green trawling nets of tall-rigged shrimp boats there are "wings up" at the eleven and one o'clock positions.

Across the vast expanse of Bayou Yscloskey from Shell Beach are the ruins of **Fort Proctor** on a spit of shell-strewn marsh. Construction of the fort's three-tiered tower (originally reached by a drawbridge over an inner moat) began in 1856 at the direction of Captain P. G. T. Beauregard. The outpost, designed to safeguard New Orleans against invasion from the bayous of Lake Borgne, is a vivid reminder of the area's strategic military importance. Outbreak of the Civil War prevented the roof and second-story floor from being built. Ironically, a garrison of black Union soldiers occupied the fort in 1865. Plans over the years to turn the fort into a recreational facility never materialized, and today the only way to visit the abandoned structure is to charter a private boat. In recent years the quiet, countrified charm of Shell Beach has caught the eye of the well-to-do. **Proctor's Landing,** for example, is a small but growing development of new, modern-style homes built on pylons with massive decks overlooking the bayou. Property values are rising throughout the community, and some have suggested that it won't be long before Waverunners outnumber fishing boats.

ST. TAMMANY: OVER THE BRIDGE AND THROUGH THE WOODS

Thirty miles north of New Orleans across Lake Pontchartrain sits St. Tammany Parish, where visitors can find the natural delights of a weekend in the country. The original inhabitants of these piney woods, which locals call the north shore, were the Choctaw Indians. The area was part of the vast Louisiana Territory that Napoleon sold to the United States in the early 19th century. At that time it was named for Delaware Indian Chief Tamanend, who was renowned for his virtue.

Even before that time, though, settlers—mostly via New Orleans—were drawn to the area by its abundant sources of water. The earliest industries were boat building, farming, brick molding, and timber. In antebellum times, St. Tammany boomed as a resort community with hotels, inns, and restaurants frequented by wealthy New Orleans Creoles who came to partake of the "healing" artesian waters in the town of Abita Springs or simply to holiday in the fresh outdoors on *l'autre cote du lac*—the other side of the lake. Daily boat excursions from the city were popular, and by 1880 people were able to travel here by rail.

For more information on attractions and special events in the great outdoors north of the lake, call the St. Tammany Parish Tourist and Convention Commission (www.louisiananorthshore.com) at (800) 634-9443.

The 1956 completion of the 24-mile Lake Pontchartrain Causeway Bridge, the world's longest bridge completely over water, made the drive only a 60-minute commute to New Orleans. In recent years, thousands of New Orleanians have relocated to the north shore, making St. Tammany the state's fastest growing parish.

There are two ways to get to the north shore from New Orleans. I–10 east takes drivers to Slidell on the east side of the parish, and the Causeway (which is off I–10 west at the Causeway Boulevard exit) takes visitors to west St. Tammany and the towns of Mandeville, Madisonville, and Covington. The following are suggestions of at least twice as many activities as can be done in a day, so take your pick and enjoy your day in the country.

Slidell

Settled in 1850, Slidell offers natural attractions and scenery. Don't miss the **Honey Island Swamp Tour** (See Attractions and Activities chapter). Considered one of America's most pristine river swamps, the area is teeming with wildlife, including alligators, waterfowl, and mink.

Mandeville

From Slidell, take I–12 west to the town of Mandeville (or go straight to Mandeville from New Orleans via the Causeway). Founded as a summer retreat by Bernard de Marigny, one of New Orleans' most prominent Creoles, Mandeville offers **Fontainebleau State Park** (see the Parks and Recreation section in the Attractions and Activities chapter) for hiking, bird-watching, and picnicking. Excellent for cycling or horseback riding, nine of the 31 miles of the **Tammany Trace,** a 200-foot wide wooded trail that follows the old Illinois Central railroad bed, passes through the park. For more information call (800) 43–TRACE.

Madisonville

A few minutes west of Mandeville (take scenic byway LA 22) is Madisonville. This quaint waterfront town, situated at the mouth of the Tchefuncte River, was established in 1810 and named for President James Madison. It is home to the annual **Wooden Boat Festival** that attracts the largest gathering of antique, classic, and contemporary boats in the South. **The Fairview-Riverside State Park** (see the Parks and Recreation section in the Attractions and Activities chapter) is also here, offering piney woods, a cypress swamp, and good fishing.

Covington

About 10 minutes up LA 21 is the town of Covington. Established in 1813, Covington scenically sits where the Bogue Falaya and Tchefuncte Rivers meet. Stroll through the shops and galleries of Covington's quaint historic district, and don't miss **H. J. Smith's Son's General Store** at 308 North Columbia St. Family owned and operated since 1876, this shop is more museum than store. It has everything from ox yokes and cast-iron stoves to plantation bells and cypress swings. Then tour the region's only winery, **Pontchartrain Vineyards** (www.pontchartrainvineyards .com; 985-892-9742), just outside town on Highway 1082, where fine table wines are produced. The tour includes tasting in an Old World, French Provençal tasting room.

At the end of the day, before heading back to New Orleans, stop back in Madisonville and enjoy dinner at **Friends on the Tchefuncte** (407 St. Tammany St., 985-845-7303; www.geauxfriends .com), in a beautiful riverdock setting. From there, cruise on back across the Causeway to the city.

PLANTATIONS: THE WAY WE WERE

Call it political correctness. Call it long overdue. Either way, a growing number of River Road plantation homes between New Orleans and Baton Rouge are beginning to acknowledge stories of the African slaves who almost single-handedly—and, it should be remembered, without any say in the matter—constructed the antebellum's so-called grandeur of the Old South.

Many antebellum homes throughout southeast Louisiana's Plantation Country offer overnight accommodations, a romantic way to savor the historic opulence, architecture, and elegance of a time when self-pampering was the order of the day—and night.

Any story of the African experience in southeast Louisiana can only make a visit to Plantation Country richer, not to mention more accurate. Some tours include visits to historic on-site slave quarters. Consider: It was in one of Laura Plantation's 150-year-old slave cabins that the West African folktales of "Compair Lapin," better known in English as the legendary "Br'er Rabbit," were first told on the American continent.

Plantation Country still offers an unparalleled glimpse of what unlimited time, wealth, ego, free labor, and architectural largesse could create in this one-time backwater territory. Ironically, the smoke-belching refineries that today dot the petrochemical corridor along River Road also remind us that time waits for no one.

DESTREHAN PLANTATION
13034 River Rd., Destrehan
(985) 764-8785
www.destrehanplantation.org
What makes this home noteworthy, at least in the historic scheme of things, is that Destrehan is the oldest documented plantation left intact in the lower Mississippi Valley. And that's saying a mouthful. This multicolumned tribute to Louisiana's antebellum glory was built in 1787 and acquired five years later by Jean Noel Destrehan, the son of a French aristocrat statesman, from his father-in-law, Robin de Logny. These names mean something down here, trust us.

Destrehan had his own statesman stash, and in 1810 he didn't bat an eye at the cost of embellishing this stately mansion with two additional wings. After all, he had the bucks. During his off time he had perfected the process for granulating sugar and, thus, helped launch the most profitable industry in the history of the Louisiana plantation economy. No layabout, he.

From 1830 to 1840 the facade and interior were changed during a major renovation, and today the Greek Revival-style house showcases Destrehan's hand-hewn cypress timbers, bousillage-entre-poteau construction, and West Indies-style roof. Destrehan Plantation, listed in the National Register of Historic Places, is also a popular site for dinner parties and special evening occasions, when only costumed guides who intrigue visitors with the history of the house and its ghosts will do.

Located 8 miles from New Orleans International Airport, Destrehan is best reached by taking I–310 to the River Road exit. Head east on River Road and you can't miss it or the house's twin redbrick chimneys. Tours are daily 9 a.m. to 4 p.m. Tickets cost $15 for adults, $5 for children aged six to 16. A gift shop sells books by Louisiana authors, locally made handcrafts, and specialty products. A fall festival is held the second weekend of Nov.

HOUMAS HOUSE
40136 LA 942, Darrow
(225) 473-9380
www.houmashouse.com
In its heyday more than 20,000 acres of surrounding sugarcane fields made fortunes for men like Ireland native John Burnside, who bought Houmas and 12,000 acres for $1 million in 1858. The British subject saved his home from the ravages of the Civil War by declaring immunity, thus avoiding occupation by Union forces. The move helped Houmas flourish as the greatest sugar producer in Louisiana in the late 1800s under Col. William Porcher Miles.

The house was built in 1840 by John Smith Preston, and movie buffs will recognize the blinding-white three-story, 14-columned home as the setting for the classic film *Hush, Hush, Sweet Charlotte,* starring Bette Davis and Olivia de Havilland. The Greek Revival masterpiece has also been featured in national magazines including *Life, House Beautiful,* and *National Geographic.* Preston pur-

chased the house from his wife's father, Revolutionary War hero General Wade Hampton of South Carolina, who had acquired the property in 1812.

The original four-room dwelling at the rear of the house, characteristic of both Spanish and rural French architecture, was built in the late 1700s by Alexander Latil after he purchased this tract of land along the Mississippi River from the Houmas Indians. The structure was later attached to the great house by a porte cochere, or arched carriageway.

The grand old home fell into disrepair after the Depression and was purchased and restored in 1940 by Dr. George Crozat of New Orleans for his country estate. Today the home, listed on the National Register of Historic Places, is furnished with the late Crozat's collection of 1840s-era museum pieces of early Louisiana craftsmanship. The formal gardens have been returned to their former beauty beneath magnolias and 200-year-old moss-draped oak trees.

Plantation tours are open Mon and Tues 9 a.m. to 5 p.m. and Wed through Sun 9 a.m. to 8 p.m. Cost is $20 for the mansion and gardens and $10 for the grounds only.

LAURA PLANTATION
2247 Louisiana Hwy. 18 River Rd.,
Vacherie
(225) 265-7690, (888) 799-7690
www.lauraplantation.com
Perhaps the most important legacy of this Creole plantation is not its opulence but rather the fact that inside its six historic 150-year-old slave cabins were first told the West African folktales of "Compair Lapin," better known in English as the legendary "Br'er Rabbit," by Senegalese slaves. This two-story restoration-in-process, built in 1805, is surrounded by sugarcane fields and is home to the largest collection of artifacts—more than 5,000 pieces—belonging to a single Louisiana plantation family. Objects include clothing, toiletries, business and slave records, Carnival and mourning heirlooms, and the retold stories of Laura Locoul, the 1805 owner-manager. All of which enables visitors to glimpse the daily work-

ings of 18th- and 19th-century plantation life, as well as a detailed look at one extended Creole family. Laura's weathered walls add an authentic air of untouched history to the 45-minute guided tours conducted daily 9 a.m. to 4 p.m. Admission is $15 adults; $5 children age six to 17.

MADEWOOD
4250 Louisiana Hwy. 308,
Napoleonville
(985) 369-7151
www.madewood.com

The origin of this wonderfully restored, two-story Greek Revival mansion constructed in 1818 on Bayou Lafourche is rooted in sibling rivalry. Madewood was built over a period of eight years by the youngest of three sons of a wealthy North Carolina planter to outdo the architectural splendor of his older brother's Woodlawn home. But, as luck would have it, the youngest brother died of yellow fever before Madewood, designed by noted architect Henry Howard, was completed.

Be that as it may, what really sets this 21-room Plantation Country charmer apart from its competitors is the reputation of current owners Keith and Millie Marshall for treating overnight visitors staying in one of the greathouse guest rooms to a unique experience: a library wine-and-cheese reception followed by a sumptuous multicourse candlelit dinner in the large dining room and, later, brandy in the parlor. Some guests opt for a more secluded stay in one of three informal suites in Charlet House, a restored raised cottage built in the 1820s on the plantation grounds, which features a family cemetery and carriage house.

Not to be outshined by nearby Houmas House, site of the movie *Hush, Hush, Sweet Charlotte*, Madewood lured Hollywood to its breezy gallery and massive white columns for the filming of *A Woman Called Moses,* starring Cicely Tyson. Tours are available daily 10 a.m. to 3 p.m. at a cost of $10 for adults and $6 for children. Madewood is located 2 miles south of Napoleonville on LA 308, 74 miles from New Orleans and 20 minutes from Houmas House.

NOTTOWAY PLANTATION
31025 Hwy. 1
White Castle
(225) 545-2730, (866) 527-6884
www.nottoway.com

If Southern grandeur has a name, it's Nottoway. That in no small part was due to the great wealth of prosperous sugar planter John Hampden Randolph, who in 1849 commissioned what today is the largest and certainly one of the finest homes in the entire South. Nottoway, simply put, is an American castle whose Italianate and Greek Revival architecture and 22 enormous columns epitomize antebellum luxury and magnificence. Randolph also saw to it that his splendid 53,000-square-foot home with 64 rooms brought innovative and unique features to the South, including indoor plumbing, gas lighting, and coal fireplaces.

Ten years after construction began, Nottoway was completed to accommodate Randolph's 11 children. Situated on a 7,000-acre sugar plantation, this aristocratic house, with its intricate lacy plaster friezework, hand-painted Dresden porcelain doorknobs, hand-carved marble mantels, Corinthian columns of cypress wood, crystal chandeliers, and 65-foot Grand White Ballroom, was saved from total destruction during the Civil War by a kindly Northern gunboat officer who had once been a guest of the Randolphs. The current owner, Paul Ramsey of Sydney, Australia, continues an authentic restoration begun in 1980.

Guided tours are daily 9 a.m. to 5 p.m. Admission is $20 for adults and $6 for children age six to 12; children under five free. A restaurant and overnight accommodations in one of 13 guest rooms, each with private bath and entrance, are available. Room rate includes bottle of sherry; morning wake-up call with sweet potato muffins, orange juice, and coffee; plantation breakfast; and guided tour of the mansion. To reach Nottoway take I-10 west and exit at LA 22. Turn left on LA 70 and follow the signs across the Sunshine Bridge, 14 miles north through Donaldsonville on LA 1.

OAK ALLEY PLANTATION
3645 Louisiana Hwy. 18,
Vacherie
(225) 265-2151, (800) 442-5539
www.oakalleyplantation.com

To stand at the wrought-iron gates to the entrance of this River Road plantation near the levee and gaze down its quarter-mile alley of 28 evenly spaced, 300-year-old live oak trees, believed to be at least 100 years older than the great house, is to experience firsthand perhaps the most spectacular antebellum setting in the entire Mississippi Valley. If nothing else, it's probably the most photographed plantation house in Louisiana.

Fluted Doric columns surround the two-story Greek Revival house originally named Bon Sejour and built in 1837 by Jacques T. Roman III, reportedly because he was so enamored of the oaks. The traditional interior floor plan leads visitors to a second-floor gallery overlooking the alley of oaks. Jefferson Hardin bought the deteriorating house in 1914 and sold it in 1925 to Andrew Stewart, whose restoration gained for Oak Alley its designation as a National Historic Landmark. The house is furnished as it was during Stewart's ownership.

Oak Alley is open for tours Mon through Fri 10 a.m. to 4 p.m. and Sat and Sun 10 a.m. to 5 p.m. Tickets are $15 for adults (age 19 and older), $7.50 (age 13 to 18), and $4.50 (age six to 12). Take I-10 west to the Gramercy exit 194 and take LA 18 (River Road) to Vacherie. Oak Alley is located between St. James and Vacherie, 60 miles from downtown New Orleans.

SAN FRANCISCO PLANTATION HOUSE
Drawer AX, Reserve
(985) 535-2341, (888) 322-1756
www.sanfranciscoplantation.org

Back in the 1820s, Elisee Rillieux had the idea to put together a large plantation out of smaller properties. Edmond Bozonier Marmillion, whose family owned some estates in the neighborhood, liked what he saw so much that he snatched it off the market in 1830 and commenced construction

two decades later. Today this galleried house, originally called St. Frusquin, a name derived from the French slang *sans fruscins*—"without a penny in my pocket"—has only a dining room and various service rooms on the ground floor. The main living room is on the second floor as was often the Creole custom. Marmillion's son Valsin and his wife, the former Louise von Seybold, whom he met during a trip to Bavaria, decorated the home in 1860.

In 1879 Achiulle D. Bougere bought the plantation, renamed it San Francisco, and in 1905 sold it to the Ory family. For a while this plantation seemed gone with the wind, but a $2-million complete restoration in the 1970s returned this belle of the ball to its rightful place on the River Road plantation corridor. Ceiling murals, faux marbling, and graining reflect the interior splendor that once was, while Gothic windows, ornate grillwork, and gingerbread trim characterize the facade. Those tracking the Battle of the Plantations take note: Flanking the exterior of the house are onion-domed blue-and-white water cisterns that look like miniature Russian Orthodox churches. Daily 30- to 40-minute tours are conducted every 15 minutes from 9:40 a.m. to 4:40 p.m. at San Francisco Plantation, located on River Road about 1 mile past the Marathon Oil Refinery. Admission is $15 for adults; $7 for children 7 to 17; kids under 6 are admitted free.

CAJUN COUNTRY: HOUMA GOOD TIMES

In the 18th century the British swept into Nova Scotia and shoved the French settlers out. This homeless band left Acadia and moved southward to set up an outpost along the coast of the colonial French territory of Louisiana. These Acadians kept their language and their culture and made new lives for themselves as the Cajuns of South Louisiana. Many of them ended up an hour southwest of New Orleans in the modern-day city of Houma, named for the Houmas Indians who originally settled the area. Houma is the seat of Terrebonne Parish, the second largest in

Louisiana. More than half of Terrebonne's 2,000 square miles is made up of bayous, lakes, and salt marshes. The area offers the closest taste of Cajun Country to New Orleans as well as ample evidence of why Louisiana is called a Sportsman's Paradise. In fact, the bounty and beauty of this rich subtropical delta so enchanted the Acadians that they named it "Terrebonne," French for "good earth."

i Looking for a Sportsman's Paradise? Cajun Country is a great place to fish and hunt. For a complete list of charters and outfitters, call the Houma Area Tourist Commission (www.houmatourism.com) at (800) 688-2732.

Terrebonne Parish is located on the last great delta created by the Mississippi River more than 2,500 years ago and is home to the largest, most productive estuary system in the world. People here have long been connected to the local bayous. Pirate Jean Lafitte and adventurer Jim Bowie were known to retreat to the mystery of the region's moss-draped waterways. Civil War soldiers adapted to the land using a local plantation home as a hospital and converted Spanish moss into sutures. The Acadians chose the area because it was so secluded.

To reach Houma from New Orleans, cross the Crescent City Connection (the Mississippi River Bridge) and continue down US 90. It's a straight shot that takes about an hour. For a good area overview, stop at **Southdown Plantation,** which houses the **Terrebonne Parish Museum** and its oral history room. Exhibits chronicle the contributions made by various cultures in the area and showcase the unique Cajun lifestyle. The house itself, built in 1858, is beautifully decorated and displays a collection of 135 Boehm and Doughty porcelain birds as well as a re-creation of local U.S. Sen. Allen J. Ellender's private Washington office. (Ellender served in Congress from 1937 to 1972.)

No one should miss **the swamp** on their visit to Terrebonne Parish. The variety of tours include those on foot, by boat, and by air—and now even by train. The two most popular tours are those offered by "Alligator" Annie Miller's Sons and Ron "Cajun Man" Guidry. Miller's sons still steer a boat full of visitors into the moss-draped cypress swamp, cut the engine and, then, as if calling a dog sing out, "Come on, Baby!" as a 7-foot alligator swims up to get its reward—a piece of raw chicken they place on a stick they hold just above the water. "When Annie's sons call," say locals, "the gators come like children to an ice-cream truck." **Alligator Annie's Sons' Swamp and Marsh Tours** (www.annie-miller.com) is at 3718 Southdown Mandalay Rd., Houma; (985) 868-4758 or (800) 341-5441.

Ron "Black" Guidry, on the other hand, is known as the Cajun crooner. While swamp-cruising visitors gaze at alligators, possums, and cranes, Guidry, a former Green Beret and Louisiana State Trooper, plays guitar and sings Cajun songs. If you're feeling lonely, it won't be for long because Guidry's dog, Gator Bait, a Louisiana catahoula who rides along, is sure to give warm welcome. **A Cajun Man's Swamp Cruise** (www.cajunman.com) is at 3109 Southdown Mandalay Rd., Houma; (985) 868-4625.

In Gibson, 15 miles west of Houma, there is another fun option for exploring the swamp and learning about Cajun life on the bayou: the **Wildlife Gardens** (www.wildlifegardens.com) at 5306 North Bayou Black Dr., (985) 575-3676. The Wildlife Gardens is a swamp zoo featuring native plants and animals including rare duck species. The walking tour features an authentic trapper's cabin and B&B cabins for overnight accommodations.

Take US 90 back to Houma and head south on LA 56 to begin a picturesque 80-mile driving tour of **Bayou Country.** Travel down LA 56 until you reach LA 315 for the return trip. Along the way are sugarcane fields, moss-draped cypress trees, the swamp maple, redbud, and various fruit trees. See eagles, egrets, herons, owls, and seabirds—all of which flock to this fertile delta located within the Mississippi Flyway, the migratory path of waterfowl and geese from 32 states and three Canadian provinces.

At the Bayou **Dularge Marina** (www.dularge .com), visitors will find a small fishing village where many locals make their living repairing boats and making nets. See miles of campboats, oyster lugger boats, shrimp boats, and various pleasure boats. The marina offers a rest stop, refreshments, fuel, visitor information, and the opportunity to experience the charm of local Cajun conversation. Five miles from the junction of LA 56 and LA 57 is **LUMCON,** a marine biology research facility. Visitors are welcome to stop and view the marsh from the facility's observation tower, free of charge.

Back in Houma, check out **A-Bear's Cafe,** which also features live Cajun music on Fri nights; 809 Bayou Black Dr. in Houma. Call (985) 872-6306.

ONE DAY AT A TIME ON THE MISSISSIPPI GULF COAST

Where do many Big Easy residents head off to when the walls start closing in? For more than 150 years the Mississippi Gulf Coast has been a home away from home for locals seeking an escape from the rattle and hum of big-city life. First-timers are easily smitten by the area's breeze-swept sandy beaches, and the raucous gulls that scout overhead for fish in the calm, warm seas. Travelers along the coastal scenic drive lined with oak-framed antebellum mansions and stately summer homes with screened verandas can look out to the horizon and see shrimpers and sailboats silhouetted in the late afternoon sun. Shopping and historic districts compete for attention with lively beach bars, brash souvenir shops, and casinos in the third-largest gambling mecca in the country.

In 2005, Hurricane Katrina's winds and tidal surge devastated much of the coastal areas. Since then, the stalwart residents and officials of the towns and cities along the Mississippi Gulf Coast have been working tirelessly and valiantly—one day at a time—to rebuild their communities. And New Orleanians couldn't be happier—or more simpatico with their Mississippi country cousins along the Gulf Coast. The umbilical cord linking the Crescent City and the Mississippi Gulf Coast reaches back to 1699 when French explorer and New Orleans founder Pierre LeMoyne d'Iberville landed in Biloxi and established the first permanent European settlement in the Louisiana Territory for King Louis XIV. Iberville established Biloxi (*buh-LUX-see*) as the third capital of the colonial French megacolony, which stretched north to Canada, east to the Alleghenies, and west to the Rockies. Prior to the Civil War, wealthy 19th-century New Orleanians rode the Louisiana-Nashville Railroad to their gracious Greek Revival and West Indies-style planter's homes located on the Gulf Coast. Confederate President Jefferson Davis spent the last 12 years of his life at Beauvoir, a national historic landmark in Biloxi, which is open for tours.

Affectionately dubbed the Redneck Riviera, the Gulf Coast stretches from Waveland eastward through Bay St. Louis, Pass Christian, Long Beach, Gulfport, Biloxi, and Ocean Springs on US 90 along a 26-mile curve of man-made white-sand beach. Variety is the spice of life on this sun-drenched Mississippi coastline where the Deep South meets the Gulf of Mexico. The **Mississippi Gulf Coast Coliseum & Convention Center,** for example, is big enough to lure heavy metal troubadours like Van Halen and just small-town enough to host local craft shows and the annual Crawfish Festival. The region has offered shelter from the storm for such eccentric and nationally acclaimed artists as the late painter Walter Anderson and potter George Ohr, who ran a Cadillac dealership in his later years. One watering hole celebrates Christmas in July (and the owner gets riled if anyone cuts in on his one-man jukebox sing-alongs). And sometimes it seems as though the casual seafood restaurants overlooking the area's picturesque harbors are as plentiful as the beach kiosks that rent waverunners and umbrellas.

Waveland

It may be years before this "Hospitality City" is once again a popular weekend getaway for New Orleanians and year-round home for Big Easy retirees, but there is still at least one out-of-this-world reason to visit Waveland: the **NASA Stennis Space Center** (800-237-1821). Since 1966 the facility has test-fired rocket engines that have taken astronauts to the moon and back, as well as those used on the Space Shuttle. Today the site's StennisSphere offers "shake, rattle and roar" tours Wed through Sat 10 a.m. to 3 p.m. of the complex's noteworthy exhibits including a real Space Shuttle main engine, a walk-through of the International Space Station, the Rocket Test Control Center, a Space Shuttle cockpit, and moon rocks. Admission is free.

To get here, take I-10 east from downtown New Orleans approximately one hour, over Lake Pontchartrain, and past the city of Slidell. At the juncture of I-10 and I-59/I-12, stay on I-10 heading east to the town of Bay St. Louis in Mississippi. Take exit 2 and follow signs on Highway 607 to the Hancock Country Welcome Center's "launch pad," where a shuttle picks up visitors and takes them to the Stennis Space Center. *Note:* Photo IDs are required for visitors aged 18 and older.

Bay St. Louis

Among the hardest hit areas along the Mississippi Gulf Coast was Bay St. Louis (www.baysaintlouiscity.com), once rated as among the best art towns in America, and known for its slow-paced way of life and homespun seafood eateries. While a lot of rebuilding still lies ahead, especially along the 3-square-block waterfront district, this resilient town's artists' community hasn't exactly been asleep at the easel. New galleries, artists co-ops and antiques shops have sprung up, including **The Shops at Serenity Place** (126 Main St.; 228-493-5712), which boasts the works of nearly a dozen artists ranging from funky original local art and semi precious stone jewelry to black-and-white fine-art photography. A must-visit venue is the **Alice Moseley Folk Art Museum** (214 Bookter St.; 228-467-9223; www.alicemoseley.com), which celebrates via paintings and video the life and times of the late local primitive artist Alice Moseley, who lived at the Bookter Street address before her death in 2004.

Also not to be missed is the '30s-era stucco **train depot,** where part of Tennessee Williams's *This Property is Condemned,* starring Robert Redford and Natalie Wood, was filmed. To reach the depot take Main Street to Toulme Street, turn left, and follow Toulme Street until it turns into Blaize Street at the bend in the road. Drive over the railroad tracks and you'll see the green building on your right.

Eateries are also making a comeback thanks to opening of such popular dining spots as **Jack's Restaurant** (136 Blaize St.; 228-467-3065), and **Mockingbird Cafe** (110 South Second St.; 228-467-8383; www.mockingbirdcafe.com), both of which serve up short but tasty menu staples of sandwiches, pizza, and more.

To get here follow Highway 607 from Waveland to Highway 90, and follow Highway 90 for approximately 15 miles to Bay St. Louis.

Pass Christian

Besides its pretty harbor, mercifully uncrowded beaches, and laid-back ambience, one of the best things about this small residential community, known affectionately as "The Pass" (pronounced *Pass Kris-tee-ANN*), is its 3-mile Scenic Drive, which runs alongside coastal Highway 90. The drive offers visitors a close-up view of waterfront antebellum mansions and Creole cottages. Many of these gracious homes were built by well-heeled New Orleans merchants in the 19th century and today rise from manicured lush front lawns shaded by towering oak, pine, and magnolia trees. Some of the homes are on the National Register of Historic Places.

The Pass (http://pass-christian.ms.us/) was once an internationally known resort area. Six U.S. presidents have vacationed at The Pass, including Woodrow Wilson, who resided in the "Summer White House" on Scenic Drive, and Theodore Roosevelt, who came often to sail, write, and visit friends.

Long Beach

Pick up Highway 90 at the end of Scenic Drive and the next town you'll come to is Long Beach (http://

long-beach.ms.us), the self-proclaimed Radish Capital of the World in the early 1900s. Two of the most popular attractions include the 500-year-old, 50-foot **Friendship Oak** (www.gp.usm.edu/oak.htm) at the University of Southern Mississippi Gulf Coast campus (730 East Beach Blvd.; 228-865-4500) and **Wolf River Canoes** (www.wolfriver canoes.com), 21652 Tucker Rd. (228-452-7666), for leisurely guided tours of the local swamps and waterways. Cost is $45 per canoe (two-person minimum); children under 12 can sit in the center for free. Call for departure times.

Gulfport

Two points of pride among the residents of Mississippi's second-largest city are (1) the town celebrated its centennial anniversary in 1988; and (2) the State Port at Gulfport is the largest banana importer in the country. That said, Gulfport (www.gulfcoast.org) is also a fun place for kids, and the best place to start is the state's first hands-on children's museum at the **Lynn Meadows Discovery Center** (246 Dolan Ave.; 228-897-6039). Turn left off Highway 90 onto Dolan Avenue and it's ½ block on the right-hand side. Simulation is the name of the game here. Youngsters can become a news reporter and make a video, shop for seafood and garden veggies at a grocery store, operate a crane, trawl the Gulf for shrimp, and even load a train engine with coal from the Dolan Avenue Depot. Youngsters with a yen for science can deflect a tornado, make a square wheel roll, and defy gravity. Not to be left out, toddlers can join a group of teddy bears on a bayou camp "picnic." The center is open Tues through Sat 10 a.m. to 5 p.m. Admission is $7 for all ages.

Ship Island is the most historically significant and visited of the four major barrier islands (the others are Cat, Horn, and Petit Bois) rimming Mississippi Sound about 10 miles offshore. Visitors can tour the remains of historic **Fort Massachusetts,** built in 1858. Travelers can surf-fish, swim, and sunbathe at the **Gulf Islands National Seashore,** known for its warm tidal pools and wind-shaped sand dunes crowned with sea oats.

Visitors will find a small beach snack bar, picnic pavilions, shower and restrooms, and rental beach chairs and umbrellas. During the War of 1812, 60 British ships with nearly 10,000 troops rendezvoused at Ship Island prior to an unsuccessful attack on New Orleans.

The island was a POW camp for Confederate soldiers and a base for the U.S. Second Regiment—one of the first African-American combat units to fight in the Civil War.

Ship Island is best reached by taking the **Ship Island Excursions** (www.msshipisland.com) passenger ferry (228-864-1014 or 866-466-7386), which departs the Gulfport Harbor daily during summer months at 9 a.m. and noon, returning at 2:30 and 5 p.m. Fall and spring departures are Wed through Fri 9 a.m. to 2:30 p.m., returning at 2:30 and 5 p.m. Call ahead—departure and return times may vary depending on season. Round-trip fees are $24 for adults; $14 children aged three to 10; and $22 seniors aged 62 and older. It's a good idea to buy tickets for the popular Skrmetta family-owned and -operated ferry excursion at least one hour prior to departure. Onboard snack bars and restrooms are available.

Biloxi

The French explorer Iberville landed in what is now modern-day Biloxi (www.biloxi.ms.us) on February 13, 1699. Since that time eight flags—namely, those of France, Britain, Spain, the Republic of Florida, Mississippi Territory, State of Mississippi, Confederate States of America, and United States of America—have flown over the area. By the mid-1850s Biloxi was arguably the Deep South's most popular coastal resort. New Orleans newspapers of the period were filled with advertisements proclaiming the amenities of the area's fine hotels: fresh seafood daily, live bands, banquets, and balls. As the most widely recognized Gulf Coast town, this city of 50,000 residents plays host to the lion's share of the region's casinos, the last home of Jefferson Davis, the historic Biloxi Lighthouse, and a museum of artworks by the late George Ohr, "the Mad Potter of Biloxi" (the late artist delighted in the moniker).

The **Ohr-O'Keefe Museum of Art** (www .georgeohr.org), housed at a temporary facility at 1596 Glenn Swetman Dr. (228-374-5547), pays homage to the Dali-like eccentric artist who used to wrap his 2-foot-long moustache around his ears while toiling at his potter's wheel. A significantly abbreviated display of only 30 pieces of Ohr's pottery is the result of the museum's decision to keep the lion's share of the potter's works in hurricane-proof storage until completion of the new Ohr-O'Keefe Museum, designed by renowned architect Frank Gehry, which is scheduled to open in 2011. The artist who went virtually unrecognized until his death and who owned a local Cadillac dealership was anything but modest. Ohr billed himself the "unequaled, unrivaled, undisputed greatest art potter on earth." Today a George Ohr pot can fetch up to $35,000—more than he earned as an artist his entire life. Orh's work, warehoused in boxes at his dealership, wasn't discovered until 1972, after his death, when visiting New Jersey resident James Carpenter bought 5,000 pots for $350,000. Today Ohr's pots are displayed in the Smithsonian, the Metropolitan Museum of Art, the Los Angeles County Museum, and the Victoria and Albert Museum in London.

It's impossible to miss the historic **Biloxi Lighthouse** (228-435-6339), one of the most famous icons on the coast—and perhaps the only lighthouse in the world situated in the middle of a four-lane highway. Located on Highway 90 (Beach Boulevard) at the foot of Porter Avenue, the towering white structure is topped by a weathervane and has been a symbol of the city's maritime industry since it was erected in 1848.

History buffs will want to set aside time to visit **Beauvoir-Jefferson Davis House and Presidential Library** (2244 Beach Blvd.; 228-388-4400), the final home of Confederate President Jefferson Davis. In 1877 the aging Davis accepted an invitation by then-owner Sarah Dorsey to write his memoirs at the 52-acre seaside estate. Two years later Davis and his wife, Varina, bought Beauvoir from Dorsey for $5,500, and in 1881 he published his memoirs as *The Rise and Fall of the Confederate Government*, followed by *A Short History of the Confederate States of America*.

Beauvoir (www.beauvoir.org), a national historic landmark overlooking Mississippi Sound, includes the 1851 Greek Revival residence and outbuildings, nature trails, a Victorian antique rose garden, and a Confederate cemetery. Beauvoir is open daily 9 a.m. to 5 p.m. and admission is $9 adults; $5 children age six to 16. The self-guided tour includes a 29-minute videotape, which provides a historical overview.

For a hands-on seafood experience, hop aboard the **Biloxi Shrimping Trip's** *Sailfish* (www.gcww.com/sailfish) at the Biloxi Small Craft Harbor on Highway 90 at Main Street, (800) 289-7908. The 70-minute tour in the calm protected waters between Deer Island and the Biloxi shoreline lets passengers participate in a real shrimping "expedition" that includes casting a net to catch blue crabs, flounder, stringrays, squid, and other sea life. Cost is $15 for adults and $10 for children age four to 11. Children age three and under are admitted free. Call for departure times.

One of the best dining experiences on the entire Mississippi Gulf Coast is to be found at **Mary Mahony's Old French House** (228-374-0163). John Grisham mentions this venerable landmark and one-time headquarters of the Louisiana Territory in his books *The Runaway Jury* and *The Partner*. French colonist Louis Fraiser constructed the building in 1737, and its original high ceilings, wooden-pegged cypress columns, heart-pine floors, and exposed walls of handmade brick are characteristic of Creole homes in the French Quarter. Diners who know what's good for them will want to try the shrimp remoulade, seafood gumbo, stuffed catfish, and bread pudding with rum sauce. Other signature dishes at this fine-dining establishment include Sisters of the Sea au gratin (fresh lump crabmeat and shrimp in a creamy cheese sauce); half-lobster Imperial (blended with shrimp in a cream sauce, teased with a hint of brandy and served en coquille). Hours are Mon through Sat 11 a.m. to 10 p.m.

Even if you don't dine at Mary Mahoney's, it's worth a visit just to see the spectacular

2,000-year-old oak tree "Patriarch" towering above the French Quarter-style courtyard. Nearby is the historic **Old Magnolia Hotel,** 119 Magnolia St., the coast's oldest extant antebellum hotel and today home to the **Biloxi Mardi Gras Museum,** (228) 435-6245. The museum tells the story of Gulf Coast Carnival celebrations and traditions with a display of festive costumes and old photographs. Hours are Mon through Sat 11 a.m. to 4 p.m. and admission is $2 for adults; $1 for seniors, students, and children; kids age six and under are admitted free.

Not to be outdone is Biloxi's triple threat of resort casinos—Beau Rivage, Grand Casino Biloxi, and the Hard Rock Hotel & Casino—that weekly draw New Orleans day-trippers for its gaming, restaurants, shows and nightlife. Among the best is **Beau Rivage** at 875 Beach Blvd. (228-386-7111, 888-567-6667; www.beaurivage.com), an $800 million, 32-story resort casino with a dozen restaurants, four lounges and bars, plus an equal number of upscale retail shops, a spa and pool. From the massive lobby arboretum of blooming azaleas, evergreens, and other foliage, all sunbathed by the sun streaming through the glass ceiling, to the fine-dining restaurants with inspired decor ranging from walls of Thai bamboo to walls lined by huge aquariums of tropical fish, this 1,740-guest room resort continues to make a splash post-Katrina thanks to a $500 million renovation. Gamblers will find every possible game of chance under the sun—and lots of them. But those who prefer to keep their hands off Lady Luck will have no problem finding fun, whether it's sunning around the Romanesque outdoor pool, relaxing at the Mediterranean-style, sexually segregated spa and sauna, or simply enjoying the Gulf of Mexico view from their guest room, with oversize bathrooms accented by Spanish and Grecian marble, hand-finished wood, luxurious bath towels, and a step-in shower for two. Others include the **Hard Rock Hotel & Casino** at 777 Beach Blvd. (228-374-7625; www.hardrockbiloxi.com) and the **Grand Biloxi Casino Hotel & Spa** at 280 Beach Blvd. (228-436-2946; 800-946-2946; www.grandcasinobiloxi.com).

i | While driving along Highway 90 in Biloxi, Mississippi, take note of the dozens of live oaks in the median (or neutral ground) that died in the aftermath of Hurricane Katrina but have been reborn as sculpted works of art by international award-winning "chainsaw artist" Dayton Scoggins of Mississippi.

Ocean Springs

If you do only one thing in Ocean Springs, it should be to visit the **Walter Anderson Museum** (510 Washington Ave.; 228-872-3164; www.walterandersonmuseum.org). Anderson, regarded as the region's premier artist, was a fierce Gauguinlike recluse whose inspired paintings and drawings of Gulf Coast animals, plants, and people put him on the map of 20th-century American artists. Anderson used to row his 12-foot skiff filled with paints and brushes 10 miles out to Horn and Chandeleur Islands to work. Andy Warhol collected Anderson's artworks, and today more than 150 examples of his carvings, ceramics, sketches, and paintings—including numerous vibrant watercolors of seashells, herons and gulls, swallow hawks and myrtle warblers, crabs and pumas—are on display. A wonderful "day in the life" mural discovered after the artist's death depicts Anderson's Gulf Coast world and is regarded as his most important work. The mural, originally painted on the walls and ceilings of a small room in Anderson's cottage, was painstakingly reconstructed and attached to the museum. The museum, located in the historic downtown district and next door to the Ocean Springs Community Center, is open Mon through Sat 9:30 a.m. to 4:30 p.m. and Sun 12:30 to 4:30 p.m. Admission is $7 adults; $6 seniors; and $5 children under 18. Admission is free on the first Mon of each month.

LIFE'S A BEACH AND THEN YOU FRY

When it comes to bagging rays close to home, New Orleanians are never bashful about piling the car with sun block, straw hats, and trashy novels for a quick fix on the Mississippi Gulf Coast. Surfers and boogie-board enthusiasts may be surprised to discover that the Gulf, rimmed by barrier islands, is flat-calm, shallow (walk out a quarter mile and you're still only knee-deep), and usually bathtub warm. Leave the wet suits at home. A lack of waves and dangerous undertows makes Mississippi's beaches, in theory at least, among the safest and most swimmer-friendly anywhere. Water sports including aquacycles, sunfish sailboats, waverunners, parasailing, paddleboats, and kayaks (plus umbrellas and beach chairs) can be rented on the beach usually in front of the larger hotels.

Free public beach parking is available from Bay St. Louis to Biloxi (although parking is prohibited from midnight to 6 a.m. in the parking bay in front of the Coliseum Holiday Inn in Biloxi). Permits for bonfires, a popular nighttime activity, are available from the city fire departments in Ocean Springs (288-875-4063), Bay St. Louis (288-467-4736), and Waveland (288-467-9353). In Bay St. Louis bonfires are permitted between Bay Oaks and Washington Street only. A $25 deposit is required and refunded if the site is cleaned before noon the following day. Permits cost $30 ($25 is refunded following cleanup within 24 hours) in Pass Christian, Long Beach, Gulfport, and Biloxi. Caution: The fine for not having a permit is $25 to $500.

RELOCATION

New Orleans is a mosaic of neighborhoods. One of the cornerstones of development here was the growth in the 19th and 20th centuries of working- and middle-class ethnic neighborhoods of immigrant populations—Irish, Italian, German, French, Spanish (including Canary Islanders, known locally as Isleños), descendents of the city's earliest Creole and African-American inhabitants, and, most recently, Vietnamese. During the past 60 years, a confluence of population growth, demographic shifts, economic upswings and downturns, and social change has transformed some neighborhoods dramatically, while others have barely been touched by the passage of time. Meantime, the development and growth of suburbs, some of which were wooded wetlands only three decades ago, has been nearly mind-boggling.

REAL ESTATE

Compared with other cities of similar size and infrastructure, New Orleans offers a sizeable and affordable middle- and upper-middle-class housing market, especially for people relocating from the Northeast, Pacific Northwest, and West Coast accustomed to inflated housing prices.

Newcomers to the area will find the state's homestead exemption a tax-friendly and money-saving aspect of home ownership. Homeowners are exempt from paying state property taxes on the first $75,000 of the value of their home. For example, an individual who lives in a $100,000 home pays taxes on $25,000 of the value; $125,000 for a $200,000 home, and so on. This can add up to a significant savings for the young family shopping for that first three-bedroom home, as well as the retiree on fixed income eager to downsize his post-work years by moving into a condo or town house.

In Orleans Parish, where property taxes are paid forward, the homestead exemption offers another excellent way to stretch the home-buying dollar. Since mortgage companies escrow a year of property taxes when a home is purchased, a reduced property tax bill enables buyers to spend less up front for their home.

Newcomers from large cities who are accustomed to long commutes will also discover it's fairly easy and economical to find suitable housing only 10 to 25 minutes from work. For north shore residents who commute to work in New Orleans and drive the Causeway bridge over Lake Pontchartrain or Interstate 10 from Slidell, the commute is about 45 minutes.

Not surprisingly, architecture varies greatly in this 300-year-old city, and a 1,000- to 1,500-square-foot house that people would still regard as "nice" can be had for $100,000-plus. Newcomers from Southern California or New York City who arrive here with heavy-duty home equity under their belts often discover they can live like virtual land barons.

But what of the neighborhoods?

NEIGHBORHOODS

French Quarter

The French Quarter is certainly New Orleans at its most colorful. But unlike Uptown, the French Quarter prefers to keep some of its most charming attributes tucked away like a secret. Tropical courtyards accented with lovely fountains hide behind a high brick fence or wrought iron gate.

Architecture dates to the 1700s, and some homes feature century-old, hand-carved cypress-beam ceilings and brick or slate floors, double parlors, paneled bookcases, floor-to-ceiling guillotine windows, and wrought-iron balconies. Renovation is a popular pastime for homeowners with the time and money—and many of the French Quarter's well-heeled residents have plenty of both. Even with a lack of off-street parking (though the creation of special parking permits for residents has helped), real estate in New Orleans' second most picture-postcard section goes for a ransom worthy of King Louis XIV.

i Among the most vexing pests is the notorious Formosan termite, which can inflict substantial and costly damage. Solution? Many wise homeowners contract with a reputable termite pest control company for regularly scheduled inspections, preventive care, and (if necessary) treatments.

Faubourg Marigny and Bywater

Faubourg (meaning "neighborhood") Marigny is the neighborhood just downriver from the French Quarter and is almost as old. A renaissance began in this area around 30 years ago when the Vieux Carre evolved into a national real estate market and many locals were priced out of it. Today, this bohemian neighborhood is a harmonious mixture of commercial and residential areas full of beautifully restored homes, good restaurants, and the city's best jazz clubs.

Bywater, as the name implies, is the next riverfront neighborhood below the Marigny. It's a little funkier, a little less freshly scrubbed. Comparatively, bargains can be found here.

Uptown

The Uptown area includes the Garden District (Upper and Lower), Bouligny, and University area. Each has a distinct personality, but what pulls them all together is the unparalleled charm

that pervades Uptown's sleepy oak-lined streets and architecture—from Victorian, Greek-, and Spanish-Revival mansions to far more modest camelbacks and Victorian shotgun doubles. A camelback features a second floor but only at the back of the house (thus the "camelback" hump), a design feature that at one time helped residents finagle out of a tax levied on homes with complete second floors. A shotgun house refers to how someone could stand at the door, shoot a gun and the bullet would go through every room and exit the back door. Simply put, every room in the house, from the living room and kitchen to the bedroom, is situated in a linear fashion.

With few exceptions real estate here fetches a pretty penny. And why not? This is unquestionably one of New Orleans' most postcard-perfect surroundings, epitomized perhaps by the sight of one of the city's leaf-green streetcars click-clacking down St. Charles Avenue under moss-draped oaks past Audubon Park on one of those mercilessly idyllic spring days.

Nowhere else does the city's characterization as an architectural "checkerboard" fit so snugly as it does Uptown amid the area's lush kaleidoscope of myrtles, azaleas, camellias, and bougainvillea. One street is filled with stately French Gothic and antebellum-style plantation homes, any of which would be right at home on the cover of *Architectural Digest*. Two blocks away and you swear you've stumbled upon a Caribbean island neighborhood, where West Indies-style wooden cottages in pastel turquoise, yellows, and greens are framed by overgrown front-yard banana trees that shade jalousied windows and a lazy pooch too busy slumbering to bark.

Old Metairie

Many experts believe that the latest local tear-down-and-rebuild craze got its start not in New Orleans but rather in Old Metairie, one of the oldest sections of east bank Jefferson Parish. With the notable exception of that part of Old Metairie nearest Metairie Country Club, the lion's share of this neighborhood was composed mostly of wooden 1940s and 1950s cottages, some three- and four-bedroom homes, and a sprinkle of Federal-style Georgian brick houses.

Today, the "new" Old Metairie is defined in part by the demolition of charming and old (or puny and obsolete, depending on perspective) homes and their replacement by two- and three-story property-line-to-property-line houses elsewhere on the east bank of Jefferson Parish is a mix of homogeneous, mostly middle-class, cookie-cutter subdivisions of single-story three- and four-bedroom brick homes. Corridors of apartments and town houses are often conveniently located near I–10 or Veterans Boulevard's strip- and anchor-store malls, fast-food drive-thrus, franchise restaurants, car dealerships, health clubs, pawn shops, and bank branch offices. Neighborhoods on the lakeside of West Esplanade Avenue, meantime, feature four-bedroom family and executive-style houses within easy reach of the Lake Pontchartrain levee trail popular among joggers, cyclists, and those out for a sunset walk.

Kenner

The popularity of Kenner, one of the fastest-growing cities in Louisiana, has grown in recent years with the addition of The Esplanade mall, the Pontchartrain Center entertainment and convention complex, and the Treasure Chest casino. Ongoing public works projects to ease traffic congestion have resulted in the widening of Kenner's main arteries, Williams and Loyola Boulevards, a new I–10 off-ramp at Power Boulevard, and a new Williams Boulevard and I–10 interchange.

i Upscale urbanites might want to check out the hot apartments and condominiums available in the Warehouse Arts District, which during the past 20 years has seen numerous old brick warehouses and factories converted into oh-SoHo-hip residences.

i Many young families buying their first home find they get more bang for the buck in one of New Orleans' numerous suburbs, where the cost of a three-bedroom house can be considerably less than the price of a comparable residence in town. These include Metairie, Kenner, the West Bank of Jefferson Parish, and St. Bernard Parish.

Lakeview

Bordered by City Park, Robert E. Lee, the 17th Street Canal and City Park Avenue, the Lakeview area is highly regarded for the mix of housing in quiet, tree-lined, middle-class neighborhoods. Lakeview is close to Lake Pontchartrain and the West End restaurant corridor, yet less than 15 minutes from the French Quarter—all for about one-half the price, or less, of its breeze-swept Lakefront neighbors only blocks away.

Gentilly

Gentilly, located on the other side (east) of City Park from Lakeview, is an interesting mix of more than 20 lower-middle to upper-middle class neighborhoods. Known for its abundance of colleges and universities (including the University of New Orleans), the ethnic diversity of its residents, and a low crime rate, the area offers a wide variety of housing stock. This includes everything from some of the city's most affordable starter homes to well-preserved Arts & Crafts architecture found in the Gentilly Terrace & Gardens national historic district. Streets are wider and have fewer potholes than many sections of town and traffic is almost non-existent in this quiet city-suburb.

A necklace of upscale neighborhoods—Lake Vista, Lake Shore (East and West), Lake Oaks, Lake Terrace, and so on—rim Lake Pontchartrain to Robert E. Lee Boulevard and are often home to the "new" rich.

West Bank

The opening of the twin span of the Mississippi

River bridge, officially named but rarely called the Crescent City Connection, has significantly opened up the West Bank of Jefferson Parish as a desirable and affordable location. Commute times to New Orleans from major West Bank cities such as Algiers (which is part of Orleans Parish), Gretna, Marrero, and Westwego have been cut in half. Once viewed as suburban sprawl, the West Bank's attractiveness has soared among homeowners looking to get the most bang for their home-buying buck and a stable resale value. Those looking for the country club life will find it at English Turn. As one Realtor pointed out, the West Bank offers "all the conveniences of Metairie without the crowds and hassle."

North Shore

Whether the result of a conspiratorial mass exodus from New Orleans or simply normal demographic shifts, development on the north shore region of the metropolitan area has exploded over the past 20 years and shows few signs of slowing. The once rural but still pine tree-dotted communities of Mandeville, Covington, Madisonville, Abita Springs, and Folsom have become bedroom communities. Convenience is a factor: These towns are linked to New Orleans by the 26-mile twin-span Causeway bridge (the nation's longest, for those keeping track) over Lake Pontchartrain.

The lured is the promise of relaxed, country-style living near the lake and solitude far from the big city. Adding to the area's popularity are modest- to fine-dining establishments (including several notable ones right on the lake and the Tchefuncte River), boating and recreation opportunities, and a manicured lakefront of sleepy oaks, quiet gazebos, greenspaces, and bicycle paths.

The north shore community of Slidell, 20 minutes east of Covington-Mandeville, has seen the development of fresh-scrubbed subdivisions, some with homes right on a lake canal highly coveted by weekend boaters and other water enthusiasts. Slidell is linked to New Orleans via I–10, and the 30-minute commute is half that from West Tammany.

EDUCATION

Public Schools

Historically, the story of public schools in New Orleans is about as happy as a Tennessee Williams play. Students routinely score below the national average on standardized tests and, periodically, newspaper articles appear telling of new businesses' reluctance to relocate to the area because of the lack of skilled and educated workers. However, since Hurricane Katrina a growing number of charter schools have been introduced that are showing marked improvement.

So, it is possible to get a decent education in public school and there are a handful of schools where students do quite well even by national standards. These successful schools generally have no more money than those schools that fail. What they do have, practically without exception, is a large percentage of students from middle-class families, a dedicated and talented faculty and staff, and a high level of parental involvement.

There are a handful of excellent public magnet and charter schools in New Orleans, the brightest star of which is Benjamin Franklin High School. The school, which regularly places students in the country's best colleges, is the kind of place private school kids transfer to when they hit ninth grade. For more information call the Orleans Parish School Board at (504) 304-5680.

Private Schools

The following is an overview of area private schools which, in the form of Catholic schools, have been educating New Orleans children since long before the public school system was established and, for that matter, decades before the United States was established. Not surprisingly, Catholic schools make up the majority of today's private institutions. There are Catholic elementary schools throughout the metro area and, generally, children attend the school in their own or neighboring church parish. However, students may choose to which Catholic high school they apply. A number of excellent non-Catholic schools are also available.

i Moving to town and suburbs bound? Contact the Jefferson Parish School Board at (504) 349-7600 to find out your district school.

Elementary through Secondary
ACADEMY OF THE SACRED HEART
4521 St. Charles Ave.
(504) 891-1943
www.ashrosary.org
Sacred Heart is a Catholic college prep school for girls in preschool through 12th grade. Founded in 1887 by the Religious of the Sacred Heart, the school educates approximately 800 students. The preschool program emphasizes development of a positive attitude toward learning as well as fundamental readiness skills. In the lower school, a whole language approach is taken to reading. Students also study math, science, social studies, religion, music, art, foreign language, physical education, and computer science. In the middle grades students continue with their core curriculum, adding a peer support program. High school students can enroll in honors classes as well as advanced placement biology. All Sacred Heart graduates generally attend college. In recent years they have been accepted at Auburn, Boston University, Dartmouth, Emerson, Johns Hopkins, and Stanford.

ECOLE CLASSIQUE
5236 Glendale St., Metairie
(504) 887-3507
www.ecoleclassique.com
Founded in 1956, Ecole Classique is a private, coeducational elementary and secondary school with the purpose of preparing students to enter college. In kindergarten through third grade,

students are in self-contained programs with a single educator. Grades four through six are completely departmentalized (students change classes) and staffed by degreed and certified teachers. Seventh through 12th grades are also departmentalized, with courses offered on three levels: honors, middle, and academic. Students are required to take both the SAT and ACT prior to graduation.

ISIDORE NEWMAN SCHOOL
1903 Jefferson Ave.
(504) 899-5641
www.newmanschool.org
When financier and philanthropist Isidore Newman founded the Isidore Newman Manual Training School in 1903, he envisioned a superior education for the children of New Orleanians as well as those of the Jewish Children's Home. He hoped to provide skilled, competent, and well-trained labor for the local workforce. In the next 100 years, this Uptown institution developed into one of the city's finest college prep schools. The population has grown almost tenfold to nearly 1,000 students in prekindergarten through 12th grade. The original Jefferson building now opens onto an 11-acre campus of 14 buildings set against a backdrop of playgrounds, patios, greenspaces, and an athletic playing field. Curriculum is infused with technology in every classroom.

The school offers a challenging academic curriculum that emphasizes sequential development of courses in basic disciplines—English, math, science, foreign language, history, the arts, computer science, and physical education.

More than 40 team sports are offered to 7th through 12th graders, and the school's debate team has won national titles. The school's library boasts 47,000 volumes, and the media center offers additional technological resources.

Most of Newman's graduates attend college. Choices have included Amherst, Boston University, Columbia, Cornell, Dartmouth, Georgetown, Harvard, Princeton, and Yale.

Parents who want their children to attend private school in New Orleans must plan ahead. Most private schools hold "Open House" for prospective students and parents between Sept and Nov (for the following year), with the application process following in Jan and Feb.

METAIRIE PARK COUNTRY DAY SCHOOL
300 Park Rd., Metairie
(504) 837-5204
www.mpcds.com

Everyone knows that the most successful schools are generally the ones with the most parent involvement. At Country Day, folks took it a step further. This kindergarten-through-12th grade school, situated on 14 acres in a quiet, residential neighborhood of the Metairie suburb, was founded by a group of parents in 1929. Country Day is a nonsectarian, college prep day school with an enrollment of approximately 700 boys and girls. One hundred percent of Country Day graduates pursue a college degree and are accepted by some of the nation's best colleges each year. The average class size at Country Day is 12 to 15 students. Honors and advanced placement classes are offered in all disciplines. An emphasis is placed on fine arts at every grade level.

Most Catholic schools offer tuition discounts for parents who regularly contribute a certain amount to the parish church. It generally costs the same, except that church contributions are tax deductible and tuition generally is not.

URSULINE ACADEMY
2635 State St.
(504) 861-9150
www.ursulineneworleans.org

Ursuline Academy was established in 1727 by the Ursuline nuns as the first school for girls in the United States. Holistic education is designed to educate the whole person—spiritually, intellectually, socially, and physically. Ursuline is a private, independent Catholic school with an 11.5-acre campus in Uptown New Orleans. The school museum displays documents from Presidents Jefferson and Madison as well as religious artifacts dating from the Spanish colonial period to the present day. The campus also includes the National Shrine of Our Lady of Prompt Succor, whose statue has been venerated by New Orleanians for more than 150 years. Many locals believe it was Our Lady of Prompt Succor who protected the city during the great fire of 1812 and the Battle of New Orleans in 1815.

Currently, the school educates 720 girls, toddlers through 12th grade, with an average class size of 20 students. Eligible high school students can enroll in honors, accelerated, or advanced-placement courses and 99 percent of graduates go on to college.

If you're moving to town with an eighth grader who will attend private school, you'll want to check out both elementary and high schools. While most private lower schools go through eighth grade, most high schools now begin there as well.

Middle School
CHRISTIAN BROTHERS SCHOOL
8 Friedrichs Ave., City Park
(504) 486-6770
http://cbs-no.org

Christian Brothers is unique in two ways: It is New Orleans' only private school for boys exclusively serving the middle grades (fifth through seventh), and it's the only school located in City Park, tucked amid the park's centuries-old oaks. The faculty consists of Catholic Christian Brothers as well as lay teachers whose approach is modeled after St. de La Salle, who conceived of education as "a fraternal relationship between the teacher and the student." The low student-teacher ratio allows educators to take a personal interest in each student, sharing "his interests, his worries, his hopes," according to a school literature. All applicants must take an entrance exam.

High Schools
BROTHER MARTIN HIGH SCHOOL
4401 Elysian Fields Ave.
(504) 283-1561
www.brothermartin.com
Brother Martin is a private Catholic school for boys in 8th through 12th grade. The school has a lay and religious faculty and is under the direction of the Brothers of the Sacred Heart, who have educated children in New Orleans since 1869. The school philosophy states: "The most important aspect of any Catholic education is the development of Christian values and the transmission of the Catholic heritage. We accept this task as the call of the Church and as the primary goal of our school apostolate." Students study basic subjects in either an honors or academic curriculum. Recent graduates have been accepted at Rice, USC, University of Virginia, and Yale. Admission is based on a student's desire to attend, overall elementary school record, recommendations of elementary principal and teachers, and an interview with the applicant and his parents.

HOLY CROSS SCHOOL
5500 Paris Ave.
(504) 942-3100
www.holycrosstigers.com
Established in 1879 as St. Isidore's College, Holy Cross (as it was later called) is the second oldest Holy Cross institution in America—beat out only by a place in South Bend, Indiana, called Notre Dame University. As has been the trend among Catholic high schools in recent years, Holy Cross has expanded to include a middle school—now educating boys in fifth through 12th grades. Average middle school class size is 22; high school is 29. The school offers a broad curriculum that includes an honors program and comprehensive college prep courses. Recent graduates have attended such universities as Auburn, Emory, George Washington, and Vanderbilt.

The Holy Cross's band program has been part of the school since 1894. The band includes several performing groups and has helped a high percentage of students earn music scholarships to college since 1989. Admission to Holy Cross is based on transcripts, standardized test scores, conduct, and interview.

ST. MARY'S DOMINICAN HIGH SCHOOL
7701 Walmsley Ave.
(504) 865-9401
www.stmarysdominican.org
The tradition of Dominican education was born in New Orleans in 1860 when seven young Dominican sisters arrived from Dublin to educate daughters of Irish immigrants. Despite the Civil War the nuns within five months had established St. Mary's Dominican Academy, a "select school" for girls, founded for literary, scientific, religious, and charitable purposes. Today the Carrollton school continues its pursuit of academic excellence through a traditional yet innovative college prep curriculum. Curriculum includes a variety of electives as well as advanced placement classes in a number of subjects.

An estimated 99 percent of students go on to four-year colleges including Carnegie-Mellon, Clemson, Columbia, Oxford, Georgetown, Harvard, and Yale. Admission is based on cumulative school records with special attention given to math, English, and reading grades as well as attendance, conduct, and standardized test scores.

Special Needs Schools
ST. MICHAEL'S SPECIAL SCHOOL
1522 Chippewa St.
(504) 524-7285
The Archdiocesan Department of Special Education was founded in 1964 with St. Michael's Special School for Exceptional Children as its focal point. The school is designed to help students with significant difficulties in learning. The program employs a low student-teacher ratio, specialized techniques in ungraded levels, and an atmosphere of love, order, and relaxation. The elementary program serves children age 5 to 16 in an academic climate. The secondary, vocationally oriented level works with students age 16 to 21. Academics are balanced with job-training skills to prepare young adults for the world

of work. After age 21, students attend the Joy Center, a sheltered activity facility at which they follow the school schedule but also take part in work-related activities.

Colleges and Universities

Ironically, for a town that traditionally has offered a less than adequate public school system, the Big Easy has a lot of colleges. Following is an overview of what degree-seekers will find in post-secondary New Orleans.

DELGADO COMMUNITY COLLEGE
501 City Park Ave.
(504) 671-5012
www.dcc.edu

With its main campus located across the street from City Park, this community college is named for Isaac Delgado, a businessman who left most of his estate to found a trade school for boys in 1909. Old Isaac wouldn't recognize the place today. Delgado currently is a state-supported, comprehensive community college educating more than 13,000 men and women at multiple locations throughout the New Orleans area. Delgado is the largest and oldest two-year college in the state and is widely recognized for its constantly expanding curriculum and involvement in community programs.

Increasingly, students planning to seek four-year degrees find themselves spending their first two years at Delgado, where transferable credits cost just a little more than half of those at state universities. Along with core curriculum courses, Delgado offers more than 70 programs in allied health and nursing, early childhood education, business, technology, and skilled labor. The school also offers a wide variety of noncredit classes.

LOYOLA UNIVERSITY NEW ORLEANS
6363 St. Charles Ave.
(504) 865-3240, (800) 4–LOYOLA
www.loyno.edu

Loyola University New Orleans, founded in 1912, is one of 28 Jesuit colleges in the United States and one of the largest Catholic universities in the South. Its rich history and Jesuit influence date back to the early 18th century, when the members of this religious order were among the city's first settlers. The school's 20-acre campus offers a mix of Tudor–Gothic and contemporary architecture, set off by broad expanses of greenspace and walkways, located on prestigious St. Charles Avenue in the university section of Uptown. The university's 4,500 students include those from all 50 states, the District of Columbia, Puerto Rico, and 49 foreign countries. Approximately 1,500 students live on campus.

Offering more than 60 undergraduate degrees as well as 10 graduate and professional programs, the university stresses the Jesuit tradition of liberal arts education in all majors. The Loyola College of Music and fine arts is nationally acclaimed for the quality of its outstanding performance and music education curricula.

In recent years Loyola has consistently ranked among the top regional colleges and universities in the South, according to *U.S. News & World Report*'s special issue "America's Best Colleges." The school was also named one of "America's 300 Best Buys" in *Barron's* "Best Buys in College Education." *Barron's* also ranked it in the top 7 percent of 1,500 colleges and universities.

OUR LADY OF HOLY CROSS COLLEGE
4123 Woodland Dr.
(504) 394-7744, (800) 259-7744
www.olhcc.edu

A small band of nuns, the Marianites of Holy Cross, arrived in New Orleans from LeMans, France, in 1853. An ambitious bunch of educators, they began establishing schools throughout the state. In order to supply teachers to the schools, the Holy Cross Normal College was established in 1916. Today, nestled on 15 tree-shaded acres, Our Lady of Holy Cross College is located in Algiers (a tiny portion of New Orleans on the West Bank of the Mississippi River). The coed liberal arts college educates 1,250 full- and part-time students. Along with education (still the school's strong suit), the school offers master's and bachelor's degree programs in business, humanities, and natural

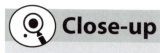

Close-up

New Orleans Center for Creative Arts

With the possible exceptions of Louis Armstrong and Mozart, great musicians are not born, they are made. And in this cradle of jazz, that creation takes place at the New Orleans Center for Creative Arts. Since 1974 high school students with talent in music, dance, theater, creative writing, or visual arts have learned the meaning of discipline and rigor in this artistic haven that has produced the likes of singer Harry Connick Jr. and Wynton Marsalis, the first jazz musician to win a Pulitzer Prize. A media arts program incorporating film, video, and audio curricula was added in 2001 and a culinary arts curriculum was established in 2009.

In a city whose public education system could politely be described as wanting, NOCCA is a real star. And so are its students. After making it through a tough audition process, students sign a contract acknowledging the academic and artistic requirements they will be expected to meet. Each year, more than 800 teenagers from 100 public and private schools around the New Orleans area take half a day of classes at their "regular" schools, then spend the other half of the day at NOCCA for practice, practice, practice. Ninety-eight percent of them go on to college, with more than 70 percent earning scholarships.

"NOCCA had a profound influence on me," Connick said. "The teachers put the tool belt on me, gave me a hammer and nails. They gave me everything I needed to build what I had to do." Of course, students haven't always crooned about every aspect of the place. Until recently, NOCCA was housed in an old elementary school where the music practice room was a piano in a closet. Drama students had no theater, and dancers were forced to "explore space" in a classroom built for third graders. In a financially strapped school system, a nonprofit

and social sciences. Nearly 72 percent of the 52 full-time and 102 part-time faculty hold terminal degrees. The student-faculty ratio is 22:1.

TULANE UNIVERSITY
6823 St. Charles Ave.
(504) 865-5000
http://tulane.edu
Right next door (and basically dwarfing) Loyola is Tulane University's 110-acre campus, marked by traditional Romanesque and Georgian academic halls dating from the turn of the last century and accented by grassy quadrangles and oak-lined walks. Tulane was established in 1884, when the public University of Louisiana was reorganized as a private school, and named in honor of benefactor Paul Tulane, a wealthy merchant who bequeathed $1 million to endow a university for the city where he had earned his fortune. Two years later, Josephine Louise Newcomb founded Newcomb College at Tulane as a memorial to her daugh-

ter, Harriet Sophie. As the first degree-granting women's college in the nation to be established as a coordinate division of a men's university, Newcomb became the model for other women's colleges, including Barnard and Radcliffe.

Tulane began with schools of liberal arts and sciences, law, medicine, and graduate studies. Over the years it added schools of architecture, business, social work, public health, and tropical medicine.

With 6,749 undergraduate and 4,408 graduate students, Tulane is consistently ranked in the top quarter of major universities and among the top 25 for value by *U.S. News & World Report*.

THE UNIVERSITY OF NEW ORLEANS
2000 Lakefront
(504) 280-6595, (800) 256-5–UNO
www.uno.edu
Established in 1958 as part of the Louisiana State University system to bring public-supported

advocacy group called Friends of NOCCA (now the NOCCA Institute) sponsored fund-raisers to pay for toe shoes, band equipment, and a visiting artist program. Each year more than 70 professional artists from around the country conducted master classes and extended residencies. But after 26 years of "making do," it was decided that enough was enough.

"When you're dealing with the arts, especially now with the proliferation of computers and all the other technology, it's important that you have a space that's designed for what you are trying to do," said Marsalis. He should know, being the only musician to win Grammys for both jazz and classical recordings in the same year.

Thanks to the State Legislature and the NOCCA Institute, in 2000 students left their dilapidated Uptown location to move a few miles downriver of the French Quarter. On the border of two old neighborhoods—Faubourg Marigny and Bywater—sits their new school, a $23 million, 125,000-square-foot facility featuring not one, but three theaters (a 300-seat proscenium theater, a fully equipped "black box" experimental theater, and a jazz performance hall). Two of the riverfront campus's five buildings are new; the other three are renovated and revitalized warehouses, part of the old New Orleans Cotton Press, where Louisiana's favorite cash crop was baled and shipped in the 1830s. The facility features a state-of-the-art writing lab, set and prop building areas, three kilns for pottery classes, TV and recording studios, three major dance studios, and a movement studio.

To many involved with the school, there was no better way to start the new millennium. "In the new century, if we hope to be competitive in the best sense of the word, we have to spur the imagination of American youngsters," said former NOCCA instructor and jazz legend Ellis Marsalis, "and there's no better way to do that than through the arts."

higher education to the state's largest urban community, the University of New Orleans sits on a 195-acre parklike campus along the shore of Lake Pontchartrain, as well as the 200-acre east campus, which houses the UNO Arena. UNO has fully accredited programs in business studies and nationally recognized programs in hotel, restaurant, and tourism administration as well as jazz studies founded by jazz great Ellis Marsalis. The College of Engineering boasts one of only five naval architecture and marine engineering programs in the nation and the only one in the South; the college of education is the state's largest and one of Louisiana's top producers of certified teachers. Eighty percent of the school's 700 faculty members hold doctorates.

UNO's 12,000 students come from all 50 states and 97 countries. Half the student body is over age 25. Most students live off campus, although the school does offer both coed dorms and married student housing.

XAVIER UNIVERSITY
1 Drexel Dr.
(504) 486-7411
www.xula.edu

Founded in 1915 by Katherine Drexel of the Sisters of the Blessed Sacrament (nuns dedicated to serving the educational needs of Native and African Americans), Xavier is the only historically black Catholic university in the United States. And that's the least of its distinctions. Under the direction of Dr. Norman Francis, who became the school's first African-American lay president in 1968, Xavier has grown into a science powerhouse, especially in the areas of pharmacy and pre-med. The campus, with a mix of contemporary architecture and Gothic design, is located in the residential neighborhood of Mid City. Current enrollment is more than 4,100 students, of whom approximately 90 percent are African American. Approximately 86 percent of the 214 fulltime faculty members hold the highest degrees in their fields.

MEDIA

Newspapers

Daily

THE TIMES-PICAYUNE
3800 Howard Ave.
(504) 826-3279
www.nola.com
Like a growing number of big cities, New Orleans is a single daily newspaper town. Established in 1837, the Pulitzer Prize-winning *Times-Picayune* enjoys one of the highest market penetration rates in the country. Part of the Newhouse family's Advance Publications group, the *Times-Picayune* has numerous strong suits including entertainment tabloid Lagniappe (Fri), Food (Thurs), and Sports (daily), as well as community-specific *Picayune* sections on Thurs and Sun, which zero in on local neighborhood and school news.

Weekly

CLARION HERALD
1000 Howard Ave.
(504) 596-3035
www.clarionherald.org
The official newspaper of the Archdiocese of New Orleans reaches an estimated 210,000 Catholics. The *Clarion Herald*, which takes strong editorial stands on a range of local and national social and political issues, has been selected by the Catholic Press Association as one of the top 10 Catholic newspapers in the country. Coverage includes local youth, school, and church news.

DATA NEWS WEEKLY
3501 Napoleon Ave.
(504) 821-7421
www.ladatanews.com
This African American-owned and -operated free newspaper, established in 1966, covers local, state and national issues of importance to black readers, as well as the areas of entertainment, health, and the arts.

GAMBIT WEEKLY
3923 Bienville
(504) 486-5900
www.bestofneworleans.com
This free weekly is as much a part of the urban landscape as the coffeehouses, record stores, and bistros through which it's distributed. The city's most widely recognized alternative tabloid keeps readers tuned in to the local art, film, and food scenes, while its often insightful investigative political reporting can be counted on to point out the good, the bad, and the ugly of local politics.

LOUISIANA WEEKLY
2215 Pelopidas St.
(504) 282-3705
www.louisianaweekly.com
Coverage of business, health, lifestyle, religion, and entertainment is the hallmark of this broadsheet founded in 1925 by local African-American businesspeople. Distributed by subscription and at newsstands, news racks, and many convenience and retail drug stores, the weekly is the oldest African American-owned newspaper in southern Louisiana.

NEW ORLEANS CITYBUSINESS
111 Veterans Blvd., Metairie
(504) 834-9292
www.neworleanscitybusiness.com
Since 1980 this award-winning weekly business publication has covered the bottom line on everything from minority-owned start-up companies and emerging women entrepreneurs to the region's huge oil and gas and tourism industries and the movers and shakers who make it all happen. This tabloid is available through newsstands and vending machines throughout the Central Business District, Uptown, and Metairie.

Monthly, Bimonthly, and Quarterly

OFFBEAT
421 Frenchmen St.
(504) 944-4300
www.offbeat.com

Locals have been keeping plugged into the city's blues, jazz, traditional, folk, alternative, and rock music scenes ever since this monthly music newspaper opened its doors in 1988. *OffBeat* rarely hits a sour note with readers with its monthly nightclub and entertainment listings, as well as its unique spin on local culture, food, art, and film. It is distributed at newsstands, hotels, restaurants, music venues, coffee shops, and other outlets.

NEW ORLEANS MAGAZINE
111 Veterans Blvd., Metairie
(504) 832-3555
www.neworleansmagazine.com
Slick city magazines come and go, but this one has been a local staple for more than four decades, thanks in part to its entertaining and informative coverage of local culture, politics, lifestyle, history, and consumer-related issues by a masthead of award-winning local writers such as Errol Laborde.

Radio
Community (Jazz)
WWOZ 90.7 FM

Contemporary
WEZB 97.1 FM (Top-40 contemporary)
WYLD 98.5 FM (urban adult contemporary)
WLMG 101.9 FM (adult contemporary)
KSTE 104.1 FM (Top-40 contemporary)
WKZN 105.3 FM (adult contemporary)
WMTI 106.1 (oldies)

i Stuck in commuter traffic but anxious to keep up with what's going on in the world? Tune to WWNO 89.9 FM for National Public Radio's morning and afternoon drive-time broadcasts of world news and in-depth features designed to keep you in the know while stuck in the slow lane.

Country
KLEB 1600 AM (Cajun)
WBOX 92.9 FM
WUUU 98.9 FM
KLRZ 100.3 FM (Cajun)
WNOE 101.1 FM
WHMD 107.1 FM
KCIL 107.5 FM

Cultural/Classical/National Public Radio
WWNO 89.9 FM
KTLN 90.5 FM

Gospel/Contemporary
WBOK 1230 AM
WIKC 1490 AM
KAGY 1519 AM
WOPR 94.7 FM
WPRF 94.9 FM
WGON 103.7 FM

Religious
WVOG 600 AM
KKNO 750 AM
WSHO 800 AM
WLNO 1060 AM
WBSN 89.1 FM
KMRL 91.9 FM

Rock/Rhythm/Soul
WTUL 91.5 FM (progressive)
WDVW 92.3 FM (alternative)
WQUE 93.3 FM (hip-hop)
WTIX 94.3 FM (oldies)
WTKL 95.7 FM (oldies)
WRNO 99.5 FM (classic rock)
KMEZ 102.9 FM (oldies)
KNOU 104.5 FM (hip-hop)
WJSH 104.7 FM (oldies)
KXOR 106.3 FM (rock hits)
KKND 106.7 FM (alternative)

Spanish News and Music
WFNO 830 AM
KGLA 1540 AM

Time for Church

Catholicism has played a large part not only in the spiritual lives of locals but also in the city's history. Here are a couple of churches worth seeing. Along with being beautiful monuments to God, they tell the stories of the people who passed through them.

St. Louis Cathedral
615 Pere Antoine Alley
(on Jackson Square)
(504) 525-9585
www.stlouiscathedral.org

This Jackson Square landmark has been a French Quarter beacon since the original cathedral, designed by architect Don Gilberto Guillemard, was built in 1794. After a devastating fire destroyed most of the Vieux Carre, the church was reconstructed and enlarged with J. N. B. DePouilly flourishes and today is the oldest active cathedral in the United States and one of only 15 minor basilicas nationwide. It was the site of Pope John Paul II's clergy prayer service during his visit to New Orleans in 1987.

With its 16-foot-wide center aisle, huge chandeliers hanging over the pews, and flags of various countries, it's easy to understand why this awesome church is a favorite among local brides. The church's large altar mural, painted in 1872 by Alsatian artist Erasme Humbrecht, depicts Louis, the saint-king of France, announcing the Seventh Crusade, which he was to lead.

The colorful garden at the back of the church on Royal Street serves as a memorial to the Capuchin priest and devoted humanitarian Father Antonio de Sedella, who arrived here in 1779 and spent the next half-century serving the poorest citizens of this budding territory. Known locally as St. Anthony's Garden, this tranquil spot, ironically, was occasionally the site of bloody duels. If you visit, look for the statue of the Sacred Heart of Jesus and the marble monument commemorating the death of 30 French sailors who died in the city's 1857 yellow fever epidemic.

Call for tour times.

St. Patrick's Church
724 Camp St.
(504) 525-4413
www.oldstpatricks.org

This Central Business District church,

Special

WBYU 1450 AM (Disney radio)
WRBH 88.3 FM (radio reading service)

Talk and News/Sports

WTIX 690 AM
WASO 730 AM
WWL 870 AM
WGSO 990 AM
WODT 1280 AM (sports)
WSMB 1350 AM
WSLA 1560 AM (ESPN Sports Radio)

Television

Local Stations

WWL Channel 4 (CBS)
WDSU Channel 6 (NBC)
WVUE Channel 8 (Fox)
WYES Channel 12 (PBS)
WHNO–TV Channel 20 (Independent)
WGNO Channel 26 (ABC)
WLAE Channel 32 (PBS, educational)
WNOL Channel 38 (CW)
WPXL–TV Channel 49 (Ion)
WUPL Channel 54 (My Network)

located a couple of blocks off Poydras Street on the Uptown side, tells another important chapter in local history, the early days of the 19th century. It was then that New Orleans began taking its first tentative steps outside of the city's original settlement (now the French Quarter). New American settlers who started arriving following the 1803 Louisiana Purchase began building what would be known as the American sector. Up went homes and businesses and a way of life very different from those of the original Creole inhabitants.

It's no coincidence that the church's construction in 1840 coincided with the growth of the city's Irish immigrant population, tired of squirming in the back pews of St. Louis Cathedral where God seemed to speak only French (and Latin, of course). It is understandable that the Hibernians, many of whom were lured here to build the growing city's transportation canal, wanted their own place of worship.

The impressive Gothic-style church features splendid murals including a depiction of St. Patrick baptizing the daughters of Ireland's King Laoghaire. The murals, painted in 1841 by French-born artist Leon Pomarede, were quite pricey, costing $1,000 each. And even the Creoles had to admit that they were good. A local French newspaper suggested that if Pomarede had been creating similar works for a European church, the event would have attracted daily crowds of onlookers. "The name 'Pomarede' would have been on every lip and everyone would have wished to know him," it read. Later, the Creole neighbors had ample time to study the artist's work when St. Patrick's became the city's main house of worship while St. Louis Cathedral was being rebuilt.

Various restoration projects were undertaken over the years, and today the church and its magnificent vaulted ceilings and arches are pristine reminders of one of the city's turning points— when the Irish built a house where God spoke English. Ironically, it is also now the only place in town where you can attend Mass in Latin. Call for schedule.

WORSHIP

From that moment in 1682 when LaSalle planted a cross in the ground claiming this Louisiana territory for God and king, Catholicism has reigned supreme. Along with the more than 470,000 of the faithful who can be found attending Mass all across the metropolitan area every Sunday, Catholicism has been woven into the fabric of everyday life here. The city's most famous party, Carnival, finds its roots in the Mother Church. Mardi Gras, or Fat Tuesday, is the final day of fleshly revelry before the 40 penitent days of Lent begin on Ash Wednesday. Also, the sea-food industry may owe much of its livelihood to hungry tourists, but don't discount the Catholics, who fill every seafood house on Friday during Lent—the traditional day of abstention from eating meat. And don't forget our football team, the New Orleans Saints, who were so named as a nod to the city's strong religious ties as well as the fact that the National Football League franchise was awarded to the Big Easy on All Saints' Day, another important holiday here.

Of course, this being New Orleans, the city has developed its own unique form of the faith.

Take St. Expedite. There are many stories to explain how New Orleanians developed the tradition of praying to this completely fictional character, so much so that there is an old mortuary chapel exhibiting his statue. The best tale is told by historian Buddy Stall in his book *Buddy Stall's New Orleans*. Apparently, as Stall tells it, a group of local French nuns received a large shipment of religious items for their chapel from Italy. One of the boxes containing a statue was marked *"Espedito"*—"send off" in Italian. Stall writes, "Thinking this was a statue of a saint named Expedite—a French word—the statue and a small chapel were dedicated to St. Expedite."

For years afterward New Orleanians prayed to St. Expedite in that chapel. Holy candles with his likeness could be found in religious paraphernalia shops. Even after the mistake was uncovered, nobody really seemed to be bothered by St. Expedite's lack of authenticity. And in a city that takes care of its own, a few New Orleanians still display his likeness in their homes right next to their Mary candles and St. Jude prayer cards—if for no other reason than the fact that it makes them smile to know that they live in a place where people have the imagination to create their own "in" in Heaven.

Mass Appeal

Until 1803 and the signing of the Louisiana Purchase, New Orleans was populated by French and Spanish colonists who (by royal decree) were Catholic, giving the Mother Church a giant head start on any other faith. Even voodoo, practiced by the city's early slaves, combined aspects of Catholicism—mostly in the form of iconography—with traditional African and West Indian rituals. Immigration in the 19th century brought mostly Irish and Italians who further bolstered Catholicism's stronghold. The early 1800s did see the arrival of a few Protestants, such as the Episcopals and Lutherans, and by the turn of the 20th century, New Orleans' federation of religions had grown to include the Disciples of Christ, the Mormons, the city's first Jewish congregation, and the Greek Orthodox. (The city's only Greek Orthodox church, The Cathedral of the Holy Trinity, is known for its beautiful Byzantine-style iconography. Take a virtual tour of the Lakefront church at www.holytrinitycathedral.org.)

In the 1900s the Big Easy diversified even more by welcoming the Southern Baptists, Quakers, Muslims, and Buddhists. Today, the Catholics, with nearly half a million members in the metropolitan area, still far outnumber any other denomination. The second largest group is the Baptists, who since their arrival in 1914 have seen their numbers grow to an estimated 54,000, due in part to the area's large African-American population.

For more information about local congregations, contact the Greater New Orleans Federation of Churches at (504) 488-8788 or check the Yellow Pages under "Churches." Also, check out "Religion News" every Sat in the *Times-Picayune* newspaper's "Metro" section for the latest church happenings and service schedules.

HEALTH CARE AND WELLNESS

In a TV commercial for a local hospital, groups of New Orleanians are shown doing what many New Orleanians do best: eating, drinking, and (yes) smoking. The narrator says, "If ever a city needed a great hospital . . ." No kidding. After all, one day the backlash from all of those artery-clogging oysters Bienville and roux-thickened étouffées—not to mention the cigarettes and booze—is bound to come banging at the front door. Perhaps it's only fitting that the city that forgot to close its bars can trace the roots of two longtime hospitals to an early 19th-century Irish nun and a World War I-era Baptist missionary. What does catch one off guard is the story of the late philanthropist Elizabeth Miller Robin. She was stricken by polio as a toddler and grew up to build in New Orleans the state's only children's hospital, designed originally to provide care to children hit by a poliomyelitis epidemic. When it comes to hospitals in the Big Easy, necessity is the mother of invention.

Numbers for Health-related Questions or Emergencies

Look to these phone numbers for help. Crisis lines are answered 24 hours a day.

Life-threatening, police, and fire emergencies:	911
AIDS Counseling:	(504) 821-2601;
	(800) 992-4379
AIDS Testing:	(800) 584-8183
AIDS Statewide Hotline:	(504) 821-6050,
	(800) 992-4379
Al-Anon:	(504) 888-1356
Alcoholics Anonymous:	(504) 838-3399
Alcohol Abuse Helpline:	(800) 214-4904
American Cancer Society:	(504) 833-4024
American Diabetes Association:	(504) 899-0278
American Lung Association:	(504) 828-5864
American Red Cross:	(504) 821-3746
Arthritis Foundation:	(800) 283-7800
Gamblers Anonymous:	(504) 431-7867
Narcotics Anonymous:	(504) 899-8840
New Orleans Health Department:	(504) 658-2500
Overeaters Anonymous:	(504) 366-3230
Poison Control Center:	(800) 222-1222

Today more than a dozen acute-care facilities of various sizes throughout the New Orleans five-parish metropolitan area provide state-of-the-art health care to almost half a million area residents. Hospital growth tempered by managed care virtually guarantees a topflight facility or satellite clinic is always nearby ready to provide treatment in a cost-conscious environment. Whether it's organ transplantation, limb reattachment, treatment for reproduction disorders, or physical therapy, local hospitals, doctors, and other health care professionals offer a broad spectrum of services, procedures, and treatments.

In this chapter we will focus on many of the hospitals within the New Orleans area and outline the uniqueness of each facility set against the local health care landscape. Remember, this is meant to serve only as an overview of New Orleans acute-care hospitals. Check the Yellow Pages for freestanding specialized treatment centers, such as physical therapy and outpatient clinics, home health agencies, alternative medicine practitioners, substance abuse treatment facilities, mental health professionals, and other health care providers.

Alternative Clinics

AMERICAN BACK INSTITUTE OF GREATER NEW ORLEANS
671 Rosa Ave., Metairie
(504) 833-2225
www.backpaininstitute.com

This institute specializes in treatment of the spine using state-of-the-art technology including the VAX–D, which has been demonstrated to be effective in 71 to 74 percent of 778 patients who participated in a recent study. Other disciplines include prolotherapy and chiropractic. The clinic also offers a large and varied referral base including conventional and alternative medicine specialists.

METAIRIE PAIN AND ACUPUNCTURE CLINIC
3216 North Turnbull Dr., Metairie
(504) 888-5449

For nearly a quarter century, this clinic has been providing patients with nonsurgical alternatives to pain management, specializing in nerve blocks and acupuncture. Dr. Jerry S. Y. Yong is one of only a few acupuncturists licensed in Louisiana to practice the ancient Chinese healing art.

i Many local hospitals offer a broad range of on-site community health- and wellness-related seminars, lectures, and workshops, often free to the public. To get the pulse of the latest trends in diagnosis, treatment, and prevention, call the hospital nearest you for a list of upcoming topics.

Chiropractic

ACHIEVEMENT THERAPEUTIC SERVICES
3320 Hessmer Ave., Metairie
(504) 366-7246

Dr. Kenneth S. Pace, DC, treats a wide variety of patients with joint pain, whiplash, sports injuries, and neck pain using the most modern techniques available to chiropractic medicine. Pace combines his extensive knowledge of biomechanics and state-of-the-art equipment and diagnostic techniques.

CHIROPRACTIC HEALTH CENTER
101 Clearview Parkway, Metairie
(504) 454-2000
www.chirohealthcare.com

Since 1986 this clinic has been treating patients requiring short- or long-term corrective chiro-

practic treatment. From junior high school students with sports-related injuries to oil rig workers with back and neck pain, the Chiropractic Health Center team provides state-of-the-art treatment. Other ailments treated include headache and shoulder pain, pinched nerves, and sciatica.

DISCOVER CHIROPRACTIC
4600 South Claiborne Ave.
New Orleans
(504) 899-2225

The team of Drs. Paul Gordon and Jeff Miller offer spinal corrections and other chiropractic treatments for a variety of disorders including disc injuries, headaches, dizziness, and migraines. The clinic, which also has a staff physician, offers emergency appointments and X-ray facilities.

Hospitals

CHILDREN'S HOSPITAL
200 Henry Clay Ave.
(504) 899-9511
www.chnola.org

Pint-size patients can count on big help at Louisiana's only full-service pediatric hospital, which opened its doors in 1955. Originally called Crippled Children's Hospital, the facility cared for the thousands of children left disabled as a result of the polio epidemics that followed World War II. The epidemics hit hard in Louisiana, which lagged behind in providing care to children. Thousands contracted polio—including the woman who would become the hospital's founder, the late Elizabeth Miller Robin. After a bout with polio at age two, she spent many of her childhood months in the hospital and for the rest of her life was dependent on crutches. Years later, motivated by the challenges she encountered as a child, Robin set out to establish a hospital exclusively for handicapped children. The daughter of a prominent New Orleans physician, she used her powers of persuasion to fulfill her dream.

"No child's case is too big or too serious," states the nonprofit hospital's brochure. Critical-care youngsters with broken bones and cancer to those born prematurely are but a few examples of the more than 6,800 inpatient and 156,000 outpatient visits in 2008. Patients, referred to this facility from more than 1,600 doctors each year, come from 40 states and five foreign countries. Developments at this 235-bed hospital in recent years include a new youth sports medicine program as well as clinics for genetic and metabolic disorders and general pediatrics. Critical care services include a 25-bed pediatric intensive care unit, an eight-bed spinal unit, and a 36-bed neonatal intensive care unit. The hospital's emergency care center is staffed around the clock by board-certified pediatricians, with the availability of a full range of pediatric subspecialists. The hospital has opened a satellite location, The Metairie Center, in the New Orleans suburb of Metairie in Jefferson Parish.

i Why not donate the priceless gift of time to a local hospital in need of volunteers? Many health care organizations have volunteer and auxiliary groups that are always looking for individuals who have a couple of hours a week to help out.

EAST JEFFERSON GENERAL HOSPITAL
4200 Houma St., Metairie
(504) 454-4000
www.eastjeffhospital.org

Since 1971 this nonprofit, 450-bed community hospital has provided tertiary care to residents of the East Bank of Jefferson Parish and surrounding communities. More than 700 primary care and specialist physicians spearhead the broad-based medical staff at this facility, which was awarded accreditation with commendation by the Joint Commission on Accreditation of Health Care Organizations, the body's highest recognition. The facility also receives vital support from more than 1,000 volunteers, some of whom have been with the hospital since its inception. Centers of excellence include Cardiovascular Services, Diabetes Management Center, The Wound Center, Regional Cancer Center, Rehabilitative Services, and Woman & Child Services.

i Today hospital-based membership programs targeted to older adults offer such perks as newsletters, access to medical information and hospital fitness centers, and various discounts. To get the most out of life in the mature lane, call local hospitals for the lowdown on their senior membership programs.

A modern outpatient facility, the 228,000-square-foot Joseph C. Domino Health Care Pavilion opened in 1997 to accommodate the large number of patients needing same-day surgeries and laboratory procedures such as gastrointestinal endoscopy. Departments occupying the pavilion's four floors include laboratory and diagnostic radiology, same-day surgery, gastrointestinal endoscopy. Other hospital services offered include an emergency department, ambulance transportation, and intensive care unit. A 38,000-square-foot wellness center for older adults offers a variety of fitness and health education programs such as cardiovascular exercises and aquatic therapy. Mature adults will find innovative programs tailored to meet their special wellness and health education needs at the hospital's Elder Advantage program.

The Yenni Pavilion houses radiation therapy, outpatient chemotherapy, and MRI.

During the past three decades, the hospital has devoted millions of dollars in community benefits such as indigent care and support for the prison medical units. The hospital also provides the Jefferson Parish Public School System with registered nurses and substance abuse and intervention facilitators, and helped fund the Jefferson Community School's science lab.

The hospital's participation in the evolving Integrated Physician Network of primary care doctors and specialty physicians, as well as partial ownership of the Southeast Medical Alliance and its insurance products, puts the facility in a good position to seek managed care contracts.

This publicly owned service district hospital is governed by a 10-member volunteer board of directors appointed by the Jefferson Parish Council and Parish President. More important, with more than three decades of service and the steadfast loyalty of the community, East Jefferson General has earned a reputation as a health care "jewel" of the East Bank.

OCHSNER MEDICAL INSTITUTIONS
1516 Jefferson Hwy., Jefferson
(504) 842-3000
www.ochsner.org

Twins born in separate years? The birth of twins Timothy and Celeste Keys of New Orleans set a world record by being delivered 95 days apart. Timothy was delivered at Ochsner on October 15, 1994, followed by his sister, Celeste, on January 18, 1995. David Watkins, a 19-year-old Louisiana State University football player, made national headlines as well when he received a heart transplant at Ochsner, not only giving him the chance to survive but also enabling him to continue his education and the hope of one day returning to athletics. The odds were against 4-month-old Guillermo Rodriguez of Honduras living to see his first birthday. The infant was born with life-threatening congenital heart disease and time was running out. But the odds took a 180-degree turn when Rodriguez arrived at Ochsner for life-saving surgery in 1996, which was performed by pediatric cardiologist Dr. Albert Gutierrez.

These and other success stories underscore the national and international reputation earned by this premiere health care facility, which opened its doors in early 1942 in a wooden complex known as "Splinter Village," a former military hospital at the foot of the Huey P. Long Bridge. The five physicians and surgeons who founded Ochsner Clinic—Alton Ochsner, Guy Caldwell, Edgar Burns, Francis Le-Jeune, and Curtis Tyrone—were all eminent specialists and professors at Tulane University School of Medicine. By 1946 the hospital had become a thriving multispecialty clinic and a nonprofit foundation responsible for running the hospital and directing the institution's research and medical education programs. Today Ochsner includes seven hospitals, over 35 neighborhood health centers,

80 specialties, and more than 11,000 employees and 600 physicians. The main campus's 443-bed teaching hospital is one of the largest non-university-based physician training centers in the country, serving not only the New Orleans community but also a large international patient base from South and Central America.

TOURO INFIRMARY
1401 Foucher St.
(504) 897-7011
www.touro.com

The oldest private nonprofit hospital in the city, Touro Infirmary was founded in 1852 by Judah Touro, who envisioned a multispecialty facility offering a complete range of general medical and surgical services. The hospital made medical history in 1888 when Dr. Rudolph Matas, the father of modern vascular surgery, performed the first successful surgical repair of an aortic aneurysm. Today this 350-bed Uptown medical complex and teaching hospital has 500 physicians who staff state-of-the-art centers of excellence including cardiopulmonary and mental health services, obstetrics and gynecology, physical medicine and rehabilitation, and cancer treatment. The hospital's chest-pain emergency room, which opened in 1993, was the first of its kind in the New Orleans area and is designed to quickly diagnose and treat symptoms related to heart attacks. A family birthing center features beautifully designed and appointed labor, delivery, and recovery rooms as well as a level-III neonatal intensive care unit, a breast pump station, and perinatology services. Fast one-stop outpatient surgery in a private atmosphere is provided at the hospital's freestanding Prytania Surgery center at 3525 Prytanian St.

i Some New Orleans hospitals specialize in the treatment of children and women; others offer general medical and specialized surgical treatment. To find out which facility best suits your and your family's health care and medical needs, always ask the hospital before making an appointment to see a doctor.

TULANE-LAKESIDE HOSPITAL
4700 I–10 Service Rd., Metairie
(504) 780-8282
www.tuhc.com

In 2005, Tulane Medical Center merged with Lakeside Hospital to become a leading teaching facility in the community. Today this 119-bed specialty center and state-of-the-art health care provider, located in Metairie on the East Bank of Jefferson Parish, has more than 250 full-time employees and 650 staff physicians. The Tulane Center for Women's Health, a comprehensive care system, offers a centralized system for coordinating patient education, screening, diagnosis, and treatment services related to women's health needs. Lakeside was the first hospital in the area with the new Advanced Breast Biopsy Instrumentation and is a regional ABBI training site. The hospital was also the first in the market to have fully digitized radiography and fluoroscopy capabilities. Pioneering procedures have included the transvaginal sling procedure used to treat incontinence as well as the direct-oocyte sperm transfer for the treatment of infertility. The hospital has ICU and telemetry units, and a state-of-the-art urgent care center.

i A historic consortium forged by LSU and Tulane medical centers, the Louisiana Cancer Research Center, has created a comprehensive cancer treatment facility in New Orleans, offering patients access to a greater number of clinical research trials and promising treatments that observers say may one day rival such regional powerhouses as Houston's M. D. Anderson and Birmingham's University of Alabama medical centers.

TULANE UNIVERSITY HOSPITAL & CLINIC
1415 Tulane Ave.
(504) 588-5800; (800) 588-5800
www.tuhc.com

Several of the world's top physicians were educated here. A 1977 winner of the Nobel Prize

Physician Referral

The following are at-a-glance physician referral telephone numbers for hospitals listed in this chapter.

Children's Hospital:
(504) 896-9460

East Jefferson General Hospital:
(504) 456-5000

Ochsner Medical Institutions:
(504) 842-3155

Touro Infirmary:
(504) 897-7777

Tulane-Lakeside Hospital:
(504) 988-5800

Tulane University Medical Center:
(504) 988-5800

in Medicine works and teaches here. Important medical breakthroughs were discovered here, not the least of which was Dr. Rudolph Matas's development of a lifesaving surgical procedure for aneurysms—back in 1888. More than 170 years of health care delivery and medical research tradition is nothing to sneeze at.

In 1834 William Harrison was president and the first Mardi Gras parade was still three years down the road. Seven ambitious New Orleans doctors banded together to form the Medical College of Louisiana, the first of its kind west of the Allegheny Mountains and the forerunner of Tulane University Medical Center. Today the medical center is regarded as one of the finest teaching, research, and patient care centers in the country.

Several divisions make up the medical center located in the heart of the Central Business District nearby the French Quarter: the School of

Medicine (with 1,700 faculty and 1,500 students), the School of Public Health and Tropical Medicine (established in 1910), the Tulane Regional Primate Research Center, the U.S.-Japan Cooperative Biomedical Research Laboratories, University Health Services, and the 235-bed Tulane University Hospital and Clinic. More than 630 hospital and clinic physicians see nearly 200,000 patients annually. Specialties include cancer and oncology, cardiology, neonatology, pediatrics, surgery, OB/GYN, international health, and infectious diseases. Seven centers of excellence include Tulane Cancer Center, Tulane Hospital for Children, Tulane Institute of Sports Medicine, and Tulane Center for Women's Health.

With its proximity to downtown and the French Quarter, Tulane's emergency department sees many out-of-town visitors who need medical assistance. Services are available around the clock.

Tulane has been on the forefront of numerous important breakthroughs, such as in 1917 when the medical school awarded degrees to its first women graduates, and in 1969 when it was the first institution in Louisiana to transplant organs, beginning with the state's first kidney transplant. In 1989 Tulane researchers developed a vaccine against simian immunodeficiency virus, hailed as a breakthrough in the fight against AIDS. Another innovation is the hospital's community outreach: The Professionals At Tulane program allows anyone to call a central number—(504) 988-5800—and receive quick, accurate, and dependable health information, physician referrals, and registration for free classes and seminars.

INDEX

ABOUT THE AUTHORS

Becky Retz is a native New Orleanian whose other work includes a weekly automotive column in her staff position with the *Times-Picayune* newspaper. Her early career also included acting stints on stage and in television commercials, stand-up comedy, and guiding tours of her beloved city. Becky lives in the Gentilly area of New Orleans with her favorite baker Steve, her son Chris, and their canine pals.

Veteran travel journalist **James Gaffney** has been a book, magazine, and newspaper writer and editor since 1985. A cultural explorer at heart, he has traveled the world writing about diverse topics ranging from the aboriginals of Far North Queensland and Mayan burial caves in Honduras's storied Mosquito Jungle to the Byzantine and Ottoman legacies of modern-day Istanbul. Since 1989 he has served as national affairs editor for a syndicated news service covering international travel and aging issues. Television credits include co-writing the 13-episode series "Quest for Adventure" for The Travel Channel. He is the author of *Keys to Understanding Medicare*, published by *Barron's*, and *Day Trips from New Orleans*, published by Globe Pequot Press, and co-author of *The National Geographic Traveler New Orleans*, published by The National Geographic Traveler. His award-winning photography and travel photography has been exhibited at professionally juried local, national, and international galleries.

Past projects include writing the pilot for a TV documentary series on Congressional Medal of Honor recipients, *In the Company of Heroes*.